COBAIN
ON COBAIN

COBAIN
ON COBAIN
INTERVIEWS AND ENCOUNTERS
EDITED BY NICK SOULSBY

CHICAGO
REVIEW
PRESS

An A Cappella Book

Published by Chicago Review Press Incorporated
814 North Franklin Street
Chicago, Illinois 60610

ISBN 978-1-61373-094-2

Library of Congress Cataloging-In-Publication Data

Cobain on Cobain : interviews and encounters / edited by Nick Soulsby.
    pages cm
  Includes index.
  ISBN 978-1-61373-094-2 (cloth)
  1. Cobain, Kurt, 1967–1994—Interviews. 2. Rock musicians—United States—
Interviews. 3. Nirvana (Musical group) I. Soulsby, Nick, editor.
  ML420.C59C62 2016
  782.42166092—dc23
  [B]
                          2015029431

Interior design: Jonathan Hahn
Interior layout: Nord Compo

Printed in the United States of America
5 4 3 2 1

CONTENTS

PART III · JANUARY TO AUGUST 1990 —UNDERGROUND DARLINGS

PART IV · OCTOBER TO NOVEMBER 1990—UK RISING

PART V · MARCH TO OCTOBER 1991—ONE TO WATCH

PART VI · NOVEMBER TO DECEMBER 1991—THE DELUGE

PART VII · JANUARY TO FEBRUARY 1992—SULLENNESS

PART XI · FEBRUARY TO APRIL 1994
—THE REST IS SILENCE

INTRODUCTION

For more than two years, Nirvana was barely worth a mention in the press or on air. After six months of practicing, the band had plucked up enough courage to play a house party in March 1987. A full year later they'd finally settled on a band name. Another year later they'd played only three gigs outside the state of Washington. Who were they? Two original songs and a cover shared via limited edition releases on a label, Sub Pop, that had only local cachet and was forever teetering on the brink of bankruptcy.

Two years after that, in 1991, Nirvana, now on a major, with a solid reputation in the underground as "one to watch," was preparing demos for a sophomore album to be titled *Nevermind*. They'd toured the United States four or five times and Europe twice, and their first album, *Bleach*, in the summer of 1989 was followed by an EP, a couple of singles, and a couple of compilation tracks. But for most of 1991 no one paid them much mind outside the same circles of punk fanatics, grunge addicts, rock aficionados, and college students who made up their normal audience.

The next two-year leap was exponential: millions of records sold, shows on five continents. Those songs of 1991 had launched the band into a stratosphere lit by paparazzi flashbulbs and stadium effects rigs. The band's front man, Kurt Cobain, was married, a father, a rich man, the acclaimed voice of a generation, writer of the anthem that rebuilt rock music . . . and was condemned as a malcontent, a bad influence, a depressive, a drug addict. By 1993 Nirvana had already prepared what, unbeknownst to them, would be their final statement, *In Utero*.

Two more years: 1995. Fans greeted the one-year anniversary of Nirvana's collapse and soon turned to commemoration of Cobain's death at his home in Seattle around April 5, 1994—only six and a half weeks after he had turned twenty-seven.

What happened?

Well, it's not like Kurt Cobain set out to become a plumber. From the start, his desire was to live from his music, to perform and to display his art before an audience, to be appreciated. The Faustian bargain was made at the outset: he wanted to be seen, to be heard, and he needed the help of radio, newspapers, television, and magazines for that to happen.

This bargain is at the heart of *Cobain on Cobain*. In this book we'll follow the relationship between Kurt Cobain, his band Nirvana, and the media that he would alternately curse or court, from the band's earliest interviews to their last. The words of the artists themselves will be our guide.

The relationship between Cobain and the media was a fraught one. After those first two years in the wilderness, Cobain measured his progress by dropping a quarter in a pay phone slot and requesting his band's first single on local radio. It's how bands function: they play, people listen, they're played, people pay, they speak to persuade more people to hear them, to see them play, to listen, to pay. The media isn't something a band "engages with"—it's fundamental to a band's existence, a part of the look, sound, concept, and image that make an artist.

And in the band's early days there wasn't enough media attention for Cobain's liking. In 1988, as far as is known, the band earned a solitary article in a local music magazine. In early 1989, scattered quotes appeared in barely half a dozen places—the band's first tour that summer raised perhaps two brief commentaries. Nirvana wasn't worthy of press comment because the group was an unknown factor; their first album didn't emerge until June 15, 1989, and the record and their touring needed more time to gain them a following.

Cobain would later cite this lack of coverage as a reason he was unhappy on Sub Pop. He would further claim that the record label presented Nirvana as rednecks or ignorant wild men. Regardless of the truth, the crucial point, the key factor in Cobain's relationship with the press, was that Cobain wanted to perform and be understood on his own terms.

It was the same reason he'd underperformed in school despite his obvious intelligence, the same reason he'd been loath to hold down any formal work in his young life—he was completely resistant to the compromises that school, family, jobs, and employers impose. Music had suggested a path via which his unmediated self could be expressed, when he wanted and how he wanted. This was something he was willing to work very hard for. To find that being on a record label meant someone else playing a role in defining who he was came as an undesirable imposition; "you're in high school again," he sang.

He was willing to bend and accept some things, however, to further his wish to be allowed to create and to retain his freedom from any nine-to-five existence. Plus he was a likeable, albeit shy, individual with no desire to upset anyone with whom he came into contact—which is why so many of his complaints and criticisms were confined to his journals, written into songs, or voiced in interviews months or years later. He wasn't one for confrontation. Also, as, in these early years, he was rarely interviewed when the band wasn't on tour, it wasn't a hardship to make time for this aspect of the music business.

The early interviews display elements that never changed. Krist Novoselic—Chris, until he changed his name in 1992 to reflect his Croatian roots—was a gregarious and talkative spokesman for Nirvana. More than that, Novoselic often shielded Cobain in interviews. Amid Krist's clowning, Kurt could veil himself, speaking only when directly addressed or when he sincerely wished to make a point. Novoselic was a deeply loyal and faithful friend, and numerous times in these pages you'll witness him stepping up to cover his quiet comrade.

The attention given to Nirvana gradually increased throughout 1989–1991. Kurt was still often known as Kurdt, the mild pseudonym he'd adopted on early Nirvana releases (and as far back as the Fecal Matter demo) and that he used in an effort to place some distance between himself and his public persona—a feature that went uncorrected given the band's limited significance at the time. In 1989 the feeble quantity of press coverage had ramped up once the band hit Europe for a month. The same happened in 1990—one or two interviews a month at most gave way to a dozen or so when Nirvana reached the United Kingdom,

Germany, and the Netherlands. About half of all interviews the band ever gave were to non-US publications, and therefore around a third of Nirvana's interviews exist only in languages other than English, because it was only abroad that they rated a more substantial level of attention from the music press.

That tendency to interview on tour also influenced the nature of coverage. Interviews were snatched at venues around the band's performance with mere minutes for journalists to introduce themselves (often in a second language), make the band's acquaintance, get the background right, then fire more substantive questions. It helped, however, that at this stage the people interested in speaking to Nirvana were hooked into the underground scene, fellow travelers, people with whom Cobain et al usually shared some musical common ground. So, though Nirvana would remain a fleeting presence prior to 1991, it was a happy one—the interviews are full of off-kilter humor, openness, and visible interest.

As late as August and September 1991 the band had no clue what was coming. Fame hit full force in the final three months—peaking while the band was engaged in its second European tour of the year. Nirvana had never toured as long nor as hard; they were exhausted. The shows had been booked long before stardom was even conceivable, so the venues were too small, the band still drove long hours between shows, they still snatched a few hours' sleep in the same ol' hotels. The audience changed from the underground crowds, with whom Cobain and his friends felt a kinship, to pop kids, hipsters, and those who didn't mind about music so long as it was "in." The change was a source of significant discomfort.

At this point, the entire power relationship between Cobain and the media flipped. Until October–December 1991 the only real media interest came from fanzines, college radio, and the European music press. Now everyone wanted a piece of the band. The number of interviews soared to upward of eighty across those three months. Interviewing filled whole days—there was no time to recover between gigs—and speaking to the press became the day job taking up tightly scheduled hours, as much a part of life as the actual performances. The band's freedom ceased to exist amid the desire for access and availability.

Until now the group had only been noted as Nirvana, a unit, rarely warranting individual interviews. Now that Cobain had become the poster boy of a rumored musical movement, the pressure built especially on him. A shift in the nature of the band's interviews occurred as a logical reaction to workload; Nirvana chose to divide and conquer, and it became common for each member to take on interviews alone. Kurt decided he would only do cover stories; Krist and Dave shouldered the bulk of the work and protected him from scrutiny. Exposure to the media changed Nirvana's interviews from a brotherhood speaking to others in the scene to a divided force repetitively answering people who had barely noticed the cream of the underground—let alone Nirvana—pre-*Nevermind*.

Rather than reacting with anger, often the bandmates chose to amuse themselves. While rarely anything other than warm and friendly toward their interrogators, they often joked and teased—sometimes to the frustration or incomprehension of the interviewer, who would involuntarily play the straight man. Having no time left to relax between gigs, Nirvana let off steam in interviews instead—attempting to turn the new day job into a source of fun.

Unfortunately, this fed a reputation for being difficult that Nirvana would spend much of the next couple of years alternately defusing or reinforcing. The year 1992 commenced with an Australian tour where, again, a substantial press pack followed. Cobain's retreat deepened; having sought freedom through music, his musical endeavors had now caused his freedom to be deemed dispensable compared to the business of being the face and voice of a lucrative commercial entity. He reacted by sidelining music in favor of a cocoon of family and chemicals.

After only a short break in January before the Australian tour, a longer break ensued. The band was more selective of the interviews it accepted; inside of a single year the group's desire for coverage had been sated. The separation of interview duties became even more prominent, with Novoselic and Grohl performing the majority throughout 1992. It was still just a case of managing workload; the media coverage was uniformly warmhearted.

Cobain and his colleagues felt that they might use the excessive attention to benefit the underground via the interest in Nirvana. To this end the band tried to ignore corporate music publications altogether in favor of speaking to amateurs, fanzines, and respected underground publications like *Flipside*. This was simultaneously a positive desire to draw others toward the scene from whence Nirvana had come and a disdain for the mainstream.

Another lesson the band took from their experiences in late 1991 was that they'd failed to exercise sufficient control over whom they spoke to. Open confrontations arose in 1992. Cobain would grumble he was railroaded into speaking to *Rolling Stone* and so, while wanting to avoid a fight with his management, he pointedly wore his self-made CORPORATE MAGAZINES STILL SUCK T-shirt, an homage to the slogan of the label SST ("Corporate Rock STILL Sucks"). While seen as a petulant gesture among mainstream journalists, it fairly reflected Cobain's feelings toward magazines who, until *Nevermind*, had barely acknowledged an underground scene existed.

MTV came in for similarly passive-aggressive treatment. Cobain accepted he couldn't avoid the nation's most omnipotent music media outlet. So, instead, he did little more than the minimum and actively antagonized the network's staff whenever possible. This started early: he hardly spoke during the band's interview on *Headbangers Ball* and then refused to do any reshoots in the band's first MTV performance. A full-scale showdown occurred before the 1992 MTV Video Music Awards, with MTV asking Nirvana to play "Smells Like Teen Spirit" and the band refusing in favor of newer songs, including the controversial "Rape Me." MTV threatened to dump Nirvana from the show, Nirvana accepted, and eventually a compromise was reached with each party settling on the song "Lithium." Still, Cobain made one last gesture of rebellion by playing the opening chords of "Rape Me" and then switching back to "Lithium" before MTV's panicked executives could cut the broadcast. Mild antagonism swirled around the *Unplugged* performance a year later, with Nirvana insisting on bringing country-punk band the Meat Puppets onstage with them and selecting a playlist of covers and non-hits. Finally, at the *MTV Live and Loud* performance in December 1993, Cobain rejigged the playlist of the *In Utero* tour to focus on noisier songs, spent the final fifteen minutes playing a noise jam, and eliminated "Smells Like Teen Spirit" (and even "In Bloom") to make his contemptuous point. His courtesy to MTV's journalists as individuals, as human beings, reflected his overall decency, but he never made his peace with the channel as an institution.

And it wasn't just MTV who suffered in that regard. On the United Kingdom's premier music show, *Top of the Pops*, Cobain was so incensed at having to mime playing that he essentially fellated the microphone while performing like a gothic-voiced robot. Weeks later on *The Jonathan Ross Show* the band slammed their way through a furious "Territorial Pissings" rather than "Lithium" as scheduled. In Belgium Cobain acted as if he was going to attack a camera that got too close on stage, and later, on Brazilian national broadcaster Globo, he exposed himself to the camera, having chased it around the stage, and spit on the lens.

Meanwhile his addictions worsened, which, coupled with his lack of interest in being asked for the umpteenth time to explain his lyrics, meant he shirked all media duties, though was rarely less than charming to those who spent time with him. His issue was a discomfort with the press as an amorphous mass, not with any individual journalist. That changed, however, in autumn 1992 when his wife, Courtney Love, gave an interview to *Vanity Fair*. Her quotes laced what was truly uncomfortable reading, a veritable poison-pen letter made up of unnamed sources making claims regarding the couple's drug use. A series of "junkie baby" headlines circulated before the birth of the Cobains' child, which resulted directly in their newborn baby being temporarily removed from their custody by the authorities and restrictions being placed on their access. Kurt and Courtney became the world's most famous addicts.

His relationship with the media now became the most brutal tension in Cobain's life. Numerous song titles penned at this time centered around words that he felt were being used to define him in the press or that he felt defined them in turn: "Curmudgeon," "Oh the Guilt," "Serve the Servants," "Nine Month Media Blackout" (an early title for the equally pointed "Radio Friendly Unit Shifter"). Most viciously of all, "Rape Me," a then unreleased "anti-rape" song written in 1990, was given a new bridge taking aim at "my favorite inside source," and telling those who voiced criticisms of his family in the press, "appreciate your concern, you're gonna stink and burn." Two journalists attempting to write a biography of Nirvana were deemed hostile to Cobain and his wife and duly suffered a half hour of vicious (and highly drugged) voice mails from Cobain, plus an assault by Love in a nightclub.

Cobain, after a year of barely speaking to the press, commenced actively seeking sympathetic media engagements. This was no coincidence; the threat to his family came via the media; therefore the media would be the stage for the counterattack. The result was a flurry of articles from late 1992 through mid-1993, while an authorized biography written by respected journalist Michael Azerrad prepared to tell the band's side. With his band and music now public property, Cobain had hoped to keep his family life wholly private. Discovering that even his home wasn't safe from scrutiny, and dearly wanting to protect his loved ones, he would give up his privacy in an attempt to staunch the wounding coverage.

The choice of publications—the *Advocate*, the *New York Times*—showed that this was no longer about the music. Previously deemed worthy of only music-press coverage or the "arts" pages, Cobain's celebrity status as a bad boy with a soul meant he warranted mainstream newspapers and lifestyle magazines. He alternated between startling candor—sharing intimate details of his life and upbringing—and blatant concealment, particularly when downplaying his drug use. Nirvana played live only about a dozen times between February 1992 and October 1993, and wrote or recorded scarcely any new music, which only fueled speculation.

Onstage at the 1992 MTV Video Music Awards, Cobain leaned into the mic and said, "Y'know . . . it's really hard to believe everything you read," then gave a lopsided and sad smile and left it there. Feeling he could trust hardly anyone to relay his words, Cobain penned his own missive in the liner notes of the *Incesticide* compilation that December. This was his most direct address in the war of words: he vented against homophobes, racists, rapists, macho men, and his media image in a sprawling conjoined scree. He learned another lesson: what he wrote would be repeated as effectively as what he said in interviews.

Amid Cobain's personal battles, Nirvana as a group had already become mired in another media storm surrounding the album that would emerge as *In Utero*. The joke title "I Hate Myself and I Want to Die" appeared in the paper with a distinct lack of amusement. Rumors of Steve Albini's involvement as producer leaked before Albini had even been asked, so he had various publications issue his statement vociferously denying the story. Then, following his hiring and the album's recording, press reports claimed it had been deemed unlistenable, that the band and Albini were at loggerheads, that the band and record label were fighting, that the album would be denied release, that the album would be remixed, and so on. The entire band was embroiled in media activity clarifying the rumors were untrue. Nirvana even rented a full page in *Billboard* magazine so they could include their own letter categorically refuting the stories surrounding the album; writing it themselves seemed the only path to the truth.

In August 1993 band business continued to ramp up. While Nirvana could have chosen to stage press conferences to get the media work over in one go, instead they reverted to the model of their prefame years. To promote *In Utero* they shouldered multiple interviews, but now with the whole band present to face each individual interviewer. On the one hand, this meant a lot of work on specific days in August, but the band's priority wasn't workload. Nirvana in 1993 felt vulnerable, wounded by regular rumors of fights and breakups. They reacted by presenting a united front, the band of brothers all in it together. It gave each member strength in numbers when faced with prying microphones.

With the promotional interviews done, the single selected and video recorded, the album ready to go, all that was left for Nirvana to do was get out and play. The band's first US tour since 1991 stretched throughout the final three months of 1993. In that time, however, the band rarely interviewed, and Cobain was noticeably absent. Even the support bands are clear that they seldom saw Cobain except when he was on stage. The media saw even less of him: he roused himself to tend to MTV in December; otherwise, silence.

The year 1994 was worse. His bandmates shouldered the work once more, but even they didn't grant vast time to the media. Cobain, meanwhile, in the first three months of the year contributed just a few one-line responses to a radio interview in January and took part in an unrevealing phone call in February to talk about guitars. In a far more telling commentary, in Paris during Nirvana's European tour, Cobain was spotted positioned at a window using a replica handgun to pretend to shoot journalists gathering outside the venue.

The end spiral of the Nirvana story now played out; medical excuses for tour cancellation, overdose and coma in Rome, the band's survival in doubt, police called to the Cobain residence, Cobain's drug issues in the spotlight—so far, so 1992. In that first year of fame Cobain had held his family close, allowing him to relinquish the musical path that had become just another job, a place where people either told him what to do or demanded answers from him. Now, at a drug intervention in March, his friends told him the consequences of his continued drug use, and his wife made clear she would leave him and take his child with her. In 1992 he had attended his child's birth while trying to persuade his wife to enter a suicide pact to avoid the pain of their daughter being taken from them; in 1994 even Courtney was saying Kurt couldn't keep on his path and keep his family intact.

Cobain made his choice. He fled rehab, hid out with drug buddies, and refused to relinquish the one thing he had left that wasn't controlled by others. Even now he felt the media eye upon him. Instead of a suicide note to his loved ones, he wrote a press release for the media to relay to the millions who now had some claim to know him and to whom he had inherited a responsibility. He knew he was launching his family and friends into yet another round of coverage, he knew he'd be picked apart in obituary columns—his note relayed a clutch of reasons for them to chew over, and to this day fans and press alike tease out whether the note was an honest declaration of feeling or just a last attempt to protect those around him. This was one of his final acts: to feed the insatiable mouth that had feasted on him for some two years and devoured his life whole. He even echoed the drippingly polite sarcasm of the bridge from "Rape Me" by ending the note thanking people for their "letters and concern during the past years." This from a man who had simply wanted to be left alone.

The desire behind *Cobain on Cobain* was to place the reader inside the key moments of this roller-coaster ride and to tell the tale of Nirvana entirely through the words of Kurt Cobain and his bandmates as they unleashed the whirlwind that would consume them for some two and a half turbulent years. This is the most comprehensive compendium of interviews with the band ever released—each interview another knot in a thread running from just after the recording of their first album, *Bleach*, to the band's collapse on the European tour of 1994. Interviews were cherry-picked to provide definitive coverage of the events of those five years from as close to the key moments as possible—to see the band reacting to the circumstances of each tour, each new release, each public incident. One limitation that impacted the creation of this volume is that a number of copyright holders were unwilling to see their interviews represented and/or possessed their own intentions for the interviews, hence they could not be included.

During those years, Nirvana toured the United States five times, toured Europe six times, visited South America for three shows, and spent a month in Asia and Australia. Capturing those moments meant circumnavigating the world to find pieces revealing Cobain and his colleagues at each point in time. The desire was to journey with them, to experience their world "live" as they gave their immediate impressions of what was happening around them. These interviews are the nearest one can come to conversing with Cobain on his journey.

My thanks must go to Elizabeth Adair for her constancy and greatness, to Isabel Atherton (and James!) for wisdom and decency, and to Yuval Taylor for having the vision of a book that would bring together Nirvana's best interviews and become the go-to volume for anyone seeking to understand the life of the last great rock band. Likewise, I must thank the many people who contributed their skills as translators to this project, allowing English-speaking audiences to explore many of these interviews for the first time. Finally, and very important, I must thank the many people around the world who have supported this quest by providing their content, connections, and enthusiasm. Thank you.

The book seeks a connection with—an insight into—a fellow human being: no fictional character, no posthumous saint, but a real person

PART I

February to June 1989—Fledglings

MEET THE LAST GREAT BAND OF ROCK 'N' ROLL'S glory years! Arrive early to beat the crowds!

Except it wasn't like that. Nirvana in early 1989 was entirely subordinate to Sub Pop's grand plan. Sub Pop wooed the UK music press, selling them "the Seattle sound," "grunge." The weekly format of *Sounds*, *Melody Maker*, and *NME* meant more column inches to fill with more new sounds, so the papers were susceptible to the exoticism of the Pacific Northwest and proved far more fervent appreciators of Nirvana's early charm than American ones. John Robb, then of *Sounds*, provides an early glimpse of Nirvana's support abroad.

The band had played exclusively in the state of Washington from April 1987 to January 1989 and were almost entirely dependent on local college media—represented here by Hanmi Hubbard's taped interview conducted for the *Current*, the student newspaper of Green River Community College, and by Phil West's piece for the *Daily*, the student newspaper of the University of Washington.

What comes across immediately is the band's way with surreal amusement, including jokes about oil tankers and potato-growing in Yugoslavia. They also play off one another in group situations—Krist Novoselic is already the band's biggest voice, but there's no sign of Kurt Cobain's later shyness, and the band members are enthused about the new record, about touring, about other releases in the pipeline. It's notable that at this early stage they still count Robert McFadden as their first drummer, a friend Kurt and Krist jammed with for a month or so in 1986 under the name the Sell-Outs. Rob would be dropped from future counts. It's also apparent that Chad Channing is a quieter presence than his comrades, but he's no less the joker—the backseat role is precisely what future drummer Dave Grohl would occupy in most of his early interviews with the group. Jason Everman, second guitarist from February 1989 until the abandonment of the first US tour, comes across as an affable presence, but the exchange on music tastes reveals the divide between his rock instincts and his colleagues' dive into the Pixies, the Smithereens, and other quirkier interests.

COBAIN CLIP

"Our biggest fear at the beginning was that people might think we were a Melvins rip-off."

—from "It May Be the Devil and It May Be the Lord . . .
But It Sure as Hell Ain't Human" by Dawn Anderson,
Backlash, September 1988

HAIR SWINGING NEANDERTHALS

Phil West | February 25, 1989 | *Daily* (US)

I had the great fortune to be covering music for the *Daily* (the University of Washington's student newspaper) when Sub Pop was beginning its campaign to put Seattle on the map. I'd met Nirvana once before the interview, one evening having gone over to the apartment of a woman named Tamera who seemed to be helping manage them. Kurt, Chris, and Chad were sitting cross-legged around a turntable in the middle of her living room, transfixed by Black Sabbath's "Into the Void." I relayed that story to a *Daily* writer on the tenth anniversary of Cobain's death, but the writer misheard and reported they'd been sitting on stairs, which isn't as good a story.

I did the interview at Sub Pop's offices in February 1989—back when the label was in an eleventh-floor office in an art deco building in Belltown. Tamera had given me their early demo tape a few weeks before the interview, and it was getting heavy rotation on my Walkman. The interview was with Kurt and Jason Everman, who'd just joined the band and would be included on the live photo on the cover of *Bleach*—released just over three months after the interview—even though he didn't play on the record. We did the interview in a side room of the office that was being used for storage. No chairs; we just sat on the floor.

Kurt (who was spelling it *Kurdt* at the time) didn't say much throughout the interview, but what he did say was funny, to the point, and quotable in the context of how Sub Pop was packaging itself, and I ended up using pretty much everything he said in the article. I could tell he was sort of bemused that someone was interested enough in the band to interview them. Jason talked most of the time, but I only used a couple of his quotes at the very end of the interview; as it turns out, Jason would eventually have the distinction of being kicked out of both Nirvana and Soundgarden. —Phil West

Nirvana transcends all the pretensions that go along with being rock stars. They come across as the type of earthy psycho scums you wished you could beat up in high school. They view music as a trend, think the SubPop movement is sincere but "the ultimate rehash" and "the last wave of rock music," and singer/guitarist/group founder Kurdt Kobain, on the average, listens to three records a month. They started out in ultimate hick-town Aberdeen, and their current Olympia base hardly qualifies them for urban art hipness.

Although Nirvana looks like nothing special in this context, they could be the greatest contribution that Seattle's grunge-oriented SubPop Records makes to society. Kurdt originated the Nirvana sound during high school days in Aberdeen.

"I wasn't thriving socially, so I stayed in my room and played guitar all the time," he said. "At the time, I thought I was inventing a new sound that would change the whole outlook of music. I've discovered in the last few years that it was just the Seattle SubPop sound."

The core of their sound is based in primal Black Sabbath and Stooges punk/metal riffing, but it carries a dark, raw, earthy, grungy tone that separates them from their labelmates. Kurdt, after a long pause, decided their music has a "gloomy, vengeful element based on hatred."

A lot of this is rooted in his adolescent small-town experiences. "In Aberdeen, I hated my best friends with a passion, because they were idiots. A lot of that hatred is still leaking through."

It's not all hatred though. Their debut album, *Bleach*, contains two straight-ahead, blow-pop tunes that attest to Kurdt's feeling that things are going his way. This newfound positivity has led to a "gay pop songs phase that will eventually die," yet they'll probably write more of them on the next album.

Most of *Bleach* contains the style which made SubPop seek the band out, after a demo that Kurdt and bassist Chris Novoselic did with the drummer from Aberdeen's SubPop predecessors, the Melvins. The album, like their initial demos, is a full mix of heavy dirge songs, which new guitarist Jason Everman has the most fun with, upbeat power grunge, guttural lyrics, scream-singing and to-the-point titles like "Swap Meet" and "Negative Creep."

Lyrics range from simple repetition about rural hick-jerks to detailed narratives of horror-torture. The end effect, epitomized in their live shows, channels Kurdt's subversive intellect into an aggressive release, while they purge themselves in search of the great exalted god riff. Even during shows like a recent Annex Theater show marred by failing equipment and an overzealous crowd slamming into the broken monitors, they lock into a larger-than-life sound on every song.

Although a national tour is planned and a wave of positive press is following them, they remain mostly unaffected. Chris and drummer Chad Channing still work as dishwashers, Jason is living off savings from four years of "commercial fishing hell," and Kurdt lives off his "nice, sweet, and wonderful" girlfriend.

"I'd like to live off the band," Kurdt said, "but if not, I'll just retire to Mexico or Yugoslavia with a few hundred dollars, grow potatoes, and learn the history of rock through back issues of *Creem* magazine."

But if Nirvana does become part of the last wave of rock, what will replace them? "I don't think we'll have to worry," Jason said.

Kurdt's a little more nihilistic. "If it was up to me, I'd get more oil tanker drivers drunk," he said. "I don't value music much. I like the Beatles, but I hate Paul McCartney. I like Led Zeppelin, but I hate Robert Plant. I like the Who, but I hate Roger Daltrey."

ON THE SUBS BENCH: NIRVANA

John Robb | March 1989 | *Sounds* (UK)

In early 1989, John Robb—then of *Sounds*—initiated the first contact between the bands of the Sub Pop scene and the UK music media, who would prove to be their most fervent supporters and boosters in those early days. The article is precisely what one would expect to find in relation to a band barely out of the starting gates—short, to-the-point, direct. Funnily enough, it was originally published on the same day that the next interview took place. Robb's latest endeavor is the *Louder Than War* online magazine, where some of the footage of this very early encounter between the press and Cobain can be seen. —Ed.

THE POTENTIAL trump card in Sub Pop's pack, Nirvana have created one primed to thrill single so far.

The grubby pop delights of their guitar maelstrom 7-inch, "Love Buzz," were quickly chewed up by clued-in punters.

But now, with Sub Pop achieving a higher profile, and Nirvana ready to hurl their debut LP at a fawning nation, things could move faster.

Frontman, Kurt Kobain explains: "The album is similar to the single in song material, but we've recorded it a lot rawer. It sounds better—harder. The single seems so commercial now. But it's bound to be, since it's a cover of the Shocking Blue song." And that's the Shocking Blue who gave Bananarama their "Venus" hit.

But what's this fuss about Seattle? Last year it was home town to Jimi "Six Fingers" Hendrix's remains and the Petrol's Steve Mack, but nothing else. Now there's an infatuation with the place.

"It's because we are secluded, out on a limb up here. The local scene has always had an element of rock in it, but it's been a gloomy element.

"That's why I reckon you guys in the UK like it—because your rock is on the gloomy side too. Maybe it's the weather—we have the same sort of miserable climate as you have!"

Nirvana's LP, "Bleach," is due out next month, and they play their first major US tour to promote it. Hopefully they'll reach Europe in September.

If Nirvana can maintain the standards set by "Love Buzz" the four-piece could well find themselves at the vanguard of guitar pop noise at its best.

"IT'S THE CLASSIC PUNK ROCK RAGS-TO-RICHES STORY"

Hanmi Hubbard | April 22, 1989 | *Current* **(US)**

The first time I saw Nirvana was at the HUB Ballroom in February 1989. I had second-degree burns on my hand, which was all bandaged up, and I was heavily medicated. I went to the show with a group of friends and promised I'd stay in the back, away from the crowd, and most certainly out of the mosh pit. But the pull of Nirvana's performance—the perfect mix of ear-candy pop and raw angst—was too much for me to resist. I soon found myself standing right in front of Kurt Cobain, marveling at his immense stage presence while clutching my injured hand to my heart as if pledging my allegiance. I was certain he was seven feet tall. And I had a new favorite band.

I interviewed all four band members at Kurt's house in Olympia for the *Current*, Green River Community College's student newspaper. I was barely seventeen, had only two interviews under my belt, and truly didn't know what the hell I was doing. The band actually asked me if I'd done an interview before, then gave me a tip for recording group interviews. We sat in Kurt and Tracy's [Tracy Marander, Kurt's girlfriend] living room, and the television was playing heavy metal videos with the sound off. Occasional non sequitur comments were made about the videos throughout the interview. Despite the sometimes sardonic answers the band members gave me, they were very kind and said it was probably their best interview to date. I kept in touch with Kurt after the interview, and when he found out how young I was, he said I should write a book about my life story. Oh, the irony.

Kurt granted my request for a copy of the band's demo tape, and Nirvana played a show at my school. With the tape and the contract, he included a note that read:

Yo, this contract is a relief of details compared to the Sub Pop agreement I just signed.
Three LPs and three long years. I feel as if I've signed my life away.
Thanks for being so prompt in sending the official documents.
We're looking forward to seeing you on the 26th.
Bye for now.
Kurt Cobain
PS. this is how I really spell my name.

—Hanmi Hubbard

Tracy Marander: The cat was playing with it earlier . . .

Hanmi Hubbard: OK, hmm . . . How long ago did you guys form, as a band?

Kurt Cobain: Jesus Christ . . .

Chris Novoselic: Maybe we should say our names so you recognize our voices—you ever done this before?

HH: Yeah . . . But then again it was just people I knew, so—

CN: Usually when we do a recorded interview—

KC: Yeah, when we do a recorded interview it's always like one person's statement meshes with the others. And then it's just one person's—

Chad Channing: Well, you're more apt to answer that because you guys were in the band way before me and Jason.

Jason Everman: Yeah . . . Let's let Chris answer.

CC: Whatever year and title you give off is gonna do it.

JE: Yeah, we'll agree.

CC: Back in 1880—

CN: 1987—

KC: As a band, we've been around for about a year. Chris and I, in Aberdeen, had been trying to form a band for about . . . gee . . . four years? Would you count "Bob" as a band, sure?

JE: Are we gonna say our names and stuff?

HH: Yeah, we could do that.

CC: You had a band called "Bob"?

JE: Jason Everman—guitar!

CC: Chad . . . And I play drums.

CN: I'm Chris, the bass player.

KC: I'm Kurt, the crooner.

JE: Who does that leave?

CN: And gee-tar picker . . .

HH: So who was originally in the band?

CN: Us two, but like, three drummers. Is Bob in? Should we count Bob?

KC: It doesn't . . . Let's just say three drummers.

CN: Yeah, three drummers.

KC: They all had moustaches.

CN: Yeah, that was weird. Dale [*Crover, of the Melvins —Ed.*] didn't have a moustache.

KC: Oh! Dale counts too. We've had four drummers. And Dale was like an honorary member of Nirvana forever—he's gotten the golden plaque. He's even going to be mentioned on the record because he plays on two tracks.

HH: Where'd you form—Aberdeen?

KC: No, as Nirvana we formed in Olympia and Tacoma.

HH: When did Bruce Pavitt first become interested in the band?

CN: How's he interested?

KC: Well, actually it was Jonathan [*Poneman, of Sub Pop —Ed.*] that was working on us for a while. (HH: When?) Almost about a year ago;

in fact, during the time when we were having troubles with our other drummer we were kind of negotiating with Sub Pop to put out a single, but we weren't quite ready. But we weren't quite ready to be a band, to be a permanent band, 'cause they weren't really sure if we were going to stick together or not so they needed some insurance. So we got Chad and played a few shows and . . . [*Kurt yawns—all chuckle*] so we got Chad and played a few shows and—

CC: And it worked out!

KC: And that's our insurance. So then we put out a single.

HH: So, OK, like, the four of you as you are now have been in Nirvana about a year now, then?

KC: Yes.

JE: Me and Chad played in a band together, a speed metal band called Stone Crow. Like four years ago.

CC: Did you know question number five?

JE: Why?

CC: That's what it is—what your earlier bands were.

JE: Yeah, I pretty much read it. I'm gonna screw up the whole thing.

CC: No, it'll be like, you answer it, and we'll see if the question's right.

JE: You could just, like, put that answer after that question and pretend like I answered it on time.

CN: Psychic!

HH: Were the two of you in any other bands?

CN: No . . .

KC: Well, we played under different names. We actually played shows with our . . . second drummer. Under such names as Skid Row, Pen Cap Chew—

CN: Bliss!

KC: Bliss—

CC: More names than I can count!

KC: Yeah, we were just known as the band that changed their name.

CN: Every show!

KC: Every show.

JE: It was a gimmick.

CC: I was in a band called Magnet Men, which is how I met those guys.

CN and KC: Yeah!

JE: Yeah, I don't—I did meet you guys at that show, that's right! Because—

KC: We played with you, and our drummer had such a crappy drum set that he borrowed yours.

CN: Yeah, and sho'nuff . . . we were amazed when we seen the North drum set. So fuckin' far out, man.

HH: Who would you say has influenced your music?

CC: Mass . . .

CN: Mass . . .

KC: Too much . . .

JE: Personal influences?

HH: Personal or other artists.

KC: Well, before I knew better I imagine Led Zeppelin [*all chuckle*] . . .

CC: The Pixies . . .

KC: The Melvins. The Melvins really influenced me because they lived in Aberdeen, and I watched a lot of their practices. [*Hanmi shows the band that the next question on the list is about the Melvins.*]

CN: This is weirrrrd, man.

KC: The Aquaman circles are coming out of the woodwork . . .

JE: Malfunkshun!

CC: Yeah, Malfunkshun, they were on the island.

JE: Me and Chad have the big Malfunkshun influence . . . 'Cause they're, like, older than us and a cool band, and we pretty much worshipped them.

KC: Basically I was a rocker-stoner. And then I got into punk rock, and now I'm into both.

JE: I was a rocker. Then I was a punker. Then I was an . . . idiot. Well, I was always an idiot.

KC: We've just always had identity crises. We don't belong!

JE: Just don't fit.

HH: Do you listen to any bands that have a particular style that may surprise your fans or people that listen to your music?

JE: I listen to a lot of rap and hip-hop. NWA.

KC: I like a lot of clean pop like the Vaselines and Beat Happening. Chad likes the Young Marble Giants—ooh, I answered for him!

JE: Oooh . . .

CC: Oh, they're great, I don't care.

HH: [*Giggles.*] Your turn.

CN: I like bands with big fat drummers. Just whatever tape's laying in my van, I'll play it.

KC: I like, umm, Lead Belly, the blues singer. He's a crooner. I'm trying to think of something new I listen to . . . I listen to a lot of kids' records. Well, just children's records and sound effects records—I think I enjoy listening to that stuff more than rock 'n' roll right now. As of now, I'm just . . . we're just kinda taking a break from listening to rock 'n' roll.

HH: Do you think that's going to affect your music at all?

KC: It probably always has because I've never really listened . . . I've never been a big music fan where I'm totally obsessed with listening to music all the time, like every day. I mean, I go through weeks of not listening to music at all. I don't think it's gonna affect us.

CC: That's kinda healthy 'cause—

JE: It's totally healthy.

CC: Sometimes it's a lot better—I dunno . . . I prefer influence over environment of where I'm at . . .

JE: Internal influences as opposed to external ones . . .

CC: So it's not really influence, it's more yours . . .

KC: A chance to create your own—

CC: It's more what I see and what game I pick up in life.

KC: I'm always afraid of poisoning myself with too much influence.

CC: That's why I don't read!

KC: I suppose it's probably a subconscious thing.

CN: [*Yawns.*] Excuse me . . .

CC: God bless you.

HH: How long ago did you start playing?

CN: When I was eighteen.

JE: Guitars?

HH: Whatever—

CN: I was force-fed accordion lessons.

JE: I was fifteen . . . I'm twenty-one now, so that's six years.

CC: I played violin when I was about fifteen. I haven't been playing drums that long, really. I started playing guitar like everyone else; I really like the bass guitar.

KC: How long have you played drums now, about six months?

CC: No! A year, you said we'd been together a year.

JE: My mom finally bought me my first electric a couple months ago, so I'm pretty psyched.

CN: Yeah! We were a mariachi band. [*Interrupted by the arrival of "Damon"—greetings all around, explanation of what's going on.*]

HH: Where do you see yourself in, let's say a year on from now? Will you still be on Sub Pop?

KC: Hopefully together. We will . . . we have definite plans for staying on Sub Pop.

CC: That's a safe answer.

KC: Yeah, that's a safe answer. [*Obvious amusement in his voice.*]

CC: That's all I'm gonna say.

HH: Has anyone approached you with like a major record deal? Or a large indie label?

JE: There's pretty much a full-scale bidding war going on right now that we can't really talk about.

CC: Nor will we say it . . . for just the change in their pocket.

HH: Are you planning to tour this summer?

All: Yeah.

CC: May!

KC: We're planning on touring a lot. Let's see.

CC: Two months in the summer.

KC: We'll be leaving June—

CN: June! Fifteenth!

KC: June fifteenth, and we don't know exactly how long we're going to be out there for sure.

JE: That's a good roundabout date.

CC: Hope so. [*All say farewell to "Damon."*]

HH: What do you have planned for the tour?

CN: Rock 'n' roll!

KC: As long as we don't go on back roads in North or South Carolina.

JE: We're taking a great big, fat, strong guy to protect us. Look, look, look! Look at the bass drum, look at that!

KC: They look like lil' lollypops—

CN: You know those Union 76 balls? [*Reference to the antenna balls from the 1980s —Ed.*] Those things are so rad.

KC: OK, so, we're going across these great United States for as long as we possibly can and hopefully more than a month.

CN: Six weeks to two months.

KC: We'll be coming back, and then we'll take a rest, then take off—

CN: For the continent—

KC: We'll be going to Europe in September.

HH: Are you planning on touring with anyone?

KC: No . . . we want to, but we haven't found a band big enough. A band that we would benefit from doing the tour with.

HH: Where do you want to go most on the tour?

JE: The Deep South.

KC: New York. The Deep South back roads—

JE: Lower Alabama!

CN: Towns that aren't spoiled like San Francisco or L.A. Y'know, where people feel cheated.

KC: Places where they don't have the attitude. Where they don't have the attitude like, "I've seen everything."

CC: Italy. I've always wanted to go there.

KC: We're looking for starving, hungry kids. Like in Ellensburg.

CN: Or in Seattle. There's hardly any all-ages shows.

HH: Have you played outside of the Seattle area before?

JE: Yeah, we've even played in California.

KC: We played in San Francisco—

CN: And San Jose.

KC: San Jose.

CC: Portland.

CN: Aberdeen.

KC: Don't say that!

JE: Ellensburg.

CN: Tacoma.

JE: Oly.

CN: Bellingham.

KC: Oh yeah . . . Enumclaw . . .

JE and CC simultaneously: We almost played Walla Walla . . .

CC: That was in stereo, by the way.

JE: Full blown.

CN: We were supposed to play in L.A., but we got sick.

KC: We all caught bronchitis while we were down there.

CC: Sleeping outside—that wasn't fun.

KC: We were scheduled to play with Living Color in L.A.

CC: But fIREHOSE bumped us off the bill—jerks!

HH: Where's your favorite place to play?

KC: Seattle. That's my choice, anyhow.

HH: Is there a particular venue?

CC: I don't mind it, yeah. People—

KC: I dunno, we've played in different places. Definitely not—

JE: [*Finishing Kurt's sentence*]—the Underground.

KC: Oh really?

JE: Raven!

CC: I think there's quite a few cool places to play in Seattle.

KC: I don't enjoy playing the bars too much.

CC: Nahhhh.

CN: It doesn't matter where you're playing!

JE: Chris, why can't you do that? Goddamnit . . .

CN: Too lazy to practice.

CC: I dunno, people are certainly a lot more into their music it seems around here than, say, when we've done San Francisco. It's just like, even when we saw a show at the Ivy—quite a big show and lots of people and it's like—

JE: Standing around?

CC: Yeah—

JE: Even though Mudhoney was rocking pretty much as hard as you can rock and people were just standing there.

CN: Just as long as there's a good crowd, it doesn't matter—it's where the good crowds are. You can be in Ellensburg and have a good show. That's what's important.

CC: There aren't any in San Francisco!

HH: Do you have a particular show that stands out in mind as particularly good?

KC: Our last show.

JE: The Annex [*Theater —Ed.*] show . . .

KC: People were voodoo dancing . . .

JE: It was insane . . .

KC: I got sweat in my eyes and it burned.

JE: Yeah, me too.

KC: I actually sweated for the first time.

JE: I had chunks of hair hanging off the headstock of my guitar.

CC: Chunks. [*Chuckles.*]

JE: It was gross.

HH: How do you manage to keep going through your whole set? 'Cause you're known as one of the most exciting bands, I guess—you jump around so much—

JE: Steroids! [*Laughter.*]

CC: Vigorous training.

CN: Exercise programs. Thirty push-ups—

JE: We got a trainer that we're gonna take on the road with us. We work out a lot, as you can tell.

KC: I've got a Jack LaLanne record; that helps me.

JE: Aerobics.

CN: Whoa. Do you do it on like 78 speed?

KC: No, it's a ten-inch, and it's blue vinyl, it's pretty cool.

CC: Actually that's why we're so thin.

JE: Did Sub Pop put it out?

KC: It's a limited edition Jack LaLanne Sub Pop thing—

JE: Single of the Week—or Month. That's excellent.

HH: Who, as far as other bands, do you like to see live?

KC: Mudhoney.

CN: Mudhoney.

JE: Soundgarden.

CN and KC: Yeah, Soundgarden.

CC: No local bands.

JE: Forced Entry.

CC: Well, if I could see, who would I like to see? I'd like to see the Angry Samoans live if that would be possible.

KC: Are they still around?

CC: I'd sure like to see Bad Brains. That show's impossible. I'd sure like to see Shonen Knife. That would be a great show!

CN: Yeahhhh.

KC: Shonen Knife. That's who we'd like to tour with in the summer. Something that our fans wouldn't expect. They'd get a big thumbs-up.

JE: I like seeing Slayer live.

CC: Yes! Slayer live, yeah, that's good for me.

KC: I wanna see Iggy Pop.

JE: I saw Iggy in Frankfurt. And Lemmy was in the audience. It was excellent. Lemmy was right up front getting into it. I saw Motörhead the next night, so it was really cool.

CC: I think Dave went to those shows; he's got like a poster thing of Iggy Pop.

JE: Yeah, he was at one of the Metallica shows I was at over there, him and Renee.

HH: How long have you been working on the album?

CC: Forever—

CN: About half a week—

JE: We've been in the studio about four months. We changed locks on the studio when we went in.

KC: We wrote three new songs the week that we recorded the album. And I wrote lyrics to two of the songs ten minutes before I recorded singing.

CC: Sitting in a car.

KC: So we didn't work on the album for very long at all. It was two days, I think.

CN: Two days and six hundred dollars!

CC: As far as the artwork and stuff, that's kind of taking a little time.

JE: Yeah, the packaging's taken way longer than the actual recordings.

CC: But I think the biggest delay is Sub Pop.

KC: It takes a long time to get things done; you have to wait for one record to come out—

JE: Yeah, you have to wait for funds, for everything to click.

CC: It's not like Black Flag, who can put out three new albums a year.

KC: We really haven't been waiting too long, I mean, we've only been Nirvana for a year. To have a single and an LP out—

JE: And Sub Pop just released the Tad album, so I'm sure they want it staggered a little bit.

HH: When you first started, where did you get the material to play live?

KC: The material?

HH: Yeah.

KC: Well, I wrote—I guess I wrote all the songs before . . . I don't understand what you mean?

HH: Like, what did you play when you first started? Did you have songs already?

KC: Yeah, we already had songs.

CN: Most of the stuff that was on our demo. Did you hear that old demo of ours? It had, like, "Hairspray Queen" on it and "Aero Zeppelin."

KC: Just songs that were outtakes from . . . [*Hanmi and Chris quietly discuss an unofficial recording of the* Bleach *sessions.*] Where'd you get that?

HH: Sub Pop.

CN: Oh . . . bootlegs out there already.

HH: It was before the test pressings; it was just a tape.

JE: It was probably the tape I made.

HH: It says "Nirvana LP"—

JE: Yeah, that's the one I made.

KC: What were we talking about?

CN: Where did we start for material. We started jamming with just junky equipment—I had a bass amp called the PMS bass amp [*riotous laughter*]; it said PMS on it, man! And what was it?

JE: Pre-Marshall Syndrome.

CN: Then I had, what? An Epiphone bass or a Hohner bass—

KC: It's the classic punk rock rags-to-riches story.

CN: The drum set was just a piece of shit.

KC: They were tin cans!

CN: We would buy parts off stoner kids who'd wanna buy a gram and then sell a drum stand for ten bucks, and it was just like "Alright!" It was just junky old Sears stuff. Then we'd still smoke pot with them after, so, y'know—

KC: We were considered a legitimate band as Skid Row for about three months with our second drummer; we played a few shows, and we wrote a lot of songs which were outtakes of what we—a lot of them are—what we play now still.

HH: This has nothing to do with the band Skid Row that's currently—

KC: Oh yeah!

CN: One original member!

KC: They wanted to buy the name from us!

HH: Did that surprise you when you saw that name?

CN: Oh yeah!

KC: Yeah, it made me think, "Wow, I'm glad we didn't stick with that name."

JE: But we might be touring with Bon Jovi now if we had. So consider that factor—

KC: There is another band from the 1960s called Nirvana.

HH: Is there?

KC: Yes, and they were not too popular.

CN: They sucked.

KC: They're bad; they were like bad early Bee Gees, and I hope they try and sue us—it'll be fun.

CC: Valerie at the diner was like, one of her boyfriends was in that band.

KC: Really?

CC: Yeah, that's pretty weird.

CN: Whoa—

KC: Oh yeah, you told me about that.

HH: Is that where you got it from?

CN: No, we didn't know about this.

KC: No, we didn't know about it at the time, and then when we heard about it we bought one of their cult budget collectible records for fifteen dollars and who knows where it is now. It was bad.

CN: I've got it.

KC: We read this—

CN: There was a story on it in *Strange Things* magazine—you ever read that magazine? It's from England.

KC: We read this story about one of the members of that band, and he seemed like a real contrived, pompous dork.

CN: Has-been.

JE: A never-was.

CC: Never was, never has been.

KC: What was some of the things he was talking about, Chris?

CN: Something about going to the Catalonia region of Spain to get inspired by Salvador Dalí's vibes!

KC: [*Laughs.*] Yeah! Stuff like that, man! And he was just so close to stardom all the time in this band, but they just didn't quite have it.

CN: [*Observing something else.*] This could be a cool postcard—

JE: It's mine, buddy!

HH: Where'd you get the band name from?

KC: It sounded good, I dunno . . . You see, I was in the middle of transcendental meditation, and I spiraled up to the ceiling, and I said, "Nirvana!" and sparks came from my belly button.

JE: Wow, it was excellent, I was there—

KC: He got blinded.

CN: Damaged eyes.

HH: Are there any plans to move to Seattle so you're all in one place?

CN: Nahhh . . . it's a rat hole.

KC: No, we like to not practice. Should we practice today? Could we swing getting you home kinda late?

CC: That depends on what you're talking about; you talking about I have to take a 2:40 ferry.

CN: 2:40 at night?

KC: Oh! 2:40 at night? No problem!

JE: Chad, Chad, Chad. You'll be home.

CC: Yeah, but still I don't wanna do that, but that's just something I can get.

JE: You'll catch a ferry before that. No problem, 'cause I'm not gonna stay that late. Probably.

KC: OK, we'll have an acoustic mariachi set.

CN: We should go play at Reko/Muse and—

KC: Or do a video—we should do a video today. I don't mind either way.

HH: [*Speaking to CC*] You don't like Saturdays?

CC: It's everybody's day off.

CN: We never practice—that's something you oughta know, we don't practice.

JE: I wouldn't say we don't practice. I practice to a tape all the time.

KC: Yeah, we all practice in our rooms to the tape.

JE: That's a serious answer. It is! It's what we do.

KC: I think the reason we don't practice is—

CN: When we play I get pissed at myself that I should practice more.

JE: In a way it's good we don't practice because we don't really get sick of the songs.

KC: The songs are so repetitious and easy it's . . . it's easy to get tired of them.

JE: Yeah, when we play 'em live they're still fun to play. That's the problem with a lot of bands that practice five times a week, they just get totally burned on the songs and—

KC: It's like déjà vu, "Oh yeah, these songs . . ."

CN: Maybe that's why it's exciting, if we're supposed to be exciting to see, I guess.

HH: Jumping around?

CN: Because we never play, so when we play we're so happy that we're playing that we just hit the ceiling.

KC: The testosterone starts a-flowing . . .

CN: We're all celibate, too, so that helps.

KC: All these pent-up sexual frustrations coming out.

CC: Devouring drugs.

JE: Heavy drugs.

KC: None of us do drugs. Chris and I are starting to drink again—if we drink two nights in a row it's a binge.

CN: I'll drink Monday night too.

CC: I smoke every now and then.

CN: I don't care anymore.

KC: We're pretty much—we're not antidrug, we just choose not to do it.

JE: That's just the way it is.

HH: Who came up with the slogans on the back of the shirt?

CN: I did.

KC: Chris did.

HH: The total opposite, then, of what the band stands for?

KC: Yeah, exactly. Not necessarily "stands for," though.

CC: We don't mind.

JE: We just wanted a totally extreme statement.

KC: We wanted to be rebellious.

CC: We wanted to be cool, and boring, and rebellious.

KC: I was thinking our next T-shirt should have flowers all over it and nothing else. To counteract that.

CC: Sure, that's a great idea.

HH: Did any of you go to college? [*All burst out laughing.*]

CC: [*Almost apologetically*] I went to OC [*Olympic College in Bremerton, WA —Ed.*] for a while.

KC: Why didn't you say, "Did any of you graduate high school?"

CC: I'm a high school dropout, but I got into OC.

JE: I graduated early from high school.

CN: I graduated a year late. Like when I was a senior, the freshmen were all like born in 1970, y'know? And I was a senior and thought, "Gee, I started school in 1970 . . . I've been at school as long as you guys have been alive. In public education."

KC: I just couldn't believe you were all math majors. 'Cause I had, like, theater studies.

JE: Yeah, math was my favorite subject for sure.

CC: History.

KC: We're philosophers. We're philosophy majors.

CN: Just get me drunk, I'll talk your ass off.

HH: Then where did you go to high school?

CN: I went to Aberdeen High School.

KC: I don't even remember high school.

JE: It's a bad trip, pretty much.

KC: I went to Aberdeen. I lived in Aberdeen all my life up until two years ago.

CC: Great place.

HH: Why did you move to Olympia?

KC: Well, I was three months behind on my welfare-stricken house, and I was afraid that the landlord was going to call the cops on me. So I moved up with my girlfriend in Olympia.

HH: Do any of you have other jobs or anything?

CN: I work at a Sizzler. [*Scoffs of disbelief.*] I do!

CC: I make $5.50 an hour dishwashing at Streamliner diner.

JE: I don't work.

KC: I don't work.

HH: You just live off shows then, or try to?

KC: [*Laughs.*] Yeah, let's just say we do.

CC: Jason is a millionaire.

JE: Yeah, I inherited millions.

KC: One of us has a very rich parent.

CC: Which one can it be? A—Kurt. B—Chris. C—Chad. D—Jason.

JE: One of us is Shirley Temple's child. [*Lori Black of the Melvins was Shirley Temple's daughter. —Ed.*] Shhhh! You don't have to put anything about that!

KC: Don't say that. Please don't say that. Seriously. [*All obviously amused.*]

HH: Why'd you name the album *Bleach*?

KC: Well, I don't—

CN: We were cruising around the Bay Area—

KC: With bronchitis.

CC: Yeah, getting sick.

JE: With Bruce Pavit

KC: And Bruce sug   d *Bleach.*

CN: It was fucking   o.

CC: We were all deliriou   and sad.

JE: We had "Merciful Fate" going on the stereo.

KC: Bruce took advantage of us having bronchitis and talked us into calling it *Bleach.*

CN: No, really, we drove to San Jose for nothing.

JE: For nuthin'! It was hot.

CC: Well actually it's cool though—I like it.

KC: It's a cool name.

JE: It's catchy.

CC: It can stand for almost anything you want it to say.

KC: Cleaning out your needles—and acid wash.

JE: Acid wash. We get lots of free advertising on TV and everywhere else.

CN: You sterilize things with bleach, y'know.

KC: I was just going to say I don't particularly like people that wear acid wash clothes, that's all.

JE: Especially if they're in Celtic Frost.

CC: Yeah . . . yeah.

HH: How long are you going to be in Europe?

KC and CN in unison: We don't know.

JE: Forever.

KC: As long as we can; maybe we'll stay there.

JE: Relocate to Germany.

CC: Yeah, we know some people we might try to—

KC: We might try to become po-ta-to farmers.

JE: Or move to Amsterdam and become junkies and pretty much live on the streets.

CN: I'm going to move to Yugoslavia.

CC: I'm gonna get a farm in Frankfurt hills.

KC: [*In Swedish accent*] Squat and tour.

HH: What countries are you going to go to while you're there?

CN: Poland.

JE: Eastern Europe—the Soviet Union!

CN: We're going to go way back, to, like, Siberia. Just weird places like in China, remote parts of China.

JE: Mongolia, Tibet.

KC: Hike with the Buddhist monks.

CN: Because we want to relay the message of rock 'n' roll. Music's a universal language!

JE: We're going to play in places that don't have electricity—it's going to be something else.

CN: We'll spread the good word, my brother!

KC: Spread the gospel, brother! [*Degenerates into all calling each other "brother" in mock voices.*]

KC: We scream that at people out our windows.

CN: I like the Smithereens—I do.

KC: The Smithereens, yeah!

JE: Metallica.

KC: The Pixies! By the way, let's go for Pixies.

JE: Pixies and Metallica.

CN: Will it screw up the tape?

JE: We'll just turn it down a little. Just for atmosphere.

KC: This record just, like, screams atmosphere.

HH: Is there any place you want to go, or anything you want to do while you're in Europe?

JE: Visit my friends, people I used to live with.

KC: I want to collect religious artifacts.

CC: I want to go to Spain and bounce on the rooftop that Damon did.

JE: That'd be cool.

CC: I wanna go to Spain and get picked up and kidnapped. Never come back here.

HH: Why is that? Do you not like Seattle?

CC: I don't like anything here, I just wanna go home. No, I want to go somewhere where I can't understand anything for the most part. Where I can say, "Wow, this is weird," just somewhere completely different. And then they'll feel the same about me, and we'll get along just fine. I want a whole new world—something to discover. [*All now in background talking about the record they're putting on.*]

KC: Hey, they're really ripping it up—he just winced.

TM: Oh, is that the new one?

JE: They're pretty high-dollar—you can change guitars every song. That's pretty cool.

KC: Who are they?

JE: Raven.

KC: Haven't they been around for a while?

CN: The legs weigh a ton, man.

JE: They're on the comeback trail pretty much.

CC: Me too.

HH: When did you record the original version of "Spank Thru"?

KC: January '87.

HH: Over a year ago—two years ago!

KC: No, I think it was '88, January of last year. When did we record the demo with Dale? Just about a year ago, right?

CN: Yeah, March—last year.

KC: OK, I guess it's March. I thought it was January. I'll find out for you.

CN: No, 'cause I was laid off. I was laid off from a painter's.

KC: January of 1988. January 23, 1988.

TM: And a week later Jonathan called.

KC: Yeah.

HH: Did you send the demo to them or—

KC: No, we made 'em sweat.

HH: Did they ask for it?

KC: No, Jack Endino gave it to them.

HH: Oh really? Who recorded it?

KC: Jack Endino. [*Everyone pauses to listen to the Pixies'* Doolittle *album.*]

KC: Pixies are my favorite band.

CC: Right now they're unbelievable. They're great.

HH: If you could choose who would produce, would you want to be produced by anyone other than Jack?

KC: No. Not me.

CC: Probably not.

CN: Quincy Jones. John Paul Jones. Tom Jones.

KC: Davey Jones.

CC: Maybe the guy who produced the Pixies' *Surfer Rosa* album.

TM: David Bowie produced *Raw Power*.

CC: Really?

JE: We'd like to maybe go into a better studio next time.

KC: But we still have to have Jack Endino looking over his shoulder all the time.

JE: Go bigger—bigger studios.

HH: What else is coming up for you guys?

KC: Well, we've thought about putting a couple of singles out before the New Year.

HH: From the album or new stuff?

KC: We're not sure yet.

HH: What about compilation work?

KC: Oh! Yeah! We're going to have one cut on this compilation from Australia with all these other bands doing just covers. That'll be cool. And we're also putting something out on a single with a band called Alphabet Swill. We're doing a Neil Diamond cover.

HH: Which song, do you know yet?

KC: We don't know.

CN: I don't know about "I'm a Believer" 'cause—

CC: *The Jazz Singer!*

CN: Yeah! It's got an organ in it—how are we gonna do that? That's like the whole part of the song.

KC: So? That doesn't matter.

HH: Just play it on the guitar.

KC: Yeah, just play the organ on the guitar.

JE: We'll get one of those gee-tar synthesizers—

CN: No! No technology.

KC: Because it's the only good Neil Diamond song! All his other songs suck.

CC: I didn't know there was good  songs.

CN: What d'you know?

HH: Is there work supposed to be coming from C/Z next month, too?

KC: Uh, yeah.

JE: Daniel House [*owner of Seattle music indie label C/Z Records —Ed.*].

KC: I've heard so. What song is it going to be? I forget.

JE: "Mexican Seafood." Wasn't it?

KC: Oh.

JE: Is that what Daniel wanted?

KC: Which is one of the outtakes from the Dale demo.

HH: Is there any way to get a hold of that?

KC: Sure. I got one.

HH: Can I have it?

KC: Yeah, I'll copy it off. It's a lot more punk rock, raw—

CN: RAW! [*Everyone starts yelling the stereo system.*]

KC: Is that all the questions?

HH: Pretty much. What about shows in the area, like in the colleges, all-ages?

KC: Yeah, that's practically all we ever play.

HH: And you have a show coming up at the Vogue?

CN: At the Vogue.

KC: And with Mudhoney at the Moore Theatre . . . June 10?

JE: Ninth, it got changed.

KC: We play with Mudhoney on the ninth.

JE: And Tad. At the Moore Theatre.

HH: Oh really? That's going to happen?

KC: June 9.

JE: Friday. Six dollars.

KC: It's going to be the extravaganza of the year.

JE: Sub Pop showcase.

HH: Anything between then?

JE: Hopefully.

KC: What was the question?

HH: Shows?

CN: If someone calls us up, we'll play.

KC: We plan on having a show in Oregon.

JE: There's a possibility of a show at the Central, May 9, too—I don't think I told you guys yet.

KC: Oh really? May 9.

JE: I'm not sure. The guy called me.

CC: Where at?

JE: The Central.

KC: We shouldn't do that.

JE: We shouldn't? I don't care.

KC: We shouldn't play during May because June is a big thing—we need to let them sweat.

JE: That's true.

HH: Would you be interested in playing a show at, like, Green River Community College?

KC: Sure.

JE: That's out in the woods, isn't it? We almost played Walla Walla.

HH: [*Responding to something from Kurt*] Yeah, when they played Nirvana the other day it was 'cause of me. No, they don't have a single—the guy asked if I could get one. Do you have any extra copies of "Love Buzz"? Do you have any at all?

KC: Yeah.

JE: Kurt's got a shitload!

HH: Could I buy two of them from you?

KC: Yeah.

HH: I owe KGRG one. I've got to get one to the radio station.

KC: Oh, they didn't send one? Jerks! I've got about twenty singles.

CC: I've got ten.

CN: I've got one.

CC: Oh, wait, I sold one. I've got nine.

HH: Well, that's about it. Any public announcements?

CC: Yeah, that I'm in love with myself.

JE: And I'm in love with Chad.

CN: Eat porhk suckah!

KC: Eat pork?

CN: Aaron, my roommate, went to this soup kitchen in Las Vegas and he's walking down these stairs, and there's this big cartoon painting of this pig in a cop uniform and in this little balloon it said EAT PORHK SUCKAH! Then he walked in there and there's like ham sandwiches, bacon, everything was like ham.

JE: Porcine.

CN: Yeah, eat por-ke sucker!

JE: Porcine meat products.

COBAIN CLIP

"Chris and I have been in TOO MANY various forms of Nirvana for the past four years under such names as Skid Row, Ying Yang Valvestem, Pen Cap Chew, Bliss, Ted Ed and Fred, and other unmentionables."

—from "Nirvana" by Joe Preston, *Snipehunt,* early 1989

PART II

September to November 1989—Old New World

THE FIRST TOUR HADN'T ENDED WELL; THE BAND QUIT and drove home with a full week of shows canceled. They immediately shed guitarist Jason Everman and became a three-piece. They would play only two shows between July and the end of September, when they set out on their second US tour and then their first tour of Europe.

Their excitement is palpable. In Cincinnati they're clearly buzzed about being on the road, and they're looking forward to making the leap to Europe. While in the interview with Hanmi Hubbard in April they spoke of a single with band Rainbow Swill that never happened, here it's a Sub Pop single of Lead Belly covers which would, again, never occur.

Cobain, with the agreement of his comrades, is keen to try to escape the "Sub Pop band" label by pouring scorn on the nature of the burgeoning interest in the label and by distancing the band from the grunge stereotype. He claims Nirvana is trying "to be less . . . categorized than most bands" and pledges his allegiance to punk, the Beatles, even ABBA, while pointing to the softer qualities of the band's latest music. The yin-yang moments continue; Cobain claims there's something wrong with the state of rock 'n' roll but denies that his band is a particularly original solution to that. He shares thoughts on US small town life and mentalities while denying Nirvana is a band with a message. Instead of just being "against," however, Kurt and the band claim to be about authenticity, emotion, honesty.

As for Kurt Cobain's relationship with the media, these still are the early days. A telling moment, however, is when he compares interviews to therapy sessions, to a form of psychological evaluation—already there's a discomfort, phrased as a joke, with the idea that he's exposing himself for an assessment and a judgment.

"TWO OR THREE THINGS
I KNOW ABOUT KURT COBAIN"

Guido Chiesa | September 1989 | *Rockerilla* (Italy)

My friend wrote an article for the Italian *Rolling Stone* magazine declaring I had known Kurt Cobain, which is only partially true. I did interview Cobain in 1989 for the magazine *Rockerilla* at the time of the launch of *Bleach* (mistakenly calling him Kobain. Sorry.). It was a phone interview; I didn't meet him in person. Later, having met a number of musician-addicts and learning the sad fate of Cobain, I thought back on our conversation and of the common triggers I'd seen in others who became embroiled in drugs.

Ultimately, the man I spoke to did not seem unhappy or uncomfortable. There was nothing in his voice or in his words, no part of my human (though distant) experience of him that indicated to me the isolation, loneliness, or abandonment that comes as part of the heroin experience. I looked at the note Cobain left when he died and the portrait it drew of a man who had lost all feeling for his art, for his creativity, for this world. It was not the man I had encountered.

The closest I came to meeting him in person was in September 1991, when I was invited by Geffen to participate in one of its showcases, a concert marking the inaugural presentation of *Nevermind*. Besides the press and numerous fans, the concert was attended by the most illustrious representatives of the New York alternative scene, including Thurston Moore and Kim Gordon, for whom Nirvana had been the opening act during their recent English tour. Prior to the gig, Moore told me, "They are amazing!" And he was right.

This testimony is the best I can offer to the memory of Kurt Cobain, whom, sadly, I never did meet. —Guido Chiesa

Introduction translated by Ilaria Colombo. Interview translated by Sabrina Ciavarella.

In the columns of the magazine *Rockerilla*, somewhere around seven years ago, the press and members of the press in our country began a minor but significant dispute regarding a musical genre designed for a short life: "new psychedelia," otherwise called "new garage rock."

In retrospect, not only was the phenomenon far more restricted than what both the partisans and the enemies of new psychedelia imagined, but the argument also demonstrated the limits of a much wider music phenomenon (rock) and came at an extremely critical stage in its existence, one in which the maximum amount of news coverage corresponded to the minimum of originality.

In hindsight, it's obvious that the discussion was nothing other than an effect of the provincialism that has afflicted the rock tastes of non-Anglo-Saxon countries since time immemorial. Just to say, though, that most of the "new psychedelia" acts moved to Europe on a professional basis, since they had so little following among the American public.

At second glance, it seems to me, however, that this discussion was concealing another problem, one more interesting and defined, but which no one had the courage to face: does rock have a future? In other words, what does the future hold for a music that at this stage, less than twenty-five years after its unofficial birth, is already compelled to recycle itself?

Seven years later, given the paltry present-day situation of mainstream rock and the unstable fortunes of the independent variety, the question is being posed more clearly than ever due to ephemeral fashions, personal interests, and one-minute wonders.

In this context, with this ongoing debate, a small label from Seattle in the state of Washington, Sub Pop, has emerged on the American independent rock scene that, inside just a year and a half, thanks to Mudhoney, Soundgarden, Swallow, etc., has earned a prominent place on the American underground scene. As already happened with new psychedelia and countless other phenomena, the audience and the critics have been split in two. On the one hand, there are those who exalt these bands' psychedelic hard rock as something like the antidote to the decline of rock and its homogenization by various individuals like Madonna and Tracy Chapman. On the other hand, there are those who believe these bands are nothing other than the worst possible blending of someone else's ideas and, again, are the symptom of the irreversible decline of rock music.

Who's right? It doesn't fall within my remit to make statements about it. I simply interviewed Kurdt Kobain, singer, guitarist, and leader of Nirvana, a band which, right here in these pages, received very favorable remarks for their debut LP, *Bleach* (Sub Pop). Nirvana will soon be on tour in Italy with Tad, another Sub Pop artist.

In the next issue, in connection with the first LP release from Mudhoney, *Rockerilla* will be staging a Sub Pop special interviewing the two label factotums, namely Bruce Pavitt and Jon Poneman. Of course, thanks to them, the wider debate will continue.

Is this not the amusement for which you read a music magazine?

Guido Chiesa: How was Nirvana born?

Kurt Cobain: It was about four years ago. Chris, the bass player, and I tried to start off Nirvana in a small county about one hundred and thirty kilometers from Seattle. This wasn't easy because in Aberdeen (this is the name of the county) it's difficult to find dedicated musicians. The population is made up mostly of manual workers and the mentality is kinda old, closed, and stupid. So, about a year and a half ago, we moved to Tacoma. Here, with help from Dale Crover of the Melvins, we recorded a demo tape that got the attention of Sub Pop's Jonathan Poneman. Then in Tacoma we met Chad, the drummer, and with him we really started Nirvana. Shortly after that I went to live in Olympia, while the other two stayed in Tacoma.

GC: And what happened to Jason?

KC: Jason was our guitarist for about six months, but we've kicked him out quite recently. At the end of the day, we began as a trio, and we were four for just about six months. I believe that the three-member formula is ideal for this music.

GC: It seems to me that in the last two years, the state of Washington has produced more bands than all other forty-nine states combined. Tacoma has given us Girl Trouble, Ellensburg has given us Screaming

Trees, and Olympia the Melvins and Beat Happening, not to mention Seattle. Are you in contact with these bands?

KC: Yeah, we're all friends.

GC: Is there a sense of community among all these bands?

KC: Yes, absolutely. Everyone knows each other well, and everyone usually cooperates with each other. For example, I play occasionally in the Go Team, a sort of supergroup that Calvin from Beat Happening brings together occasionally. Recently, Chris, Mark [*Lanegan —Ed.*], and the drummer from Screaming Trees [*Mark Pickerel —Ed.*], and I recorded a single for Sub Pop consisting of two covers of Lead Belly. It'll be part of the Sub Pop "Singles Club" series.

GC: Have you ended up recording for Sub Pop because it's the only label in the area, or is it the one you feel closest to?

KC: When we started playing, about three years ago, we didn't even know that there were labels in existence interested in our kind of music. Then when the first Sub Pop records came out, we were taken by surprise and we said, "This is the best label we could record for!"

GC: Do you feel close to other groups on Sub Pop?

KC: Yeah, actually we all play more or less hard music at a moderate tempo. All Sub Pop bands have their own distinct sound, and I don't like to be all tangled up with the others as if there were no differences. I don't think that all of the Sub Pop bands are that similar.

GC: It's true, as you said, that nearly all Sub Pop bands (maybe with the exception of the beautiful and underestimated Walkabouts) play hard rock with a steady rhythm. Another common element to these bands, and perhaps in general, in today's post-punk America, is the mixing of three genres into a single unique sound: hard rock, psychedelia, punk. What do you think?

KC: I totally agree. It's really hard in the late 1980s to come up with wholly original ideas, so the only alternative is to just rely on your own

influences and make do with them. Thank God, in this respect Sub Pop—
and this generally applies to the state of Washington—the influences that
have been adopted are among the most honest and pleasing.

GC: It's almost as if you'd come to the end of the life of rock music—

KC: Exactly. The last example—

GC: And you had decided to take the good things rock has produced,
put it all together, and try to create that illusion once again.

KC: This is just what I'm trying to explain. Maybe rock has had its
day. After all there's a limit to the notes on a guitar . . . Rock has
been around for thirty years, and when you play with a four-four beat,
you run out of ideas sooner or later; it all becomes unoriginal at some
point. This is precisely the problem that contemporary rock is facing.
We haven't had a really different band getting up on stage for at least
three or four years.

GC: So you're not either?

KC: Yeah, we're not either. But maybe we represent the greatest originality that you can attain at the end of the 1980s.

GC: How would you define the originality of Nirvana, in your words?

KC: I can't. It's inside of us. We just are. The influences are there, clear
as the sun. We're something original, and I can't explain it because it
all takes place on the inside.

GC: Clear as the sun, but not enough to avoid the obvious question: Tell
us about your influences.

KC: First and foremost, the Beatles. For the first eleven years of my life
I did nothing else but listen to the Beatles. Their influence on how I
write the chords of my pieces, it's undeniable. So then I started listening
to Led Zeppelin and Aerosmith, and finally punk changed my life. And
when even that phase was over, I started putting everything together
into something that I could create that was my own.

GC: From another point of view, however, it's also true that you do nothing but continue the long wave of punk . . . or rather, live in the wake of punk . . . Or at least, live in the wake of what punk has set in motion.

KC: Yes, although I don't think I'd be able to explain how. Punk has set us free. I discovered punk when I was eleven, and I immediately wanted to be part of it. I was reading *Creem* magazine, and the sadomasochism and the colorful appearance of this music exerted an immediate fascination on me. I wanted to be part of it at all costs and pretended to be a punk, although in my town no one knew what that was. On the other hand, I was also scared, because I was nothing more than an ignorant hick like everyone else in the end. I only really came into contact with that music when I was around fifteen years old.

GC: After all, for kids as young as thirteen from your small town in Washington, even today, punk hasn't offered up a really different form of rebel—although that word has changed meaning and significance. Now Guns N' Roses have also ended up on the cover of *Rolling Stone* . . .

KC: Yeah, in that sense, the Sub Pop bands are an easy introduction to the rebellion that punk has embodied. It's definitely more of a pop music than punk is, but it maintains the same spirit. The punk I listened to as a kid, like *Damaged* by Black Flag, it was too extreme and it alienated the majority of the youth who paid it any attention. No one could understand it.

GC: Yes, but what you say only holds if you've lived through the time of *Damaged*. Now, unfortunately, there's the desert behind you. It may be that you are a good introduction to something more extreme, but something that has already passed. The music from Sub Pop is the most extreme form of post-punk we have a chance to listen to nowadays.

KC: It's true. I'd like to think that bands like ours have occupied the place left vacant by the open door that was punk. At the same time, however, I understand that we are nothing other than a shadow of something that was already there. Every time I write a riff, I can't help but realize that it's an imitation of some other piece, that it's not original, that I've heard it already. "Love Buzz," for example, it's nothing but a Shocking Blue piece rewritten. We just changed half of its words and the bass line.

GC: This isn't meant to be provocative, but given you're the first to admit that every time you write a piece you realize you're robbing someone, why do you keep playing?

KC: On the one hand, because I can't do anything else and there's nothing else I want to do. I don't have any other goals in life, nor other activities that interest me. I don't want to be a doctor or a journalist. And then, on the other hand, there's always the possibility that between three hundred ideas I've subconsciously stolen from another musician, one would come up entirely from me. It's a great challenge [*and you'll win it, Kurt* —Rockerilla *Ed.*].

GC: It is this kind of existential nihilism that provides you with an opportunity to produce music so sincerely tormented and pained. As if there were no tomorrow?

KC: Yeah, especially when you live in America. They remind you constantly, twenty-four hours a day, what kind of world you live in: a ridiculous society, only able to produce frustration and knuckleheaded people. The United States is made up of knuckleheads. My judgments may seem extreme, but to be convinced of the truth of this I just have to turn on the television or walk down the street and hear them shouting insults at my back about the color of my hair.

GC: It's almost as if you felt part of a minority on the brink of extinction . . .

KC: Yes, and I abandoned all hope of changing people's mentalities. When I was a kid, I was involved in the political wing of punk . . . It was kind of a breath of fresh air, the feeling that you could change humanity, or you could do something concrete. But after a few years I realized that not only is it impossible to change the majority of people, but besides, I don't have any interest in trying to save these people because they don't deserve it.

GC: Is this the sadomasochistic aspect of punk you said you were fascinated by?

KC: That must be it. After all, it's the only form of sadomasochism I like.

COBAIN CLIP

On Touring

"I'm seeing America for, like, free and only having to work for two hours a day. It's weird though. I'm not homesick yet."

—from "White Heat" by John Robb, *Sounds*, October 1989

"YOU NEED WATER,
YOU DON'T NEED RECORDS"

Mark Shafer | October 6, 1989 | WAIF Radio (US)

Murphy's Pub in Cincinnati had just started doing shows, and my interview with Nirvana took place outside the back door of the dart room annex. The bar was closing for the night, so we sat on the cold concrete wall in the parking lot with the chill conducting right through our jeans. It kept the interview short and sparked a palpable nervous energy, mainly because our teeth were chattering so much. It aired the following Friday on the "An Electric Fence" program on WAIF 88.3 FM, somewhere between midnight and 2 AM.

Since that long-ago interview there's been a cultural shift in how humans communicate, akin to shunting from Iron Age to Bronze. The Information Age was being formulated; we're still living in the middle of it. For that final moment, though, we plugged in live and direct: we used fanzines, networked, used cork message boards, picked up fliers in stores, had record parties, traded mixtapes, bootlegged shows, connected with pen pals—and WAIF meant we had a community station letting us share knowledge.

The journey to the interview kicked off in June 1989. I visited Pittsburgh with a friend, Steve Snyder, who worked at WRCT. Our objective: the Sonic Temple—a former Masonic temple, now a record store-performance venue. We'd timed the visit for the arrival of the Nirvana and Mudhoney LPs—we took them fresh from the shipping crates. We each had cash for a single LP, but we knew we'd copy them for one another—Steve went for Mudhoney on purple vinyl, and I settled for *Bleach* on white vinyl. As soon as the needle hit the platter, however, I lost any doubt that I'd made a good selection. I played the entire record on my show that week.

Nirvana was booked to visit Newport. We went there toting my ancient Panasonic boombox. (My mom bought it on installments from a gas station in 1980. I can't imagine the bands had much faith in me when I dropped this relic in their lap.) But Nirvana canceled—a no-show. It was me, Uncle Dave Lewis (soundman), Peter Aaron (Sub-Fudge Productions/Chrome Chranks), and this redhead kid called Mike, but still, we had a good night watching Cows and Blue Othello, with Shannon of the Cows playing with both arms in plaster casts and his trumpet taped to the top of a mic stand. Come fall, no mistakes. Peter booked the Murphy's show; I talked to Nirvana's roadie and he introduced me. Poor guy was the brunt of many a joke; he'd been brought along as a potential second guitarist, but they never let him play. Later on, as we sat on the wall, the guys seemed excited about heading behind the Iron Curtain—that mysterious dividing line between "them" and "us." The fall of the Berlin Wall a month and three days later, while the band was in Hanover, wasn't the last time that Nirvana would display this uncanny knack for being in the right spot when real change happened in the world. —Mark Shafer

Mark Shafer: We're down here at Murphy's Pub; we just saw a pretty good show by Nirvana. They're at the end of a tour here. Go ahead and say where you're going next and what's up with you.

Chad Channing: Kansas City. Lawrence, to be exact, at this place called the Outhouse. I guess it's in the middle of a cornfield, way out there. (Chris Novoselic: Oh yeehawwww . . .) I think it's with 24/7 Spyz (Kurt Cobain: Sounds like fun.)

CN: 27/4 Spiders.

CC: No! [*All talking over one another.*]

KC: Two hundred and forty-seven spiders.

CN: Two hundred and fifty . . . something spiders.

CC: One million guys in a van. I don't know

CN: I saw them on MTV once.

CC: Have you ever heard of them? [*Mutters*] 24/7 . . . is it Two Hundred and Forty-Seven Spiders?

MS: I've never heard of them.

KC: You haven't? You should have; they're supposed to have a fantastic concoction. I think they're on a major label with a rip off of . . .

MS: That's a problem as well; I wouldn't have heard about it.
(CC in background: It's broken! MS replies: You can get shot of it round here.)

KC: Well, majors creep into every nook and cranny of the world. Even I cannot handle, I mean, I can't even get away from it.

MS: I've been pretty good about it . . .

CN: 'Cause you're a strong man.

MS: Well, it's 'cause I don't have cable.

CN: Oh, there you go! Y'know I like getting antenna TV.

MS: Is, hmm . . . I was gonna ask you about [*stumbles*], discography. I know you've got the *Bleach* album that came out a couple months ago. (KC in background: Hey, watch your cigarette, you could burn me with it!) And I've got one of your white ones . . .

CN: Oh really? Those are worth fifty bucks!

KC: [*TV sales voice*] Those are worth "Fifty Bucks!"

CC: Fifty whole bucks!

CN: Fifty bucks!

CC: You hear that, Chris? I'm getting one right now!

KC: You can retire!

MS: Oh really? Wow, I bought it for seven.

CN: Good, I'm glad.

KC: He bought it at the Sonic Temple—at that record store where we played? [*July 7, 1989, in Wilkinsburg, PA —Ed.*]

MS: Dave's gotta run to the record store. Yeah, they're starting a new record store. (CC: In Cincinnati?) No, it's in Pittsburgh. They're starting a new record store and a place to play. Over in Pittsburgh.

CN: Well thank God, I mean, crawling up three flights, (CC: Four stories, man.) four flights of stairs . . .

MS: That's a pretty rough deal . . .

KC: Well, they were willing to help us.

CN: We had a lot of helpers.

MS: Yeah, this is just one floor down. People'll play in the basement, I think.

KC: Our discography . . .

MS: Yeah, I know you've got *Bleach,* then the Sub Pop thing [*Sub Pop 200 compilation —Ed.*], Teriyaki Asthma [*compilation on C/Z Records —Ed.*] . . .

KC: We had a single out before that, which is "Love Buzz" and "Big Cheese," and on our European release it has . . . it replaced "Love Buzz," which was on it . . .

MS: It was on Glitterhouse [*European record label —Ed.*]?

KC: No, it's on Tupelo [*UK record label —Ed.*]. They replaced "Love Buzz" with "Big Cheese" on that and on the CD as well.

CN: We have a, uh, twelve-inch EP coming out (KC: It's a promo EP for Europe) pretty soon! Just in Europe only; it's going to be out in a week or so.

KC: It'll have two new songs on it off a record, an upcoming record.

CN: Two new songs, plus "Love Buzz" from *Bleach* because I guess they're really popular in Europe. Like a four-song EP. It's going to be released to coincide with our tour. We're doing really good in the charts over there too. (CC: We're really looking forward to going.) We're leaving in a couple of weeks.

KC: A month and a half with Tad. (MS: Oh really?) In the same van. (CC: Tad 'n' us.)

MS: Tad in the same van? (KC: Yeah.) Uh-oh . . .

KC: We're going to rent him a U-Haul and put him in it.

MS: You gotta get a ventilation system in there. (KC: What?) You'll have to get a ventilation system in there.

CN: He farts and laughs a lot.

KC: And he snores realllllly loud! Like this! [*Impersonates vast snoring like a pig.*]

CN: Well, he snores and then, he was on this floor on (MS: The pig-man!) the Lower East Side in New York and he just . . . [*more impersonations*] just shooting, gee gosh! Gosh, b'gosh . . . He's a great guy, though, I mean, y'know.

KC: Oh yeah! The whole band, we're looking forward to it. Really fun to hang out with.

MS: Are you going to be on the mainland or round the isles? Both?

CN: All over the continent man, all over. We've got a week in the UK, then we're going over to the Netherlands—about four, five shows. Then we're doing Deutschland. (MS: You're playing Amsterdam?) Yeah, we're doing Amsterdam. (CC: And Austria!)

MS: Where you playing there? (CN: What?) In Amsterdam, do you know?

CN: A place where they serve marijuana brownies, yeah . . .

KC: Hash brownies [*starts mock coughing and choking*].

MS: That's just about everywhere.

CN: We're going to Budapest, Hungary. Rome, Milano, Paree!

MS: They've talked to you about going behind the Iron Curtain?

CC: Yeah, that'll be fun!

CN: Hungary's cool. They just, er, they just loosened up there.

KC: I wonder if they can get our records there. It's like, you need water, you don't need records.

MS: There's probably one person in the world has one over there or something.

CC: We should sell bottles of water while we're out.

KC: Yeah, I'm going to wear, like, four pairs of jeans and sell them for fifty bucks apiece.

CC: Get some extra money.

MS: You could sell Nirvana blue jeans or something, yeah. Get them printed off.

CN: They'd be bleached, stonewashed jeans.

CC: Bleach shirts, bandannas 'n' . . .

MS: Just say it's a conceptual thing?

CC: Bottles of water and stuff . . .

MS: "We have our blue jeans on sale here . . ."

CN: Conceptual—cash-ceptual . . .

CC: Buy level—ting! Buy level—ting! Ting-ting-ting-ting-ting!

MS: This is probably the first interview I ever did where I'm shivering to death.

CC: Really? Wear a coat.

CN: And it's not because you're nervous.

MS: Trying to get used to the weather out here. Actually, I have my coat, but it's kind of a pain to wear it with my arm the way it is.

CN: Oh, that's right! [*Female voice screams, "Come onnnn! Get in the van, let's go!"*] How'd you mess your arm up?

MS: Broke it, falling down.

CN: Drunk?

MS: No, was playing football.

CN: That's not funny, man.

MS: Got my movement back this week, so I'm happy.

CC: Yay!

MS: Well, I'll let you guys get moving here. I appreciate you taking the time after the show. It's quite late.

CN: Well, thanks for the interview, and could we do the radio call? What station is it?

MS: WAIF.

KC: Good night, WAIF, and God bless.

CN: You're listening to—

All together: You're listening to W—A—I . . .

KC: Or Y?

MS: I.

All together: W—A—I—F.

CN: In (**CC:** Cincinnati?) Cincinnati. Is Loni Anderson—

CC: What's the call numbers? What's the call numbers?

CN: Is she your . . . is she one of the receptionists at the station?

[*Chris and Kurt start singing badly in the background.*]

CC: What's the call numbers? Is it ninety something or eighty something?

KC: Good night and God bless.

"YOU'RE JUST NIRVANA?"

Lena Jordebo | October 27, 1989 | Sveriges Radio P3 *Bommen* (UK)

It's strange when you look back. How did you go about arranging radio interviews with a tiny American band before the Internet? I can't remember. But I know my boyfriend and I were in London in October 1989 to see various Sub Pop bands doing their first European tour. And I know I had interviews booked with both Nirvana and Tad, to be broadcast in *Bommen*, the radio show I hosted. To be honest, the band we were really looking forward to seeing was Tad. Sure, *Bleach* was OK, but we liked Tad. The heavy ones.

So we arrived at this strange location, some kind of university, and everyone was outside in a yard. There was no backstage area or changing rooms. I was supposed to interview Nirvana first, and we sat down in the band's tour bus. I probably asked to interview one or two of them—with only one microphone, that's easier—and they probably refused. My memories of the interview are vague; they talked about ABBA, and that's about it. They were just skinny boys in T-shirts, jeans, and unfashionable jackets, having a laugh. It was twenty awkward minutes, and I mostly felt relief when it was over—they probably felt the same. After Nirvana, Tad was next. We sat down outside somewhere, and yes, we had a really good time. The guys in Tad were so funny and smart. That's what I remember best from that day.

The interview took place in English; that's why the voiceover summarizes key points for Swedish-language listeners—a common practice with foreign-language broadcasts. —Lena Jordebo

Translation of voiceovers by Jonas Sorensson.

[*Nirvana song "Blew" plays under Lena's opening remarks —Ed.*]
Lena Jordebo: Nirvana now consists of three young guys. The fourth member, who played the guitar on their debut *Bleach*, has been fired. The

bass player is tall, the guitarist is skinny, and the drummer is short—and they all have an "average" look about them. We're sitting in their tour bus chatting away, and the atmosphere is a little frosty. They're joking, and I'm trying to ask intelligent questions. One thing is for sure: they do not like to be called a "Sub Pop band."

Chris Novoselic: We're a band before we are a record label so, y'know, I'm not really concerned with the record label as much as I am with our own music and uh, so . . . [*clears throat*] . . . Sub Pop, it's a lotta hype and stuff, but there's good bands there too. It's not just all hype.

LJ: What do you mean with "hype?" Why?

Kurt Cobain: Promotion. Over-promotion, it's just, it's kind of amazing how it has become such a popular label within the year and a half it's been together. And a lot of people are claiming that it's so much hype that they don't have any substantial bands to back it up.

CN: Some people will walk into a record store and ask, "Do you have anything by Sub Pop?" and just buy it! I mean, y'know? (KC: Yeah.) Why don't I just walk in, "Do you have anything by, uh, Warner Brothers?" "Yeah, here's this new ABBA record." "Wow, thanks a lot, that's great." Y'know?

KC: Are ABBA from Sweden?

LJ: Yes, they are.

CN: I like 'em, I like 'em.

KC: Fantastic. I do, too.

CN: They're fantastic.

KC: They're brilliant.
[*Band members continue talking in the background—KC: "They have some good melodies"; KN: "We like the image. See, we're very concerned with image and rock's soul. We love their music totally—the band had a lot of image. . ."—as Lena comments over the top in Swedish. —Ed.*]

LJ: A lot of the media coverage of Sub Pop is fake—it's commercials and tabloid gossip, even if a lot of the bands are great, says Nirvana. And, by the way, what is the competition between all these bands playing 1960s and 1970s rock like? Kurt claims they are mostly inspired by punk. The punk music is better today than it was before, although Nirvana does not wish to communicate a specific message.

KC: Maybe we're more like the Stooges type of punk rock. Before punk rock was a trendy fashion statement and where people would expect to try to act as punk rock as possible. It seemed like, when Iggy was playing to his audience, he dove out into the audience and cut himself up because he wanted this audience to act like that, or he wanted to create an environment the way that he felt, and at the time the audience response was just basically heckling and, um, there for their entertainment, not to really get into the music, and so now nowadays I think that the . . . the band and, and the audience participate together in that. And it just seems more like the way punk rock really should be or the way punk rock finally has become—to where people have a little respect for each other and try to have fun at the same time, other than throwing bottles at each other and sticking pins through their noses.

LJ: And what about messages?

KC: Messages?

LJ: Yeah, messages. Well, in lyrics for example? [*Kurt hums thoughtfully.*] I mean, that's what punk was about as well. Ten years ago—well more than that, as a matter of fact, thirteen years ago.

KC: That's true. Hmmmm . . . [*Sniggers quietly.*]

CN: Messages? We don't have a message, y'know?

KC: We definitely don't have a message. [*Laughs.*]

CN: We're not like U-T, uh, U2 or Joan Baez; they can give people . . .

Chad Channing: That's why we're not punk rock. [*Laughs all around.*]

KC: Is that why?

LJ: You're just Nirvana, hmm? [*Agreement from the band.*]

CN: I mean, rock 'n' roll, I love rock 'n' roll a lot but . . .

CC: [*Interrupting*] You know it is dead?

CN: It's a . . . [*laughs at Chad's comment*] it's not that important, I mean, there's a lot more important things in life. (KC: Oh yeah?) Yeah.

LJ: Like what?

[*Kurt and Chris speak simultaneously.*]

KC: Like what?

CN: Like love.
[*Nirvana's "Been a Son" fades in and out before Lena's voiceover in Swedish. —Ed.*]

LJ: There are much more important things in life than rock 'n' roll, says the bass player in Nirvana—things such as love. However, their music is hardly love ballads and romance.

CC: Thank you.

CN: Have you heard our new song?

KC: Soft and . . . (Chris still speaking: Our EP?) Frustrated. Yeah. And romantic. [*Laughs.*]

CC: Soft and romantic. All the time.

LJ: No it's not. I think.

KC: I think it is. (LJ: Yeah?) Yeah. I think it has a lot of compassion. Even though it may not have a message in the music, the feeling and the vibes that we're giving out, I think, has a lot of compassion 'n' emotion. And I would consider that soft and romantic. [*Laughs*] Even though it seems negative and hateful.

LJ: So the band, playing with Nirvana is a way of getting your feelings out?

KC: Sure.

LJ: Yeah?

KC: Yeah, exactly.

CN: Yeah, that's true. You feel a lot better after you put on a good show—feels really good.

LJ: Like going to . . . therapy?

KC: Sure! (CN: Yeah.) Exactly! Interviews are therapy, you're . . . you're an analyst right now. (CN: Yeah, we're like, like a . . .) We don't really dwell on thinking about things until we're actually interviewed and then it's just like, "Uhh . . . Gee, should we have said that?" We don't know what we are! We're trying to figure it out. (CN: Yeah we are.) I would say that we're trying to be less . . . categorized than most bands. I think. We—we have an influence—we may sound like the 1970s, or the 1960s, but . . . but what else can you sound like? Because they were such a forceful time—they were such forceful times.
[*Nirvana's "Love Buzz" plays to fade-out —Ed.*]

SWEET LIKE HONEY: NIRVANA

Sebastian Zabel | November 1, 1989 | *Spex* **(Germany)**

In November 1989 I went to Rotterdam to watch Nirvana playing a small club called Night-town. They were touring with Tad, and I can't remember who was headlining that night. What I do remember is a furious band and an intense singer, who stood there like a tensed bow and shouted out his soul, who blew my mind—and forced me to write that this brand-new Sub Pop band would soon be "bigger than the Pixies."

What I loved about them was that they were not just another of those grunge bands: they were sweet as honey. They were rocking hard and fucking melodic; they were much more pop than any other rock 'n' roll band coming out of Seattle. And Cobain seemed to be overwhelmed by himself, pure emotion on stage.

Backstage it was different. After the show I did an interview with all three members of the band—Krist Novoselic was friendly and funny, joking about Kurt Cobain's size. As we were taking pictures for *Spex* magazine, the sulky singer had to climb a bar stool to compensate for the difference in heights between him and Krist. He didn't like it much. And he didn't say much. He seemed shy and scornful at the same time. "I am that Negative Creep," he grunted.

I met him again two years later—Nirvana was playing the as-yet-unreleased "Smells Like Teen Spirit" at the Monsters of Spex Festival in Cologne in August, and Cobain was polite and joking. He seemed to have a great time. A few weeks later my daring prophecy came true: Nirvana was bigger than the Pixies. —Sebastian Zabel

Translated by Inga Owczors and Jon Darch.

Sebastian Zabel: And what is Jack Endino like?

Kurt Cobain: He's constantly eating chocolate bars, sardines in oil, and crisps, all mixed together.

The rich, clearly structured Nirvana sound, which is neither interspersed with annoying overtones nor sweet distortion, but simply comes across as a sensual tough-guy vibe—that's Trash Pop, big sebi sex, you know. [*"Sebi" is a joking reference the author is making to his own name —Ed.*] Three (formerly four) boys from the American Northwest, who are cool enough to play divine show-off riffs and, only when the subject matter makes it unavoidable, to let their sensitive side show (on "About a Girl," for example). But Kurdt Kobain wants none of it, cuts me off dead, and raves about the Buzzcocks.

"Sometimes I think," muses Kurdt, resting his chin on his hand, "that our music is maybe dance-rock or something like that."

"All my friends say I'm too negative," Kurdt tells me later. "But essentially I'm just amused by lots of things that I find ridiculous. I've got a permanently black sense of humor."

Chris Novoselic: Our songs sound deep and heavy, because that's the way we play them. Plus, it's also down to the instrumentation itself. With acoustic guitar and pipe organ they'd definitely sound lighter, but they'd still be the same songs. We're a songwriter band with a fairly traditional understanding of the pop song.

KC: We want to produce records that you listen to, not just ones you rock away to. So not a record where you can drop the needle down anywhere. And it'll always be a hard, fast rock 'n' roll sound.

SZ: Do you think that *Bleach* had this versatility?

KC: In its own way, yes.

COBAIN CLIP

"SOON we will need groupie repellent. SOON we will be coming to your town and asking if we can stay over at your house and use the stove. SOON we will do encores of 'Gloria' and 'Louie Louie' at benefit concerts with all our celebrity friends."

—from Sub Pop press bio for Nirvana, 1989

PART III

January to August 1990—Underground Darlings

IN THE SPRING OF 1990, KURT COBAIN CLAIMS NIRVANA "don't have any interest in a major label." It's a year of transition, with the band saying in April that there's only been one lineup change—by this point they're ignoring the early drummers altogether—then in August they have their old friend Dale Crover back, having dumped Chad Channing from the band. But there's no sign of what the future will be; Cobain is either lying to the *Dirt* fanzine or honestly believes that the band's next album will be out on Sub Pop later that year.

A lot of Cobain's later weariness with the media is understandable given the education the band receives. By the end of 1990 they're still answering questions about an album recorded in the last days of 1988 simply because that's all most people know about the band. This isn't the age of instant information—the members of Nirvana need to fill people in almost from scratch because most of the fanzines and radio stations they've spoken to in the United States have only a local reach or audience. Cobain mentions the same challenge with "distribution"—whether words or records, the benefit of a major would be to get them to more places more quickly and easily.

A crucial feature of Nirvana's conversations with the press was the desire to champion and promote other friends in the underground, other musical enthusiasms. This is very much on display in the following interviews—as is their wide palate: they're fully aware of most of the major players in rock music across its thirty-year history at that point.

Oh, and remember that new album? It's going to sound just like Nirvana always has—but with one or two more pop songs. The reason is revealing: Cobain states that "Love Buzz" is, in his view, Nirvana's best song. It's also the song most in line with what was to follow, the Nirvana "formula" of loud intro, quiet verse, roared chorus. For all the talk of Nirvana cribbing its next new sound from the Pixies or Boston, perhaps it's fair to say Nirvana stole its own sound and just fine-tuned it.

"THAT'S NOT ROCK 'N' ROLL"

Bill Reid | January 28, 1990 | KITS Radio *The Independent Hour* (US)

I conducted this interview late on a weeknight in 1990. I was working on-air at a mainstream rock station in Seattle, and producing and hosting *The Independent Hour*. I recorded the show in Seattle and mailed it on reel tape to KITS in San Francisco, where it aired every week. Seattle was a great place to produce the show in the late '80s and early '90s as the Sub Pop–Seattle scene was huge, first in the underground and then as a mainstream sensation. They were calling Seattle "the new Liverpool."

I'd arranged this interview through Sub Pop and had no contact with the band members until that night. They were to show up at the studio at 10 PM and were already there when I rolled in. I had to leave a Smithereens show early to do the interview. Kurt and Chris were floored that I'd leave a Smithereens show early to interview their band, as they were big fans of the Smithereens. I was amazed that they were surprised by that, as Nirvana was far and away my favorite group at the time. The band was already an underground phenomenon in Seattle ("Seattle Famous," as we say here). They were "our band." The *Bleach* album had recently come out, and the band had just returned from a thirty-six-date European tour.

It is a source of embarrassment to me that Chris, Chad Channing, and I did most of the talking. Kurt was the quietest guy in the room. Kurt's most memorable contribution, for me anyway, comes at the end of the interview when we're bemoaning the fact that rock 'n' roll had become something that both parents and kids could enjoy together. —Bill Reid

Bill Reid: [*Laughter*] I wasn't going to ask Chris to count! Well, here we are in San Francisco with Nirvana! [*Round-robin of "Yeahs!" from Kurt, Chris, and Bill.*]

BR: Good to see you guys.

Chris Novoselic: A great town. We're hanging out at Haight-Ashbury, beat up some Deadheads . . .

BR: [*Laughs*] That was . . . if there are any Deadheads listening, that was Chris over there. Where you guys from?

Kurt Cobain: Seattle, Washington.

BR: Yeah? You record, I think you're on Sub Pop?

KC: We're on Sub Pop.

CN: We're Sub Pop recording artists! [*Some sniggering.*]

BR: Sub Pop recording artists, Nirvana. How'd ya hook up with Sub Pop?

KC: We recorded a demo in Seattle at Reciprocal, and sure enough, Jon Poneman, head honcho of Sub Pop records, called us up about a week after that and sort of negotiated putting out a single.

CN: [*Interrupting*] You can't buy the single if you wanted it anyway, so what does it matter? It's like a limited edition [*puts on radio advert voice*] "Sub Pop Limited Edition Single!"

BR: The tough part about Sub Pop is that sometimes you can't get ahold of their stuff because they make so many collectors' singles and things [*chorus of "right" from Nirvana*]. So you just rented out, called Reciprocal to buy some time there. Did you work with Jack EnDIEno?

CN: EnDino, Jeek EnDino.

KC: Gia Kineval . . .

Chad Channing: He's the one who records us . . .

KC: He's got middle names.

BR: The stuff I've heard is what Jack has produced.

CC: Yeah, yeah. He's the one who recorded the demo Kurt was talking about. Got off on it, then gave it to the head honcho.

BR: Who else has . . .

KC: [*Interrupts*] Jack has worked with Soundgarden, Mudhoney, the Fluid, Tad . . .

CN: He's in England right now recording Blue Cheer!

BR: Seriously?

CN: Yeah, and he's recording, he's also . . . While he's over there, going to Holland, and he's going to record a band called Love Slug.

BR: You mentioned Blue Cheer; that's one of my favorite old 1960s bands. Have you guys been listening to a lot of Blue Cheer?

KC: Sure.

CC: They're right on. They're cool.

CN: "Vincebus Eruptum." They're from San Francisco.

BR: Yeah they are.

CC: Eruptus?

KC: Eruptum.

CN: Yeah, they played taverns and stuff here in San Francisco.

BR: It's crazy. So who else you guys been listening to?

CN: The Vaselines. They're from Scotland.

KC: Young Marble Giants. Smithereens.

CC: Shonen Knife.

BR: Shonen Knife, seriously? Chad, why don't you explain what Shonen Knife is because seriously I'm not sure how many people really know.

CC: Well, like, the meaning of the name perhaps? Well, Shonen Knife . . .

KC: The band.

CC: Well, they're three girls, three Japanese girls that take time off from their different jobs and stuff, because they all work and stuff, and they claim that, like, their band and their music is like their hobby or something, just what they do for a hobby. But it seems they're getting more and more into what they're playing and stuff. Like they're supposed to be coming out with another album real soon and hopefully . . . They're negotiating to get it released over here again, 'cause they're having a bit of trouble with that. But they recently played in L.A., and they had a huge turnout, so I think they'll probably have no problem with it. I dunno. I first heard them in . . . '84 I believe it was? When I got this cassette, I just thought, "Ah, that looks really interesting," because it's like written in Japanese saying Shonen Knife. And I've always been into, like, Japanese things, and I looked at it and said, "Wow, I've got to get this." So I picked it up, and I put it in, and it was just like the most perfect, beautiful Barbie-doll-bubblegum-candy rock I've ever heard.

BR: Yeah?

CC: It's just amazing! Great!

BR: You guys do any Shonen Knife covers?

KC: We want to. We do Vaselines covers, we do one Vaselines cover. But, heck! That's a good idea. We're gonna do.

CC: Oh boy, I dunno, there's so many groovy tunes that they do.

BR: So the records I have from you guys, I've got *Bleach*, which is Sub Pop domestic. And I've got *Blew*, which is . . . it's on Tupelo, it's import, an EP . . .

KC: It's a promo EP. For our last tour.

BR: Oh really? That's why it didn't come out in the States?

KC: Yeah . . . Well, actually, it is available in the States, but not too many of them got here.

BR: Now let's . . .

CN: It's out of print now too.

BR: It's already out of print?

CN: Yeah, it's like, just like a [*radio advert voice*] "a promotional vehicle to help the band on its European tour."

CC: And we didn't even get one.

CN: Who wants to hear your own record anyway?

BR: Well, it'd be nice to have it in the collection, wouldn't it? You wanna play it for your mom, don't ya?

CN: Yeah, I gave one to my little sister; she likes it. My mom doesn't really care for it. She's like, "Well, uhhh, I dunno, Chris, I . . . Uhhh . . . I don't really like it." "OK, mom, well, you like Julio Iglesias."

BR: Yeah, it's like when my mom listens to me on the radio, and I'm playing, like, the Butthole Surfers and stuff. For some reason she can't get into that either!

KC: [*Putting on a voice*] "No, I don't get it, I just don't understand!" There's a big generation gap . . .

CN: Yeah! Rock 'n' roll is like mainstream now, man.

KC: Well, like I was talking about the generation gap; I don't get it. This is the first time in rock 'n' roll history where parents and children listen to the same stuff. Y'know? This is the first time it's happened in thirty years. It's amazing. That's not rock 'n' roll! It's not supposed to be . . .

BR: Rock 'n' roll to me is supposed to be something that your parents ought to hate. Every generation, I thought, needed its own music that their parents hated.

CN: Hi, my name is Chris Novoselic from Nirvana, here's my carrrrd . . . [*Purrs smoothly.*]

BR: OK, thanks for stopping by, you guys. That was Nirvana on *The Independent Hour.*

COBAIN CLIP

Cobain and Novoselic "Explain" Nirvana's Origins

Chris Novoselic: It was a long story. Kurt and I had a job tree-planting, and we got in a fight with these Mexicans.

Kurt Cobain: We were hired by McDonald's to plant trees.

CN: Because they feel guilty, because cows exhale, like, methane or something.

Colleen: So it's been on McDonald's conscience. You guys were hired to ease McDonald's conscience.

CN: So we were digging through the dumpster, trying to find the bag where they throw the good food away. Because they only let it be in there for like ten minutes, and they just throw it out. And we had massive Big Macs, McDLTs, everything, you know? We were feasting.

Colleen: You guys ate so much, you said, "Hey . . ."

CN: "Let's start a band."

—from WORT Radio, April 9, 1990

LONG HAIRED NIRVANA GUY SHAVES HEAD! NATIONAL HYSTERIA ENSUES, NIRVANA KEEPS ON GOING

Laura Begley Bloom and Anne Filson | April 27, 1990 | *Dirt* (US)

In April 1990, we interviewed Kurt Cobain before Nirvana's sound check for a concert in the dining hall of Hampshire College, in Amherst, Massachusetts. We were DJs for WOZQ, the tiny radio station at Smith College that had been recognized by the industry for its commitment to emerging bands. Sub Pop arranged our interview with Kurt (who was spelling his name *Kurdt Kobain* at the time) for our station's biannual fanzine, *Dirt*.

A year and a half earlier, Nirvana's "Love Buzz"/ "Big Cheese" single was on heavy rotation at WOZQ. When we interviewed Kurt in 1990, many of our most beloved punk and indie bands were starting to sign with major labels. The evolution of an industry was quite the affront to our twenty-year-old idealism and punk ethos, and we lamented the increasing exposure of an underground scene that felt so intimate. We could not have fathomed that, shortly after our interview, Nirvana would follow suit by signing with Geffen Records.

Nirvana had driven up to western Massachusetts from New York City after a show at the Pyramid Club, which went so badly it prompted Chris (a.k.a. Krist) Novoselic to shave his head in penance. (The show couldn't have gone that badly, though, because Geffen A&R man Gary Gersh was in the audience that night.) While waiting our turn, we watched the band load in as we sat meekly alongside two British writers, who clearly had a more high-profile interview scheduled with the band. As the equipment made its way into the cafeteria, we didn't really know which one was Kurt but assumed he must certainly be the tall bald guy—until the very slight blond guy approached us for the interview. We recall being disappointed, at first thinking we were interviewing the drummer. We weren't entirely sure until later, when Kurt Cobain came onstage in a dress and blew away the small audience of about one hundred people.

At the time, the band members were still traveling around in a van, and Kurt admitted that they had done very few interviews to date. He was humble yet hilarious in the driest way possible. Looking beyond our Gen-X sarcasm being volleyed back and forth in the interview, there is a glimpse of how earnest, intense, and precise Kurt was about Nirvana's music.

Soon after, we watched with surprise and amusement as this band that we met in a college cafeteria made its epic explosion into the mainstream. And then we mourned with the rest of the world when Kurt ended his own life, just four short years later. We had no idea we were catching Kurt at such a specific and seemingly innocent moment in time, right on the brink of the massive stardom that would come with such tragic repercussions.
—Laura Begley Bloom and Anne Filson

This interview was given with Kurdt Kobain, lead singer and guitarist of NIRVANA, this past April when the group played Hampshire College. We were squeezed in between a previously scheduled interview with some annoying, pretentious British snots from the magazine, "Sounds," and NIRVANA's soundcheck.

KURDT: I had the worst dream on the tour bus. I have these same dreams. I'm going insane. It's like a curse. There's like a voodoo curse on me because every time I fall asleep I'm awake and I can hear the conversations going on in the band. And I look at myself through the corner of my eyes, but I'm paralyzed and I'm going, "You guys, I'm paralyzed and I can't move." It's a dream, but I'm still awake. I feel like I'm on the verge of dying because my lungs are collapsing. (After listening to Kurdt babble about his dreams, we launch into a completely different conversation. There's about six bands playing tonight, and rumor has it that Nirvana might not get to do a sound check.)

DIRT: What's going on tonight? They won't let you soundcheck?

KC: Bad organization as usual.

D: Does this happen to you guys a lot?

KC: Yeah. Seeing bad organization on such a small level makes me realize why the world is so fucked up.

D: Do you think if you were playing at bigger venues people would be more organized?

KC: No.

D: You guys are known, actually, as being a "SubPop band." What do you think of that?

KC: Well, when someone walks up to me and says, "You're my favorite SubPop band," I think—geez, we're you're favorite out of five bands? What about the rest of the country? I don't know. It just scares me. I wonder whether they like us because we're a SubPop band or because we're ourselves.

D: What do you think of the other SubPop bands?

KC: I love 'em. It's not like I have to say, "Oh our label's great. We have good bands." I really like the bands on the label. It isn't because Jon and Bruce (who run SubPop) are marketing geniuses. It's because they have good bands on their label. They do a good job of promotion.

D: I heard they based the whole label on the Motown idea . . . the regional thing . . . taking a lot of bands from the same region and marketing them all in one packaged deal.

KC: It's not as if they've all packaged all these bands and told us to all go out there and play fuzz guitar.

D: Were you influenced by each other?

KC: I don't really think so because most of the bands have been around. They didn't all start up around the same time. I think every Seattle band is just influenced by punk rock. There's always been a good, strong punk rock scene in Seattle. So it's been around for a while.

D: So, how long have you guys been together as a band?

KC: About three years.

D: Didn't they start with MUDHONEY?

KC: MUDHONEY wasn't actually the first to put out a record. They just became the most popular because they went on tour with SONIC YOUTH and they got a lot of exposure.

D: Were you one of (SubPop's) first bands too?

KC: Yeah. In fact, we were together before MUDHONEY.

D: You guys were playing together before SubPop even started.

KC: Around that time when it was just starting up; when they put out the SOUNDGARDEN EP. I mean, we definitely didn't have an impact on anyone in Seattle because we were totally unknown. We'd had a few shows, but we weren't really serious about it. We just decided to record a demo. We didn't even know SubPop existed when we did our demo.

D: Any major label interest?

KC: We don't have any interest in a major label. It would be nice to have better distribution, but anything else that goes on major labels is just a bunch of shit.

D: Does NIRVANA have another album coming out soon?

KC: In September 1990.

D: Is it already recorded?

KC: We recorded seven songs with Butch Vig, a producer that does KILLDOZER and a lot of Amphetamine Reptile bands. He's a great guy.

D: How do you think the album is going to sound?

KC: Well, it doesn't really sound different. We recorded seven songs. There's five that are typically raunchy, heavy NIRVANA with even more guitar and there's two that are manic depressants. So it's a little bit varied.

D: The token slow songs . . .

KC: The token reggae song . . .

D: Any covers on the album?

KC: We don't know. We recorded a VELVET UNDERGROUND song. The songs will be more poppy sounding.

D: Trying to get on the radio?

KC: No. Not at all. That has nothing to do with it. I like pop music.

D: Do you like doing covers?

KC: We made a mistake with "Love Buzz" (on the group's last LP, "Bleach") because it's our best song as far as I'm concerned. There's nothing worse than when a band does a cover that's better than the original. Basically we took the rim—the bass line—and rewrote that song. We stripped it down.

D: I thought that song sounded a little bit different than the rest of the stuff on the album.

KC: It's a lot more simple pop.

D: So, have you guys ever played out here in Western MA before?

KC: I don't know. I'm here in this room. I didn't get to walk around. You see, we don't really get to see the sights. We mainly see the road.

D: What cities do you like to play?

KC: I'll tell you what cities I don't like to play. No, really. The cities I like: San Francisco. Ann Arbor. That's a really great place. People are enthusiastic. They're organized.

D: Have you been drawing more crowds since the LP was released?

KC: It depends on what city. In some places we're popular. Some places no one has heard of us. It's weird. We don't have much promotion. I can probably count on my hand how many times we've had an interview.

D: Do you think it's worth it just to play even if you don't have much of an audience? Do you still enjoy it?

KC: Sure. I like playing just for the hell of it. But not for seven weeks. Playing the same set every night is as boring as a construction job. You get tired of it.

D: You don't vary the set at all?

KC: We don't have enough songs. We dropped five songs (from "Bleach") off the set the week after we recorded it. We're not playing them anymore because they're boring. It's just the same set. Fun. Fun. Fun. But in Europe we're bigger than breakfast on an underground level.

D: That's like when Dino. Jr. went to Europe. They got an incredible turnout.

KC: Dino. Jr.'s big over there. They accept underground bands over there.

D: So, what was the deal with Jason Everman (NIRVANA's ex-guitarist now in SOUNDGARDEN) last summer?

KC: We kicked him out 'cause he didn't like to do the songs that we like. He wants to play slow, heavy grunge and we want to write pop songs.

D: Are you getting a bit sick of hearing the grunge sound?

KC: Yeah. There's only so much distortion you can take. A lot of bands now are going in different directions and writing different styles of songs. Everyone's experimenting. We don't want to milk the sound as far as we possibly can. The FLUID recorded with Butch Vig in Madison, also. TAD recorded with STEVE ALBINI in Chicago.

D: Has NIRVANA gone through any other band member changes?

KC: No. Just one and Jason didn't play on the record. He joined the band a week after we recorded it. But we put his name on the record anyway.

D: Is he from Seattle?

KC: Yeah. He's a really nice guy. We met him maybe a couple of months before we recorded the record and really liked him and started hanging out with him. I started thinking that maybe I'd like to do a bit more singing and didn't want to worry about guitar playing that much. It wasn't a very good idea. We had to practice more.

D: There's a lot of bands that are doing it with three people.

KC: It's kind of hard. (A fourth person) can help a lot though. It would be easier to just stand there and sing.

D: Do you make a concerted effort to jump around on the stage?

KC: Yeah. We choreograph it. There's tape marked all over the floor.

D: You know, I thought you used to all have long hair. When I saw you guys the last time, I swear all of you had long hair.

KC: Yeah. Hair grows, then you cut it. Chris (Novoselic, the bassist) just shaved his eyebrows and his body. All of us had to stop him.

D: When I saw him at first, I thought he was one of the security people.

KC: A Nazi. Yeah, he's really into MINOR THREAT. He just heard it for the first time yesterday. And he's even questioning that.

D: We saw FUGAZI two weeks ago. They played here—a benefit concert for a women's shelter in Northampton. Are you guys into any politically activist movements?

KC: We don't agree with it at all.

D: How did you spend your Earth Day?

KC: We collected as many plastic and polystyrene goods as we could find and built a big bonfire.

D: Do you recycle on tour?

KC: Sure do. We throw everything right out the window. Actually, we recycle at home. I think there should be mandatory recycling laws.

D: But you said you're not into political causes.

KC: Oh no. Not at all. I don't think it should be related to music. Nobody wants to hear a preacher. If you play guitar, you're supposed to have fun.

D: That was like at the FUGAZI show. It was cool, but Ian MacKaye got up there and lectured to everyone.

KC: I mean it's fine for some people. But even if we wanted to be politically correct, we couldn't because we're too stupid. We were just a bunch of stoners in high school.

"IT WAS REALLY COOL ABOUT 1985"

August 25, 1990 | CiTR Radio–*Discorder* (Canada)

This interview occurred at the last show Nirvana played with Dale Crover guesting on the drums. It's an interesting meeting of old friends—Crover ribs his comrades a tad about their current status as if grounding them, reminding them where they came from. A month later there would be one show with Dan Peters on drums; a month after that would come Dave Grohl's inauguration. The single "Sliver"/ "Dive" would come out just a few weeks after Nirvana returned from this tour—their first release indicating the future. —Ed.

Some say heavy, distorted, grunge rockers Nirvana are among the better Sub Pop offerings. One of the few bands on the label to mix poppy melodies with heavy riffing, they've managed to stir up quite a bit of interest with their debut album, *Bleach. Discorder* caught them at the New York Theater on tour with Sonic Youth, where they ripped through a powerful set bristling with energy, despite it being the tail end of the tour. Chris on bass and Kurdt on vocals and guitar are founding members of the band, but their old drummer seems to have mysteriously disappeared, so I started off by talking to their temporary drummer and possibly longtime friend.

Discorder: You're from the Melvins?

Dale Crover: Yeah.

D: What's your name?

DC: My name is Dale, and all I can say is . . . WOW!

D: What happened to the other drummer?

DC: He got shit-canned!

Chris Novoselic: Long story, don't wanna take up your valuable time. Man, it just didn't connect, man, just didn't connect . . .

DC: He's out of the band, that's it.

CN: What other drummer?

D: Um, the one who played on most of the album.

CN: He drowned in a swimming pool.

DC: He spontaneously combusted on stage.

CN: He choked on vomit and died.

D: But what's this I heard about the drummer from Dinosaur Jr. joining the band?

CN: Nah, nah.

D: Why are there all these wild rumors going around?

CN: Yeah, they're WILD rumors. You know, John Bonham is gonna be our drummer.

Kurt Cobain: Jason Bonham.

CN: Jason Bonham. We were kind of talking to Jay about it, but it never materialized. That's how things go, y'know what I mean? That's life for you; you never know what's gonna happen. I mean, one day you could be walking down the street and the next day, boom, you drop dead. Who knows?

D: So when are you coming out with another release?

CN: We've got a single coming out next month.

D: What tunes?

CN: We've got two new tunes: one song's kind of poppy and one song's kind of heavy, so it's the best of both worlds.

D: So what musical direction are you going in, then? Or are you just making it up as you go along?

CN: More melodic.

KC: Speed metal's coming back with a vengeance next ye

D: I noticed you had some metal overtones, especially o "Negative Creep."

CN: Yeah, but we hate heavy metal. We like to play . . . he

DC: There's nothing wrong with a little metal influence, but who wants to limit themselves? We wanna do everything, and anything.

KC: The song got retitled "The Negative Crepe," with berries and whip cream.

CN: We're not really gonna have any gloomy-doomy songs like on the last record.

D: It's one thing to have metal influences, and it's another to be a metal band.

CN: There's good metal.

DC: There's Black Sabbath and then there's bad Danzig stuff . . . There's nothing wrong with a little bit of metal. Anybody that doesn't like even just a little bit of metal is penis-less

KC: They're penis-less?

CN: That means that girls don't like metal . . . But is just a small penis?

DC: [*Laughing*] Yes,

KC: What about hermaphrodites?

CN: But weren't all men born women and then XYZ chromosome came along and then . . . [*Laughter*]

D: Yeah, something like that.

CN: What I'm trying to say—

DC: What I'm trying to say—

CN: When a person leestens to heavy metal music—

DC: If you do not like a leetle bit of the heavy metal, then you are stupid.

CN: You are el stupido. You scum.

D: You've probably had this question a million times, but what do you think of the whole Sub Pop phenomenon?

CN: Mmm . . . it's alright. I don't think it was a movement or anything. It was just a bunch of bands on this label, and those guys played the media hype: "Yeah, yeah, yeah, it's right on!"

DC: After seeing what it turned the audience in Seattle into, it's the worst thing that could've happened.

D: What do you mean by that?

DC: Because, they're just—

CN: He's not on Sub Pop. [*Laughter.*] The Melvins aren't on Sub Pop.

DC: Well, the Melvins aren't, but I play on a couple of songs on their [*Nirvana's —Ed.*] record, so therefore I am on Sub Pop. There's nothing wrong with the bands or anything like that. It's just that all the people up there just take it for granted. They think, "We are so cool."

KC: Social politics involved, man. Everybody just all of a sudden said, "Oh, we have a scene. It's really cool and new so now let's act really cool and hip." All across the nation we've talked to people who say, "I'm moving to Seattle because there's a scene, and it would be really great, and there's a whole bunch of great bands." But really there are only just as many bands in Seattle as there are in any other town. It isn't like a big explosion of great bands in an awesome unity togetherness type of scene like when punk rock was neato a few years ago.

DC: As far as I'm concerned, the media and everything else missed the scene. The scene happened in 1985. And it was really cool about 1985.

D: So you think Sub Pop is a bit media-created and there are a lot of posers now? I don't like to use that word, it's kind of meaningless, but . . .

KC: There's really no such thing as a poser, anyway.

DC: All I've got to say is . . . WOW!

CN: Next question.

D: Yeah, sorry. That was a boring question.

CN: We had one interview where everything the guy said I would say, "No! Next question." We gave the guy a really bad time.

DC: Everybody asks that question, but you haven't asked it before so it's OK. I think everyone gets asked that question anyways, every band: "So what do you think of Sub Pop?"

KC: That must prove there's mixed feelings about it.

CN: There's cool bands, I mean, Mudhoney's a cool band, but anybody who buys a record like "Oh, this is a Sub Pop record so I'll buy it" is kind of screwy.

KC: People don't walk around wearing Sub Pop T-shirts, they wear Mudhoney and Tad T-shirts.

DC: Yeah, but what's on the back of them? A big SUB POP.

D: Just like a big commercial?

CN: Yeah, I don't know.

DC: There's some good bands on there, and that's why it's popular, because there are some good bands.

D: Like you guys?

DC: [*Sarcastically*] Yeah, we're just fuckin' great, goddamn we're the best.

D: How did you end up on a tour with Sonic Youth?

CN: They called us up and said, "Do you guys wanna go on tour with us, just do some West Coast gigs?" And we said, "Yesiree, Bob." And that was all there was to it. It was really great. I guess they caught a few of our shows, heard our record, they liked it, and we liked them, and we said, "How cool, how totally cool. Let's go on tour."

DC: All I got to say is . . . WOW!

CN: That's it, they just called us up and asked if we wanted to do it, and after one millisecond of contemplation we answered yes, we will do it. It was great, big shows.

DC: There was like 4,500 people at the Palladium in L.A.

D: How long have you been on tour with them?

CN: A week or so. This is the eighth and last show. We had one live show where we played but no Sonic Youth: STP didn't play [*an all-female New York punk band who toured with Sonic Youth and Nirvana around this time —Ed.*]. We were all the way down in San Diego so we did a total span of the West Coast of the United States from San Diego, which is like ten miles from the (Mexican) border up to Vancouver. We played Las Vegas. We were all around.

KC: There's swingers in Las Vegas.

CN: Fuck yeah.

KC: A lot of them. People that just swap partners and they can't decide who they wanna have sex with; it was really interesting to watch.

D: You went to some swingers' clubs?

KC: No, they were "swinging" while Sonic Youth was playing. Girls would go back and forth between these two muscle guys and kiss them and then they'd touch each other's genitals. They couldn't decide. I thought they were all going to go home together. But then I lost interest and forgot about them.

CN: They were smoking and drinking.

KC: I couldn't understand what they were doing there at Sonic Youth. But it was kind of neat to watch, y'know. Sonic Youth in the background and these people, like, wanting to breed.

DC: WOW!

PART IV

October to November 1990—UK Rising

IT'S SAID OF CHILD ACTORS THAT IT MUST BE hard for them to go through puberty in the public eye. Well, here we witness Kurt Cobain's end of innocence. The last interview in August concluded with him discussing watching "swingers"; the first interview here from October 1990 has him recounting one of the only groupie stories he ever told. By November he's already sworn off such behavior; there's a "no groupies" rule while traveling. He's growing into the music scene in other ways too: the long conversation about drugs, the rules of long drives, and so on.

Dave Grohl had entered the band about a month before; he takes part in the interviews with Push and with James Sherry. He remains a cheery background presence, like Chad in many ways—younger than his two friends, not the voice of Nirvana. He's also perhaps not as firmly ensconced in position as later retellings would suggest—the comment made to Fraser McKay is, "I won't introduce you as we seem to be going through more drummers than Spinal Tap at the moment." In fact, they'd gone through five drummers (six if you count Bob McFadden) and that summer had sounded out numerous individuals as potential drummers while staging auditions with at least a half dozen individuals; it's fair to say there was caution about whether Grohl would last.

It's also notable that the dynamic of the interviews is changing. In Push's piece, instead of having to explain who the band is, Nirvana now has a release that's well enough known, at least in the United Kingdom, that Cobain is called on to explain one of his songs. Until now it hasn't mattered—interviewers might ask about the band's history or about the *Bleach* album, but "Sliver" is the first original song the band releases that catches people's eye.

The band members also exhibit defensiveness over being overanalyzed, a simple reflection of their relative lack of egotism—they're regular guys and a bit stunned anyone might consider their hair length anything special. Then again, they're under observation, and perhaps it's coy of them to feign surprise when they're asked to explain themselves—no one dyes their hair to go unnoticed.

Nirvana now openly admits that they're chasing a major-label deal, though they're still on Sub Pop, soon to leave, mulling over options, not yet sparking interest from Geffen. They are going places, and the level of ambition is rising visibly: "Well we have some songs that could be a Top Forty hit . . ." They are no longer just talking about this single or that EP or the next tour—they're thinking about getting a song on the charts. Some form of success is finally imaginable.

"WHAT HAPPENED TO REBELLION? WHAT HAPPENED TO ROCK 'N' ROLL?"

James Sherry | October 23, 1990 | *Metal Hammer* (UK)

People make a difference in this world—the cynical prefer to say that "it's all about who you know." *Metal Hammer*'s eye was firmly on hair metal bands and other end-of-the-1980s detritus when a package arrived from Anton Brookes, who worked at Bad Moon Publicity and was handling Sub Pop at the time. Nirvana's *Bleach* album fell out, and I fell into step with their strange groove on first listen. With the encouragement of my then editor, Chris Welch, I was able to start working underground sounds into the magazine. So when Nirvana came on tour, the friendship I'd established with Anton—plus my status as the office's resident fan of the Seattle scene—meant I was able to secure an interview with the band. It started as goofily as it continued—they got a tad lost on the way to the office, and I had to go out on the street to find them, eventually spotting Chris's lanky frame and guiding them in. Kurt maintained an enigmatic distance throughout the proceedings, toying with a cigarette, occasionally interjecting, maintaining a heavily eye-lined background presence. His companions, however, guffawed their way through our time together with easy bonhomie before half-inching my recorder to stage mock interviews with the staff. They say you should never meet your heroes. Well, these guys weren't mine at the time, so that's OK, but maybe my obvious enthusiasm and interest helped give them a stage to breathe easy, have fun, and just enjoy the attention. —James Sherry

[*Long bout of coughing.*]
Chris Novoselic: . . . Bloody mess. [*More coughing.*]

89

James Sherry: Lots of people have had the tape that's going around . . .

CN: That pisses me off, man! [*Laughter.*] We'll have to kill Anton [*Brookes, Nirvana's press manager —Ed.*] now. You're on our death list! [*Listening to recording of what it seems is a tape of Nirvana's first ever recording session —Ed.*] Do you have a shitty copy of it?

JS: No, I haven't, actually, I've only heard a bit of it.

CN: We've got a DAT copy. Do you know what it is? It's a dub off of my stereo, of a tape we got from the studio that Kurt has on his junky hundred-dollar stereo [*interruption*] . . . No, he sent it to Anton and now people are copying off of that so it's all SHHHHHHHHHH . . . Thank God for degeneration.

JS: So is that how your first album first started? You've changed a lot in that time.

Kurt Cobain: Well actually we're going backwards to what we sounded like; we were a lot more experimental, punk, we've never really been that technical, more like . . . we sounded more like the Butthole Surfers.

CN: That's not by choice! Oh "Mexican Seafood," have you heard that? That's one of our first songs.

JS: I've only got the . . . [*Inaudible —Ed.*]

CN: "Paper Cuts" is from a little bit after that.

JS: So what's the music scene like over in the States right now?

CN: Y'know, it's really weird. The music scene seems like all these bands out of nowhere have been signed to major labels.

KC: Yeah, major labels are taking over the underground. Then you come out with a record, come out with a video—and that's it. It might be a great record, but what the fuck are they going to do after that?

CN: There's like . . . They're "made" into an underground band.

KC: They're cultivating underground, alternative images for certain bands. The majors are. See one of the differences between—

CN: [Interrupts] Hey, you know what's weird—

KC: All the college radio stations revolve around alternative—

JS: We don't really have that over here.

CN: Tell you what, though, when was the last time you heard a "pledge drive" on a college radio station?

KC: Ages . . .

JS: To get money?

KC: There's KAOS. But you have a station like KGRG, which is like a total corporate, it's like an alternative station but it's—

JS: It's done by a college?

KC: It's mainstream alternative college radio. They only play major-label, bland, tame music.

CN: What's weird too is the charts here. 'Cause, if you're, like, on an independent label in the charts here, indie chart and major chart, you won't be on the indie chart even though you sell at least a decent amount of records, and you won't be on the major chart because you have to sell astronomical amounts of records to get in that chart. So, you can be out here and you can try to be active, but you won't be on any charts. You're, like, in this limbo land. It's a fine line.

JS: Do you get much press at all these days?

CN: Little bit. Well, we went on the Sonic Youth tour and got a bit. That's another thing; we don't have anybody who, like . . . like at Sub Pop, we didn't really have anyone who organized any press for us. So we'd be on tour like seven weeks and only did one interview, and I can't remember who it was.

JS: What's it like for groups out there, though? Do you manage to get a lot of tours and stuff?

Dave Grohl: In America, where one night you play New York City and the next night you play wherever—Richmond, Virginia—and still you've only got three hundred people. Here you've got halls with, like, a two-thousand capacity place, or maybe a thousand capacity—not every city has those. I think that helps a lot. Here, as far as bands, y'know. I mean, for the Pixies, if the Pixies were to play in America somewhere they'd probably be playing a college auditorium or something. Whereas here they can play a hall.

KC: Most of the time you play in bars.

CN: [*Sings*] We put on women's clothing and hang around in bars . . . [*Laughter*]

KC: Yeah, you can't play to a younger age group.

JS: [*Inaudible —Ed.*] . . . Laser show?

CN: We're going to have a new booking group soon, so we're going to emphasize all of that.

KC: Oh, we're definitely going to make sure all our shows from now on are all-ages gigs.

JS: Yeah? It's not fair if most of your audience are going to be under twenty-one and eighteen.

DG: I'm from Washington, DC, where Minor Threat started, and it never really blew up in DC; it was, whatever, it was Minor Threat, but it was California was where it went next.

CN: We played with the Jesus Lizard—

KC: We played with Jesus Lizard; they're a great group. The Melvins—Buzz [*Osborne —Ed.*]. Total metalheads.

CN: Opinions are us! They're great guys.

KC: They're our friends. They're a heavier band as well. They're the only future for heavy metal. They're the heaviest thing ever. They're slow, they're heavy, they're smart. They're brilliant. And all-round nice guys.

DG: We got called a couple weeks ago about a heavy metal radio show in New Hampshire, and all the kids wanted to know how to get the *Bleach* record, or they wanted to know more about Nirvana and—

KC: There's plenty of good heavy metal; it's just a shame it's all old.

JS: Yeah.

CN: Right on.

JS: Which English bands go down well in the States?

CN: Labels are always picking up these, like, pop and la-la-la—

KC: The Manchester bands . . . Soup Dragons . . .

CN: The Charlatans are really good.

KC: That stuff's really tame, though.

CN: Nothing really shit-hot, though.

KC: I consider it as lame as Jocelyn Brown, or the Carpenters.

JS: All that Manchester scene . . .

CN: How can you totally rip off "Hush" by Deep Purple? How can you do that?

DG: They can beca[u]se [n]ody re[ali]s. [*Chorus of agreement.*]

KC: That's the be[auty] of plagiarism; [h]e hears in between.

DG: Right, MC Ha[mmer]'s doing "Su[perfr]eak" [*sings the "U Can't Touch This" bass line —Ed.*] [and everyone's] [g]oing "woooooo!"

KC: "Hey, this is a great song."

CN: Vanilla Ice is doing "Under Pressure," that Queen/David Bowie song. Oh, and he's also sampling Prince "When Doves Cry."

DG: For which song? "Pray"? [*Agreement.*]

KC: That's the music of the future. There's going to be DJs who do nothing but bring back new dance mixes of old hits. People will be considering them rock gods.

DG: I think that if you do it right . . . because I consider Public Enemy a really good band, y'know? Because the way they do things, they've got this edge to them. I don't know what it is. But they've taken cuts, bits and pieces, from James Brown and—

CN: Sure, what you're seeing there is that quality is there somewhere. If you listen to Patsy Cline, that's really good. That's quality, and Public Enemy is quality, y'know?

KC: People can usually sense that.

DG: If you're sampling stuff, so long as you've got half a fucking brain, and you use it, and you try to do something different instead of using eight bars from a riff that was written—

JS: [*Inaudible —Ed.*] . . . Rave . . .

DG: How does a fourteen-year-old kid get that and want to go "Yeahhhh!" For example, when I heard AC/DC I'd jump all around: "Rock!" Now it's [*impersonates light, jazzy house music —Ed.*] . . . it's like fuck, man.

KC: What happened to rebellion? What happened to rock 'n' roll?

CN: Let's go get high and drink some wine! Throw up, skip school, y'know?

KC: You're out of it, and if you don't, you're a born drug abuser, because you're supposed to be. [*Laughter all around throughout exchange.*]

CN: Well, I inherited alcoholism . . . I like people who go, "It's genetic!" People who go to—

DG: A codeine habit: "It's genetic!"

KC: My fucking dad was a codeine freak!

CN: You know what my dad did? My dad was a Vicks nasal freak.

KC: My grandma swigged NyQuil all the time. Cough medicine.

CN: Why? He just . . . you get used to the sort of chemical in there; you get addicted to it.

KC: You get a tolerance or something?

DG: Probably.

CN: You know how people walk up to you, they haven't touched a drop of alcohol in five years, since they had that cure, 'n' say, "I'm an alcoholic." It's part of their anti-drinking brainwash-type thing, y'know? Some of them are so extreme inside the first five minutes you meet with them they lay the trip on you. They're still in a daze from the cure, y'know? [*Makes electricity sound effect*] Zzzzzit! "Ya gonna drink?!"

KC: It's a hard thing to quit!

CN: Then they press . . . They put these things in your eyes.

KC: Eye drops . . .

DG: That'll be the name of the next big English rap band—Cattle Prod [*impersonating an upper-class English accent*].

CN: Cow Pie! . . . Hair Pie . . . [*Sings*] "She's my . . . you heard that song yet? By Warrant?

JS: Oh yeah, I have. I have.

DG: Oh fuck . . . that's typical American shit! Fucking Warrant . . . It's just a circus. And we're all into heavy metal, but all this is is this big circus . . . fucking crap. Dancing around.

CN: They're not musicians. They're not musicians. They're manipulators. They don't have any feeling. (JS: Songs you're bored of after ten minutes.) It's so bad, and they sit there acting it up. It's so bad that we should hate those guys, we should tell them right to their faces "fucking dicks!" And they're assholes! They're prostitutes!

JS: What do you think of all the thrashy stuff—thrash metal?

KC: It's bullshit.

JS: At least it's got some energy to it. (KC acknowledges: Yeah.)

CN: At least you can piss off somebody.

DG: When "Hell Awaits" first came out . . . oooo, Slayer, "Hell Awaits." And that first riff: "Ah man, this is thrash metal!" And then everyone turns to like, "Wow, look at Candlemass, they're so slow." (CN: That guy sounds like Tom Jones!) And now it's just, y'know? Now you've got fucking Anthrax covering a fucking Joe Jackson song, it's like, what the hell? [*Chris sings a bit of Joe Jackson's "Is She Really Going Out With Him?" —Ed.*]

JS: Oh no way!

CN: No, no, they're not doing that song. It's "Got the Time." But I mean . . .

KC: [*Inaudible —Ed.*] . . . Is influenced by . . . [*Inaudible as they all talk over one another. CN: No way! That's so goofy. —Ed.*] It's what he plays all the time.

DG: I went and saw Anthrax open up for Ozzy, and I'd never seen Anthrax before, and I thought, "Yeah, OK, whatever." So I go see Anthrax in my first heavy metal arena show—it was about two years ago—and I go and Anthrax comes out, lights come on, and they've got this huge goofy-ass-looking fucking cartoon caricature of their faces and stuff, and the singer's like sitting off to the side and I can see the singer sitting under these stairs that are all lit up or something, waiting to come out, and he, like, comes out, it's his cue, and he comes out from under the stairs and he goes like [*makes explosion noise and they all dissolve into hysterics*] . . . smacks his head, comes out like, "Allllllrighhhhhhttttt!" [*Falsetto metal voice*] And then Ozzy comes out, like, Ozzy Osbourne,

Mr. Ozzy Osbourne, he comes out, he's got fucking, he's got the lyrics of his songs on these huge pieces of paper taped to the floor, it's like, "What are you doing?!" He's so fat, between each song he's going, "I love youuuuu!" Everyone's like, "Yeahhh! He loves ussss!"

KC: Ozzy was so great in the early 1980s, though, when he shaved his head and bit off the heads of bats—just wired!

JS: He's popped to hell, though; he doesn't know what he's doing!

CN: On the *Speak of the Devil* tour he'd walk out and go, "I love you!" He'd grab the mic and shout, "Alright!" Then he'd walk off. His eyes were just so wired!

DG: Well, that's cool. He was in one of the coolest bands of all time. [*Chorus of agreement.*]

JS: He's so funny, though, kids love it.

KC: Yeah, he's like Gary Glitter, like Gary Glitter wearing a big tent. I liked it when he went skiing in Japan.

JS: The way he moves on stage is brilliant, all hunched over. "I'm fucking crazy!"

DG: He's wearing that polyester . . . and their drummer came out and did this drum solo where he's got this drum set with all these like electric drums all over it, like on the outside of it, and he's sitting there doing this [*impersonates jackhammer-like drumming*] double-bass thing where they go [*impersonates drums*] and he's looking around like [*more sound effects*] and he gets out in front of his drum set and he's got these huge . . . he's standing with his back to the audience and he's standing in front of his drum kit and hitting these pads and he's got like lightning sounds, thunder sounds, he's going like [*impersonates storm*] and everyone's like, "Whoaaa . . ." Fucking smoking up a storm.

JS: Those big metal shows are so funny. I went to the "Clash of the Titans" one, Slayer and Megadeth and Suicidal Tendencies.

DG: Oh God.

CN: Shows from Hell.

DG: Suicidal Tendencies, man, they're about a fucking . . . they really were ruined. They just . . . because that first record they put out it was like this quality hardcore punk record and then all of a sudden they start just . . . fucking up.

JS: There's a space of about four years between the first one and the next one; it's a really long time.

DG: They were thinking how they could fuck it up!

JS: What next?

CN: What next for our band? (JS: Yeah.) Sign our big deal. Tour.

KC: That's it.

JS: Enjoy it?

CN: Well, what we want to do is . . . yeah, it's alright if it's little hops here and there. What we want to do is we just want to hit some money so we can get some recording equipment and a place and just get secure. Instead of living from hand to mouth every month, so we can relax and really make some songs and work on 'em.

KC: Once America goes to war we're going to live up in the mountains.

CN: I can hardly wait. I hope it triggers a full-on economic collapse. There's hope for it yet.

JS: That'd be cool.

DG: We need to be Top Forty to be ready for a hit like that!

KC: Well, we have some songs that could be a Top Forty hit, but they just wouldn't be.

DG: Well, I don't know, if we just play the game . . . in America you have to have a [*inaudible*]—you guys'll just have to yuk it out with what's her name? [*All guessing.*] Julie Brown! "OK, it's Julie Brown . . ." [*Impersonating TV personality.*]

KC: Get the fuck out of here, bitch! Fuck you!

CN: To everybody on the . . . Go to heaven, break some wood or something.

JS: There hasn't been a band in ages that's got really big on their own without playing the normal game that's needed.

CN: Yeah, you can't do it in the United States, believe it or not.

JS: The same thing will happen over here. Five, six years ago you had Dead Kennedys and Fugazi and all this kind of stuff. I'd like to see that happen again.

DG: What are Fugazi doing, are they into anything?

JS: Well, all these bands were really big in the indie charts and get just in there in the major charts. Fugazi came over the other month and played the festival at Kilburn, which is fucking huge. A really big place and they filled it out, and they've been doing really, really well. But it's not possible to do it in the States?

DG: Well, I think things are changing.

CN: A video on MTV.

KC: If you have the right support. Still, I think people have good judgment, and people know when it's bullshit.

DG: I always get so disillusioned coming over here because the music scene here in England seems like everyone's so much more open-minded, there's so much room for people to do what they wanna do instead of having kids, follow the herd. Then you go back over to America . . . You come over here, everything's so great, and you think, "Wow, things are going to change!" Then you go back to America.

CN: Oh yeah. Our last show of the tour was kinda weird.

KC: We were on tour for seven weeks. It was too much. (CN: A hell tour.) Tired. I only had one guitar that made it through the tour; I'd broken all the others. I just wanted to go home. It was our last show.

CN: That was a hell tour, never again some shit like that, crammed in a van as Tad drives.

DG: A lot of the time it's fun to stay at somebody's house so long as something exciting and dynamic happens. Like a . . . truck gas leak. You can break their stuff and not necessarily have to pay for it.

KC: Or we'll break our stuff, or get our windows bashed out of the van.

CN: By a drunken crazy Rasta man.

KC: This guy took a hammer and smashed in all the windows on our van because he thought I was having an affair with his girlfriend.

JS: Where was this?!

CN: In Columbus, Ohio. I told this guy, "Fuck you, asshole!"

KC: It was so scary too! I was in the van, I was in the van! It's pretty hairy.

CN: It cost two hundred dollars to fix.

DG: Why? Why? Because you'd been boning his wife?

KC: Not his wife, his girlfriend. Well, she told me they were broken up.

CN: He was a nice guy! He was a nice guy, then he gave us his address and we called the cops on him. That cop was so pissed off.

DG: Wait, the guy who busted the windows was a nice guy?

KC: Yeah, he turned out to be a nice guy.

CN: We talked to him afterward, and I started calling him names at one point because we came by his house like, "Get out of here!" "Fuck you, man, kiss my ass!" And we went and called a cop. And he said, "You know what people's problems are?" The cop goes, "Well, some people are screwed up." And he goes, "No, everybody is screwed up." And he gave us his card and said, "If you guys want to try and report it, here's my card, go downtown, you guys have to fill out a report, I'll have to fill out a report." Forget it. We went to some ritzy hotel and for breakfast there was—

KC: Pink salmon toast. It was really expensive.

CN: Calories and carbohydrates on every meal. But it was the only place within walking distance of the glass repair shop—and there's still glass in the hold of the van.

JS: Which ones did he break out?

CN: The roof . . . on the side, the sideboard, the door.

DG: What did you do when he did it?

KC: I was butt naked covered in glass. I just stood up and went, "Don't kill me!"

CN: I was totally hungover.

DG: Did he say anything?

KC: He said, "You're a bitch, and I'm not putting up with this anymore!" Then he went away. And she said to me, "Oops . . . yeah."

CN: Craig [*Montgomery, Nirvana's soundman —Ed.*] was there when that happened. Craig's seen a lot of shenanigans.

KC: We're better off when he's taking control. "Oh now look. Calm. Down. OK, call in the plastic place, Craig . . ." Here we are totally hungover, dead at six o'clock in the morning.
[*Inaudible exchange between James and Kurt —Ed.*]

CN: We had a Peel session yesterday. We played cover songs.

KC: A Devo cover, a Wipers cover, and two Vaselines covers.

JS: How long do you get to do them?

CN: They give you about . . . maybe ten hours?

DG: But we did it in five. We recorded all the songs in about an hour.

JS: How long do you think it's going to be before the album comes out—your next album?

KC: Probably about February. [*Various sounds of mental impairment.*] Can you get codeine over the counter here?

JS: I have no idea.

CN: I had a bottle of liquid codeine and I was meant to have a teaspoon. I drank a whole shitload; I was like uhhhhhh . . . Then I ran out and then I cut to, I had to go through codeine withdrawals. Wake up in a cold sweat. Middle of the night.

KC: I'd never really heard of that!

CN: Oh yeah, you know Janis Joplin at the Monterey Pop Festival? She was walking around with like a Jack Daniel's bottle and it was full of codeine cough syrup, man! "Oooooo! Baby!"

DG: That's how she got that scratchy voice—all that cough syrup! Can you imagine a pile of puke, just cough syrup? [*Much sniggering.*]

KC: Codeine puke . . . I should use codeine.

JS: I've got to go get some—now.

CN: I've got to go to that Music Room place. Get an amplifier. I've got to get it on this tour 'cause . . . I'm just going to test it out.

KC: You've rented a head?

CN: No, but I want to.

KC: Your head's not working?

CN: It's not loud.
[*Dave commences screwing with the mic, and in a Hammer Horror voice says, "KILL, RAPE, TORTURE, REFUSE MEDICAL TREATMENT . . ." —Ed.*]

DG: Hey, now let's go interview people in the office . . . Hello! Now, what do you do?

Unknown: I don't give a shit about nuthin'.

DG: And hi, what's your name?

Unknown: My name's Alexander.

DG: Hello, Alexander, and what do you do here?

Alexander: I'm reception. I've been receptioning.
[*Tape ends with Chris singing Joe Cocker's "You Are So Beautiful," random vocal drum effects, random chat about "Lawnmower Death," and other cheerful inanity. —Ed.*]

NIRVANA

Fraser McKay | October 29, 1990 | *Eye Sore You* (UK)

Like many teenagers in 1989, I had been swept along by the rise of indie music in the wake of the Stone Roses' breakthrough but found the loud riffs and sweaty stagecraft of the Sub Pop roster far more thrilling to see live.

I had gone to see Nirvana and Tad at Norwich Arts Centre after seeing their label mates Mudhoney play one of the best gigs I had seen at that point. Although Tad, quite literally, had a larger stage presence, Kurt Cobain rolling around on the floor shouting while summoning gargantuan guitar sounds was far more mesmerizing.

When I heard Nirvana was returning to Norwich's newly opened Waterfront venue in 1990, I knew I just had to interview them for a fanzine I was producing with my friend Matthew Ivany. Arranging an interview was relatively simple in the days before the Internet—a call to Nirvana's tiny PR agency was all it took, and we were in.

Looking back at the interview, I am startled to see how tolerant Kurt and Chris were. That session backstage at the venue was more like chatting with music fans in a pub than interrogating the following year's alternative rock giants. Chris answered most of the questions, while the shier Kurt was initially happy to just chip in with witty remarks while he was busy redesigning the sleeves of *Blew* and *Bleach* with assorted mohawk hairstyles and fetuses. After I had exhausted my list of prepared questions and Kurt had finished "updating" my record sleeves, the chat became even more jovial—or it may have been the beers they thrust into my hands every few minutes. When I asked who the tall chap with long, dark hair who had said hi on the way to the dressing room loo was, Kurt said, "Oh that's our latest drummer, Dave; I won't introduce you as we seem to be going through more drummers than Spinal Tap at the moment." —Fraser McKay

Nirvana played in Norwich a long time ago now, but they will soon be releasing a second Sub Pop album and we can't see any reason not to cash in on that fact. We talked to Chris (bass) and Kurdt (songs and guitar) about lots of things, and we even mentioned music once in a while. For insights into Noise Heaven read on . . .

Fraser McKay: How did you get involved with Sub Pop?

Chris Novoselic: We just had an idea to go into the Reciprocal recording studio in Seattle. We were living in Aberdeen (not Scotland!) at the time, it took us two hours to get there in this beat-up old Chevy truck with a stove in the back. The camper on the back had a smokestack! Did you know that?

Kurdt Cobain: No!

CN: Yeah! Dwight's truck, that beat-up old Chevy . . .

KC: It had a smokestack??

CN: Yeah, it had a wood stove in the back of it and it had a smokestack!

FM: Oh, come on! What about Sub Pop?

CN: Anyway, so we drove out there and we did this tape with Dale from the Melvins and then Jack Endino happened to be the producer, and he turned it on to Jonathan Poneman from Sub Pop; and Jonathan Poneman from Sub Pop called us up and about a year later I think we finally put out a single. And then we put out our record and then everything just started to roll and that's how we did it. I mean we never even really played in Seattle before that. Jonathan got us a show at this place called The Vogue, that was with Dave, another drummer, another Dave . . . another drummer and, erm, he wasn't in the band for very long.

FM: How are you (and other Sub Pop bands) perceived in the States?

CN: It's totally different to here. It's such a big country it seems like everything's like big corporations . . . Actually that's a very strange question! Y'know—perception is a really weird thing. Like for example people will perceive that it's alright to eat a cow, but at the same time they'll also perceive that it's not okay to eat a dog.

FM: What is the coverage of Sub Pop like in America?

CN: There's no real music press to speak of, you guys are so lucky, you have two papers coming out every week. That's why there's so much hype and stuff—they *have* to do that or they'd be really boring. They have to make up all kinds of stuff and get people jacked up on something, so people will buy their music magazines. Think about it, when your magazine's as big as "Sounds" you'll understand!

FM: How do you like the "Waterfront", compared to the Norwich Arts Centre last time you came?

CN: I liked that other place better. It's really neat, this old church. The Waterfront is just like any other club and you don't get to play in a 500 year old church very often, but this really is just like any other club. It's not that I don't like it, it's just there's nothing really remarkable about it. It's not like "Have YOU been to the Waterfront in Norwich?" And it's not like it's a really awful place either, but "Have YOU ever played in that old church? There's tombstones there from 500 years ago!" Here's a question for you—what happens when your car overheats and the weather's not very hot?

FM: Please tell us!

CN: What is something you should look for to correct the problem? The thermostat could be shot, the timing could be off . . .

FM: Touring's a world of wonder then?

CN: Yeah . . . the waterpump might be shot . . .

KC: We have very strict rules about that—every 300 miles we have to stop for snacks and a feed. Pull over to the side of the road and take all of the equipment out of the van and check it on a checklist, to make sure it's there still . . .

CN: Then when we stop to refuel we have to check the oil, check the air, check the water.

KC: We have to go to an excellent fuel station.

CN: And in the van you can only look forward, you can't turn sideways, you can't talk to anybody at all.

KC: No groupies, friends, roadies.

CN: Nobody but the band.

KC: No radios, no eating. We have a trailer to tow around, for the groupies!

FM: Do you have any favourite British bands?

CN: The Vaselines are my favourite band now. Hey, what's your favourite Rolling Stones record?

FM: Erm, "LET IT BLEED."

CN: Yeah, I like "Let It Bleed" too.
(Someone from the corner of the room: "Let It Be"??)

CN: "Let It Bleed"! That's a good one, yeah.

KC: My favourite is ". . Satanic Majesties . ."

CN: I like that one too.

KC: It's so fuckin' bizarre.

CN: I really like "Flowers" too.

(Out comes the sleeve of "Sub Pop Rock City," searching for autographs.)

FM: Oh—there he is! There's the Legend (Everett True, fact fiends!)

CN: Oh wow!!

KC: Gee, that guy really gets around. That picture was probably chosen because he was in it!

(Everett True is on the back of *Sub Pop Rock City*, in case you were wondering.)

CN: The Legend's right up front, man! He's right up there! Good old Mr Donuts himself!

FM: Last question, how does the band keep going?

CN: Once a week, write a song.

KC: Or you'll turn into crap.

CN: C.R.A.P.—crap! "They're very prolific," somebody said that about a band and I thought it was really horrible (. . who shall remain nameless). "They're very prolific" y'know. Oh jesus!

And that was Nirvana. Prolific or what?

HEAVEN CAN'T WAIT

Push | November 1990 | *Melody Maker* (UK)

I wrote this Nirvana piece for *Melody Maker* at the end of 1990, having reviewed the *Bleach* album for the *Maker* when it came out the previous year. I guess I must have met Nirvana on half a dozen occasions between 1989 and 1994, but this was the only time I interviewed them. The interview took place in November 1990 at a small, shabby B and B on Shepherds Bush Road in west London. I remember sitting on a single bed with the three of them in one of their rooms. I think it was Dave's room. Kurt was in good spirits, laughing and joking and very chatty, and Dave was pretty relaxed too, even though he'd joined the band just a few weeks earlier. I can't recall anything about Krist's demeanor. Kurt had dyed his hair green just before I got to the B and B, but it was a bit of a mess, and I remember him bending over the sink in the room and insisting that Dave and I add more dye to some of the bits he'd missed before we started the interview. If memory serves me right, most of it ended up on my T-shirt. —Push

Nirvana's "Sliver" is probably the only single to rise above the traditional Christmas turkeys this year. Push talks to the Sub Pop band who is being chased by all the majors.

Nirvana's new single, "Sliver," weighs in at a fraction over two minutes and is one hell of a pop song. No messing.

Kurt Cobain: We like to think of it that way too. It's probably the most straightforward song we've ever recorded, but we don't really care if people say that we're spinning off at a tangent. We've always tried to accomplish something new with every track and we've always liked the idea that each one sounds as though it's been written by a different band.

The glorious guitars and vibrant vocal harmonies of "Sliver" are a careful progression rather than a radical departure from their highly acclaimed "Bleach" LP—and anybody who thinks otherwise can't have listened very closely to "About a Girl" or "Swap Meet." But even during the darkest, most leaden moments of "Bleach," those times when the bass rumbles and Kurt howls in mock sympathy, there's still a chance that a melody will suddenly spring forward to alter the mood. Nirvana are experts in the art of surprise.

But there's another sting in the tale of "Sliver." It tells of the traumas of a child away from his parents for the first time and Kurt believes it could be perceived as being as scary as it is poppy.

KC: Mom and dad go off somewhere and leave the kid with his grandparents, and he gets confused and frightened, he doesn't understand what's happening to him. But hey, you mustn't get too worried about him—grandpa doesn't abuse him or anything like that. And in the last verse he wakes up back in his mother's arms.

Chris Novoselic: We now specialise in happy endings. No, that's not true. We actually didn't really know what we were doing with the song when we recorded it. We did it on a whim.

KC: Yeah, Tad were in the studio at the time and we called them up and asked if we could come over and record the song during their lunch break. It took about an hour, and we used their instruments while they sat around eating. But that's nothing new—we approached the recording of "Bleach" like it was a radio session. The key to a successful album is to get the fuck out of the studio before you're sick of the songs. I hate "Bleach" so much now.

Dave Grohl: I still love the album, but that's probably because I've only been in the band for six weeks. I'm sure I'll get sick of it soon.

KC: So am I.

———————

Dave Grohl has already been with Nirvana longer than the last drummer, Dan Peters, who joined the band in time to record "Sliver" and left as the tape cooled down. Dan is better known as a member of fellow Seattle Sub Popsters Mudhoney. There had been speculation about him switching allegiance for ages, with the likelihood of Mudhoney splitting up as a result.

So how come Dan was in Nirvana for only a matter of days?

KC: It wasn't that we were unhappy with Dan's drumming, it was just that Dave has qualities which match our needs a little closer. He takes care of backing vocals for a start. We were blown away when we saw him playing with this band called Scream a few months ago, and Chris and I agreed that we'd ask him to join Nirvana if we ever had the chance. Ironically, that chance came a week after we got Danny in. It was a stressful situation, but it now looks like Dan will rejoin Mudhoney and they'll carry on as before. They're one of our favourite groups, and the idea of that band stopping because of Dan coming over to us had caused us considerable distress.

Dave says one of the best things about being in Nirvana at the moment is the fact that more and more major record companies are taking the band out to dinner to discuss a possible deal. What's the latest?

CN: Well, I don't eat red meat and I'm trying to give up chicken and turkey, so there's not a lot of choice for me.

KC: There are six or seven labels interested in us now, but we're keeping all our options open. It's mainly a question of who understands us best, which A&R man's personality is most compatible with ours.

DG: But we have to remember that a major wants you to make money for them, and if you don't do that they can fuck you—and they fuck you hard.

CN: Oh sure, but also bear in mind that we've got a good lawyer. We have the same lawyer as The Rolling Stones, Poison, Kiss, The Bangles . . .

KC: The Bangles? Wow, that's really neat. He's also got Peter Frampton and we saw him sitting in the office only the other day. He was huddled up in a corner with a plastic tube poking out of his mouth, dribbling everywhere and making those weird wah-wah-wah noises. I couldn't understand a fucking word he said.

———————

Whatever label Nirvana's second album appears on, Chris wants it to be a box set of seven seven-inch singles, each containing a pop tune on one side and a grungy track on the other. The idea sounds almost as much fun as the band's John Peel session a few weeks ago, for which they recorded irreverent versions of songs by Devo, The Wipers and The Vaselines. Leonard Cohen, Beat Happening and Fear are being considered for the next time they're in town. Nirvana also appear on the recent Velvet Underground and Kiss covers compilation LPs, contributing "Here She Comes Now" and "Do You Love Me?" respectively.

CN: That Kiss track was a bit of a joke. We drank a load of red wine and went into this college studio for free. We even let some student mix it for us. The next time we heard the song was on that fucking album. Mind you, who'd want to be serious about a track like that?

KC: Yeah, the whole idea of a cover is to have some fun, to try out something a bit different. We've never tried to do a straight copy and we've never bothered to pull a song apart in order to learn it properly. We'd rather just get on and do it.

DG: The Vaselines songs we recorded sound nothing like the originals at all. Having never heard any of the records until after we came out of the studio, I had no choice but to drum and sing the backing vocals my way rather than theirs. But the Vaselines themselves said that they enjoyed what we'd done to their material and that was quite a thrill. I'd like more covers in our live set, but Kurt has problems remembering the words to most of them.

CN: What the hell does that matter?

———————

Nothing, it would seem is precious to Nirvana. Not even Kurt's long blonde hair, which he's recently had chopped off. Although Mudhoney's Mark Arm beat him to that idea, he's gone a step further by dyeing what's left of it green.

KC: I didn't do it to prove that we're not a Sub Pop big hair band, I did it because I wanted to.

CN: I hate the way that every single thing you do or say is seen as being of such great importance, just because you're in a band. We've been portrayed as redneck illiterates just because of where we're from, and while I don't mind admitting that we're from a redneck town, we've always had trouble dealing with the attitudes which prevail out there. By the same token, we're not an underground band because we've had records out on Sub Pop and we're not a teenage pop group because we now want to sign to a major label.

KC: We're just some guys playing some music.

And modesty has rarely sounded so good.

COBAIN CLIP

"Punk is musical freedom. It's saying, doing and playing what you want. In Webster's terms, 'nirvana' means freedom from pain, suffering, and the external world, and that's pretty close to my definition of Punk Rock."

—from David Geffen Company press bio for Nirvana, 1991

PART V

March to October 1991—One to Watch

HALF THE FUN OF A SURPRISE IS SEEING SOMEONE unaware of what is about to happen. In Nirvana's case the surprise is total. At one point Dave casually mentions that "Smells Like Teen Spirit" "seems like—it's got that heat," indicating the band members still don't realize they've recorded the anthem of the decade. Even in October, interviewing for a local newspaper in the United States, the praise only goes so far as to say that Nirvana *might* become "a household name among the alternative rock set." Worldwide mainstream glory still isn't visualized.

There's an echo of how positive they are toward Sub Pop in how they talk about their new label; the frustrations and limitations of engagement with any commercial company haven't yet set in. Similarly, Cobain rephrases the entire past two years of interviews as having warned everyone Nirvana was going pop. He's right in the sense that it had been an ongoing part of the conversation, but he's wrong in that he'd never said how far Nirvana was going to take it. Still, at this point, he clearly welcomes the shift, the challenge.

There are significant changes, however, in the nature of the interviews. In March they are a band talking about their Sub Pop-era releases; that soon ends. Similarly, with the amount of information about Nirvana piling up in more accessible music magazines, the questions being asked are more probing—school life and childhood, not just band business.

So here they are now: Kurt Cobain on the cusp of stardom confessing he's living in an old van behind Krist Novoselic's house—the band as a whole about to go on tour with a cheap mattress tossed in the back of a rental van. There's no hero worship of Cobain, no excessive focus on him as the front man. Nirvana is still a unit, tired though aware the touring has barely begun; unaware the madness has barely started, and is nowhere near its zenith.

"MOST THINGS PISS ME OFF, I CAN'T HELP IT"

Stephen D. and Garth Mullins | March 9, 1991 | *Offbeat* **(Canada)**

On March 9, 1991, I spent an evening with a little-known band that was gigging in the sleepy college town of Victoria, Canada. I was a DJ at a community radio station and an albino punk antiwar activist with a foot-high platinum mohawk.

I first heard Nirvana on a cassette my friend brought back from Seattle. They were a little band—just like the ones we all played in. We interviewed them for the local alternative weekly, *Offbeat*. Steve brought the tape recorder. I brought the beer.

We talked with the band over dinner at a moderately fancy restaurant—on the record label's tab. At first the maître d' wouldn't let us in. Our punk/grunge uniforms failed the dress code. After the road manager secured us a table, Kurt su̶̶̶̶̶̶̶̶̶ll order the most expensive things we could find. We took turns reading of̶̶̶̶̶̶̶̶ crust English accents. Unable to expense booze, Kurt asked for̶̶̶̶̶es. Really.

After we ate, Kurt reflected on the musical influen̶̶̶̶he metalheads w̶̶̶g around his dad's trailer when he was in fourth grade.

Nirvana played a loud set in a little basement club w̶̶a̶̶̶ceiling. An A̶̶̶̶̶er band opened for them. There was much bullshitting, beer, ̶̶̶̶̶e all hung out in their cheap hotel room. Kurt periodically yelled out ̶̶̶̶̶̶̶̶t people in the alley: "Shuddup down there! We gotta work in the morning!" Just two months after the interview, Nirvana was in the studio recording "Smells Like Teen Spirit." I couldn't help but wonder if my being an albino put the idea for that lyric in Kurt's mind. I guess I'll never know.

Nirvana blew up around the world.

Suddenly, everybody was buying up pieces of a culture that we had made, that we thought was ours. Punk was a commodity, available at a shopping mall near you. I've been watching the process ever since: the rebel sell. That was the beginning of the end of the little community I knew. It was hard on all of us. And I think it was also quite hard on Kurt. Nobody knew then what was coming. —Garth Mullins

[*The article was originally titled "Nirvana" —Ed.*]
Garth and Stephen were just finishing off the last of their generic beer in the alley behind the Forge when three guys came sub-pop-boppin' down the way.

Hey, are you guys Nirvana?

With looks of slight confusion, a shrug and a sniffle the reply came: "Yeah, I guess so."

Stephen D.: We're from some cheesy alternative radio station-CFUV, and we're here to get in free.

Garth Mullins: And to do an interview.

S: Oh. Yeah.

So the introductions were made. Chris (bass), Kurdt (guitar and vocals) and Dave (drums) agreed to let G&S ask them what they anticipated as the same grovelling, butt-kissing questions that Nirvana has been prodded with since their first hint of success. But oh well.

Later, the road manager invited Garth and Stephen to join Nirvana in the consumption of a lot of really expensive food paid for by the unknowing (yet generous) Geffen record label.

Now, with the road manager, the sound dude, and Chris (bass), Kurdt (guitar) and Dave (drums) (Nirvana, stupid!), Garth and Stephen proceeded to the neo-fascist Sticky Wicket where all were promptly rejected for not meeting the "Victorian" dress code (they had jeans on).

Yet after the huge gigantic road manager "conferred" with the weasly whiny restaurant host they were seated in a back corner.

Dave Grohl: Here's the menu.

Kurdt Cobain: What's the most expensive thing?

Chris Novoselic: Well . . . um . . . char grilled New Zealand lamb chops in a golden provincale sauce . . . hmm . . . or baked spring salmon served with tiger prawns on a bed of spinach . . . or . . . wait . . . actually the cajun style baked red snapper served hot 'n' spicy . . . with creole sauce . . .

KC: Any King Crab?

CN: . . . or a blend of westcoast seafood in a puff pastry shell enhanced with a lemon hollandaise breast of chicken served on a cheesy bun.

GM: The whole thing sounds pretty cheesy to me.

Everybody ordered the most expensive thing they could think of.

G&S: So what's up with you guys and Sub Pop?

KC: We cut our hair and they dumped us. Actually, we talked to them for the first time in four months last week. If they weren't such scammers they'd be cool . . .

G&S: What do you mean?

CN: Scamming every fucking thing, everybody, just not taking care. They had all kinds of action that could have made them really something, but they just wanted to play big fish in a little pond.

S&G: Any other bands ditch Sub Pop recently?

Nirvana: . . . Fluid, L7 . . .

CN: Sub Pop actions are not deliberate, they just don't know what they're doing.

KC: I could run a business half the shit they are, or are.

CN: They only wanted to take bands that they thought were cool and make a record for them . . .

DG: . . . that's not so bad . . .

S&G: So who is the creative core?
(Everybody points at Kurdt.)

S&G: And your motivation?

KC: My inspiration to write is mostly to stay sane. Typical punk rock; nothing new, but nothing wrong with it. You've got to write about the truth. Most things piss me off, I can't help it.

S&G: What did you guys think about the war?

CN: Ugh! Not while we're eating.

KC: People are sheep. (A chorus of "Baaas" ensues).

CN: Bush did a really good job re-Americanizing everyone. Boy. We can be proud again. Now the U.S. can do whatever, whenever, however to whoever it pleases.

KC: The best thing about this tour is we haven't seen an American flag for days. What a relief.

CN: I'm sick of it, those goddamned yellow ribbons everywhere . . ."Oh tie a yellow ribbon . . . 'round yer neck . . . baaa."

G&S: So what do ya think about a popular socialist revolution?

CN: Oh yeah, absolutely, we've got to rip down this shit system before we do anything.

S&G: Any striking distinctions from city to city?

DG: Yeah, different forms of THC.

S&G: How did the tour in England go?

KC: Really good. The best tour we've ever been on. Eleven dates just past October with Tad. And we played our last show in England with Mudhoney and Tad.

S&G: Where do you see the impact of *Bleach*?

KC: In England we got a lot of airplay. But I don't really know about the States and Canada. We're just figuring it out. We've been on a few tours in the States playing clubs about this size.

S&G: With the tour over in Vancouver tomorrow . . . what next?

CN: We're going to Madison Wisconsin in a few weeks to start recording. And then starting a tour with Jane's Addiction.

G&S: Keeping the distinctive sludge-pop sound?

KC: Definitely . . . sure . . . it's not going to be concretely that way. We always mix it up. I'm sure after the next record we'll weed out a lot of die-hard grunge freaks—and that's all they like. If they can't appreciate our pop stuff then fuck 'em.

S&G: Love Buzz is a cover—right?

KC: Yeah, by a sixties band called Shocking Blue. They wrote that Bananarama "Venus" song. Shocking Blue's first album rules. I love it.

S&G: Do you like the pop stuff better?

KC: Well . . . not right now. I did a few months ago but I go through phases. I mean . . . I was listening to R.E.M. There's a lot of good pop music. I've always liked it . . . bands like the Beatles, XTC, stuff like that. We won't completely lame-out and convert to that style . . . but I wish people would appreciate a diverse range of music.

S&G: How long have you been a band?

KC: About three-four years.

S&G: And what line-up changes have occurred over time.

KC: Jason Everman was in the band for about six months. We recorded the lp without him but at the time the record came out we decided to put his name on it 'cause he was in the band. THEN we went on tour with him and realized what kind of personality he was. Which was a heavy metal rock 'n' roll kind of attitude, so we kicked him out.

S&G: Regrets?

KC: It was kind of a shame we put his name on the record, now people think he's the guitar player. We just kicked Chad (Channing) out.

G&S Why?

KC: Musical problems. We just weren't clicking and it was getting really stagnant. We just felt we needed a heavier drummer and a technically better drummer. Then Dave (Grohl) came along, and you just couldn't ask for more . . . no way . . . he's the best. And he sings back up, which is good.

S&G: You guys even have a history with the Melvins.

KC: We all lived in Aberdeen (Wash.) and we were friends for the last few years in high school. They were a band, we weren't. Just friends hangin' out so we saw a lot of Melvins' practices.

S&G: Did you jam with them?

KC: Dale did the first demo with us . . . we couldn't find a drummer . . . so we practiced for a couple of days and then recorded. And within a week, Sub Pop was on our butts. Even a little while ago when we were on tour with Sonic Youth Dale played drums for us cause we had just booted Chad.

S&G: Considering you appreciate a diverse range of music, you've probably been influenced by diversity.

KC: All through grade school all I listened to was the Beatles, except for a few singles like, "Seasons in the Sun." There were a few songs I got to hear. My aunt gave me a bunch of Beatles records and I listened to them all the time.

Then I moved to my dad's and hung around with these older stoner guys . . . sorta like right out of the movie *Over the Edge.* Ever seen it? It's great! That's what these guys were like and they'd come over to our trailer and play Aerosmith and Led Zeppelin and Black Sabbath. I was in the fourth grade at the time so I thought it was really neat.

They mainly came over to use my house as a place to fuck their girlfriends and smoke dope but they really turned me on to some really neat music.

S&G: Whence came punk?

KC: Ninth grade. I remember I sold my whole rock collection for twelve bucks to see D.O.A. I didn't like anything else but punk rock for a while. I never really got into hardcore when it came around. It didn't thrill me too much.

G&S: What else stands out now?

KC: The Melvins are fantastic. There are a lot of bands I still listen to, old punk rock stuff. A lot of new bands I don't care for at all.

I like the Pixies, R.E.M., the Vaselines . . . Shonen Knife. Basically a lot of shit we don't play.

G&S: Your hometown?

KC: Aberdeen Washington, a really small secluded redneck logger town. Around 50,000.

S&G: And now . . . ?

KC: I've been living in Olympia the last four years. It's really cool. Totally liberal college. There's an all ages club. Really good scene with shows every Thursday. It's a kind of conservative, clean city, but the cops are Nazis.

S&G: Wow. Sounds like Victoria . . . clean city . . . liberal college . . . Nazi cops. Same shit, different city.

COBAIN CLIP

On Welcoming Success

"The main thing is that we're just as happy playing our music now as we were when I was cleaning fireplaces in Aberdeen. There's still the same excitement, so the level of success we're on doesn't really matter to us. It's a fine thing, a flattering thing, to have major labels wanting you. But it doesn't really matter. We could be dropped in two years, go back to putting out records ourselves, and it wouldn't matter. 'Cause this is not what we were looking for. We didn't want to be staying at the Beverly Garland Hotel. We just wanted people to get the records. And we did do it on an independent level. That's the beauty of it."

—from "Better Dead Than Cool" by Gina Arnold, *Select*, interviewed June–July 1991

(Published January 1992)

COBAIN CLIP

On Sharing Enthusiasm

"I asked my four-year-old sister, 'what's the biggest problem in the whole world, Brianne?' And she said, 'People need to concentrate more.' It was so awesome! She's gonna grow up to be something really great . . . And it won't be the President."

—from "Nirvana Be in My Gang?"

by Keith Cameron, *NME*, August 1991

THE GOLDEN TWENTIES

Marcus Koehler | August 16, 1991 / August 30, 1991 | *No Trend Press* (Germany)

When I heard *Bleach* for the first time, it blew me away—just like the title of the album's opening song suggested it would! At that time, in 1989, nobody would have predicted the pioneering role Nirvana would play for a whole generation of music fans. When I first met the band members at their show in the Schwimmbad Music Club in Heidelberg in November 1989, they seemed to be nothing more than a bunch of slackers with a deep passion for loud, heavy music plus a punk attitude. Hooking up with them again nearly two years later in West Los Angeles, at first glance nothing seemed to have changed. Flannel shirts, lots of booze, and loud distortion tracks. But there was a sort of excitement and suspense in the air. They had just finished the recording sessions for *Nevermind*. The concert was supposed to be the live showcase premiere of their new songs. Also, they were handing out flyers to gather extras for their "Smells Like Teen Spirit" video shoot, which took place the day after in Culver City. Among those who lived through the era, Nirvana's gig at the Roxy on August 15, 1991, is considered the best rock show they've ever seen—a peak. I agree. Totally! It always gives me goose bumps when I recall it! –Marcus Koehler

Translated by Inga Owczors and Jon Darch.

Who'd have thought it? Nirvana storming the *Billboard* charts! Not me, that's for sure. Otherwise, probably only a handful of people, and definitely not the band themselves. *Nevermind* is seriously anything but commercial, and I'm certain that those people currently accusing it of being precisely that would never in a million years have said so if it had come out on Sub Pop. And in any case, all the tracks were created before or just after *Bleach*. So, there you go! And that's not some justification based solely on circumstantial evidence, but an indisputable fact, as bootlegs that appeared at the time quite clearly prove. Period!

On the day of their first gig after the album was recorded, which was at Roxy's in L.A., we got the whole of the band together in front of the mic to find out what they'd been up to over the last twelve months. Then, of course, due to the usual technical gremlins, things didn't go as planned and everything had to be pushed back about eight hours. We therefore had to have the first part of our chat during a party at the Wool commune (ex-Scream band members and others) somewhere in a far-flung district of North Hollywood at an extremely ungodly hour (4 AM). And as Kurdt couldn't be there due to a chronic stomach problem, there then had to be a second chat, which took place about two weeks later in a tour bus at Nuremberg's Serenadenhof (with interview assistance provided by a hack from the *Gurtel* and Nirvana traveling companion Ian Dickson). This time all three of them were together again. And, in contrast to the first meeting where, let's say, there wasn't exactly any lack of yelling, for their part at least they're in somewhat fresher condition—astutely taking the mickey out of each other every now and then, and always talking with a due degree of cynicism. Three rogues, like their music, generally likeable but sometimes also seeming rough at the edges, all twenty of them.

North Hollywood

Marcus Koehler: Why did Chad leave the band?

Chris Novoselic: Because he's now living in a commune, a sort of religious community. On Bainbridge Island. Being with us was getting too much for him. From now on he wants to concentrate almost exclusively on his life there.

MK: But despite that he's playing in a band again . . .

CN: That's right. It's called the Fire Ants and is made up of some of Andrew Wood's younger brothers. [*Wood, who died of a heroin overdose* *in 1990, was the singer with potential breakthrough stars Mother Love Bone and Malfunkshun —Ed.*]

MK: And what's the music like?

CN: Fairly heavy, yet at the same time funky as well. You could even say it's very much in the style of Malfunkshun [*One of the first of the new generation of Seattle rock bands, which consisted of Andrew Wood and his brothers and broke up due to Green River being formed —Ed.*].

MK: He couldn't tour anymore, either.

CN: He simply had too many commitments he had to fulfill. He wouldn't have been able to deal with them. He's living there now, happy and content. They've got a big garden there, animals . . .

MK: And how did you then come to take on Dave?

Dave Grohl: I was playing in a band called Scream. We were just returning from our European tour and had decided to hook another US tour straight onto the back of it. It was supposed to be booked in just a couple of weeks, as we wanted to get back on the road as quickly as possible. But, of course, it was all planned far too much at the last minute and so practically everything then went wrong. When we were appearing here in Hollywood, we stayed for a while with some relatives of our singer and guitarist. Well, then at some point our bassist announced he was off.

MK: Which was the reason for the split.

DG: Yeah, I carried on living here, as I had no way of getting back to Washington, DC. Then one day, I heard from Buzz Osborne of the Melvins, a good friend of mine, that Nirvana were looking for a drummer. I then gave them a call and because they liked Scream and had even seen them live once, they said I should come over. So, I promptly hitchhiked my way up to Seattle and have been living there ever since.

MK: Where did you find a place to live there?

DG: At first, with Kurdt in Olympia, a smaller town about an hour's drive from Seattle. But now in Seattle itself, on the outskirts. A wonderful city. When I was touring before with Scream here in the States, we never played there at all, so I didn't know the place. But I often previously used to ponder where, apart from Washington, DC, I could see myself living. And when I arrived there I thought, yeah, this is a possibility.

MK: Chris, where are you living at the moment?

CN: In Tacoma. It's about half an hour's drive from Seattle. Kurdt lives in our worn-out tour bus directly behind my house. He really likes it.

MK: How did you actually come to sign to Geffen Records?

CN: At the time there were a load of labels who would have liked to sign us, but we thought Geffen would be the ideal choice. They might not have as much money as the others, but their staff, the people who work for them, are fully committed to the thing and totally dedicated to their work in practically every respect. A lot of companies that are only just starting to get involved in alternative music probably wouldn't have known yet how to handle it.

DG: You got the impression that the people from Geffen were really interested in the music. Many of the others that we spoke to seemed to have dollar signs in their eyes and were just thinking: "Yep, there's definitely a lot of money to be made out of this!" The guys at Geffen, on the other hand, really liked our music.

MK: Lately there have been quite a few campaigns launched against the record industry, which, in the view of many fanzine producers, independent labels, and others who really know their stuff in this area, is destroying alternative music. I'm thinking above all of SST and their slogan CORPORATE ROCK STILL SUCKS! What do you guys think about this?

DG: On the one hand, I do have to agree with them. I'm from the punk scene, after all, and so I've always had a good insight into this area and have formed my own view on it. At the moment the situation is really critical for the small labels, with more and more of them looking set to disappear. But, on the other hand, we'd also have liked *Bleach* to be available in as many record stores as possible, which sadly is not the case. Quite the opposite, in fact: you can hardly get it anywhere. So we then get people coming up to us after a concert saying: "It was great, only I'd also like to listen to it at home as well. Have you released any records?" To work with a bigger label means, on the other hand, having to deal with a load of crap, but at the same time that your music gets made accessible to a lot more people.

MK: But in the end the music is bound to suffer.

DG: I wouldn't say that necessarily. Whenever a group switches from an independent to a major label, people immediately write them off: "Oh, they're now with a huge label! You can forget about them!" And that's without listening to the music at all, even if the songs had been written a long time before.

MK: It's generally the sound that gets given a bit of a polish.

DG: In that respect, Geffen are more than obliging. After we'd recorded our album, we began to work on the mix. About halfway through, Geffen said we should stop, we weren't mixing it right. We thought they'd say it wasn't sounding professional enough, or up to the standard of a major release. But it was precisely the opposite. They said it wasn't rough or heavy enough.

MK: So it was effectively you yourselves who wanted to adapt to the major label sound.

DG: It was our producer, Butch Vig. He'd never worked for a relatively big label before, and I think he was therefore always worried about making the record sound too unpolished. In any case, the label reacting in that way again confirmed our previous impression: They knew where we were from, where our roots were. They understood that we were not especially accomplished musicians and that before then we'd actually never worked professionally at all, that we were simply scruffy . . .

CN: White trash.

DG: They understood that and didn't want to make us into anything better.

CN: We all come from broken family backgrounds. [*Laughs.*] That's true! Every one of us, even Chad.

DG: Everyone had divorced parents.

CN: It could even be cited as a decisive influence. Our top twenty influences? Uhh . . . deaths in the family, divorces . . .

DG: Divorce fraud . . .

CN: Getting thrown out of high school—exactly, high school would be another important influence.

MK: Can you still remember any stories from that time?

CN: Oh shit!

DG: Stupid, fucking . . . being drunk . . . being caught doing it . . . Mom being angry because you're completely wasted . . . just stupid . . .

CN: Smoking pot on the high school steps.

DG: Yeah!

MK: Did you really do that?!

DG: Fuck yeah!

CN: It was pretty crazy, but we did it.

MK: And after that you were thrown out.

CN: They didn't catch us.

DG: I was at a Catholic high school. For two years. You had to always wear a uniform, with a tie and all that. I don't, by the way, belong to any faith; I'm not religious at all.

CN: What? You don't believe in God?!

DG: No. In any case, I was only sent there to mend my ways, as I was a very bad boy. One time we were completely stoned and had to go to a mass. There was a guy preaching away at the front and we were just sitting there in our pews going, "Woww!" Man that was so crazy. It'd be interesting to hear what your school system is like in Europe.

CN: I was at school in Yugoslavia for a while, so I can draw some comparisons. Do you know how things work here in the United States? You get a work sheet to take home after school each day, and on it you have to check A, B, or C. The next day it then gets corrected, and that's it.

MK: You're kidding me!

DG: No, that's how it is! And I tell you that's the reason [why] Americans are really stupid. My mother's a teacher at [a] a very capable teacher. She comes home every day and [tells me how] laughable the whole school system actually is and how a sixtee[n year old] was able to pass without being able to read.

MK: What?!

Both: Yeah!

DG: You can graduate from high school by cheating from beginning to end. You don't need to listen during class, be able to read, or have the faintest idea about math, and despite all that you can still pass. And it's no wonder, either. The schools are so big. In Washington, DC, there are some that around five thousand students go to. Each day, every teacher there has six different classes each with something like fifty kids. It's like working at a filling station. You could never remember every individual face.

MK: And you get your grades from start to finish via multiple-choice tests?

CN: A, B, or C . . . perhaps D as well.

DG: There are easier subjects and more difficult ones. You can pass by taking cooking or playing football.

CN: In my last year I took three gymnastics courses. I was doing pommel horse, parallel bars, and high bars. And then I also had mandatory subjects like "Washington State History." In terms of standard of education, the United States are eleventh in the world. Actually, I think it's even worse, something like fifteenth.

MK: Very different from their position as an economic power.

CN: We've simply got the knack of stealing from other people.

DG: The United States designs their school system like that only because all those people who leave high school mentally deficient have to work afterward in mass-production motor or drinks industry factories, thus taking care of our economic boom.

CN: [*Letting out an earthy belch*] That's a shithole, that's for sure!

MK: Before we finish, can you briefly tell us the main impressions left by your first European tour?

CN: Eleven people in one Fiat bus . . . schnitzel, French fries, the Berlin Wall . . . Fiat bus . . . aahh . . . good beer in Germany . . . freaks in Austria, good wine in France [*some girl interjects, shouting something about France*]. We were only in France for one day! Smoking a lot of pot in Switzerland . . .

MK: In Switzerland?! Not in Holland?

CN: [*Addressing the girl*] Are you from Switzerland? . . . Absolutely! [*Now talking to Dave*] Can you remember that weird Swiss girl in London?

Nuremberg

The *Gurtel*: What do you think about the fact that there's no record label in Europe that feels you're relevant to them or knows who you are?

CN: Shit happens!

Kurt Cobain: Who cares!

DG: At least people in the bigger countries ought to . . .

TG: Germany is the biggest country in Europe.

CN: The countries we've actually targeted are ones in Southeast Asia; Cambodia, Thailand, Vietnam, and so on. Get it? That's where the money is, where you can really make a profit. The people there were living for years under the Khmer Rouge or the Hanoi government. They've been starved of decent music! If you started selling records there, the appetite would be voracious.

MK: And do you know what you could undoubtedly make just as much money with? Video rental! In Cambodia, *Rambo* would fly off the shelves!

TG: What, anyhow, I can't comprehend is Ariola not even knowing who you guys are.

DG: Who doesn't know who we are?

TG: The record company that distributes your album here, Ariola!

Nirvana: [*Embarrassed silence, until one of them says:*] As we don't know them either, it's no big deal. It evens things up.

CN: After all, we've got a manager who has to deal with all that crap. The main thing we concentrate on is knowing whether our guitars are properly in tune and when breakfast time is.

MK: How can you afford to destroy so many instruments? [*In L.A. they had broken a guitar and a bass, in Nuremberg another guitar —Ed.*]

DG: We can't.

MK: So who pays for them, then?

DG: We do.

CN: We fund it by going into stores and plundering collection boxes. And when we've nicked enough, we've automatically got the new guitar.

DG: We take the money from disabled kids for a good cause.

KC: We involve old ladies in it, too. The kind who take valium. They often dye their bleached white hair blonde and when they then take their valium it suddenly turns purple. You just have to look out for old ladies with purple hair, cleverly ingratiate yourself with them, and then pinch their handbag along with all their valium. That's actually very easy, as they're generally so spaced out on the valium that they don't notice.

MK: What is it actually that's shown on the back cover of the *Blew* twelve-inch?

CN: No idea. Probably a list of song titles and our record label's logo.

MK: No, I mean the picture that you can see on it.

KC: My ex-girlfriend took the photo when she was at Planned Parenthood to get an abortion. Afterwards, she then also took several of the dead fetuses in trash cans.

CN: That's not right at all! Kurdt's preserved the fetus, old Kurdt Junior, in a jar in his bedroom.

MK: For every letter of the word Seattle, name something that is characteristic of the city and the people who live there.

CN: [*Starts yelling out loudly*] *S* stands for sea, the shining sea! *E* because they eat a lot of eggs, *A* is for answering those fucking questions, double *T* is for . . . because they drink tea ten times a day, *L* is for licking buttholes like a dog licks his own and he eats Gravy Train . . . and the *E* again stands for eeeee! And that's what Seattle means.

MK: If Sub Pop invited you to do a complete cover of any of their previous releases, which one would it be?

KC: Blood Circus.

CN: Blood Circus. Yeah!

MK: What would you do differently?

CN: Nothing. That record is religion. Playing anything from it differently would be like painting a moustache on the Mona Lisa. That perfection is unattainable.

MK: When you are at home and you look out of the window, what do you see?

CN: [*Hums to himself*] Outside my window . . . big trees . . .

DG: I live on a hill and so I can see the city.

CN: I see broken-down cars, a big pile of garbage, cats tearing each other's eyes out . . .

MK: You said trees as well.

CN: Two. Yeah, two beautiful trees. [*Adopts a Sherlock Hemlock* Sesame Street *type of voice*] One had boxing around it, which broke apart suddenly due to goblin-like roots shooting out of the earth. I got several splinters from the wood, which were terribly painful. After that, I lived like a recluse and shut myself away for six months in my closet in order to wait there in combat-ready position for whatever might happen next. They'd already reached my room and were sending slimy white cream through my closet door. And they didn't have any bowls or such like in which they could have conserved it. No! They just kept on shooting and shooting with their fingers. All I could discern was this bubbling fluid that was continually spraying out of these weedy fingers and soon seemed to have spread over the entire floor. Eventually I got so hungry that I ate the stuff.

MK: What do you see, Kurdt?

KC: I don't have a home.

MK: I know, you live behind Chris's house in your old tour bus. But still.

DG: He sees Chris's house, of course.

CN: And this one slightly retarded guy, who jerks off every Sunday morning when the girl next door walks around her room naked. He's a pig. His whole bedroom is papered in nothing but *Hustler* centerfolds.

MK: Why did you choose Nirvana as the band's name?

CN: Because it doesn't rhyme with anything.

DG: Yes it does. It rhymes with marijuana.

CN: True.

DG: And with Madonna.

CN: [*Again in that strange voice*] The reality is that one day we were walking along a street carrying a piano above us. Then at some point it broke over our heads and all the keys got stuck in our mouths, and it went "Myee!" It looked as though they were long, pointed extensions of our teeth, just horrible. Well, at some point a guy then came along and said "Nirvana" . . . and that's how it came about.

MK: Last year, when I was at Sub Pop, I saw in their bathroom a trophy that Nirvana had received for the best newcomer band or something similar . . .

CN: I've heard of that. We put it there.

MK: But you'd said you didn't know anything about it and even that you were appalled.

CN: We'd just forgotten it. You've refreshed our memories. (Humbug!) Incidentally, it's not a trophy. It's a kind of "splash-o-meter" that measures the different lapping sounds. You can tell if it's a guy or a girl and also determine their weight. You can measure exactly how many pounds per unit of pressure there are. This is really helpful, as it can also tell you lots about your personality, you see. People can read hands, cards, and now the toilet as well. If in one man's case it sounds like a waterfall, it's quite obvious he's a very busy guy. Whereas if it's more of a drip, that man's without doubt a laid-back sort of person. It's really extremely interesting. I can tell you things about yourself using this device that before you didn't even know yourself.

MK: Do you guys play any sport, or are there any sports that interest you like they do the majority of Americans—football or baseball, for example?

DG: Not at all.

KC: We detest any kind of sport, even checkers.

CN: Hang on there! I like bowling.

MK: And how about walking or mountain climbing, in the Olympic Mountains, for example? I mean, in the area where you guys live it's perfect for that. You could also go looking for the Yeti. That'd be a challenge, wouldn't it?

DG: What? Yeti? You don't mean Bigfoot, do you? Jesus, I reckon you've been watching too much TV, Marcus.

KC: We heard the Yeti shouting on the back of the Loch Ness Monster.

DG: We've found the Yeti already. He plays bass for us.

MK: What sexual practices do you favor? Not what you imagine, but what you actually do?

DG: As far as I can remember I've never done anything extremely perverse. Tied anyone up or done anything painful to them. What I normally do is throw drinks on the girl while we're doing it.

MK: Whole bottles?

DG: No, of course not whole bottles . . .

KC: My biggest sexual perversion is to avoid any sexual contact at all.

"WE'VE READ A FEW REVIEWS OF THE SINGLE AND THEY'RE MORE THAN POSITIVE"

James Sherry | August 24, 1991 | *Metal Hammer* (UK)

My next encounter with the band was in the back garden of a local pub in Hammersmith with families dining around us. Kurt seemed so much happier; he talked extensively, sharing his thoughts on everything from the recently completed sessions for *Nevermind*—which the entire band was clearly enthusiastic about—to whether Nirvana might get a second guitarist on board, andne even spared kind words for Guns N' Roses. He'd relaxed since our encounter the year before; his gripes about the semi-celebrity attention the band was receiving in the underground didn't seem to be deeply held dissatisfactions, and he seemed to have a genuine desire to see what would happen next. That's what's so wonderful about this interview: that sense of three guys, taking pride in their work, with absolutely no clue what the future held. They were truly innocent about what might come. They were just like any young artists—hopeful that people might see the quality of what they'd just created. They hoped they might become Sonic Youth, but little did they know . . . —James Sherry

James Sherry: So, how fucked up were you at Reading when you played? Because it was total chaos. It was fucking excellent, I thought.

Chris Novoselic: I had a good buzz going, but I wasn't really fucked up.

Dave Grohl: I was sort of, I had a nice little buzz going, then once I got on stage, looked at how massive everything was, I sorta, like, sobered up. Boing!

Kurt Cobain: Yeah, yeah.

JS: You looked like you were having loads of fun anyway.

DG: Yeah, it was great fun.

JS: Have you played festivals like that before?

KC: First time.

JS: Was it really nerve-racking or . . . ?

[*Dave tries to interject.*]

KC: I was really relaxed. I don't know why . . .

DG: I was really nervous at first. I mean, I woke up that morning really early, like my fear of playing in front of so many people woke me up. I woke up like, "Oh my God, I'm going to play in front of twenty thousand people!" Like, Jesus . . . but then after like the first two songs everything was alright.

JS: That's cool. Did you think the festival was good overall? Did you enjoy it overall?

KC: Yeah, definitely.

CN: Excellent. We were only there for the first day, we had to leave. But—

KC: But that night after we played, Sonic Youth played, all our friends were there, y'know? Babes in Toyland and Mudhoney and Hole. Everyone was there so we all got drunk and had a great time.

JS: Fucking brilliant idea. (DG: Yeah . . .) So how's it going with Geffen? Is everything going really cool with them?

CN: Going great. [*Chorus of agreement.*]

JS: Has anyone . . . have you had many sello[ ]iven you've moved to a major label?

KC: No, no one's accused us, no one's actually come up to us and said, "I hate you now!"

JS: Yeah, "You've signed to a major now," because some bands do get that.

KC: Yeah, it's expected, too. I used to think the same thing a few years ago. But I think we've been a pop band even before we recorded the *Bleach* album. "About a Girl" is really the only pop song that ended up on the *Bleach* album, but we had written many like it before so we've always liked pop music.

DG: And also I think if people who just bought the *Bleach* record, like you say, a couple months ago and they think, "Wow, this is great," then they see that the new record is on a major label they'll think, "Gee, there's such a big difference, what a bunch of sellouts." But I guess, what, it was two years? Y'know? There's been a massive time.

KC: Over two years now . . .

JS: What made you choose Geffen?

CN: Sonic Youth was on there . . . We talked to a lot of different people and a lot of different labels, and they seemed they really had it together for what we wanted to do. And they really understood where we were coming from.

JS: I mean, they've been signing a lot of good bands.

CN: Yeah, they just did Teenage Fanclub, and I hear they're chasing Nine Inch Nails. I hope that turns out.

JS: What? Geffen are . . . ?

KC: Yeah . . .

JS: Have things changed a lot for the band since you signed to a major?

KC: Not necessarily.

CN: We are more relaxed with what we can do now, we don't have to worry about our record company.

KC: We've got a manager finally and so the manager deals with all the business.

JS: So you don't have to deal with that kind of stuff.

KC: Well, but he still keeps in contact with us every day and we make the decisions. It is just nice that he has to take all the phone calls and tell people to fuck off.

JS: Yeah. Do you find people have treated you slightly differently since you're on a major label? People in the business and stuff like that?

DG: We got a really nice caterer while we were in Germany.

JS: So when does the album get released?

CN: September 24.

DG: Twenty-third.

JS: What kind of reaction are you expecting from it?

KC: I dunno, hard to say really.

DG: Hopefully a good one.

KC: We've read a few reviews of the single and they're more than positive. Better than I expected.

JS: I think, since the "Sliver" single anyway, people are going to kind of expect the kind of stuff that's going to be on there. It's not going to be like some huge surprise.

KC: Yeah, I don't think so. I think we've been warning people in every interview we've done over the last two years.

JS: So how much time did you spend on the album's production, to make it brilliant, basically?

KC: We spent about three weeks.

JS: Who produced it?

KC: Butch

JS: Are you all pleased with the production overall?

[*All in unison, chorus of "yeah," "yeah!" "great!"*]

KC: It's a good mixture of commercial accessibility and still steamed grunge.

JS: A classic has got to be "Territorial Pissings." I think that's fucking excellent.

DG: You like that one?

KC: That's one of our favorite songs.

JS: I didn't think you were going to do that one live, but when you played it, it was insane. So, when are you going to put a tour out there?

KC: We're coming back in November.

CN: We're going to go all the way down to, like, Italy and Austria. We're going to go back to the United States and we'll be in the United States about five weeks, and the day the tour's over, or the day after the tour's over, we fly out here.

KC: Start all over.

CN: Keep cranking.

DG: I suppose that's probably going to be the real big difference being on a major. (CN: Oh and jet lag! Aggghhhh . . .) Everything's all of a sudden . . . everything's so scheduled.

KC: Everything's so organized. We're actually working constantly.

JS: How tiring is it overall? Is it pretty . . .

DG: So far, so good.

CN: It gets pretty mad.

DG: When we come here next time I'm sure we'll be fucking ragged out.

KC: Imagine this, though: I'm home, we've been here for two weeks, we've got quadruple that amount of time to go! Way more than that. Tenfold. Every day we're going to have interviews. Jesus!

DG: I quit!

CN: See, we've been playing live shows for a while, really, we've got no new material. I mean, we've been playing new material but not out; we've been playing these new songs that we're really excited about and people's reactions are just kind of a little reserved because, you know, when you're playing new songs somebody'll be just kind of listening.

JS: And if they don't know it . . . (CN: Yeah . . .) and then as soon as you go into a song everyone knows it's like . . .

KC: So, it'll definitely spice things up.

JS: But the new songs have been going down really well so far? [*Chorus of agreement.*]

DG: "Teen Spirit" especially, "Smells Like Teen Spirit" seems like—it's got that heat.

JS: People I've played the album to and people who have heard the album have just said there's such a buzz about it at the moment, everyone keeps going on about it so . . . shit, so when it finally gets out it should be fucking explosive. So have you got plans for a follow-up yet or anything? (CN: A record?) Have you written any new songs . . . recorded?

CN: Well, we've got some songs . . .

KC: Yeah, we have some songs.

CN: We've kind of got some ideas that we want to do.

KC: We're thinking of recording a few songs, going back into Reciprocal and recording on the same equipment we recorded *Bleach* on for a few songs. It'll be very different than this one.

JS: In what way?

KC: In both of the extremes as far as being mellow and being heavy and abrasive. It'll be like there's no middle ground—so far, that's the way the songs have turned out.

JS: What kind of stuff do you prefer doing? Do you have any particular style you prefer?

KC: Yeah, I like doing all of it. I mean . . . um . . . the more abrasive stuff is, sometimes, can be more boring because we've been doing it for four years. But that doesn't mean we're going to stop. It's just that we're going to experiment with it more. I dunno . . . Like some of the songs sound like the Raincoats and some of them sound like Big Black.

JS: How do you feel about the way that the press is finally waking up to all this kind of stuff? (CN: It's great.) Now that these bands are getting major deals and things like that they seem to be opening their eyes a bit more—

CN: It's good for the public to be exposed to them. Because I think the music is valid music, really high quality, really valid music. Compared to a lot of stuff that you see in the magazines, that's kinda popular.

JS: Corporate rock stuff that's . . . [*Drowned out by Chris.*]

CN: If someone's going to go out and buy a record, they're really going to get their money's worth. Really get something out of it. Instead of the ol' redundant stuff . . .

KC: That stuff seems to be dying out.

CN: I'm happy that we're getting a lot of exposure and stuff; hopefully our record will get out there and people'll spread the gospel about all these cool bands.

KC: When I was fifteen I would have loved to have read about any kind of underground bands.

JS: Do you have kids coming up to you for autographs and things like that? [*Murmurs of agreement.*] Like rock stars?

KC: It's calmed down now. At first we were floored by it, we couldn't believe that people—punk rock, supposedly punk rock people—wanted our autographs. It seems like the underground has completely reversed itself. There's still a lot of good vital things going on in it, but the rock star part of it—I don't necessarily think it can simply be thought of as "We're rock stars and they want our autographs," it's just that they appreciate our music so much that they wanted something extra. They just wanna . . . it's an excuse to come up and talk to us also. I just assume, I would rather just talk to somebody than give them an autograph, so usually when I do give autographs I usually just take their pen and put an *X* on their program.

JS: Is it, I would have thought, is it mainly more metal kids that come up and do that kind of stuff?

KC: It's hard to even tell between punks and metal kids anymore at our shows, es[...]ates because it seems like there's this new breed of people [...]lly like both of the styles. And a lot of them have . . . a lot of th[...]ss like Mudhoney and have middle-length hair, and they just like rock 'n' roll and they don't even care to be classified anymore. So it's a mixture of the rock star and the punk rock thing at the same time, and it's not as boring as the crossover thing.

JS: So are you going to stick as a three-piece band, or is there any thought of getting a second guitarist or anything like that?

KC: It's been . . . we've been talking about it lately. There's no way we would get another guitarist in the band unless we were 100 percent positive that they would work out. It would have to be someone that has an original guitar style. I couldn't think of any musician in any band right now who I'd want to play with, so we'll just have to come across—we're not going to seek out anyone—we'll just have to come across someone, then we might consider but . . . we weren't a four-piece when we recorded the *Bleach* album, we told you that probably, so . . . We've always done it as a three-piece. But y'know, you're pretty limited that way. It's hard for me to concentrate on singing and playing . . .

JS: Having fun, rocking out . . . Was it you who threw yourself on the kit at Reading or . . . ? All I saw was, I looked away and suddenly there was these two feet poking out. When you play, do you do that kind of stuff? Because it seems like recently, watching bands, they're doing that kind of stuff and trashing equipment and being stupid, and its getting much more popular with bands—which is good I think. (KC: Yeah . . .) Mudhoney played the Astoria, to a totally packed Astoria, and just pissed around for about thirty minutes—that was fucking brilliant.

KC: It's great, it's a good time. I think it's a natural thing too. It's really natural for rock bands to throw their equipment around and fall down . . .

JS: Do you think it's something about the Seattle bands? What do you think it is about Seattle that's brought on so many of these bands? There's so many bands in one area and so many things going on in that one area; what was it that happened there that made it all sort of explode at one time?

CN: I don't know . . .

KC: I think for a long time, in the back of everyone's minds, while they were pretending to be punk rockers they all liked, hmm, Aerosmith and Alice Cooper, but it wasn't cool or hip to admit that. Then, all of a sudden, the Melvins and Soundgarden started playing the slow, heavy stuff, and it sounded a lot like . . . well, similar to Black Sabbath and stuff like that. Then everyone said, "OK! It's cool now. I can finally admit it." It wasn't something that everyone just jumped on, it wasn't like a trend at all. It was just something that was taboo that no one talked about until someone finally did it and everyone went, "Yeah, we're free!"

JS: So how far do you want to take the band? Do you see it as a Top Forty single band, a huge thing?

KC: It doesn't matter . . . it doesn't matter. I don't really like playing on really huge stages where there's a barrier dividing you and the audience from each other. That's not very fun.

JS: But that's going to be inevitable in time, isn't it? If the band gets huge those are the kinds of places you're going to have to play.

KC: Yeah, well, I think we'll have to think of something like we'll do two weeks at [*inaudible*] . . . that kind of thing. We do that a lot, stuff like that. But when we do play the larger venues we'll have to work out some kind of agreement with the security and the venue to take away the barrier or at least move it in closer, so we can be closer. Because I have to jump into the audience at least every other show, and if I can't even jump twenty feet over the top of a security guy, what's the point?

DG: Could you have cleared that at the Reading Festival?

JS: How big was that? You don't really see how big that pit is—

CN: There's a whole, like, twenty feet—

DG: Plus the stage is like eight feet high.

CN: Then there's like a little press walk—

KC: So I jumped out into the press part and then I was this far away from everyone, and I tried to jump up into the crowd, but they were so violent that they just grabbed onto my guitar, my hair, my arms, and just started pulling on me.

JS: Oh shit, isn't that kinda stuff pretty scary?

KC: Well, yeah, 'cause I didn't understand . . . I'm only just the fucking guitar player, so why rip me apart? I just want to jump on top of you, y'know? No, the only thing that annoys me about it is that they don't have any respect for my effects pedals, they always jump onto my effects pedals, rip my guitar out. But there's no sense in there being a rock show where there's seats and you can't even smoke. That's the way it is at this venue called the ████████tre in Seattle. The bouncers are Nazis, you can't even have fun, ██████ barely move without a bouncer running you out and beating you out. It just puts a damper on the whole evening. So we're never going to play that place again.

JS: It used to be a bit like that at the Astoria. They used to have a bit of a bouncer problem. Do you have your own ████████all?

KC: No, we don't, but you do have the opportunity at times to hire (**CN:** That'd be a good idea!) people, and you can do that. Like, I think that's what Mudhoney did last time we played with them at the Astoria.

JS: Yeah, I think they had their own security on when they played here recently as well because the security were actually helping people over the barrier to dive but controlling it so they didn't run all over the stage and stomp up and down on the effects pedals.

DG: But do you know what was amazing, the first time I'd ever seen this, when we played at the Pukkelpop Festival in Belgium? There's the barrier—there's probably something like twenty thousand people there—there's the barrier and just maybe like twenty or thirty security guards standing by the barrier. Now, if someone was to come over the barrier, they'd just get mauled. They had to pull people over the barrier because people were being crushed and someone would just raise their hand up like, "Pull me out," because they're crushed and it's so hot. And two guys would just pull them out.

CN: And wasn't it where they were passing people when somebody had passed out and there were medics there and they'd grab them and put them on a stretcher. An ambulance . . .

DG: Now I can see how kids were being killed at the . . . Donning Festival or something. (JS: Donington.) If you were to pass out you'd just slip in . . .

JS: Yeah, that was during Guns N' Roses' set—two kids died; it was such a total crush.

KC: Really?

JS: Yeah, it was totally horrible.

CN: That sucks.

KC: Can you imagine dying for Guns N' Roses? Such a waste.

CN: What a waste!

KC: Yeah, those guys probably didn't even, like—

DG: Stop playing.

KC: Send the family flowers or anything. Like when the Who, when that . . . when was that again?

CN: Eleven people died. Cincinnati. 1979.

KC: Yeah, the Who concert, those guys were really affected by that. Felt terrible.

JS: I mean, Guns N' Roses got into so much hassle over that. They were banned from, they played at Wembley Stadium on Saturday, and they were banned for swearing on stage; they're never going to be allowed to play there again.

KC: For swearing?

JS: It's true! London Council sent them this letter, or someone did, saying that "if you swear on stage . . ." And the band ended up signing all these contracts saying they wouldn't swear on stage, and Axl walked out on stage with his contract saying, "Fuck, fuck, fuck, fuck, fuck . . ." All this kinda stuff. That kinda stuff's cool.

KC: That's great, yeah.

CN: That's awesome.

KC: There are a few rebellious rock 'n' roll qualities Guns N' Roses have that I kinda like.

JS: Do you ever see yourselves playing with bands like that?

KC: Yeah! We're thinking about going on tour with Guns N' Roses for a couple of weeks just for the hell of it. Because it'd be a ridiculous thing, just so funny. If you have the chance, go for it. It's not a career move necessarily; it'd be funny. We'd never have to worry about meeting the band or anything because they never hang around with each other anyhow. Yeah. It'd just be kind of a thrill to play in front of that many people, it'd be like a joke.

JS: And also their reaction as well. To having a band like that when you'd be expecting a normal safe rock band and then they get their blown off . . . So, I mean, this single that's coming out off of the album, is this the only one you're going to release, or are you going to release a couple more and try (KC: We'll have a couple more.) and go for a hit single and see what happens?

DG: I don't know if that's the intention.

KC: We're planning on releasing three singles. Three videos this year once the album is out.

JS: Yeah, I was going to ask about videos—what kinds of ideas have you got? Are you going to just do a straight performance video or something a little bit different?

KC: Well, we just finished a video, our first video, for "Smells Like Teen Spirit"—it came in American formats so they have to transfer it, then you can see it tomorrow. But it was kinda typical, we just . . . it was pep assembly themed. We invited a few hundred people to come down, fans, sit in the bleachers and watch us. We filmed them watching us, we were playing, we had four cheerleaders with anarchy A's on their sweaters, and they were trying to rile up the pep assembly kids. The pep assembly pupils start dancing and falling on top of each other, and they eventually mob us and knock us over and start dancing together just . . .

CN: We have to get going now . . . sorry.

JS: That's alright.

NIRVANA: THE SHORT TRIP UP

Paul Kimball | September 19, 1991 | *Hype* (US)

One evening in 1991 I drove my Toyota Tercel from Olympia to Tacoma to interview Nirvana for *Hype*. I'd never been to Chris and Shelli's place before, but we'd all hung out at various shows so the setting was pretty relaxed. Chris and Kurdt (which is how they were spelling their names at that time) were clearly enjoying themselves throughout our conversation, despite having done several other interviews that afternoon. In retrospect, it's obvious that I was lucky enough to capture them during the brief period where the novelty of being signed to a major label pleased them in a sweetly uncomplicated way. It was a fun, loose conversation, and it enabled me to satisfy my genuine curiosity about the details of their recent step into the big leagues.

The last time I ever spoke with Kurt was at the '91 Halloween Paramount show, and he was entirely complimentary about this piece, saying I'd "got it right." He did, however, take pains to clarify that Fitz of Depression did not steal anyone's gear, which he thought the article suggested. Of course I knew that, but I saw his point. Sorry if I created the wrong impression, Fitz guys! –Paul Kimball

I remember hearing of Nirvana for the first time about three years ago. They had just played a party out at the Caddyshack in Olympia with a local band called Lush and everybody was raving about them. I was very skeptical. I mean, come on, Nirvana? That's the most stupid name I've ever heard! Like some kind of bad seventies cover band or something. And they're from where? Aberdeen? Jesus, what a joke. The fact that no one raved about my band like that might have had something to do with it, but I doubt it.

In the months that followed I had a few chances to see them, and whether I liked them or not depended entirely on how drunk we were (they and I). The sound was really heavy back then, much less poppy than the more recent material, and very repetitive. Something about it was interesting, but I couldn't put my finger on it. I continued to be a skeptic. I couldn't stand the guy's voice.

Then the Sub Pop thing happened. One minute I heard they had a single out and the next minute I couldn't find one in the stores anywhere. It was pretty good. I still thought the vocals were too whiny, but it sounded big and hairy in a way that reminded me of vintage KISS, so I was won over. I had met the guys in the band shortly before the single came out, so I was a little more inclined to like it since I knew who they were. But the next time I saw them play, in Olympia's Capitol Lake Park, with My Name, Swallow, and Soundgarden, I was not particularly impressed.

Then my band had a gig with them at a new place in downtown Olympia called REKO MUSE. It was an old garage bought by an eight-woman collective for photography shows, but rock helped pay the bills. We played a good set and I took a cool-down toke on a pipe offered to me by a friend while we waited for Nirvana to set up. They were sporting a new guitar player that night, the near-famous Jason Everman. The sound was huge with the extra guitar and I became an instant convert. The vocals were all there this time and sounded very powerful. I stood on a chair at the back of the room and let myself get swept away. It was rock 'n' roll transcendence at its finest.

After Bleach came out (with a cover photo taken at that very same REKO MUSE show) it became harder to see them at parties; the few they played were so packed that breathing was difficult and movement was out of the question. They played a great show with the Melvins and Beat Happening out in the Grange Hall on Steamboat Island around that time. Chris was in a hippie dress and Kurdt's arms were horribly scarred with needle tracks, causing more than a little shock amongst those of us in the audience who didn't realize that they had been painted on prior to the show. Nirvana started turning up on huge bills in Seattle, where it was rumored that they had become the biggest draw in town. They had lost their second guitarist on tour long ago (he was here a minute ago . . . ?) and later replaced Chad, their third drummer, with Dave from Scream. They could now be found smashing equipment in crowded rooms all over the country. It seemed only a matter of time before they took the next step in what could only be described as "up" and sign on to a multinational record label.

This has now come to pass. Nirvana's major label debut, Nevermind, is out on DGC and god only knows what's next. I have heard it a few times, and it can only be described as an incredibly strong record from start to finish. I was able to talk to Chris and Kurdt the day before they left to go on tour to support Nevermind about where they're at now in a career that many eyes and ears have followed.

Paul Kimball: How do you like dealing with DGC so far?

Kurdt Cobain: Well, our Geffen rep in Seattle is really nice. She lets us drink in her house, she buys us drinks, and she let me destroy a Nelson gold record . . . we took all the Nelson CD's and made a huge domino thing in her front room. It was real extravagant. But I did not put the Nelson tape in the toilet and clog it up, though she thinks I did.

PK: Your schedule was pretty tight for tonight. Have you guys been doing shitloads of interviews?

Chris Novoselic: Yeah.

KC: Constantly, everyday.

CN: We're gonna fly into Toronto Thursday night, all day Friday we're gonna do interviews until soundcheck. It's just something you gotta do if you wanna get promotion.

PK: How much does the record company do for you?

CN: Oh, shit. Promotion wise, they do it all.

KC: We don't have to be burdened with the everyday boring part of being a band. We don't have to hope and hope that you're gonna get an interview sometime this week, call up your label and hound them about it three or four times . . .

CN: They just take care of everything. They call us up and say, "You have to do this-and-this many interviews," we just do 'em. We have a lot of fun.

KC: They do everything for us, they buy us drinks, they burp and diaper us, tell us when to wake up . . .

CN: And on occasion smoke us out . . .

PK: You're heading to Toronto tomorrow. Is the tour beginning there, or what?

CN: Yeah. The tour's for five or six weeks.

PK: Are you headlining?

CN: Yeah, headlining tour.

KC: The Melvins are going with us for a couple of weeks, then Hole, Sister Double Happiness . . .

CN: Is Hole gonna do shows with us?

KC: Yeah, they're doing a few, I think.

CN: Oh, wow! And Urge Overkill.

PK: What were you guys doing when you were out of town last spring?

CN: Last spring . . . um . . . we recorded a record last spring!

KC: Yeah, we stayed at a McDonald's-like apartment chain.

CN: You can get a furnished apartment for a month in L.A.

KC: It's a place where kids who are auditioning for *Star Search* stay.

Shelli Novoselic (Chris's wife): Yeah, they had a piano bar, there was free beer and wine, and we saw a show they put on, little kids singing songs from Les Miserables.

KC: Fitz of Depression booked a tour and came down and stayed with us for a few days. We had to have a Fitz of Depression benefit show to get 'em back home.

CN: Yeah, and we got all of our guitars stolen.

PK: Some benefit. So, are you getting some kind of tour vehicle from DGC?

CN: Yeah, just a rental van. They took two of the back benches out and we're just gonna throw a futon back there. We got a trailer, and that's it, really.

KC: We'll have a lot of comforts; a foot massage, a water pick, a humidifier.

CN: Yeah, we're gonna be using a humidifier all the time 'cause we're so sickly.

KC: We're gonna be shooting up aloe vera and warm milk speedballs.

PK: I saw the CD single "Smells Like Teen Spirit" and it's got the Sub Pop logo on it, what's the deal with that?

KC: That was part of the buy-out agreement. In order for us to get out of the contract they got so-much money and the privilege of having their name on the back of our next two albums. Which is fine. I mean, promoting Sub Pop is fine with me.

PK: Is Geffen booking your tour or . . .

CN: We have our booking agent, Triad. We keep all the money from the shows. DGC has nothing to do with it. A lot of bands they do. It was part of the deal.

KC: We get to choose who goes on tour with us and how long we tour. If we just wanted to do a two-week tour this whole year there's nothing they could do about it.

CN: But they have their ways of doing something about it. They can say, "Okay, you guys don't participate, neither will we." All of a sudden, no promotion. You gotta work together with them.

PK: Was it fun to take time to put together something as professional as this record is?

KC: It was fun, yeah. It was very, very casual.

CN: Yeah, that was the best thing about it.

KC: We drank Jim Beam everyday and lay on the couch for hours. We wasted a lot of time. We could have recorded three Bleach records in the time we were just playing pinball.

CN: We had the studio locked out for two weeks, but it probably would have taken four days, working continuously.

KC: But we didn't really spend that much money on this record. Not even a quarter of what most bands on majors spend.

PK: When you record are you going for your live sound or what?

KC: When we recorded this record I wanted it to sound like a studio, like a Pretenders album or something like that. I wanted it to sound very tight.

PK: Are you going to have trouble recreating those studio sounds live?

CN: Oh no, I think it comes across really well live. We've been playing those songs for a while and they sound fine.

PK: What appealed to you about DGC in the first place?

KC: It didn't seem like anyone cared or knew about us, that's what appealed to us.

CN: But there were some people there that worked at, like, Rough Trade and SST . . .

KC: Who generally seemed to know about underground music.

CN: And Sonic Youth is there too, and that's cool. We went on tour with them in Europe. We just happened to get the same manager.

PK: Sonic Youth had vinyl out for their last record, are you going to do that too?

Both: Yeah.

KC: As [image] we want.

CN: We already have this [picking up the 12″ version of the Teen Spirit single].

KC: The only screw-up that DGC has made so far is the tongue on our smiley face logo. The tongue was supposed to be up like he's licking something, not like he's on drugs.

PK: So where are you taking it from here?

KC: (Singing) "One day at a time, Sweet Jesus . . . "

CN: Well, the gospel record. We're gonna cover that song. Then we're gonna do Vegas.

It seems to me that Nirvana is playing it pretty cool right now and just waiting to see what will happen next. I've heard a few people expressing the usual dismay about a local band turning big league, but I've always felt that the music speaks for itself. In Nirvana's case, the music is still sounding very true to itself and it rocks unquestionably. But, of course, I never doubted them for a minute.

"NO WAY CAN WE TOUCH THE PLASTIC ONO BAND"

Marc Coiteux | September 21, 1991 | MusiquePlus (Canada)

Since the inception of MusiquePlus in 1986, the channel has made an indelible mark on the musical culture of Quebec. MusiquePlus was the world's first French-language channel devoted to music and was a pioneer among the region's specialized television stations, constantly aiming to be the reference point for all musical trends in every genre of music. MusiquePlus has helped propel a significant number of local and international talents to wider fame, as well as providing a stepping stone for many presenters who have gone on to further glory and remain media fixtures at numerous television and radio stations. Musique-Plus continues to embody the lifestyle of a generation—in tune with its loyal audience via constant interaction through MusiquePlus.com and its social media presence. —MusiquePlus

Saturday, September 21. I had been working as a VJ and journalist for a full year at MusiquePlus. We had heard of Nirvana, but the Manchester scene in the United Kingdom was still top billing at the time—Nirvana had sold barely thirty thousand copies of their first album; they were still unknowns. I got the advance cassette of *Nevermind* only the day before the band arrived, along with a blue sheet of paper with two paragraphs describing the release. For most bands we had pages of context before talking to them; for Nirvana, just a slim file, a small number of clippings and features—no Google back then.

I dropped by the venue, and the record company guy called Cobain over and said, "Hey, do you wanna do an interview?" Kurt replied, "Fuck no."

What did I care? I was going to leave, but the band members changed their minds or were persuaded to. It was a strange interview; I had to try to get to know them right there and then.

Krist was goofing around, Dave was in the background, and Kurt was . . . Kurt. The whole of the next two and a half years was summed up by how he behaved here—brilliant, yet sombre; polite, yet unfriendly. At one point he even said to Krist, "We're avoiding the question, what were you saying . . . ?" After the interview was over, we spoke a little and he eased up—we chatted about the city a while, shook hands, and he left me with the impression that once the camera had been tucked away, we could have stayed there like that, just talking. —Marc Coiteux

[*Kurt attempts to hand-roll a cigarette and manages to drop the tobacco on himself. Studiously restarts —Ed.*]

Marc Coiteux: Well, since it's your first interview with us—you've got an album about to be released; we cannot not talk about that first major label deal. So, tell me . . .

Dave Grohl: That's a double negative . . .

Kurt Cobain: Catch-22.

MC: I ask it so many times to so many bands that have been on independent labels before and then on major labels before, that I'm always wondering if it's redundant at some point. So . . .

KC: [*Interrupting*] Do you like the B-52s?

MC: I love them.

KC: Do you like Blondie? Do you like Devo? Do you like the Cars?

Chris Novoselic: Do you like the Plastic Ono Band *Live in Toronto*?

MC: That was OK. I didn't hear the live album though.

CN: [*Chris impersonates Yoko Ono —Ed.*] Yeah, that's how we got on the subject of the B-52s.

KC: All those bands are on major labels too. And the Ramones. And the Clash! And the Sex Pistols! [*Voice rising to a squeaky pitch—Dave echoes "And the Sex Pistols!" —Ed.*] Not to say we're half as good as any of those bands but . . . pretty much . . .

CN: No way can we touch the Plastic Ono Band.

DG: Pfft! Not with a ten-foot pole!

KC: There's our answer to the major label question.

MC: Does it change anything?

KC: Yeah, it gives you more freedom because you have more money to waste. (CN: Burn!)

DG: Waste, yeah . . . I bought a kick drum pedal today, which I never would have been able to do if . . .

MC: What do you say about bands like Mudhoney that come from Seattle but don't want to be on a major label?

KC: (DG: That's great!) Well fine, that's their prerogative, y'know?

CN: Each to their own. Be a better place if we each subscribed to that philosophy, huh?

KC: It would be.

MC: Did it change anything from *Bleach*? Doing that album, was there a big change?

CN: Yeah, there was a change in the way we went about it.

DG: Well, there was two years, first of all.

CN: Two years between records. You mean the way we recorded it or the way . . . our material?

MC: Your material.

CN: Oh yeah, two years as a band. *Bleach* was recorded in December of 1988 and now it's pushing December 1991.

KC: [*In background*] Yeah, there was two years of unrecorded material to choose from . . .

CN: Now we even have *Nevermind* behind us and we're blazing new, exciting frontiers.

KC: Sacagawea!

MC: Does it change any . . . how do you say that?

KC: Sacagawea!

CN: She was Lewis and Clark's guide when they . . . they were two explorers and they . . .

KC: She was a trailblazer.

CN: They trail-blazed and went all the way and discovered the West and opened up the West. Sacagawea was their Indian guide. Yeah, Sacagawea . . .

MC: So what about him?

KC: It was a her.

CN: Well, we were blazing new frontiers and they were blazing new frontiers! We're the Lewis and Clark and the Sacagawea of modern-day rock 'n' roll. [*All sniggering.*]

DG: We were going to name the album *Sacagawea* but . . . [*Shrugs.*]

KC: But our distribution company wouldn't go for it . . .

MC: Well, why did you entitle the album *Nevermind*?

KC: I don't know. So I could brush off the question. Forget it, doesn't matter. [*Smiles as Dave and Chris chorus "Nevermind, doesn't matter."*]

MC: Any specific things you wanted to talk about on that album? I listened to it just a couple of times as I've had it just a couple of days ago. I saw the video, uhhh . . . "Smells of Teen Spirit"?

DG: "Smells *Like* Teen Spirit."

MC: "Smells Like Teen Spirit." Were there things that were more obvious in that album than others? Not statements, I hate talking about statements, but especially that first song, that first statement, that first video . . . ? [*Pause.*]

KC: . . . What? [*All burst out laughing.*]

CN: Statement is like, every month I get a bank statement—I'm usually overdrawn.

DG: So we're not into making statements.

CN: I dunno . . . statements can be made anyway, anywhere. There's a lot to be said for subtleties. Y'know what I mean? So . . .

KC: There's a lot to be said for being cryptic also. Mysterious . . . because we can't explain ourselves, we don't consciously think about our music so we can't explain it. Therefore [*shouts*] "Interviews are worthless! Let's go!"

MC: What do you think about interviews?

KC: What do I think? Did you hear my reaction when he asked did I want to do one? I said "Fuck no." I said "Heck no."

CN: We were in *Interview* magazine, right next to Shonen Knife. And do you know who was on the cover? Matt Dillon.

MC: Yeah, well, that's funny because Cameron Crowe's doing . . . (CN: I look like Matt Dillon, thank you!) a movie with Matt Dillon in Seattle (All: Right! In Seattle!) and there are many Seattle musicians in that movie. Are you part of it at all?

CN: No part whatsoever.

KC: Definitely not.

DG: We opted not to delve in the movie industry . . .

CN: 'Cause I saw *Cotton Candy,* directed by Ron Howard. It's about this rock 'n' roll band, and what was the evil rock 'n' roll band's name?

KC: Is that the one with Leif Garrett in it?

CN: I've seen all these rock 'n' roll movies and it's always . . . the star! There's either Leif Garrett in it or . . .

KC: No clue. There's never been a really good documentary on rock 'n' roll bands . . .

DG: Except *Spinal Tap*. *Spinal Tap* was the only rock 'n' roll movie worth watching.

KC: Except for *Spinal Tap*. Oh, and *Don't Look Back* by Bob Dylan— have you seen it? (DG: That's true!) Also very, very good. Makes a fool out of Donovan.

CN: Oh, that's a good movie—it's old, it was made in 1964.

DG: It's a rockumentary.

MC: So were you approached? Were you asked to be part of that movie?

CN: Nobody asks us anything! Y'know what I mean?

KC: Oh, no, they did ask us.

CN: Really?

KC: Yeah, they asked John [*Silva — Ed.*]. I said no before even asking you guys. That's because I'm the leader of the band . . .

CN: [*Mock annoyance*] You blew my chance, man! I'm gonna roll into Hollywood . . . I'm gonna have a star on Hollywood Boulevard . . . and I'm gonna have a big house with a swimming pool and all these cars . . . and I'm gonna get divorces and stuff—and I'm gonna have a big drug—

KC: Like Jethro on TV's *The Beverly Hillbillies?*

MC: Well, tell me about that Seattle thing everybody's been talking about. I mean, there's been that Manchester scene, that Seattle scene now, is it relevant at all?

KC: All scenes are relevant. But they all, eventually, phase into nothing, or they go away after a while.

DG: They eventually become a parody of themselves.

KC: People put too much emphasis on scenes. I mean, just 'cause there happens to be a town with a few really good bands in it—big deal! It's happened all over the place, in Minneapolis, L.A., New York—all over the place, so it's really no big deal; I don't understand this "community patriotism" that everyone is boasting about in Seattle because . . . they're claiming that they finally "put Seattle on the map" but, y'know, what map? [*Shrugs.*] Everyone's moving to Seattle. I mean, we had Jimi Hendrix, heck, what more do we want?

CN: We went to his grave once. And there was guitar picks and beer bottles all over it. Then we went to Bruce Lee's grave at like, 1:30 in the morning. It's really wild; it's like in a Chinese part of the cemetery.

DG: With punji sticks and nunchucks lying all over the place.

CN: We thought for sure there were these ninjas creeping behind these tombstones—woah! But then again, the state of mind we were in at the time . . . I'd be like, "Turtles!"

MC: You get that sense that everybody's been talking about Seattle; did you feel that it helped you in any ways? Getting that recording contract or . . . it has nothing to do with it?

KC: Yeah, it might have. I suppose it did. And we're grateful for it, I guess. I mean, we were never seeking out a major label contract in the first place, it just happened—I don't know if it would have happened if we weren't on Sub Pop or not but . . . I dunno. We got a lot of press in Europe because of the Sub Pop scene, and it wasn't necessarily because Jon [*Poneman —Ed.*] and Bruce [*Pavitt —Ed.*] were these mastermind guys getting a lot of interviews, like, using their talents to get interviews. I mean, they were in ways, but also a lot of the journalists over in Europe happened to like the bands sincerely, sincerely like 'em, so they wrote about 'em. It wasn't as much of a hype as everyone thinks it was.

MC: Since the album's going to be released in a few weeks, are you doing that tour—are some parts of that tour being done without those people knowing about the album? Or are you planning to go back and do cities or . . . ? Don't you feel it would have been a good thing to wait until the album was released?

CN: [*Nodding heavily*] Yeah. It's about a week or two too early.

MC: You've been complaining about that?

KC: Yeah.

MC: How many dates do you have on that tour?

KC: I don't know, I haven't even looked at the itinerary.

DG: Well, the album comes out on the twenty-third . . . Today's the twenty-first? Oh yeah.

CN: The album comes out next Tuesday.

KC: Kids'll be buying it practically the day that we play in every city—just barely being familiar—becoming familiar with it. So it would have been more wise to wait a little while. Yeah.

MC: Do you feel that radio may help you? Do you feel that the music might fit that mainstream thing that everybody's talking about?

DG: I think that people sort of get sucked into the single that we have out now, with the melody of the song, and they don't realize it's so heavy because they're singing along to the song or whatever. But if you listen to it in a succession of songs, it's a lot heavier than most stuff on the radio.

CN: There's a bunch of other bands breaking into commercial radio and stuff. We're not just kinda following in . . .

KC: It happens every ten years; the new wave gets thrown into the mainstream and they try it again.

MC: Tell me about that "Teen Spirit" song, because it's the first video, the first single out. I just watched the video—we received it yesterday. I loved it, but tell me did you have anything to do in elaborating it, doing it?

KC: Oh yeah, I thought of the whole idea. Our idea was to have a pep assembly scene that's gone bad. That's gone bad!

MC: Anything you've experienced before?

KC: No, it's just more or less like a fantasy of ours for that to happen in high school while we're sitting at a pep assembly bored off our skulls. So after a while we resorted to skipping the pep assemblies, not going to them at all, but I dunno, it was just an idea. To use the youth theme.

MC: I mean, how do you feel about youth, since you talk about it in the song?

KC: Well, Sonic Youth's a great band . . .

MC: But what about teen spirits . . . ?

CN: I hate seeing all these normal-looking teenagers. They dress like their parents, they have the same values.

DG: It's a shame.

KC: Our parents are in control of the entertainment industry, and there's no generation gap anymore because the kids and the parents like the same music and it's really frightening to us, so maybe that's what we tried to incorporate into the video.

MC: How do you feel that the parents of the kids listening to your music will react?

KC: Well . . . [*Laughs*] well, we haven't done any good, have we? No, I don't think we've done a damn dent in the wall at all. I'm really ashamed of that. Hang our heads in shame.

CN: Shame on you, Shane!

MC: Are you serious?

CN: Shannnnne! [*In high female voice.*]

KC: Oh, that's a good movie. That was a Western movie. We're avoiding the question, what were you saying?

DG: But it was called *Shane*.

MC: I don't know, we were talking about teen spirits, but I think I got material on that . . . Alright, well anyway, what about that show tonight? Is it different from one night to another? Is it something you like—being on tour—or would you just like to stick by the recording studios and do some more songs?

KC: Touring

DG: You get to travel . . .

KC: You get to eat on the road, you get to sit in a van like this and be jostled for like eight hours a day.

CN: You get free alcohol every night. Who can ask for more? It's a party every night.

DG: We've been getting cauliflower the last couple nights . . .

CN: In cream cheese . . .

DG: Or some sort of chive dip. It's been right on.

CN: See, you've got to keep solid if you're krogging down those beers, y'know? So it's good to eat a lot of veggies and cheese and stuff because I think my insides start to swell after a while and it's not a very pleasant experience. Well, it's pleasant when I'm drunk but . . .

MC: Thank you, guys!

DG: You're welcome.

"WASHINGTON'S POUNDING 'TEEN SPIRIT'"

Randy Hawkins | October 17, 1991 | *State Press* (US)

This piece was published on Wednesday, October 23, 1991, to coincide with Nirvana's arrival in Tempe, Arizona, for a show that evening. The *State Press* newspaper had arranged a meeting several days prior between its reporter, Randy Hawkins, and an exhausted Dave Grohl. By this point the band had been touring since mid-August with just a brief week-and-a-half break after the conclusion of the European leg in September. This interview was in the archives of the *State Press*, Arizona State University's student-run news organization. The newspaper has a long history of in-depth coverage of arts and entertainment, and this piece had lain undiscovered since its initial publication. —Ed.

"Nirvana: any place or condition of great peace or bliss." —Webster's New World Dictionary

It's 2 p.m. in a Kansas town, and Dave Grohl, Nirvana's drummer, has just rolled out of bed. He's exhausted after playing a sold-out show to a bunch of "SGA's," or Student Government Association-types.

"It was fun," Grohl says, in his detached monotone. "It was one of those sterile, play-at-the-college things."

Grohl, along with vocalist/guitarist Kurt Cobain and bassist Chris Novoselic, make up the Washington band, which plays either punk rock or hard rock, or alternative rock, depending on who you ask.

When asked to describe the band's sound, Grohl sighs.

"I hate that," he says, but grudgingly volunteers his 2-cents-worth anyway. "I don't know, it's just really heavy pop songs played by punk rock children. I think that to give it a definition would be a contradiction.

"Punk rock is just freedom."

Punk rock or not, Nirvana's latest release, *Nevermind,* boasts an incredibly tight sound that rockets back and forth between acoustic strumming and all-out thrash guitar attacks, sometimes within the same song. The first single, "Smells Like Teen Spirit," has been getting some airplay and threatens to make Nirvana a household name among the alternative rock set.

This increase in popularity is hardly a threat to the band's "I don't care" attitude, but it has had an effect on the crowds that show up at Nirvana's concerts.

"The crowds are a lot bigger now," says Grohl, who adds that every day he sees more and more "kids" and "12-year-old girls" at the shows.

It's ironic that the youth of America are hanging out at Nirvana gigs, considering the fact that "Smells Like Teen Spirit" is about the apathy of today's youth. "Here we are now/Entertain us," screams Cobain during the chorus, an anthem for kids everywhere.

The live shows, as could be expected, are "just like chaos," says Grohl. "It comes across really well. There's 20 times more energy and it's about 20 times as loud as anyone could listen to it at home."

Grohl isn't shy about naming the band's influences, which include Black Flag and Bad Brains, who Grohl says was "the most incredible live band I had ever seen." Nirvana also feels a kinship with "(Washington) D.C. hardcore outcasts" The Void, who "were so bad, they were the best."

In stark contrast to the sonic anarchy exhibited on much of *Nevermind,* the song "Something in the Way" is a beautiful acoustic piece, complete with cellos. "It's not like we had some scheme," Grohl says defensively. "It's just a song."

Grohl refuses to examine the song any further. "We're the last ones to analyze anything we're doing," he says. "Other people are a lot better at deciding what we're thinking than we are . . . Let them spend their own time doing that—I've got better things to do."

Nevermind may be the perfect album title for Nirvana, since it seems to accurately reflect the attitude of at least one band member. Even the story of how the band chose their album title is a telling example of this apathy. According to Grohl, the band members were stuck between *Nevermind* and *Sheep* as album titles. When finally confronted by an exasperated record company executive, they just said the title that came to mind first.

"That's how all of our decisions are made," Grohl says, not the least bit sheepishly.

This apathetic attitude carries over somewhat to the songwriting. Grohl and Novoselic allow Cobain to come up with the melody, then the trio starts jamming. "We keep on doing it until verses, choruses, bridges come out of that," he says.

This unique songwriting approach has its drawbacks. "We've written so many songs that we've forgotten about," Grohl confesses. "We know nothing about music. I mean, none of us know how to write it."

To keep from losing any more songs, the band has taken to tape recording its practice sessions.

Although the band has only three members, Grohl doesn't think the minimalist lineup inhibits the band in any way. "It should be exactly the opposite," he says. "There should be a lot more space."

The small roster isn't about retention of creative control either, insists Grohl. Continuing his neverending championing of the punk ideals, Grohl says, "We're not into 'control.' We're into 'creative,' but I don't think there's any such thing as 'creative control.'"

Grohl suddenly develops an indifferent sort of interest when he hears about After the Gold Rush, the club Nirvana is playing at tonight. After learning about its disco-meets-metal decor, Grohl interrupts, "There's nothing wrong with a good disco ball."

In fact, after listening to a '70s compilation disc he purchased recently, Grohl goes so far as to say, "I realized disco wasn't so bad after all."

A secret love of disco isn't Grohl's only surprise. One of his favorite memories of Nirvana's latest tour is the visit he paid to the Bowlers Hall of Fame in St. Louis. "That was amazing," he says, "I bet *you* didn't know that bowling went all the way back to ancient Egypt. *Did* you? *Did* you?" he smugly persists.

Other than traveling to wonderful places like the Bowlers Hall of Fame, Grohl says the band isn't aiming for much of anything in particular. "We don't have any goals. Once you start setting goals, you start expecting things and you can get disappointed."

Pausing, Grohl adds, "I just don't really care. I think that's what sets us apart."

COBAIN CLIP

Novoselic Endearing Nirvana to MTV

"Because we have our big bandwagon and we have a buncha Clydesdale horses— multi-colored horses pulling it and people are just jumping on and it's kinda like a King . . . Ken Kesey acid-trip type thing . . . passing Kool-Aid around and—we're like the Merry Pranksters."

—From MTV Headbangers Ball by Riki Rachtman, November 1991

PART VI

November to December 1991—The Deluge

ONE GLANCE AT THE TABLE OF CONTENTS TESTIFIES TO what happens over the course of Nirvana's second European tour of the year. Days line up with interviews on every one; days of multiple interviews; interviews in city after city as the band dashes around the continent. Europe possesses a thriving music press, and the media is out in force—*Ciao 2001*, *What's That Noise*, *Tutti Frutti*, *OOR*. Local radio stations join in, but now the local mainstream media are finding space for Nirvana too.

The bandmates are being questioned on a vastly expanded range of topics: their lives, their music, the Sub Pop/Seattle scene, the overall music scene, the wider world. In August they were complimenting other major-label alternative bands for having opened the doors to acceptance of Nirvana's music; by the end of the year it's become a truism that the door wasn't open before Nirvana came along with *Nevermind*. They comfort themselves by beginning to suggest that their success will lead people to their friends, to other bands.

The interviews show all facets of the band's reactions. They're working hard, touring hard, and, like anyone doing a job, their mood varies from dawn until dusk. They respond to this cycle of interrogations by being blasé, open, even cheerful in conversation—or by being awkward or just plain exhausted. They're still unaware of what's happening back in the United States, as they explain to Lucio Spiccia and Bram van Splunteren. Nirvana's members rely on phone calls home as their only window into what's going on there. In Europe the venues were all booked long before the band's fame, so they're hearing stories, they're buried in interviews, they're seeing the crowds unable to enter venues.

Old themes are stated with greater urgency. Cobain tells Lucio Spiccia that he hates interviews—by December he explains to Robyn Doreian his new policy on them. Normal questions of future intention come up; to Annemiek van Grondel, Nirvana is predicting a new and more experimental album by autumn 1992. Amid this, however, Cobain tells Gilbert Blecken that he might consider a break from music; to Frédéric Brébant the band members are already refusing to define meanings to songs.

And the band's first media squabble has occurred. Journalists, like any other human beings, often learn their information from other publications, then react to that information in the absence of anything to the contrary. Cobain is asked several times in these interviews about drugs—he makes light of the topic, equivocates about his past usage, says he doesn't use now. He tells Angela Zocco, though, that "English music papers are a bunch of bullshit, y'know? They're a big lie all the time." He tells Niels Delvaux of Studio Brussel that the English press "like to exaggerate things and make a big sensational story." He's reacting to pieces portraying Nirvana as wild drunks—the traditional sex, drugs, and rock 'n' roll approach. By December, when the band members have to reexplain that parts of their official band press bio are jokes, they're already caught having to spend significant time saying what they are *not*.

NIRVANA: THE CREEPS

Luca Collepiccolo | November 1991 | *Blast* (Italy)

I did this interview right around the release of the *Nevermind* album. We were on the phone for less than thirty minutes. The interview came out in *Blast* magazine—one of the few examples of hardcore/underground-based publications at that time in Italy. (If you need a rough idea, it was similar to *Flipside* fanzine.) The back cover of the issue had Poison Idea on it, so when I gave a copy to Kurt and Dave after the Castello show in Rome, they were enthusiastic for Pig Champion and co.! —Luca Collepiccolo

Translated by Alessandra Meineri.

In the beginning there were four: Kurt Cobain, Chris Novoselic, Chad Channing, Jason Everman. They sounded like a mix between Black Sabbath, Black Flag, and Hüsker Dü. After some dazzling appearances on some of the local indie compilations that were predominant in the Seattle scene and on Sub Pop, the band started off its long run with a vinyl LP that, in its own way, has made history in the American underground. *Bleach* was a bitter business, nestled in darker moods, its furrowed brow expressing not just anger but also the savage genius of this American fourpiece. Shortly before this vinyl release, Jason Everman left the band (we meet him again later in the role of bassist in Soundgarden, but he would only tour with them, as he was replaced by Ben Shepherd prior to the production of *Badmotorfinger*). Nirvana now remains, permanently, a trio. I retain one image of Kurt Cobain, a real madman at a Rome gig with Tad, destroying his six-string as if it were nothing, then attempting to jump from the top of an amplifier. I remember his fiery eyes full of hatred, an episode I will surely never forget. It's no wonder, as every self-respecting Nirvana gig ends this way, with liters of sweat spread to the far corners of the stage, empty beer cans stacked up behind the amps, a few joints scattered here and there, and the guitar Cobain has smashed against the amp dumped over to the right. Nirvana is definitely a throwback to the transgressive attitudes of the early 1970s—behaviors clearly not planned and constructed, unlike those of some contemporary artists. How can the instrumental destruction not remind you of the legendary the Who? But there was also a period of stagnation for Nirvana after that European tour when, for reasons never clearly specified, drummer Chad Channing defected and the band had to rapidly replace him. Here comes Dan Peters of Mudhoney, at this point also on its way to splitting up (this was around the spring/summer of 1990), but his stay in the band was very short, and now Dave Grohl of the legendary band Scream fills the vacant position of drummer. The rest is history. *Nevermind* is a wonderful album that redesigns, in every color of the rainbow, the very coordinates of post-punk made in the USA. We have prepared for you a pleasant discussion with singer/guitarist Kurt Cobain hosted in the British offices of MCA.

Luca Collepiccolo: There's a new band member in the team; could you introduce him?

Kurt Cobain: This is Dave Grohl, former Washingtonian Scream's drummer. We're old friends, so when we needed a drummer to replace Chad (Channing, the drummer who had recorded with Nirvana the album *Bleach* and a handful of singles), it seemed logical to get in touch with him.

LC: It's rather curious. During previous interviews you've always mentioned Scream as being one of your favorite bands. How do you explain it?

KC: I think this was just a random circumstance; we're now playing with Dave by chance only. I mean, I could never have imagined Scream was going to split. Anyways, it's a band we'll love forever. Recently we've been able to meet former members of Scream; we really had a good time together, we're definitely great friends. It's really cool what's happened with Nirvana; it's really great to play with a person and a musician that you've always admired.

LC: What happened to the other members of Scream? Do you know by any chance if they've put together a new band?

KC: Oh, they've put together a new band. They're playing as Wool and moved to Los Angeles, where they now live on a permanent basis. They're a really good band; they played a couple of gigs with us and I can assure you that they are absolutely amazing when playing live. Musically they really resemble Scream's later work—their music is very hard, particularly heavy.

LC: What happened to Dan Peters (the drummer of Mudhoney)? He only played with you for the "Sliver" single on Sub Pop . . .

KC: Dan Peters was in the band for only three weeks. He contacted us personally by phone, and we really couldn't refuse his offer because at that time we really needed a drummer. Danny is obviously a good drummer, you know what I mean? But Dave is qualitatively superior, his style blends perfectly with the sound of Nirvana, his drumming is definitely heavier. Also he's able to make a vocal contribution to the band; you know we need a person, especially live, who can sing choruses.

LC: *Nevermind* is your first album for a major label. What are your feelings right now considering the fact that this is a major step into the music business for Nirvana?

KC: There weren't actually any major swings, as signing this big contract didn't change our mentality. We haven't suffered any kind of pressure from the label, we have a good manager, and we're working for a label that shows competence from every perspective. We're supported from a marketing perspective; it's given us the ability to conduct a lot of interviews . . . it's the kind of relationship we were looking for. We're doing some great things with Geffen Records and, at the same time, we're having enough fun.

LC: Even if it is a major, Geffen Records has an enviable stable: Sonic Youth, Warrior Soul, White Zombie. I think it's positive that they're pursuing this kind of policy.

KC: I agree. Geffen has just signed a decent Scottish group, Teenage Fanclub, you ever heard of them?

LC: Yes, they're not bad. With all sincerity, do you believe the independent rock scene is now dead?

KC: No, I don't think the independent rock scene is dead. It's impossible because there'll always be new bands emerging from that circuit, ready to make records on independent labels and to be supported by a certain type of audience. There'll always be grunge bands ready to scrape together a few hundred dollars to self-produce a seven-inch. The independent scene isn't dying.

LC: What's your current relationship with Sub Pop's management? You're still friends with Jonathan Poneman and Bruce Pavitt?

KC: Yes, of course we're still good friends. There was a time after we terminated the contract with Sub Pop during which we spoke with them pretty often. The separation was really hard for both parties basically because we respected each other. It was hard for them to believe that we had taken that road; for a time we felt guilty for what happened. Now finally things are back to normal.

LC: In the future, if you have another opportunity to make a single with Sub Pop, what would you choose?

KC: I haven't the faintest idea. I'd probably do a cover of a song from the compilation *Sub Pop Rock City*. Do you know, we've never seriously considered this kind of thing.

LC: What type of music is going around Seattle recently?

KC: Basically the same as what was circulating about five years ago. There are a lot of new bands, new grunge bands, and I think they're all really excited about the fact that there are so many chances for them to be able to perform gigs. The scene's not dead and buried, I think it's still alive and kicking, and the same ol' Sub Pop continues going strong, putting out brilliant records. I think there's a big musical scene across Washington State, some really strong bands like Beat Happening, Giant Henry, Bikini Kill . . .

LC: Some time ago I spoke with Mark Arm (Mudhoney's vocalist), who was rather annoyed that there were so many mediocre hard rock bands playing in Seattle all aping Guns N' Roses . . .

KC: There are always bands like that in every city, not just Seattle, bands trying to play that shit. But this is the same Seattle that gave birth to Mudhoney and they're a really valuable group. Anyway, I'm not interested in this sort of thing, I don't care about that kind of music. Mudhoney are currently kinda popular, and that's because their music is fundamentally original. If you give birth to a new type of music, if you put together a group, you have to put yourself into it, so the only choice you have to be successful is to make music that's authentic.

LC: Do you think the sound of Nirvana was influenced in some way by bands from Washington, DC? I'm referring in particular to the post-punk scene revolving around the label Dischord.

KC: I personally have never been involved in the hardcore scene in Washington, DC. I've not had the opportunity to hear the latest works from Dischord, so I don't feel I can give any opinion on today's scene. I'd say I feel more connected to the era before this type of band. I always really admired bands like Faith, Void, and Rites of Spring (the former band of Guy Picciotto, vocalist with Fugazi), not to forget the always amazing Bad Brains, too.

LC: I found the lyrics of the new album really interesting. I was particularly struck by the song "Lithium." In this song you recite the verse

"I'm so happy, 'cause today I found my friends . . . " What is the value of friendship for you?

KC: Friendship is one of the biggest things I can think of. Relationships are more important than anything else. I think everyone should go all the way in trying to strengthen their personal relationships. For me, it's very important to have friends who understand your needs and who'll help you in difficult times. The value of friendship is immense, and it should be thought of that way.

LC: What is being referred to in the lyrics of "Territorial Pissings"? Does it have anything to do with the situation of American Indians?

KC: There's no exact plot to that song, so I can't really explain it. Let's say there are different themes, different images in the same song. On the one hand, there are references to Native Americans, to all those people living in the North American reserves, people smashed by the raging Americans' attacks. At the same time the song is about appreciating women. I'm standing on their side because I hate the violence they suffer, the daily injustices resulting from belonging to a different sex. Mainly this song was about just wanting to express my love toward women and the respect I have for them.

LC: Do you think the name Nirvana still retains its religious significance?

KC: Yeah, I think it still has that. It's a name belonging to the Indian religion and refers to a sort of divine consciousness. I've never really worried about the meaning of the name and I've never really asked myself, "Why name the band Nirvana?" All in all, I found a name that's well suited to the shape of the band and it sounds pretty good, by the way.

LC: When talking about the new album, in *Nevermind* I seem to have detected two different personalities in Nirvana, one closer to the folk tradition, such as the song "Polly," and another closely linked to the approach of early punk—in this regard you could mention harder songs in the collection like "Breed." What's your opinion about this?

KC: To tell the truth I've never paid much attention to folk music; I can't find any folk reference in "Polly." I believe several songs on the new album have seen a degree of influence from the Beatles and Love, bands that roughly speaking belong to this breed of music. On the other hand, we're quite influenced by groups like Young Marble Giants, Beat Happening, the Vaselines, bands that undoubtedly exerted a sort of influence on me. For some songs I was really openly inspired by these bands. Ultimately, I think Nirvana has two different vibes, one closer to pop and the other to the rush of punk.

LC: In the opening song, "Smells Like Teen Spirit," especially in the slow parts, I was reminded of early Police.

KC: Hmm . . . (Kurt twists his mouth) I've never liked the Police. I can't! There was only one song I particularly liked and now can't even remember the title, but it had to be from their third album, the one with the black cover. I've always thought of the Police as an artificial band who used punk and new wave just to become a commercial group.

LC: What's your opinion about drugs and alcohol?

KC: Well, I used drugs and alcohol for several years, but I've never become a big user, I never became addicted to either alcohol or drugs. But I know people who have been. I wouldn't encourage anyone to take drugs; at the same time, I can't forbid anyone to use them. For a time, for me, drugs were something good, positive, an incentive to create something good. I wrote several songs under their influence. Now I'm not using drugs as freely as I once did; I use them less frequently.

LC: I remember your performance two years ago in Rome. That night you were out of your mind, trashed your guitar, tried to jump from the top of an amplifier . . .

(As soon as I mention this incident, Kurt explodes with laughter.)

KC: Yeah, actually, I had a big burnout that evening. We were on the road in Europe for about seven weeks with the band, we'd had no chance to sleep properly as we stayed in uncomfortable rooms, and we'd only had two days' rest. We'd been really exhausted by all this, totally tired, that evening we were particularly flipped out.

LC: You're being ironic when you write things on the back of your T-shirts like FUDGE PACKIN', FLOWER SNIFFIN' MOTHERFUCKERS, and CRACK SMOKERS?

KC: Yeah, definitely. They're just jokes; we had fun playing around with the words. A few really humorless people took them seriously. I don't know why but a lot of people in Italy have got it completely wrong. They think we're all drug addicts because we perform the way we do. We don't use often, but when we do we feel better and it's all fun. Anyway, the words shouldn't be taken so seriously.

LC: You're interested in politics in some way?

KC: I'm completely ignorant on the subject. Everyone should have their own political consciousness, but I don't consider myself a political person because I've never received an education in that sense. I mean, no one has ever told me that in their opinion a particular policy was the right one to follow. Anyways, everyone should be sensitive to the subject.

LC: If I asked your opinion on the Russian situation, what would you say?

KC: I have no definite opinion on the subject; I've not had a chance to read up on the subject sufficiently, as we were on tour with Sonic Youth at the time. It's difficult to understand the situation of the Russian people, their history, how it's evolved. In the end I understand there's an infinite number of problems. People have been waiting for change for a long time, but I think that Gorbachev was a great head of state for Russia in recent years. It's been great to see some change in the lifestyle of the Russian people anyway.

LC: We're finishing. Do you have a few comments on the latest edition of the Reading Festival?

KC: What can I say? It was a great event as usual. Our performance went down the best way it could, we did well, it was really energetic and fun. Backstage, Mudhoney were out in full force, members of Hole too—we had a great party at the end and we were all completely drunk. It was great fun; we had some great moments in the company of our best friends.

"I FIND IT EMBARRASSING TO HAVE SUCH GREAT EXPECTATIONS PLACED ON US"

Gilbert Blecken | November 10, 1991 | *Freakshow* **(Germany)**

When I met Kurt Cobain in November 1991, I was a twenty-two-year-old fanzine writer from Berlin who usually didn't have his interviews organized by record companies. Instead, I waited in the concert halls for the bands to arrive to do their sound checks, and asked them personally. This was also how the Nirvana interview came about. Frankly, I was an unlikely person to do this interview, because I'd been a fan of British pop rather than American rock. Still, there was a big element of pop to *Bleach* and *Nevermind*, meaning that even I found it hard to resist. So I decided to try to get an interview with the band. When Nirvana arrived late that afternoon, I went straight up to Kurt and asked him if he would agree to doing a spontaneous interview. He said yes without hesitation. Sometimes interviews can be a bit tough with two different parties suspiciously watching each other's steps, but with this one everything was calm and relaxed; nobody had to prove anything. After the interview, I also took a few photos—again, all very easy; it seemed Kurt even enjoyed posing for some of them. My encounter with Kurt Cobain was nothing spectacular, but it left me with lots of good memories that I am still very thankful for.

If I'd known that Kurt would become a legend, I might have paid more attention to detail back then—I just remember it as a nice experience. When I greeted him and asked for the impromptu interview, he didn't have to be asked twice, and we started immediately. Kurt himself gave me an amazingly balanced and concentrated impression, though Krist Novoselic annoyed with occasional interjections—apparently he didn't think much of the fact that I had my interview with Kurt alone. Perhaps Krist felt a little superfluous ego. David Grohl, meanwhile, didn't say a word; he seemed entirely self-sufficient. Cobain said good-bye to me with a handshake and the words "Nice to have met you." Perhaps it was just a phrase, but at that moment it felt sincere and irony-free to me. The so-called mainstream press found the band difficult to deal with back then, but at least when dealing with fanzines, Mr. Cobain certainly knew how to behave. —Gilbert Blecken

Translated by Inga Owczors and Jon Darch.

Gilbert Blecken: I read a few days ago that now even Ozzy Osbourne likes your album *Nevermind*. Could you have imagined that he'd be a fan of yours?

Kurt Cobain: I can understand him liking us, as we have a few things in common, at least with his former band. Sure! I respect the man, and I like his music too, apart from his last few albums. Incidentally, Ozzy mixed his new LP in the same studio as we did. We didn't have the opportunity to talk to each other, but we did sometimes see him in the corridor. He was always staggering so much that I had to press myself up against the wall each time or he wouldn't have been able to get by. The guy is pretty fucked up. He also asked us to go on tour with him, but we didn't want to. Although it might have been exciting and kinda funny to have been there at his last few shows, playing as the support act in such big arenas would definitely have not been right for us.

GB: Over the last few weeks, I don't think any other band has been referred to as often as you guys as "the next big thing." How does it feel to be constantly surrounded by people telling you how famous you're about to become?

KC: I find it embarrassing to have such great expectations placed on us. And in any case, it's a very superficial description to declare a band the next big thing. It just leads to the band being seen in a lesser light if, despite those expectations, it doesn't happen. And it's not our goal in the first place. People are pushing it on us, without us wanting it.

GB: Are you nevertheless prepared for a life as superstars, which could now potentially await you?

KC: No, we're not prepared for that, because it's not going to happen either. We're prepared to destroy our careers if it happens.

GB: That almost sounds like a variant on what Jane's Addiction said. As you know, their singer also announced to the press that the band would split a year before it did. Do you really want to go that far?

KC: If that becomes too much of a problem for us, it could be OK. I don't know, it depends. However, in Jane's Addiction's case I heard there were major problems between the band members, which we don't have at all. We'd probably just break up, only to then carry on under a different name. We love playing together and I've no wish to play with anyone else. Maybe one day I'll do a project on the side, but that would be it.

GB: Are you aware that you are the first band for years to breathe new life into rock music?

KC: That's a very flattering comment, which also kinda rather surprises me. I tend more to think that we sound like Black Sabbath and the Bay City Rollers. In general, however, I believe it's very hard for a band to describe itself. You're probably the last people to realize who you've nicked stuff from and who's influenced you. After all, most of it happens subconsciously.

GB: The comparison with Black Sabbath and the Bay City Rollers is something you mentioned before in the band info that you wrote yourselves. But that biography is probably more of a joke, isn't it?

KC: Yes, most of it is pretty obvious. I wanted to try writing the biography in a different way to most of the ones we'd read before. Most bands take themselves far too seriously in those and just show how egoistical they are. So we just decided to do something that was more fun.

GB: Do you think you can retain that way of looking at things?

KC: We have to. Strangely, you'll usually find just two extremes in music. Either you're simultaneously serious, sad, and depressed like Morrissey, or you present the band as a big joke, like the Butthole Surfers. I think there's still enough room in between for us.

GB: Is it conceivable to you that one of the reasons your record label Geffen Records signed you was to enhance their reputation?

KC: I guess that plays a part in it. On the other hand, I'm convinced that the people there honestly like us as a band. So it's not as if it's something they'd stage, just to become hip.

GB: I heard that you guys also have some experiences with drugs behind you. So tell me, what was your first LSD trip like?

KC: I laughed far too much. The next morning I woke up with a stomach-ache, because I laughed so much.

GB: Which other drugs have you tried?

KC: I think I've tried every drug I could get my hands on. PCP, Quaaludes . . .

GB: Is there any drug experience you particularly remember?

KC: They all suck. Quaaludes was probably the worst time I've ever had on drugs, because it left me unable to control my balance. I didn't feel good at all—every time I tried to walk, I kept falling down. Eventually I fell asleep. It wasn't fun at all.

GB: Back to the music. What I find quite remarkable about *Nevermind* is that unlike on *Bleach* almost every song has quiet passages alternating with loud ones. Are you no longer so keen on thrashing songs out all the way through?

KC: Yeah, I think we've focused more on dynamics on this album. On *Bleach* everything was still totally straight ahead and simple. However, after a while it becomes boring just to play that kind of music all the time, so we decided it was better to split our songs up more. There were already certain predictors of that, I'd say, on *Bleach*, but now we're much further on with accommodating both of the elements of soft and pretty and hard and aggressive in our songs.

GB: Being frank, do you have the impression that you've found your style already, or could you still imagine musically going in a totally different direction again one day?

KC: Oh, definitely. The next album will be completely different. We've, in fact, already started working on a completely different sound. What we've written so far doesn't sound anything like *Nevermind.* I think that for making music to remain exciting you do need to change and experiment.

GB: To be specific then, what direction are you going in?

KC: It's going to sound a lot more psychedelic, raw, unique, and crazy. Great song structures will then no longer play such an important role. Nevertheless, we're not going to start putting any particularly great emphasis on the technical side of things, as is usual with all this jazz shit. I think "Aneurysm," the B-side of "Smells Like Teen Spirit," is a good example of what we're going to sound like. And on the CD there's also an extra track that most people don't know. That's because after the twelfth song there's first of all twelve minutes of absolutely nothing and then comes the thirteenth song, which is about seven minutes long. It sounds like an abortion. Very noisy. I think our next album is going to sound something like that.

GB: What would you like Nirvana to be remembered for?

KC: Good music and good songs. That's all I can say in answer to that, because that's more important than anything else.

GB: Alright, last question. Would you describe yourself as somebody who would go mad without music?

KC: I used to think that. But now that we're playing almost every night on tour I feel that I'll probably also want to do something else one day. If I keep on like this for another five years, I might burn myself out and no longer have the desire to just keep on playing guitar. I don't know if this is something that I'll do forever. There are so many other things that I enjoy just as much. Sometimes I just want to hang out with my friends. I also really like writing, and maybe I'll even act in a movie one day. There's so much that I can imagine doing. Maybe I could also be happy being a janitor. I don't know yet. But while that's the way I feel at the moment, I'm sure that after two months off, I'd probably then get to the point where I wanted to make music again.

TITLES, THESES, TEMPERAMENT, AND GRUNGE AS POP

Jens Kirschneck | November 11, 1991 | *What's That Noise* (Germany)

Curtain up. It's cold, wet, and misty as photographer Sabine and I trundle along the 270 kilometers of motorway in my old banger. What lies in store for us? Wasn't there a story where, in response to a totally innocuous question, bass player Chris Novoselic let rip at a reporter, while singer and guitarist Kurt Cobain was setting the tour bus curtains alight and pontificating on the controllability of fire? I don't like it when people yell at me. And pyromaniacs are alien to me.

Of course, it all turns out very different. I park my aforementioned old banger in the parking lot behind the Markthalle, the car slips into gear, and I practically still have the steering wheel in my hand when I find myself standing face-to-face with Chris Novoselic in a glaringly lit room. To be more precise, a professional interviewer spotter, who earns her corn with Nirvana's label, Geffen, identified us as we entered the lobby by our camera bag and Walkman, checked us off as number seven of seven on the list of interviews, and shipped us immediately to that room. The way he looks, nobody from his school days would have predicted he'd become a pop star: he's too tall, too thin, too bearded, everything about him is somehow *too* . . . A pair of friendly eyes looks down on us. "Hi. I'm Chris."

After twenty minutes, Kurt Cobain enters the room, picks up a copy of *What's That Noise* lying on a chair, and flicks through it. There's no missing some initial signs of the Nirvana phenomenon fading among those who aspire to listen to cool music. That, however, changes nothing about the fact that Nirvana has made the best record of 1991, even if, with charming modesty, Mr. Cobain would gladly pass on this crown. "This band should be No. 1," he says, pointing to a Beat Happening review. He toddles off again, leaving the thread of the conversation somewhat lost. Novoselic gives me one or two more tidbits (yes, they're still good friends with Sub Pop, or at least with a couple of bands, no comment about the label's financial difficulties. Yes, their new drummer is the guy from Scream) but seems relieved when we soon end the conversation. Just under an hour later, the man is enjoying being a pop star, which I deduce from the fact that while playing bass he repeatedly jumps into the air while grinning enthusiastically at the audience. His band's act triggers a collective outpouring of adrenaline, the like of which I've not experienced for a long time. A permanent level of noise and occasional hysterical squeals permeate the audience. The guys on stage have simply got it: power, tenderness, and verve. —Jens Kirschneck

Translated by Jon Darch.

Jens Kirschneck: When you look at what's going on here—the crowd of people and all the interviews—could you have anticipated that a year or two ago?

Chris Novoselic: No, no. To be honest, I wouldn't have dared to imagine it even two months ago. It's not as though we consciously tried to get to this situation. It simply happened.

JK: And how much of that is to do with the major label deal with Geffen?

CN: That's certainly got something to do with it. Thanks to Geffen's radio division, for example, we got played on the major stations, which gave people the opportunity they'd otherwise never have had to ask, "What's that?" As a result of lots of people asking, we naturally got played more often. And people bought the record.

JK: Which could, of course, also be down to the fact that *Nevermind* is a lot better than the first LP?

CN: I'd say they're very different records. I think each has its own value. The new one, however, is accessible to the mainstream ear as well.

JK: Though it nevertheless has little in common with the crap that otherwise gets played on, for example, MTV.

CN: I'd certainly like to think so!

JK: Does all the hype going on around you guys ever get on your nerves?

CN: To tell you the truth, we don't notice that much of it. We've now been on tour for nearly two months and not much has changed from before. We're not playing in stadiums—we're still playing in the same small halls.

(What's That Noise *Publisher Note: Although a month after this interview, with 800,000 copies of* Nevermind *reportedly sold, it has to be said that soon this too will probably be a thing of the past, while two years ago Nirvana in all likelihood would not have sold out the Markthalle with its capacity of 1,200.*)

JK: However, you guys are still able, for instance, to say: "I don't really feel in the mood right now, I don't want to give any interviews today."

CN: Yes, we can certainly still do that. And that's reasonable. I don't actually see a great big point in interviews. You've got to talk about yourself and analyze yourself. Not that I've got a problem with a bit of self-analysis, but if it was down to the record company we'd be doing ten interviews a day, seven days a week. And you've always got to answer the same questions. You try to remain cordial . . . you . . . try to remember what on earth you were just talking about.

JK: And in fact, music of the type that Nirvana produces actually speaks for itself. There's no need to keep talking about it.

CN: That's right. I mean, all we've done is make a record. We're not any great image band. We're not rock stars in the true sense. We're slowly getting known, but aren't yet really famous. And I don't even know if we like it. I don't think we like being chased by people for autographs. What's that all about?

JK: At what point did you notice that the new record would be a killer hit?

CN: Never. But, naturally, I'm now happy about how it's done. We worked hard on it. And then we were pleased by the praise and the sales figures. But actually that's all unimportant. The record is done. Out. What counts now is that we're playing live and the people are coming. They've heard the record and want to see us on the stage.

JK: Where does the biggest difference lie between the new LP and the first one—with the songs or the production?

CN: Both play a role. The first record was an eight-track recording done for six hundred dollars, while *Nevermind* was done for thousands of dollars in a twenty-four-track studio. And the songs . . . the ones on *Bleach* are edgier and some are slow, doleful, and dark. *Nevermind* has more melodies and there's an interplay of the vocals and the individual instruments. It's brighter and . . . more cheerful.

JK: But wasn't it the case that you said to yourselves: "So, now we'll make a cool, pop record?"

CN: No, no. It somehow evolved. Not pop in the sense of populist, but pop like the Beatles or the Byrds. On *Nevermind* there are also some riffy songs, like "Breed," "Stay Away," and "Territorial Pissings." For us it's simply about staying interested and not always playing the same old crap. That would be boring. Then again, lots of bands are constantly thinking about their image, their attitude, and their sound. By contrast, we're just three guys who write songs.

JK: So therefore you still feel closer to Mudhoney than, for example, to Guns N' Roses?

CN: Definitely. You can bet your life on that. Guns N' Roses are nothing more than a mainstream pop phenomenon. Musically they've got nothing to offer and live solely off of their bad-boy image.

JK: Although they're again a good example of how the rock business works. And I'd at least give them credit for the fact that, unlike some of their contemporaries, they'd never dispute that they're using this system.

CN: That may well be. I've not bothered myself with them that much.

JK: Excluding your current success for one moment, do you think that such music could storm the charts on a broader front or will it always remain a minority thing?

CN: We want to keep the door open. Just like Sonic Youth and Jane's Addiction did before us, we want to smooth the way so that other bands can follow: Dinosaur Jr., Mudhoney, and whoever. Eventually there has to be an end to the whole boring Guns N' Roses and Hanoi Rocks shebang. An end to this never-changing, dreary hard rock stuff. Guns N' Roses are from Hollywood Boulevard. Jeez, there are zillions more dreadful bands like that.

THE SUM OF TEN YEARS OF ALTERNATIVE ROCK, NIRVANA'S NAME IS ON EVERYONE'S LIPS

David Kleijwegt | November 12, 1991 | *Algemeen Dagblad* **(the Netherlands)**

Monday, November 25, 1991, was a crucial date for rock music in the Netherlands. That morning the daily papers ran obituaries for Freddie Mercury, the flamboyant singer of Queen, who died of AIDS. That evening Nirvana played what was to be its only gig in the country after *Nevermind* happened. It's an event that's been well documented, with long articles in Dutch magazines and even a documentary called *Nirvana/Nederland/Nevermind*.

I was writing for a daily paper at the time. For upcoming events of importance it wasn't unusual to travel ahead to see a band, maybe even speak to a musician or two. And so photographer Paul Bergen and I traveled to Frankfurt. We stayed the night in a typical German hotel. Upon arrival we could smell the beer the old-timers nursed for years and years in the dark corners of the deep brown furniture. The Nirvana gig a few hours later had quite a different atmosphere, electrically charged with an energy I still long for but rarely find at concerts. In the dressing room afterward we found Chris Novoselic, with whom I had an interview, in not too bad a mood; a hyper Dave Grohl; and a completely monosyllabic Kurt Cobain, who did nothing but shrug at my appearance. Eventually we made it back to the hotel. In the window of the restaurant, Bergen and I saw three silent silhouettes, which we immediately recognized as the most popular band on the planet, but they might as well have been the saddest creatures on earth.

A few days after Nirvana arrived in the Netherlands, my article appeared. The most tangible artifact of Nirvana's stay was the incredible photo Michel Linssen took of Kurt

Cobain during the 2 Meter Sessies, a Dutch equivalent of the Peel sessions, on November 24. That photograph, in which he intuitively captured the adolescent that remained at the core of Cobain, later graced the cover of every music magazine that paid tribute to Nirvana when they were history. (The session itself went so badly it wasn't even aired.) A day later, on November 25, Nirvana took the Paradiso in Amsterdam by storm. I was there; Linssen went to see the Ramones instead. —David Kleijwegt

Translated by Elizabeth Adair.

Frankfurt—Sold Out

It can be read in two languages at the door of the Batschkapp, the most important club in Frankfurt. Outside, dozens of people are nagging your head off for a ticket. Inside it's almost unhealthily crowded. You can hardly move. Nirvana is on a day trip to Frankfurt.

The same scenes will undoubtedly play out on Monday at the Paradiso in Amsterdam. All the tickets for Nirvana's concert were sold out within fifteen minutes. In pop circles, the name *Nirvana* is on everyone's lips. The American trio from Aberdeen, a boring suburb of Seattle, is not the future of rock 'n' roll. The music of Nirvana sounds more like the definitive last chapter: very loud, passionate, heartbreaking, and yet accessible.

Force

The gig in Frankfurt isn't great, but it's good enough to let everyone in the room feel seventeen years old again. And that is the universal power of Nirvana. In just a short time, the band's second album, *Nevermind,* a masterpiece, has sold a million copies so far, states bassist Chris Novoselic. "Nirvana has exploded," explains the tall musician. "We haven't asked for it, it just happened. I didn't see it coming. There must be some kind of vacuum that we filled with Nirvana."

Nirvana has, whether the group likes it or not, built a bridge from underground rock to the more beaten track. "We're the sum of ten years of alternative rock," says Novoselic. "Nirvana is a reaction to hearing the same retarded music over and over again that gets played on American radio."

"Semidangerous rock like Poison and Mötley Crüe isn't to be laughed at?"

"A band like Bon Jovi will be remembered as the Herman's Hermits of the 1980s and prove to be nothing more than a joke, and a bad one at that. Our music will live on. The albums by the Pixies, Mudhoney, and Sonic Youth are the only true pop music of this era. The rich, fat record bosses at the top have tried to hold us back for long enough. Now they can't do anything about the change. Slick as they are, with Nirvana in mind, they will jump on the bandwagon. Because they smell money."

Trashcan

According to Novoselic, rock 'n' roll mythology belongs in the trashcan. "A band like Guns N' Roses is the blueprint for that kind of absurd myth. They aren't musicians, they're doing party songs, drinking and grabbing at everything that comes into their vicinity. For them, music is just a matter of the right pose to adopt; riding a Harley-Davidson through the streets of Hollywood, bandanas in their hair and tattoos on their arms. Only to replay guitar parts that were already recorded twenty-five years ago."

With Nirvana, Chris Novoselic says they're trying to wake the sleeping youth of America. The classic single "Smells Like Teen Spirit," heading toward the Top Forty in our country, is a step in the right direction. Stupidity is sung about in this song as if it were a contagious disease. "Americans are in a state of suspended animation from the time they're sixteen," says the twenty-six-year old Novoselic. "There's no generation gap anymore; kids think exactly like their parents. They accept everything as it comes. In the first place, the youth wants to be entertained, give us videos with Tom Cruise, give us meaningless music, give us Nintendo games. They consume popular culture like it was McDonald's hamburgers. There's a thick layer of apathy covering American youth. It's almost impossible to get through. The schools are expertly crafting silence. The media also lends a hand."

Energy

Nirvana is taking a stand. The group is somewhere far left of the center. People who hold a different view, according to Chris Novoselic, better stay away from the trio's concerts. "I refuse to play for someone who supports George Bush," he says with emphasis, "or anyone who's a supporter of the Ku Klux Klan. Our ideas about social issues or politics are reflected in the energy, the frustration and the anger of the music. If you sell as many records as Nirvana has at the moment, you have power. It'll be good to give things a good shake out, mentally and musically."

This is what Nirvana will keep doing. Even though the musicians suddenly became accepted heroes, not much will change. Novoselic: "What will I do with my money? Buy four new tires for my car and possibly buy a new bass. In the 1970s there were rock stars who after a few hits bought a castle and a fast car. Now they don't even have a toilet, so they do what they need to do. I prefer a modest lifestyle. I don't need a limousine to buy my bread at the bakery. I prefer to walk."

ATOMIC

Lucio Spiccia | November 19, 1991 | *Ciao 2001* (Italy)

Writing about my encounter with Nirvana in Rome in November 1991 means winding back the clock many turns, especially given the pace of my life. I was able to get that interview mainly because of Urge Overkill, the support band for the European tour, with whom I had made friends when I lived in London, but I must also thank Francesco Adinolfi and Jacopo Benci, chief editors for the magazines *Ciao 2001* and *Music & Arts*, for which I wrote.

After Kurt's suicide, a lot of people asked me about the evening I spent with him, and to this day the younger generations I meet through my current job want to hear about it—staring at me as if I myself were a former member of Nirvana—wanting to know their idol through words unfiltered by the often dubious perspective of the media. It's on these occasions that I become aware that it was an exceptional event; I realize that I came into contact with a piece of rock history, with a musician who, because of his untimely death, would become an icon for generations to come—as Jim Morrison was for my generation.

Upon entering the hotel room that housed the band, the first image that came to my mind was that of the still little-known Nirvana I had seen in Rome two years before who, after half an hour, had ended the concert by destroying their instruments, climbing the amps like little monkeys and jumping down before repeating the whole thing again and again while the bouncers tried to stop them.

My new meeting with Nirvana, though it was taking place in a different context, didn't differ much from the previous run-in and was lighthearted and amusing; the musicians welcomed me by shooting at me with a plastic suction-cup gun and started swinging from the chandelier uttering animal cries. They seemed to be the same big kids, maybe just a bit more grown up. There was a major difference, though—*Nevermind* was at the top of the charts. Perhaps it was this fusion of fun and music that brought them to "nirvana," ecstasy and pure spiritual enjoyment.

I spent nearly two hours alone with Kurt (Chris and Dave made only a few brief appearances), both of us lying on the bed in a relaxed, almost suspended mood, very different from the interviews I was used to, far removed from the pressure and boredom that musicians experience during typical encounters with the press. I met Kurt again in London about one year later. We exchanged only a few words, but I got the distinct feeling that he felt like a fish out of water amid all the hype that had swelled up around him. –Lucio Spiccia

Translated by Alessandra Meineri.

Lucio Spiccia: *Nevermind* shows your strong desire to grow and explore new avenues, breaking away from the sound and the heavy and gloomy moods of *Bleach*, the typical "Seattle sound" . . .

Chris Novoselic: Do you think *Bleach* had a typical "Seattle sound"?

LS: Why, wasn't that your aim with *Bleach?*

Kurt Cobain: No [*in unison with Chris and Dave*], because we never felt we were part of anything, and we had written songs for *Bleach* long before we'd ever heard of a "Seattle sound." In fact, there was no "Seattle sound" at the time we put out that album.

Dave Grohl: At the same time, I don't see how anyone can consider that Mudhoney sounds like us; their sound has nothing in common with Nirvana's! I think it all comes out naturally. We're not trying to follow something else. When people talk about "the Sub Pop sound" I think there's a lot of confusion . . . not all the bands sound like the Walkabouts, Mark Lanegan, Beat Happening . . . and Mudhoney doesn't sound like any of the others. Each band has its own sound and none of them sound like the others.

CN: We have nothing in common with Mudhoney!

KC: *Nevermind* is the logical evolution of the past two years of rehearsing, experimenting and playing different music. But I don't think that we've completely left the sound of *Bleach*; I think of *Nevermind* having some songs, like "Breed" and "Smells Like Teen Spirit" or even "Stay Away" . . . songs that have the same sound as the first album. I don't think we've completely changed our sound.

LS: On this new album, I think you're following the same trail you blazed with a song such as "About a Girl" on *Bleach* . . .

KC: Yeah, you're right, but I think that other songs on *Bleach* followed that path and had that kinda simple structure. But people, you know, always tend to generalize. They take a song and think that the whole album is all like that. On *Bleach,* there was "Sifting" and the other slow, boring song "Paper Cuts," two very slow songs, with less feedback, so they stick in people's minds and they forget about the rest of the album . . . I read reviews about *Nevermind* that said, "Nirvana are playing acoustic guitars and their songs are very quiet," but in reality there are only two slow songs with acoustic guitars! But they always tend to generalize. We mixed this new album and it came out as it is!

LS: I even remember you playing the song "Polly" at your concert here in Rome two years ago . . .

KC: A few of the songs on *Nevermind* are old.

LS: There's no doubt, however, that the main trend of this new album is mixing pop and raw guitar sounds . . .

KC: We always have done. Some of the songs on *Bleach,* like "About a Girl," for example, have a lot of pop elements.

DG: I think the songs on *Nevermind* have far stronger pop melodies than those on *Bleach,* but if you listen closely to some of the songs on the first album you realize that there's a lot of pop there too, but most of the people never catch that.

LS: Some journalists have written that you're following the path started by Hüsker Dü and the Replacements . . .

KC: Well, I've never been a fan of the Replacements, and I only like two albums by Hüsker Dü . . . neither of those bands has had a big influence on me. People just don't understand. They see an album released in 1989 and believe that the group started to play that kind of music exactly in that year, but it's not like that! I used to play this kind of music in 1985, having never heard of Hüsker Dü before. What I mean is that people think that the original sound of a band has been invented at the exact time when the album comes out . . . I mean it's a buncha crap. There are a lot of bands in the underground that play "hard rock music" with a punk attitude.

LS: Let's go back and talk about Seattle again. A couple of years ago, many people saw Seattle as a "golden town" for American underground music. Do you think it was correct?

CN: No, Seattle is not a "golden town," it's very green! [*Laughs*]

KC: I've always liked Seattle. I think it's a fine town, there are some good people there, you can find a good cup of coffee at any time. A couple of years ago the music scene was more exciting, we were meeting new people, making new friends, and there were a lot of good bands that were putting out records.

LS: Not long ago, I interviewed Skin Yard and Mudhoney, and both of them have told me the same thing: it's all over in Seattle today, the spirit of two years ago is gone, now there are hundreds of bands but many of them are pretty bad . . .

KC: It's like a slowdown, that happens in every city, that happens everywhere; at the beginning it's all exciting and then it goes out and then comes back again. It happens in any place. It doesn't mean that Seattle is dead, it just means that there's a lot of monotony at this point in time.

CN: There were bands that released good records and that brought a lot of attention to Seattle, so a lot of bands arrived from other towns and a lot of them are kinda shit . . .

KC: Just like in any city. It always has been and it always will be . . . That's the nature of rock 'n' roll—a handful of good bands and a bucketful of shitty bands.

LS: How important was the work of Sub Pop to you?

KC: They put out our record and other people's records. It's like any other record label. People put too much emphasis on Sub Pop and Seattle when in reality there were only just a handful of good bands and there's nothing extraordinary, and it's nothing new, not anything that doesn't happen in Los Angeles or New York too, or in other places over and over again. The people responsible for this quasi-worship are the guys who write all these particular stories on the "Seattle sound," but it's just a bunch of bullshit, you know . . . it's too romantic and I never agree with them. It's really easy for a kid to read an article about Seattle and think, "Hell, it sounds like Utopia!" but that's crap. I personally have only liked just four or five bands from Seattle, you know, even though, you know, for most of my life I've been going up to Seattle to see shows, but there's always been only a few that I really liked. Most of the bands I really love come from other cities.

LS: Many journalists have written that the "Seattle sound" and bands like Nirvana, Soundgarden, and Mudhoney have brought new life to heavy metal. Personally, I don't agree with this, and I think your new album is an example that this statement is wrong. I think that you're all just playing rock 'n' roll.

KC: Yeah, you're right. We've never been fans of heavy metal, but if kids who are heavy metal fans like our music, it's fine . . . just don't call it heavy metal, please!

LS: I saw you smashing your instruments after just a half hour of performance during the concert in Rome in 1989, and I know that you do that often. Don't you think, though, that perhaps with this kind of behavior you're subconsciously retracing a rebellion that died in the 1960s?

KC: I never followed the 1960s vibe. I think the rock music of that period was just devoid of energy; it was really innocent and people just thought about lying around in couples. We're closer, if anything, to a spirit like that of Berkeley in '79. I remember one of our concerts where the bouncers were all dickheads and were beating some kids in the audience. So we stopped the bouncers and gave the microphone to one of them and asked him why he was doing that to the kids and he said he was just doing his job. At that point I told the entire audience to get up on stage and take over the bouncers . . . and the audience did, they took the stage and began a kind of dance and had fun and the bouncers left and hid backstage. We defeated the bouncers and it was really fun, and so there was a sort of a revolutionary spirit that night, without explanation, without a reason. It's fun!

LS: Is it just fun?

KC: Sure, sometimes we're happy and there's no reason, it's fun, it's something to do. I have no respect for guitars, I think they're just pieces of wood . . . I'm not one of those musicians that polishes his guitars and uses them as a tool to worship. They're just pieces of wood and nothing special for me. To go back to what you asked me about the 1960s, I honestly cannot answer, because I wasn't a teenager in the 1960s, I was a teenager in the late 1970s. If I were a teenager in the 1960s I would have definitely followed bands like the Stooges and Blue Cheer . . . and I would've hated Cream, you know, and most of the bands that were in the Top 40, they were all shitty bands. I think that in every age of rock 'n' roll, more or less every ten years, there are only a handful of really good bands.

LS: What does rock 'n' roll mean to you?

KC: It means hanging out with my friends, playing some music, eating food, riding on a bus for eighteen hours . . .

LS: Yeah, and then you can also set the bus on fire . . . [*Laugh together.*]

KC: I was very drunk . . . but it did only happen once! [*Still laughing together.*]

LS: A lot of people argue that rock 'n' roll is dead, saying that everything has already been written. But listening to *Nevermind* and seeing what's happening these weeks, I think we can easily refute that claim. Your band manages to fully embody the freshness, vitality, energy, and especially the emotional impact on young people, all qualities rock 'n' roll only has when it's alive and kicking . . .

KC: It's really great what you're saying, thank you! As long as there are fifteen-year-old kids there'll always be a need for rock 'n' roll! But at the same time, there'll always be shitty bands like Poison that gather these kids . . . and that's the downside.

CN: We don't play rock 'n' roll . . . rock 'n' roll is Eric Clapton, Phil Collins, and Bruce Springsteen.

LS: Jack Endino told me that your new album is a "good commercial album," stating that *commercial* shouldn't always be considered a bad word.

KC: No, *commercial* is not a bad word. There are a lot of shitty commercial bands, of course, but everyone knows that there are good ones . . . It's always been that way and it's just the same today as it was in the past.

LS: Although you say that Seattle today isn't what it was two years ago, the media hype that has been created around the town has been really important and the majors have started to become interested in bands from the town. That's how an album like *Nevermind* was able to get to the top of the American charts.

KC: Well, what happened is, after a lot of years, the majors have finally started to give underground bands a chance again. They've started to sign independent bands. So now you can easily find good music even at the top of the charts.

LS: I think the success of *Nevermind* was quite unexpected for you.

KC: Yes, absolutely, we would never have thought that the album would do so well or be able to reach the top of the charts! And this success is entirely due to the fact that now, with Geffen, it's much easier to find our records, unlike in the past with the Sub Pop . . .

LS: How does it feel now to stand at the center of the big music business machine?

KC: I don't know, it's pretty easy. And it's also really easy to ignore most of the assholes that revolve around the music industry who we have to meet and shake hands with, you know. It's really easy to just say, "Hey, hello, how are you?" and be told, "You played very well, it was a great show tonight!" and we reply, "Thank you, we're glad that you enjoyed it." There's no problem, you know?

LS: Maybe now that you're in the typical rock lifestyle you don't like to do interviews anymore.

KC: I've never liked it, it hasn't happened right now. I hate interviews . . . but you're nice to me, I like you!

LS: Do you think then that everything is the same as before, that nothing is changing in your life?

KC: No, nothing is changing yet, because when all this happened we were on tour, we've been on tour for three months. Our manager called us on the phone and told us that *Nevermind* was at Number 4 in the *Billboard* charts, that's all! There's no basic difference for me; I still haven't received money from the sales of the album. The only difference is that now there are kids at the concerts who ask us for grass more often! [*Laughs.*] We're very happy and we're aware that all this may not last long, maybe tomorrow we'll be back to anonymity; this is something that we've never looked for, and it wouldn't be nice to go back to an independent label. I think it's really important to have good distribution on a label, because it means people can easily find your album.

LS: Are you satisfied with *Nevermind* or is there anything you would've liked to do differently?

KC: Absolutely satisfied! Now we're with Geffen and they, too, know exactly what kind of band we are and what we want to do.

LS: David Geffen was lucky with you . . .

KC: No, I don't think so. I think we were pretty smart to choose Geffen. Of course, luck played a part . . . We had talked to several record companies and then we chose Geffen. A lot of record companies are really narrow-minded and don't realize how much potential underground bands have.

LS: Now that you have it within your grasp, can you tell me what success is for you?

KC: Writing good songs, having friends, staying in good hotels, eating good food like we're finding here in Italy . . . I love Italy, I love it so much. It was really fun going to the Vatican riding a motorbike, and then . . . the food is wonderful, the food here is amazing, I would come to Italy just for the food! And don't forget how warm the audience is.

LS: I believe that the audience will soon be quite different from what you were used to, here in Italy and elsewhere.

KC: For now it seems to be more or less the same kind of audience that we had before starting the tour. After all, the venues where we're playing now are still the same as two years ago in terms of size. I don't know what will happen when we go back to our country, because the album is selling a lot in the last couple of months in the United States. When we do the next tour we'll probably find our audience has doubled, and I'm sure there'll be a lot of dickheads and stupid people, even though there are a lot of them right now among our fans . . . but we've always respected these people, though. We're still the same band, we're not doing anything different, we're in the same hotels we were in when we put out our album with Sub Pop, we eat the same food when we're here in Italy, we're playing the same venues as ever, even though now they're maybe too small. In fact, all the shows we've done on this tour were sold out and there were a lot of people that wanted to come and see us, but the venues couldn't accommodate them all. It's very frustrating, all of this, just like it happened a couple of days ago in Trieste, for example, where four hundred people were outside trying to get into the venue and they just couldn't. It all really sucks . . . standing outside of the venue trying to listen . . . and probably a lot of these guys had come a lot of miles to get to the place; that's shit and I think the promoter has his faults . . .

LS: What do you expect tonight?

KC: I have another show ahead of me; generally we get the same reaction at every show, you know . . . some people sing along to our songs, other people dance, it'll be another typical rock show, it'll be a lot of fun.

LS: If Europe is like this, what do you expect to find when you go back to the States?

KC: *Nevermind* wasn't at Number 4 in *Billboard* when we left the States, it was in the Top 40, so I don't know, I really don't know what to expect! I just know that our manager and our friends have told us that our video is running continuously on MTV and that the album is selling a lot of copies. I don't know, I really don't know what to expect. We sold a million and a half records up until now. The only thing I can think right now is that when we go on tour next time we'll play in the biggest venues.

LS: The first time I heard of you was during a long chat with Chris Cornell and Soundgarden, shortly before the release of *Bleach*. Chris told me that you were the Seattle band that he loved the most and advised me to buy your album that was about to be released.

KC: There's a mutual respect between us; I think that Soundgarden is a great band . . . and that they're really nice people. I like them a lot; we hung out for a long time in Seattle.

LS: Something I've been curious about for some time—is Nirvana just a name like any other, or do you have an interest in Indian philosophy and you want your music to have the same meaning as *nirvana*?

KC: It's just a name . . . however, we do have respect for Indian religion. I loved the name; it's really a nice name!

LS: What bands are you listening to lately?

KC: There are very few new bands that I like. The bands that I prefer are Half Japanese, Urge Overkill, Melvins . . . I love Mudhoney, the Breeders, the Pixies.

LS: What kind of music do you feel closest to?

KC: I'm into all kind of music, but I think punk rock from the mid-1980s was probably the most important musical influence for me.

LS: In recent times most of the punk audience has been following you, Soundgarden, Mudhoney . . .

KC: Yeah, you're right, in fact, it's the punk scene that follows us in the States, whereas here in Italy the public is a lot more varied.

LS: Do you have plans for the future? Have you already sketched some ideas for the next album during this long tour?

KC: I've got no idea for the future. Maybe I'll write more poems or a book or I'll make a movie . . . definitely I'll continue to write songs and collaborate with some friends. As far as the band goes, it's really hard to predict the future and what we'll do.

LS: You said that perhaps you'll write more poems. Is it something that interests you a lot?

KC: I like to write poems and I love to read them. I like it a lot, but I don't really have a favorite poet. I've purposely kept myself away from being influenced by any poetry, even if I've always had the chance to read a lot. But I don't like to be influenced, just because I write for my own pleasure and I love doing it, especially after a show, you know, when I'm in a hotel room . . . it's a lot of fun, it's kinda like doing a crossword puzzle. And if some people someday wanted to publish that stuff I write, it wouldn't be a good thing, because I get enough enjoyment this way, it's a kind of a personal thing, it's a recreational thing. I've only skimmed through most of the popular poets and I really don't care for any other. I mean, I like poetry, I've a lot of respect for each poet, but I want to avoid being influenced by someone. I don't want to be influenced by anyone because I want to try to develop my own style, without having any idea of what poetry is really supposed to be like, because I think that poetry should have no definition, you know . . . I think devoting myself more to poetry is something to do when I'm old! [*Laughs.*] There are also poets among the singers, and some of them are great poets . . . now it occurs to me Patti Smith, perhaps because I love her so much. She's really written some good poetry and also her songs are very poetic.

LS: Does your love for poetry influence in some way the songs you write, your lyrics?

KC: Not really. I've been influenced by the things I read, but that's not a sort of slavery . . . I don't think that my music, my songs are inspired by the things I read, you know. My lyrics are pieces of my poems, lines . . . sometimes I've got no idea about what the subject will be until it's finished. I've always written, even before forming the band, since the days of high school . . . I was sitting in my room writing things, reading things, watching TV, listening to music.

LS: It almost seems like you wanted to isolate yourself from the rest of the world; did you feel alone?

KC: It was a way to escape from what I had been surrounded by, to vent . . . I didn't like my environment and the whole school environment that I attended and so I tried to create a world of my own . . . I'm sorry, Lucio, but we have to stop now! It's terribly late and our concert has to start!

NIRVANA

Giancarlo De Chirico | November 19, 1991 | *Tutti Frutti* **(Italy)**

The Setting: Theater/Cinema Castello—We met Nirvana during the band's amazing Italian tour. Aside from what happened in Turin (the concert was canceled after a gas station strike was announced), nobody was expecting such a large crowd of people; some clubs had to turn people away as the venues were packed. After a couple of long hours of waiting, we managed to physically stop Kurt Cobain, Chris Novoselic, and Dave Grohl at the exit of a Roman restaurant where they went to have some pasta before their concert. They were still soaked from the rain, but they were all excited after their wine and dinner. As it kept raining, we moved inside the Arena Castello (it became an adult cinema soon afterward but today is owned by the Vatican and shows only religious documentaries), where the stage was still under construction. Nobody noticed our presence, and in any case there was nothing that we could do to stop the staff working on the stage, as the concert was about to start in about two hours. During the interview, there was a great amount of noise—screams from the staff, carts being moved around, and sound systems being tested—creating a constant racket in the background. —Giancarlo De Chirico

Chris Novoselic: Hi, what's up? If only we had the chance to spend more time here our music would be way different! Not so noisy, not so loud, no desperate screams, no frustrations. It wouldn't be possible as the food is so good!

Giancarlo De Chirico: I guess so; how come you're all soaked?

CN: We rented some motorcycles to do a tour around the city, but then it started raining and we got caught in the middle of the storm!

Kurt Cobain: We're soaked, for sure, but we're good. At least now our bellies are full of delicious food. The world seems different.

Dave Grohl: Yeah, but I'm still cold! And I can't wait for the concert to start so I can warm up a bit.

GDC: What's behind your piercing notes from the guitars and all the furious screams in your songs? What are your musical roots?

DG: Punk rock, without a doubt. That's the energy flowing inside our songs.

KC: A revived punk which we see as a form of musical freedom. A spontaneous feeling, with no rules or categories. It allowed us to melt hard rock, punk, and psychedelic influences.

CN: I would like to underline that it all came out naturally, without us thinking about it. You can hear echoes and some flavor of Black Flag but also from Black Sabbath in our music. We don't believe they're so different from one another. We shouldn't ignore other musical realities, as sooner or later they'll all belong to us.

GDC: Can you clarify? What do you mean exactly?

CN: You see, I hate some pop songs that I listen to, but then I can't keep them out of my mind. "My Sharona" by the Knack, for instance. It's shockingly commercial! But it's amazing. It really sticks in the heads of people who listen to it. You can't forget it.

GDC: Indeed, aside from punk and rock there are some pop music influences on *Nevermind,* your latest album. Maybe this is the reason behind your recent commercial success?

KC: Yep, maybe what you're saying is right, almost true, but it depends on the fact that our music—deep inside—is really simple. We've also got a refrain, a solo, a standard structure that allows people to follow an entire song. Just don't forget that our perspective is quite different.

GDC: Were you surprised to find yourself at the top of the American charts? I heard some journalist talking about taking you to the next Sanremo Festival, so we're sure that will be as the headliner . . .

CN: A true miracle! We didn't believe in miracles up to now, but see—

KC: I'm not aware of the music executives' intentions, but we most probably will be coming back to play here but at much bigger venues. That's for sure, even though we do like the atmosphere of cozy little clubs.

DG: Everything is happening so quickly that we don't realize it. We were already happy about the fact that we put an album out with a major record label. We're still learning a lot on the technical side, and we have to worry about responding to our success. At this point I'm lost.

GDC: Everybody knows that nirvana refers to a mystical state of illumination that, once reached, brings peace, calm, and happiness. What's the link between this Asian philosophy, Buddhism, and your music, which is made up rather heavily of aggressive, loud sounds that don't even give you the time to think?

KC: The secret is all about letting go. It's because through our music we release our tension, our rage, and all our frustrations. We find at the end that we enjoy it and most of all that we make other people feel good, people that come to our gigs.

CN: Yeah, this is our nirvana; being set free from pain, worries, suffering. And we can only make it there through our music.

GDC: The official video of "Smells Like Teen Spirit" is amazing. It's something like a crescendo occurring live between your band and the public.

KC: It took us twelve hours to finish the video, so we need to thank all our friends who we invited over to help with the video. There were about two hundred people, and it went amazingly well. We were all so excited despite all this artificial smoke that was stopping us from breathing.

GDC: On your album's cover there's a baby swimming underwater; he's very determined to reach that one-dollar bill. Is that image an accusation aimed at American society, against the culture that we grow up with in school and at home?

CN: Exactly that. That baby isn't a human being, it's a consumer. From the moment we're born, we're only taught to think about the importance of money. Nothing else.

DG: OK, fine, but I believe we're all guilty. Every one of us, somehow, is influenced by shopping. It seems we're not capable of doing anything else!

GDC: What other things make you angry?

KC: Greed.

CN: Stupidity.

DG: Materialism.

GDC: Something makes me believe the American flag will never be on your stage . . .

CN: We don't feel like Americans. We're all the sons of a genocide that was perpetrated against the American tribes a long time ago. Plus, Americans have no appreciation for art, only for the color of the money.

"IT'S NOT AS DRASTIC A CHANGE AS EVERYONE IS CLAIMING"

Angela Zocco | November 20, 1991 | Radio Città Fujiko (Italy)

In November 1991, a radio colleague (Massimo Mosca, guitarist in the band Three Second Kiss) asked me, "Are you coming to the Nirvana gig? They're going to play at Kryptonite in Baricella [a very small town near Bologna; the venue no longer exists] on November 20."

I never missed a gig, and still never do, so I said, "Yes, of course, why?"

"Because I'd like to interview the singer; you might help me if we're lucky enough to meet him."

"Yes, why not?" was my answer.

Nevermind had just been released, and Nirvana was on the verge of becoming an international phenomenon. In fact that night, as I arrived in front of the club, it was evident that the capacity of the venue—just five hundred people—was insufficient for all those waiting outside, pushing to enter. It was physically challenging, but we were among those who got in. After a while we saw a young, blond, attractive guy hanging around. He could have been one of the guys in the audience waiting for the show—same clothes, same age, same attitude—but he was Kurt Cobain. We asked him if he could answer some questions for radio, and he said yes. He was quiet and smiling, very kind and focused. He suggested we sit on the stairs in front of the bar and so we did. We pushed the REC button on our cassette recorder and started the interview.

I never could have imagined back then that this short and naive conversation would become a sort of relic. Recently, someone asked me if I had taken any photos of the occasion, and I smiled, thinking of an age when you went to gigs without a cell phone in your hand and only the photographers took pictures. —Angela Zocco

[*Voice in Italian, background noise as Urge Overkill takes the stage. —Ed.*]
Angela Zocco: How come there's this change in your musical direction with your second record?

Kurt Cobain: I don't think of it as a drastic change. I don't think of it as much as other people have claimed it to be. It's like two years of evolving and practicing together and having different drummers and admitting that we like pop music more than we did at the time the *Bleach* album came out. So it's not as drastic a change as everyone is claiming it is.

AZ: How do the people in Seattle now think of you, your music, when the Sub Pop style is still prevailing, this different sound?

KC: Mmm. Our audiences have grown; we're a lot more popular than we used to be, so I think everyone is accepting it and liking it a lot.

AZ: How are your relationships with Sub Pop now? Are they still going good or are they a bit worse because we see on the record the name Geffen, y'know? So there are some changes in the future, or you will continue with Sub Pop?

KC: Oh, we've . . . we're not on Sub Pop anymore. We've signed to David Geffen Company, and the reason the Sub Pop label is on our album is because it's part of the contractual buyout that we had to make to get off of the Sub Pop contract. Because we were signed to them for seven years and we had to give them a bunch of money, but our relationship with them is just fine, y'know? We're still good friends with them and we talk.

AZ: No problems?

KC: Oh, no problems at all.
[*Italian interviewer speaks —Ed.*]

AZ: Sorry for the question you could have heard many times before, but do you feel better with a three- or four-member lineup?

KC: Oh, definitely with three, yeah. Because we'd never thought of Jason, the other guitar player, as a permanent member of the band. We recorded the *Bleach* album as a three-piece, and while the album was being released

we decided to put Jason's picture in and his name on the album stating that he played on the album, but he never did and so . . . and he was only in the band for like six months and then we kicked him out.
[*Italian interviewer speaks —Ed.*]

AZ: This is the second time for Nirvana in Italy?

KC: Yeah, right.

AZ: Do you think there's something different, apart from that you're more popular now than you were before? What about the people? Do you think that there's something different in the audience?

KC: Oh, not at all! In fact, well, we only played in two shows—we only played two shows the last time we were here with Tad, but the crowds were actually bigger than they are now, so I haven't noticed if we might be more popular or not, I dunno . . .
[*Angela speaks in Italian to her colleague —Ed.*]

AZ: I read an interview in . . . *Melody Maker,* I think . . . the description of your band was like the "sex and drugs and rock 'n' roll" lifestyle, is it correct or no?

KC: At times it is, but not as much as the person who wrote that article would like everyone to believe. I mean, it's obvious that all English music papers are a bunch of bullshit, y'know? They're a big lie all the time, so don't accept anything you read in an English paper.

AZ: It's not true?

KC: It's not true all the time; it's not as exaggerated as that article would believe.

Italian voice: Grazie particolare, Kurt, thank you!

"IF WE WEREN'T FRIENDS I WOULDN'T WANT TO BE IN THIS BAND"

Niels Delvaux | November 23, 1991 | Studio Brussel (Belgium)

The only available recording of the interview for Studio Brussel has been edited, removing the questions from the clip. Paragraph breaks indicate where there's an obvious cut in the recording. Where it aids in understanding Cobain's responses, I've stated in brackets the questions Niels Delvaux might have asked. Kurt is clearly unwell: he coughs, sniffs, and clears his throat repeatedly throughout the interview. I've retained mention of it to emphasize this as a specific conversation taking place at a particular point in time with an individual not at his best. He's talkative, though, and gives detailed replies. —Ed.

[*Clears throat.*] Attention. This is Kurt from Nirvana. This is the update on Studio Brussel.

Well . . . I suppose I should say yeah, I'm surprised but, umm, Poison sells five million records and, er, they suck. They don't deserve it. So I don't really care. Yeah, we're music lovers. We're musicians. We like music. We appreciate all different kinds of music—as long as it's good. Doesn't matter if it's on a major label, doesn't matter if it's on a tape someone made on their home boombox, or a recorder like this. It doesn't matter. It doesn't matter even if someone hasn't even recorded something to even have it distributed to anyone. If it's good, it's good, we just like it so, y'know? We'd be just as happy playing in a basement, y'know . . . sometimes that's the most—that's the most appreciable time we have with music is just being together. 'Cause we're good friends, and we play music.

Oh, we're definitely friends—if we weren't friends I wouldn't want to be in this band. I wouldn't want to be in any band if they weren't my friends. We hang out together even when we're not doing anything involving the band.

Chris and I have been playing together for about four and a half years now [*coughs*], with a few different drummers. And Dave has been in the band for a year. This is the first time we've ever felt like a very definite unit. Umm, the band is finally complete because all the other drummers we had pretty much sucked. [*Laughs.*] As far as tempo, y'know? Like, just, it's really hard to find a good drummer. I'm really not the type of person who likes to emphasize on musicianship [*coughs*], I really don't care how sloppy a band is, but, umm, it's really distressing to play in a band when the drummer can't keep time.

I've been writing songs since I was about fifteen, since I first bought my first guitar and, umm, Dave and Chris never thought of themselves as songwriters; they've never had that feeling to ever want to do that so . . . umm . . . I became the songwriter of the band. But we've collaborated a lot more. I usually come up with the basic idea for a song and then we'd go into a practice room and play the song over and over and over again until it's finally finished. So it is pretty collective.

Sometimes we just get drunk, y'know? And we want to have fun, and it's really boring to be on tour for three months and, er, be in these same kinda hotel, same hotels, and these same backstage areas and playing your show and, umm, and then just going straight to the hotel afterward to sleep and then start it all over again. And not eating regularly and driving on a bus for eight hours a day—it's really boring. And so we do everything in our power to keep it exciting, and sometimes that involves, umm, having a bit too much fun. Well? Err, not even, I mean . . . every time we've destroyed something we've always been in a really happy, jokey mood where we're drunk off our asses and throwing things around and wrestling and having fun, y'know? Umm. I don't give a shit if it's a cliché or not, or if it's been done by bands before. I think [*coughs*] any rock 'n' roll band has those tendencies to do stuff like that just to keep themselves sane. But, umm . . . obviously if you've ever read an English paper you know they like to exaggerate things and make a big sensational story out of it, so . . . it's not as extreme as everyone thinks.

[*Asked about the band's reputation for wrecking their equipment at the end of a show —Ed.*]

Y'know, when we feel like it. It's just fun too. It's part of the act. [*Laughter from interviewer.*] We did it a lot more a few years ago than we have now. We haven't been doing it very much lately because everyone expects it. We usually just play real cheap equipment, and a lot of times before a show we're scrambling for guitar parts and gluing things together just to have a guitar for that night and, uhh . . . I dunno, it's just one day at a time, sweet Jesus. We appreciate beauty just as much as we appreciate violence and . . . I mean, we don't even appreciate violence but, y'know? Obviously it's an emotion; it's just another part of emotion, negative energy. We like to divide those two, mix them up, make a nice salad.

[*Asked which bands he appreciates —Ed.*]

Half Japanese . . . Beat Happening . . . the Raincoats . . . Young Marble Giants . . . Shonen Knife . . . the Melvins . . . Jesus Lizard . . . I still think R.E.M. are good songwriters. I like the Pixies. I like the Breeders a lot.

"ACCEPT ME, GENERAL PUBLIC, BECAUSE I NEED THE CASH"

Frédéric Brébant | November 23, 1991 | RTBF *Félix* (Belgium)

In November 1991, I was working freelance for RTBF, the Belgian French-speaking public TV network, on a show called *Félix*. The producer asked me to interview "a new American band," but this was pre-Internet, so you couldn't easily find information. Plus it was my first rock interview and my first interview in English! My obsession became to get Nirvana to explain the word *grunge* to me.

It was a surreal night in Ghent. My team and I arrived and encountered the band already "in another world": Courtney Love and Kurt Cobain were chasing one another in and out of the restrooms, shouting and laughing like kids. We had just twenty minutes before the concert to get the interview done. My first (stupid!) question was: "How would you define the music of Nirvana?" Kurt seemed very tired and said nothing, looking at me as if I were a stupid little man. Then something extraordinary, something physical, happened: Chris Novoselic started to beat on the table, Dave Grohl impersonated the sound of a guitar, and Kurt concluded their answer—"with a twist of lemon"—squeezing the fruit in his hand.

The interview continued in this vein, with a disinterested singer plus two musicians playing it cool and doing the talking. Then, in the middle of the interview, Kurt fell asleep altogether! I guess he was stoned—drugs or alcohol, I really don't know. After the interview, we filmed part of the concert and witnessed this man up, active, and full of energy again!

In 1994, hearing of his death, I found my interview and watched it again. I didn't remember asking, "How do you see Nirvana in ten years?" In the video, there's a close-up of Kurt asleep, a terrible image—he looks dead. Every time I see that close-up, I get goose bumps. The interview remains, however, the best souvenir of my young professional life.

Peoples' eyes light up when I tell them I interviewed this icon. I know for a fact that the images will never leave me. —Frédéric Brébant

Frédéric Brébant: How would you define the music of Nirvana?
[*Chris commences a solid drumbeat on the table, Kurt joins in, Dave and Kurt sing a spiraling guitar line.*]

Dave Grohl: Something like that.

Kurt Cobain: With a twist of lemon! [*Snatches a lemon from the table and squeezes it in his fist.*]

FB: In "Teen Spirit" you seem to complain about the apathy of our generation, is that right?

KC: Whatever you want to make out of it. It's up to you. It's your crossword puzzle.

FB: And do you share this lack of engagement yourself?

KC: What, being apathetic? Sure.

FB: Why?

KC: Why? Because we sleep too much.
[*Cuts to Nirvana performing "Sliver" live.*]

KC: Punk rock should mean freedom, liking and accepting anything you like, playing whatever you want, as sloppy as you want. As long as it's good and has passion.
[*Cuts to Nirvana performing "Lithium" live.*]

FB: How many guitars did you destroy since your first concert?

Chris Novoselic: I don't think it has anything to do with the music.

KC: And that isn't necessarily violence either. It's fun. It's pure fun.
[*Cuts to Nirvana song "Territorial Pissings" with footage of stage destruction.*]

FB: What do you get by smashing guitars in this scene?

KC: Satisfaction, climax. [*Cuts to footage.*] What?

CN: Don't have to do encores.

KC: Yeah, there ya go, it's a good excuse not to have to do an encore. [*Cuts to footage.*]

FB: And how do you see Nirvana in ten years?

CN: I see us on stage playing, dorky clothes, and uhhh . . . just totally wrinkled and just like having, trying to relive our past and [*puts on old 1960s hippie voice*] trying to remind people of the good ol' days, how things used to be! Y'know, cruising in yer car or, y'know, smokin' pot and listenin' to music—heyyyy . . . those were the times, y'know? [*Switches to old-school radio sales voice.*] It's called "Children of the Revolution," twenty of your greatest hits by Nir-va-naaaa! "Floyd the Barber," "Smells Like Teen Spirit," and on the future, in the future, we'll have songs like "Accept Me, General Public, Because I Need the Cash," or that one notable one, "Hey Baby Baby, Pay for My Limousine."

HYPE, BUT NOT REALLY?

Annemiek van Grondel | November 25, 1991 | *OOR* **(the Netherlands)**

November 25, 1991. We are at Paradiso, a former church and a hippie squat that in 1968 was proclaimed the Pop Temple of Amsterdam. It's fifteen minutes after the show. I have about twenty minutes with the drummer of Nirvana, sitting under the basement stairs that lead to the podium. It's next to the dressing rooms where his peers are partying after an amazing show in the overcrowded, crazed venue. It's my very first interview, ever. In a slightly discomforting but gentle way Dave Grohl, while shaking hands in the "catacombs," warns: "Let me tell you first that the best interviews with Nirvana are the ones that are really comfortable and that are just sitting and chatting. The ones that aren't are about statistics."

I remember Dave looking remarkably fresh despite the band ending the show with Dave and Kurt massacring the drum set as their spectacular and irrevocable finale. This is not something I could say of Kurt Cobain, who seemed exhausted, gulped his beer nervously, and stared at the crowd in the locker room with a hazy look in his eyes that said, "What are they all doing here?"

Their breakthrough on a worldwide level, from unknown and unwanted to pampered pets of the progressive rock audience, has done the trio no harm. Yet the pressure of their rapid success seems immense. Dave explains: "The life we live, being constantly on the move and performing, it's heavy—and hectic. I have friends who don't go to rock shows very frequently. If they ever go to a Nirvana concert and come visit us afterward, in our dressing room full of boozing and dope-smoking guests, they give me a slightly puzzled look. Still, you get used to it. I simply have to be active. If I go back to America again, I'm fatigued. Within no time I'm bored to death. That restlessness always drives me to get back out on new tours." —Annemiek van Grondel

Annemiek van Grondel: In Washington, DC, you were a drummer in punk rock bands Dain Bramage and Mission Impossible before joining Scream. How did you get involved in Nirvana?

Dave Grohl: Kurt and Chris had seen me play and asked if I was interested in their band. When Scream was history, I called them and the case was settled pretty quickly.

AvG: The last album was meant to be distributed by Sub Pop. What's the reason why it wasn't?

DG: We were still under contract to Sub Pop and had to pay ourselves out of that contract; a large sum of money, and rightly so. They're just normal people who live in Seattle, not cunning businessmen but normal people who love music. We are still good friends, though. The one thing that really disturbs a relationship is business. We don't like to consider any of this business, even though obviously it is. We sell records and make money, and that's a business, but nobody considers it a job. And we don't do it for the money, we don't do it for the business.

AvG: It seems to me a contradiction to still choose to join a major label.

DG: I already mentioned the bad distribution. Sub Pop was full of normal music-loving people, who at one point had to sell so many records that they went completely berserk. It just got crazy and they started losing money and throwing money away. They ended up in debt. The label almost collapsed and disappeared. Now they're way back on the right track, but at that time it was near bankruptcy. We tried to get out of it by negotiating with larger record companies. There were eight major labels that were interested and they offered us incredible amounts, ranging from five hundred thousand to a million. Instead, we deliberately chose Geffen, who offered us less money but were willing to give us total artistic freedom. As far as the music and lyrics of Nirvana, we want to take the decisions ourselves. People on our current label understand that. We signed to DGC because they were the record label with employees who knew where Nirvana was coming from. For instance, Geffen already had Sonic Youth. They know the underground and respect the whims of the subculture. I mean, we signed for a small amount of money and all of that was budgeted towards recording and video, and the money we had to give to Sub Pop. Some people are under the impression that we signed to a major label for the money, when in reality we didn't get any money.

AvG: So you could still keep your independence . . .

DG: Totally! If we couldn't have, we would not have signed. I mean, you know . . .

AvG: Nirvana as a group doesn't stand for the baby on the cover of *Nevermind,* going against the flow trying to achieve the Big Money?

DG: No! It's the image of a little baby in blue water, which is just beautiful. Your gaze is naturally drawn to it. It's a catchy image.

AvG: But what does that dollar bill mean, dangling on a hook?

DG: It just sort of symbolizes the entire American culture, the materialistic upbringing that children receive. They're taught to worship the dollar bill. To Americans a dollar means happiness, success, and freedom. The cover says it all. Money is the root of all evil. We want to expose this, because we're antimaterialists. Money is the reason why there are borders and wars. Money divides people, money makes the upper class, makes the lower class.

AvG: Why was second guitarist Jason Everman kicked out of the band?

DG: That was before I was in Nirvana. He was only in the band for six or seven months and he didn't play on *Bleach.* That album was recorded before he joined the band.

AvG: But his name is mentioned on the cover.

DG: I know. Because they recorded and then Jason joined, and they put Jason's name on the record because he was in the band and they wanted it to come out.

AvG: In the future, are you looking for a second guitar player?

DG: No, we're happy with the way it is.

AvG: Do you feel musically related to other bands in the Northwest music scene, like Mudhoney, Soundgarden, Screaming Trees, the Wipers, and Tad?

DG: Sure. They're all great friends of ours. I mean, the whole Sub Pop thing . . . when people describe a band from Seattle, they say: "Oh, this band has the Sub Pop sound." But that's not it. See, everyone is friends. You go out and hang out with Mudhoney, you drink with the Screaming Trees. But Nirvana doesn't sound like Mudhoney, and Screaming Trees doesn't sound like Tad.

AvG: One can detect some musical similarities.

DG: Well, it's all loud, distorted rock 'n' roll. It's not the sound, more the attitude and lifestyle. The one thing all those bands have in common is the ability to write a good song. That's what's important to everyone.

AvG: Who came up with the name Nirvana? Is it inspired by the Rastafarian or Indian cultures?

DG: That was Kurt's idea. It comes from the Indian culture. For me, it means deliverance from pain and suffering, a kind of higher plane of ecstasy. But above all it's just a name that sounds good and looks nice.

AvG: Can you cope with this busy life, now that the record sales of *Nevermind* are going up like crazy?

DG: We've been on tour for three months and have a lot more gigs to do. So I'm really, really tired right now.

AvG: Don't you want to go home?

DG: I do wanna go home! I wanted to go home a month ago. [*Laughs.*] We came here on November 3 and go home on December 15. We started touring on August 18. We've been on tour since August. So we are very tired.

AvG: Do you already have a new bunch of songs collected for a new record?

DG: Yes. Maybe that will come out in a year; next September, October. Right now we're focusing on touring and trying to keep sane, trying to keep from going completely mental. Just trying to keep our heads together.

AvG: Last question: Could you give me some insight into your personal background? When did you decide to become a professional musician?

DG: Uh . . . well, I grew up . . . my mother was a very liberal, open-minded schoolteacher. She taught English to high school students. I have a sister. She is really into art; she's very creative. My father used to be a classical flutist. He played flute in the Cleveland Orchestra. My mother was in a singing group called the Three Gals in the 1950s, and she bought my father a guitar for Christmas. He never played it. They got a divorce when I was seven. And so there was this guitar in the house, all my life. I picked it up and started playing when I was ten years old. I played guitar in bands till I was thirteen, and then I started playing drums, because all the drummers in my bands sucked shit. [*Laughs.*] Guitar players are a dime a dozen; there are a million guitar players. But it is really hard to find a good drummer. So I played in punk rock bands, like Mission Impossible and Dain Bramage. When I was in high school—I was seventeen years old—I joined Scream. And I stopped going to school.

AvG: How old are you now exactly?

DG: Twenty-two.

AvG: Sorry, go on.

DG: And started touring. So my first time in Amsterdam I was seventeen years old, playing in a hardcore band, touring the world. So from the time I was seventeen until the time I was twenty-one, I was on tour. Scream was always on tour.

AvG: How did the members of Nirvana discover you?

DG: On the last tour Scream did, we were halfway across the country and our bass player quit. He flew home to Washington, DC, and we were stuck in California. We couldn't go home, we had no money, no food, no nothing.

AvG: Didn't you try to find a new bass player?

DG: We tried, but we couldn't find one. Nirvana had seen Scream play in San Francisco and they needed a drummer. They thought I was really good, but at the time I was in Scream. And then when Scream broke up, I called Nirvana. And flew to Seattle.

AvG: You don't regret it, I presume?

DG: No, I certainly don't regret it! It's just fate, destiny. A very strange thing; I never expected this—

AvG: Madness.

DG: Yes. All of this has happened since we've been on tour. I still find it strange; the success has overwhelmed us. For four months we're touring, the record came out two months ago, sold one million copies in America . . . it's just crazy! We haven't seen any reaction, yet. Well, on tour we have; our shows are sold out and the people like our music, but we haven't been in America since we've sold so many records. So I think maybe when we go home everyone will finally realize what's happened.

AvG: Aren't you afraid of being more or less burned-out before your thirtieth?

DG: Well, you know, anyone who expects to be in a rock 'n' roll band all their life is full of shit. When I was nineteen years old, I knew that I was going back to college by the time I was twenty-five. I stopped school at seventeen years old; that's not enough education for me. I wanna know more. So, I want to go back to school. And maybe, if I make money from this band, I could go and pay to go to school and—

AvG: Learning for what profession?

DG: This is all I know. For five years this is all I've done; touring and playing music. So, I don't know. When all of this is over, I just sort of think for a year: what do I want to do? If I've earned some money with this band, I definitely go back to school. Because there's nothing worse than a person who's been robbed of an education. And I'll do OK. I am happy. I don't wanna do this forever. This is fun, but it is like a phase, you know. It is a phase that you go through and it's great! I am not complaining. [*Laughs.*] All my friends wish they could do what I do! I am lucky, I am totally lucky. So I have to be happy!

AvG: Thank you very much for this talk, Dave.

DG: Thank you! I'm sorry we had so little time. I hope it's OK.

"KURT'S A MIDDLE CHILD, THAT'S WHY HE'S SO MALADJUSTED"

Bram van Splunteren | November 25, 1991 | VPRO *Onrust!* (the Netherlands)

I remember filming my Nirvana interview backstage at Amsterdam rock club Paradiso. Krist and Dave were sitting on a flight of stairs while Kurt was taking a nap in the dressing room right around the corner. They told me he was tired and not in the mood for an interview. I was very disappointed, of course, but the interview went well and the two of them proved to be good talkers. Later when we filmed the concert (on five separate cameras), I deluded myself into thinking that Kurt made up for his nonappearance with me by playing a very intense show. There was a classic moment in the middle of one song when he suddenly looked straight into the camera that was standing on stage right next to him and for a moment threatened to attack it with his guitar—ultimately, of course, he didn't. The concert footage we shot was later sold to Geffen, Nirvana's record company, which put it on a DVD with other live concerts. The sound was recorded with a twenty-four-track mobile unit and was also sold to Geffen to be put on a CD of live recordings from that era. —Bram van Splunteren

Dave Grohl: I dropped out of high school. I never went to college.

Chris Novoselic: We're all dropouts, really.

Bram van Splunteren: Is that so? [*Both nod in unison.*]

CN: Kurt's a middle child, that's why he's so maladjusted. Because, see, I'm the oldest—

DG: And we all come from divorced families.

CN: [*Gesturing at Dave*] He's the baby.

BvS: Is that so?
[*Interview cuts —Ed.*]

CN: I get a lot of my ideas from listening to early punk rock and reading fanzines and, uh, just gathering literature, just underground literature, talking to people of different persuasions, and talking to people who were just dwelled in one issue. Like just talking to somebody who's just totally into animal rights or talking to somebody from the Socialist Worker Party, y'know?

BvS: So how does it feel now to have penetrated with your group into the commercial system with your record? In a way you've made a big penetration there by having your own record in the American Top Ten.

CN: Yeah, I haven't really come to grips with it yet. We've been in Europe ever since everything's happened.

DG: We haven't been back to America since this whole thing's blown up, so we really don't know how insane it is over there yet.

CN: The tour was booked months ago, so we're playing small halls where we would have played before any of this would have happened. So we can't really tell what's changed, but—

DG: If anything, it sort of gives me a little faith in the, y'know, the [*makes quote marks in air and puts on sarcastic voice —Ed.*] "CONSUMER." (CN: Yeah, that's right.) Y'know, it's just like, hopefully, so many more people are receiving our record, maybe they'll get something out of it, and this'll be the first time they've been exposed to anything different.

CN: They'll hear our band and then they'll say, "Oh wow, I really like where these guys are coming from," and we'll say, "We like bands like Sonic Youth or Dinosaur Jr. or L7 or Hole or . . ." The whole underground scene where we come from is just so right on and maybe that's the way we justify why we've pursued this so far on this level is to maybe open doors, some doors that have been opened for us, by bands who've made dents, who've preceded us.

[*Cuts to "Polly," then to clips from commentators and further live footage —Ed.*]

DG: And it's the kind of stuff that sticks in your head because the songs are so simple, basic, sort of "stark" and, y'know.

CN: Yeah, they're really basic songs, pop.

DG: Just like the children's songs you learn when you're a kid; you remember those all your life. Just because they're so simple.

"THEY SCREAMED 'SELLOUT' AND SPAT ON US"

Robyn Doreian | December 7, 1991 | *Hot Metal* (Australia)

This was the second phone interview I did for the Australian monthly *Hot Metal*. The first had been in September 1991, to promote *Nevermind*. Fatigued by the mushrooming press obsession and unknowingly on the brink of unimaginable stardom, Kurt was only doing interviews for magazine covers. Hence, our twenty-five-minute chat was the cover story for *Hot Metal* issue 35, January 1992, promoting Nirvana's headline slot on Australia's first Big Day Out music festival. The following piece is not the article that appeared in *Hot Metal* but a transcript of the tape.

I stayed at the *Hot Metal* office until 7 PM, as I needed to record from its speakerphone. Nirvana was touring the United Kingdom, so it was morning for Kurt when we spoke. The previous night the trio had performed "Territorial Pissings" on *The Jonathan Ross Show*, which Kurt coined "a half-assed David Letterman rip-off."

When Kurt answered the connect call, he sounded tired. But as in our previous interview, I was struck by how polite he was. He didn't swear, and despite my (then) inept interviewing skills, he regarded me with respect. In retrospect, my lack of skills led to lateral topics, such as ant farms and his reverence for Mel Gibson, a.k.a. the Road Warrior, whom he termed "a hunk." During my previous interview, I had failed to comprehend Kurt's humor. His deadpan delivery of jokes made me conclude he was possibly pretentious and on the wrong side of weird. But I soon realized it was linked to intelligence coupled with a knowledge of art, and an appreciation of kitsch and popular culture. Fortunately for me, he didn't back away from any inquiry (even the most cretinous) and answered every question with honesty. Not long after we began our chat, he paused to answer a knock at his hotel room door. —Robyn Doreian

Kurt Cobain: Can you hold on a second, there's someone at the door? [*Walks to the door.*] That was my high-powered manager, Ruben Kincaid (manager of 1970s TV show *The Partridge Family*) about the next interview.

Robyn Doreian: Has he got Danny with him?

KC: Yeah, we keep Danny in a box. A shoebox.

RD: The photo on *Nevermind.* Is that you, when you were younger?

KC: No, it's not. [*Minor laugh at the idiocy of my question.*]

RD: Have you had any trouble from the PMRC [*Parents Music Resource Center —Ed.*] for having a willy on the cover?

KC: [*Energized tone*] No, surprisingly not. There has been no problem at all with it. We were prepared to alleviate that problem, if anyone were to freak out about it, by putting a sticker that said, "If you are offended by this, you must be a closet pedophile."

RD: What does a typical gig involve for you these days?

KC: Well, we just played a show at the Kilburn National [*Ballroom —Ed.*], and we asked a couple of friends to dress up in custodial outfits. We armed them with feather dusters and had them to come out on to the stage in between songs and dust off our guitars and spray us down with cleaning solvents and sweep the debris off the stage.

RD: How did the audience react?

KC: They screamed "Sellout," and spat on us. They didn't get the joke. I'll never understand English humor. I don't think I want to.

RD: I don't think many people understand your sense of humor.

KC: [*Sounds excited*] Why is that?

RD: People don't understand what it means to glue macaroni on a board with glitter. [*Alluding to the press biography for* Nevermind, *which wrote about Chris Novoselic and Kurt Cobain bonding over a love of crafts, specifically when Novoselic asked Cobain's advice about a macaroni mobile he was working on, to which Cobain said to "glue glitter on it." —Ed.*] That is great art.

KC: [*Laughs under his breath.*] Well, I can only feel sorry for them.

RD: What don't you like about TV shows like *Benny Hill*?

KC: [*Laughs.*] Oh god, give me a break. There are only so many times when you can see the scenario of two balding fat men looking at a pair of boobs, holding ice cream cones in their hands, and then thinking they are binoculars and then sticking them in their eyes. Have you ever seen that?

RD: Oh, yeah.

KC: I've seen them do that in so many episodes.

RD: Are you feeling physically wrecked from nonstop touring?

KC: Oh, absolutely. At this show in Edinburgh, my throat was so swollen and sore that while I was singing I was vomiting.

RD: Was that from screaming?

KC: Yeah. It's from screaming for three months straight. We only have another week, and I managed to get some good cough medicine today, so hopefully that will put a Band-Aid over it for a while until I can go home and start going to herbal stores and can buy the wing of a bat and put it in water and drink it. [*Laughs.*]

RD: What else have you found that's been really taxing?

KC: That's about it, except for autographs. I don't mind compliments from people, but autographs are becoming really obnoxious for me. I'm planning on having an official Kurt Cobain autograph stamp made up.

RD: I believe you are tired of doing interviews.

KC: [*In louder voice*] YES, I AM! We've been blowing off a lot of interviews lately, which has been pissing off our record company, but that is the only thing we can do to keep ourselves sane. I've decided that I'm only going to do interviews for when we are guaranteed [*laughs*] to be on the cover of a magazine, or for a fanzine, an authentic fanzine, the kind that are Xeroxed and stapled together by students and fans.

RD: Why did you decide that?

KC: Well, because it's just a waste of time to elaborate on my personal life and our music to the majority of the magazines that we are having interviews with. Most of the magazines are glossy, bullshit magazines that I would never be interested in reading myself, so it seems like a big waste of time. I don't want any more promotion. We have gone so much further than we ever expected that there is no reason to make our lives miserable.

RD: Don't you think people want to read about you?

KC: Well, I guess they just have to buy the issues that we are on the cover. [*Laughs.*] Or they will have to buy fanzines. It's just a waste of time to me, as I can't talk about myself twenty-four hours a day.

RD: Even though maybe you'd like to?

KC: [*Serious tone*] Of course not!

RD: How do you feel about selling 600,000 copies of *Nevermind* in the United States alone?

KC: Um, we've sold 1.4 million in America.

RD: Are you planning to build a replica of Graceland to live in?

KC: No, I'd rather have a Dolly Parton Land. Or a Boxcar Willie Land. He's a country-and-western hobo.

RD: To what can you attribute the success of *Nevermind*?

KC: A lot of payola. No, I have no idea. When we signed to DGC, we thought a realistic amount of records to be sold by the end of the year would be about 200,000. We would have been very happy with that. To sell almost 1.5 million is beyond anything we ever imagined. I can't say it's a thrill because we never wanted it in the first place. Whether you believe that or not, it's true. At least the good side of it is there are a lot of kids who have gotten to hear our music and who have bought a record and liked it. Hopefully they will look into other kinds of underground music. Hopefully they will buy the Black Flag back catalog.

"RACISM, SEXISM, AND NATIONALISM ARE DRIVING US TOWARD IGNORANCE"

Aline Giordano | December 7, 1991 | *Uzine* (France)

Of all the photographs taken during this interview, I like the ones by Richard Bellia the best, and one in particular. For me, this photo shows that we were taking part in a theatrical spectacle. All of us, amateur and professional journalists, swarm around Novoselic and Grohl—thrusting our microphones toward them but not necessarily looking at them, intently checking our sound levels. Bellia shows this. I was there as a fan: a fan privileged with a press pass. I did not ask questions. I was so humbly delighted, so overawed to be allowed to be part of this gathering that seemed to me so intimate and so meaningful. I tried to take my photographs of Novoselic and Grohl, and I failed to get even one decent image—any image worth preserving. But Bellia, he did it; he captured what was really happening: he shot the historic moment when grunge became a commodity. His picture also shows our complicity, our abdication—we fans, who revere or even worship others for their capacity (as we see it) to say what we feel and think and cannot articulate for ourselves. Bellia sealed in time the voracious passivity and emotional avidity that presaged the successful mass-marketing of Nirvana.

The press conference was translated from English into French for the fourth issue of the fanzine *Uzine*. Recently it was translated back again to feature in this collection of interviews. Things are gained and lost. So these are not the words of Grohl or Novoselic, but rather what I faithfully believe to be the truth of it all. —Aline Giordano

Translated from English to French by Sandrine Maugy.
Translated from French to English by Estelle Raso and Aline Giordano.

Transmusicales 91: The press conference was planned for 4 PM, but these "rock stars" of Nirvana had asked to postpone it so that they could get some rest! Well, that's fine, OK guys . . . we'll wait for you! The tension rises, the journalists start stamping their feet, and then we're told that Kurt Cobain (guitarist and singer) won't come—too bad. Around 5:30 PM, people whisper, "Here they are," and indeed the interview can start with almost all journalists still here to listen to these "new heroes" of the Seattle scene.

Question: Do you represent a threat to the system?

Dave Grohl/Chris Novoselic [*No record exists of which individual replied —Ed.*]: Threat . . . To a certain extent, yes, because what we want is to try to develop people's awareness. The largest weapon the government has is ignorance, and if through our songs people start realizing what's happening, maybe they'll react. You have to realize that in the United States, there's a lot of apathy, ignorance, so instead of jumping on any specific political bandwagon, what we want to do is just tell them: be aware of what's happening.

Q: What do you think of the parties involved in politics?

DG/CN: Since we're dealing with a year of elections in the United States, there's no way to avoid politics. It's obviously everywhere, especially since we've been living under the same political regime for quite a few years already! So, people listen to bands to know what they actually have to say; the current generation, sadly, has no spokesperson. When we think of the 1960s, there were a few, and music was just a backdrop for political discussion. Today, we haven't got that, but maybe if we help people to open their eyes, someone highly qualified and intelligent will stand up and propose an alternative.

Q: Nirvana has no political allegiance; however, you're anti-macho in contrast to some other groups . . .

DG/CN: Yeah, that's true that it's a man's world, but sexism, to me, seems as bad as racism. We must accept each other, and that's not easy. This press conference is taking a bit of a political turn. To be very clear, it seems obvious to me that racism, sexism, and nationalism are driving us toward ignorance.

Q: So, how do you like to chill out?

DG/CN: By just playing music, being with friends, partying, going to the beach when the weather is nice, practicing relaxation . . . like everyone else, in fact.

Q: You come from Sub Pop; do you still have links with the other groups who stayed on there?

DG/CN: Of course, yeah; we still feel really close to the other bands. They're our friends more than anything. You've got to understand that Seattle is not such a huge music scene. We all know each other, more or less, and it's not because we're now on a major that we're going to disown everyone; that'd be completely appalling, pompous, and arrogant. We've just done a few dates in England, we talked to magazines like *NME*, and in the end, we got sick of interviews; that's why we only talk to fanzines and college newspapers. In 1989 they were the only ones to talk about us and support us; we would be total fools to forget that and turn our backs on the past. Now we're on Geffen, but we still like the bands from Seattle, and turning our back on them is out of question.

Q: People can't really position you as a band . . .

DG/CN: That's true, to the English we're a heavy metal band, but we've got absolutely nothing to do with that. As soon as they hear heavy guitars, it's immediately heavy metal! Anyway, the heavy metal, thrash, death metal, all of that, it's the same thing which ends up by biting its own tail to die eventually.

Q: What perception do you have of European bands like Ride or My Bloody Valentine . . . of noise pop?

DG/CN: We don't know them. We listen to American stuff mainly. It's maybe our fault, I don't know, we are sorry, but we don't live here, we're on the other side of the ocean . . . but it's true—we haven't tried to listen to those bands, sorry.

Q: You speak about ignorance, but the Americans, they are at home and never make the effort to see what is happening elsewhere . . .

DG/CN: In fact, we haven't had the opportunity to really discover European bands and, even less, French ones. If you go to a record shop, there won't be French music. In fact, it's really a matter of being able to access it in the first place . . . well, having said that, we listened to stuff from Manchester. In the end that's music—full stop.

Q: What do you think of Straight Edge? [*There are some questions that it's probably best not to ask Nirvana, because they almost got upset.*]

DG/CN: Well, listen, if you're happy to not smoke, not drink, that's your problem, your body. Sometimes it happens that there is a person who gets up on a pedestal and who would like to show everyone how to change the world. He regards himself as the new messiah, he believes he holds the sacred wisdom. OK, I heard what he had to say, now as far as I am concerned, I smoke, I drink. Everyone does their own thing.

Q: What do you think of stage diving?

DG/CN: Yeah, it's cool, but the guys, they mainly do that to impress their friends, it's just more to get on stage and then say: "Look at me! I'm on stage." He's going to get on stage several times and maybe screw up a few guitar pedals, and in the end it gets annoying, especially when we can't control him. We kinda get the impression that he'd rather blow off some steam than listening to music. Personally I'd advise him to find himself a good hobby like climbing.

Q: What was Nirvana's evolution? Has this sudden celebrity arisen gradually or was it a surprise?

DG/CN: A song like "Polly" was written before *Bleach* came out; lots of songs from *Nevermind* were written in the spring of 1990, like "In Bloom" and "Lithium," whereas "Smells Like Teen Spirit" was written one month before the recording session. In reality, that's the problem with labels; they take forever to put records out. Besides, we had a few issues with our previous drummer. The band is changing, and if you listen to the demo tape that we made in the beginning—please don't buy it, the sound is really bad—you can really tell that there were already all these elements there from the start. With regard to the next album, it'll certainly be more experimental. As for the difference between *Bleach* and *Nevermind,* it's that the first cost six hundred dollars and the other one a hundred thousand dollars!

Q: In your biography, it's written that you come from different fine arts schools.

DG/CN: Not at all! That's totally wrong. People shouldn't always believe the bios. That story about fine arts schools, it's just a silly cliché. Hey, do we really look like we'd be painting in fine arts schools? Yeah, what's the biggest rock 'n' roll cliché? The musician who gave up fine arts! Anyway, that's all bullshit—paintings of blue seashells and soft toffee, it doesn't mean anything!

Q: There is a newspaper which said that Nirvana as a band are as dumb as Mudhoney; is that an insult or a compliment to you?

DG/CN: It's a compliment, of course, because they're not stupid at all. Rock 'n' roll isn't meant to be intellectual at all. But with bands like Yes—the arrogant type—people tend to think that rock 'n' roll has to be intellectual. We certainly come back to this cliché with people who gave up fine arts! Hell no, we've got to be more down-to-earth than this!

Q: Does the sleeve of *Nevermind* offer a fair vision of the United States?

DG/CN: It is obvious that there's something about this sleeve which is clearly antimaterialist; it's the one-dollar bill. The rest remains open to interpretation. There's a fishhook, a baby, so some people come and ask us what the meaning is. Or they explain to us what they see; my favorite one comes from a guy who asked us if the baby represented the group signing to a major label—and for one dollar—forget about it! There's also that version of a circumcised baby, so we were asked if that had something to do with the Jews! I was even asked if I was circumcised.

Q: And are you?

DG/CN: Yeah, everyone is in the United States.

Q: Don't you risk, because of your success, becoming one of the spokesmen to whom you were referring earlier on?

DG/CN: I don't have the mental capability to be the spokesman of my generation, and besides, there are people like Jello Biafra who are doing a pretty good job already. Jello is an interesting guy, but we, we're just a rock band, and also, well, some bands are already doing it, like the Dead Kennedys. But it's true that with success you can become a vehicle to express something, and that scares me a little, because the risk is that you start preaching. Well, I respect these bands who stand up and take the floor, but me, I don't fancy doing that. There are bands who tell the public, "Forget about all your problems." Us, we absolutely do not! It's as if I was arriving at a press conference and was saying, "Go on, ask me questions on a problem, and I am going to tell you what to think about it." On the other hand, there's so much apathy in the United States, people are so addicted to materialism, they enjoy a nice life, a big car, affordable gasoline, but they don't even know where Africa is on a map, or how many continents there are in the world. In the United States, 15 percent of people aged seventeen are illiterate. With the Gulf War, people were over the moon because the United States was number one in the world, but from an educational standpoint it's a catastrophe. In reality, we nearly have the status of a third-world country.

Q: Last question: what do you think of the United States?

DG/CN: You've really got to understand this; you consider the Americans to be ignorant people, well . . . ME TOO.

COBAIN CLIP

On Past Employment

"I do love kids, I know that sounds weird, but I do. I have a little sister who's four years old. And I was a lifeguard, and I taught preschool kids how to swim; and I worked at the YMCA and did daycare; and I babysat during my teenager years. Which was all kind of a strange thing in Aberdeen, because mostly males don't babysit that much."

—from "Better Dead Than Cool" by Gina Arnold, *Option*, January 1992

COBAIN CLIP

"My favorite guitar in the world is the Fender Mustang. They're really small and almost impossible to keep in tune. They're designed terribly. If you want to raise the action you have to detune all the strings, pull the bridge out, turn these little screws under the bridge, and hope you've raised them the right amount . . . But I like it. That way things sound fucked-up, and I stumble onto stuff accidentally. I guess I don't like to be that familiar with my guitar."

—from "Kurt Cobain's Well-Tempered Tantrums" by L. A. Kanter,

Guitar Player, February 1992

PART VII

January to February 1992—Sullenness

PEOPLE ARE NOW CALLING ACROSS THE WORLD TO INTERVIEW Kurt Cobain; it is not even six months since the release of *Nevermind*, and suddenly people are willing to pay the charges to do a phone interview—this in the days when international rates were steep. Note in these interviews that Nirvana's manager, the tour promoter, and company PR representatives are suddenly a presence—there's a wall going up that hadn't previously existed.

This section contains all but three of the interviews Nirvana are known to have given during their tour of Australasia and Asia. They capture how fast times are moving; on January 23 the idea of having a new album out in the fall, something the band had spoken of eight weeks earlier, is suddenly looking difficult, and by February 13, in a conversation with Sujesh Pavithran, Kurt Cobain declares, "We're going to take our time, there's no date set." The band's cheery message of "once a week, write a song" from October 1990 has turned into Cobain's mention of how impossible it is to write on the road. They've been touring with only a few weeks off since mid-August, and they can no longer juggle it all. That still doesn't excuse the total noncooperation displayed in their interview with Jen Oldershaw, which probably best represents how Nirvana earned a reputation for cantankerousness. But it seems to be a feature primarily when they're together as a group—as individuals, they're courteous.

Note that it's still mainly music journalists asking the questions; therefore, there's none of the burrowing into biography that happens later when Nirvana are bona fide celebrities; the biographical details slip out, but the guys are not yet being pumped for the stories of their lives.

Cobain is now a functioning addict, but he's no zombie. Despite falling asleep mid-interview in November and being asked his thoughts on drugs, even in late January the furthest a reporter goes in print is Youri Lenquette's speculation that "substances" might be a factor in Cobain's pallor. But still, the interview load has fallen. Instead of the long runs of interviews during the European tour, all are concluded in the first few days in Australia, a couple of days in Singapore, and just one day in Hawaii. Cobain is absent from about half the interviews, but when he's willing he leaves a warm impression on all who meet him: humble, welcoming, coming to terms with being something he hadn't imagined a year before.

"IT'S SORT OF SAD WHEN THERE'S YUPPIES DANCING TO OUR SONG"

James Sherry | January 1992 | *Metal Hammer* (UK)

I never met Nirvana again after August 1991; my final interview took place on a phone line from London to Chris at home in Seattle. He was certainly amused to hear that Nirvana, having been around some five years, had just won *Metal Hammer*'s "Best New Band" award. It was Chris, though, a guy who always found the silver lining, who could tell that something had changed in the music scene and that the divisions between hard rock, punk, and metal had all given way in the face of what Nirvana had unleashed the previous year. His responses perhaps showed how confusing things were for the band at that moment in time; his thoughts on the future were sometimes tentative, he sometimes seemed to protest too much how happy the band members were with their choices, and he was very openly fed up with tabloid journalism and the gutter press. Just over two years later I was in the studio drumming with a band when the news came through that the whole thing had come crashing down—that Kurt was gone. That first encounter with *Bleach* had helped steer my whole future path in music; then I'd been so delighted for them when *Nevermind* did so well, and it felt like such a victory when *In Utero* emerged and proved such an awe-inspiring achievement. But I'd felt trepidation and a solemn hope that these sweet blokes were doing all right as the less palatable tales racked up. In the end it just wasn't all right. But what was left was awesome, and I've never lost my respect for them or my love of that music. —James Sherry

Chris Novoselic: Hello!

James Sherry: Hi, Chris?

CN: Yeah!

JS: Hi, it's James from *Metal Hammer.*

CN: Hey, how you doing?

JS: Hi, how's it going? You've won *Metal Hammer's* Best New Band poll.

CN: We're the best new band?

JS: Yeah.

CN: Well, that's cool. We're flattered. Hopefully a lot of these heavy metallers'll find out where we're coming from, y'know? And they'll see, like, a Sub Pop label on our record and, y'know, check out Sub Pop bands. I know you're responsible for turning on a lot of those people!

JS: Yeah . . . Yeah, hope so.

CN: Onto Sub Pop and kinda stuff . . . More offbeat stuff, y'know?

JS: Yeah.

CN: So, hmm . . . We just hope we can turn on people to that.

JS: Is that one of the main reasons that's, like, keeping you going at the moment through all the hassles at the moment?

CN: Yeah. Yeah, kinda for us person . . . for me personally it justifies what we're doing. Well, maybe we can kinda help expose a lot of bands now that we have all this exposure, y'know? Spread the wealth a little bit.

JS: Have you noticed any of the effects yet?

CN: Not yet.

JS: No?

CN: No. Well, I haven't really been watching, so I don't know . . .

JS: I've noticed it a bit in England definitely.

CN: Oh, right?

JS: There's a few bands that have definitely been helped by you, like the Senseless Things have just got a Top Twenty single and all this kind of stuff.

CN: Right! You know it's not just us; things were going to change sooner or later, man, and we were just in the right place at the right time. We were just successful enough for the mainstream to grasp.

JS: Definitely. Are you enjoying the success in any way?

CN: Sure! It's really interesting to see what the heck's going on . . . something different.

JS: Is it different to what you expected in the way you're treated by people and stuff like that?

CN: Mmmm . . . lot of people walking up, "Hey, you're the bass player from Nirvana, aren't you? Whoa, can you sign my shirt?" "Well . . . I don't really want to ruin your clothes . . ."

JS: Do you get a lot of that, then? A lot of people coming up to you all the time? You must do really . . .

CN: Yeah, it's getting me more and more. Especially after doing TV shows and stuff.

JS: Are you doing many TV shows in the States? You did quite a few when you were over here.

CN: Yeah, we just did a *Saturday Night Live.*

JS: Was that good fun?

CN: Pardon me? [*James repeats.*] It went over great. It was a lot of fun.

JS: Excellent. So, do you ever have any regrets signing to Geffen and all that kind of stuff? Any regrets at the things you've done so far—

CN: [*Starts answering before James can finish*] No, no. No, I don't have any regrets yet. We're really happy.

JS: That's really cool. When can we expect the follow-up to *Nevermind*, then?

CN: Probably late winter.

JS: Yeah? Any plans for it yet?

CN: Yeah, we've been kicking things around. We'll see. We're going to do this Australia/Japanese tour, then we're going to take a couple months off, kind of get together, start jamming, making a buncha noise.

JS: So have you got any plans for it yet? Do you know what kind of stuff it's going to sound like, how it's going to sound, or anything like that?

CN: We've got a rough idea; we've been kicking some thoughts around.

JS: So, I mean, it's going to be weird. What I mean is one problem might be, with *Nevermind* being such a huge album, is people might always see it as, whatever you do next it's going to be such a hard album to follow. Are you worried about that at all?

CN: No, we're just worried about putting out a record that'll satisfy us—if we think it's great. I mean, if we start catering to the public you're just a total sellout. If you start compromising just because of record sales, I mean, you're just fucking a dog.

JS: How do you feel about the way the band's being portrayed by the press and everything like that? The way people think of you.

CN: Well, first off, we were portrayed as a bunch of drunks and just nihilistic troublemakers, y'know? And we got some thoughts and ideas we couldn't express. Just to take advantage and to exploit the media—OW! [*Cat wails, Chris yelps.*] Stepped on my cat's foot.

JS: Is it alright?

CN: [*Fussing over cat*] Yeah. He's a little shaken, but he's OK! [*Humorous tone.*] Y'know, might as well throw my two cents into the ring, you know what I mean? Take it for however you want. So now we go as far as stuff that I could handle intellectually. I try to be aware of what I'm saying, so I don't off a bunch of crap, at least hopefully not. I probably do!

JS: You must get quite a chance now to express yourself on TV and stuff like that—especially the TV stuff you did over here, playing a different song on one of them, smashing up gear . . .

CN: Nahhh, that's just fun! If I was in charge of that TV show I'd think that was great. That's good TV, y'know? Exciting!

JS: I would have thought it's brilliant, especially when you came and did *Top of the Pops* as well, and Kurt sung in that voice. That was just hysterical.

CN: That was fun! You've got to do something different, shake it up a little bit, see what happens.

JS: Just to get different reactions and stuff like that. You don't ever plan to do stuff like that? Are they all just things that happen at the time?

CN: Just last second, "Hey, man, what if we did . . . ?" "Yeah-yeah-yeah, yeah, yeah!"

JS: People seem to be making quite a big deal about the gear smashing and stuff like that.

CN: Well, that's media for ya! It's not what the band's about.

JS: It's just because they've not seen anything like it for a while.

CN: It's a lot of fun.

JS: A lot of people are also saying you're not particularly enjoying the success, and you're pretty pissed off at the way things have gone, and stuff like that.

CN: We can get fried.

JS: The pressure must be huge.

CN: Yeah, I mean, it's got its good and bad points. But it's only going to be here for a few more years and then that's it.

JS: Do you think this is just a fad or do you think it's more than a fad?

CN: I think it can be a fad, to an extent—I've thought about that. We're just the new popular group and people'll get sick of us. [*Mutters "Goddamn cat . . . "*] It's sort of sad when there's yuppies dancing to our song, it's like, gee, they're still yuppies. "Well, here's that new band with that new song, hey, that's it!" But I think there's a lot of people who really enjoy the music, judging by the letters we get from people. They've taken enough time to write and just express how they feel about us.

JS: I think whatever happens in the next couple years you're always going to have a following anyway. Just maybe not the same media attention. Because a lot of people—

CN: That's alright by us. Whatever happens is gonna happen; we're not out there fishing for record sales.

JS: A lot of people are comparing your last tour to, like, the Sex Pistols over here and stuff like that.

CN: Ya think so? It's probably been blown out of proportion though, exaggerated. A lot of that Sex Pistols stuff was just an exaggeration. But they did come out of nowhere and made a big splash—and I think we did to a point, but not as . . . as . . . I don't know. I just have too much humility in my thoughts to go boasting and comparing ourselves to the Sex Pistols—I can't do that.

JS: What happens if you start ending up in tabloids and gossip columns and things like this? Celebrity! It's bound to start happening.

CN: That's just crazy! It's garbage! Yeah, I guess it's going to start happening, but . . . when I hear about other people I don't pay attention. I've never paid attention to that stuff, so . . .

JS: What's the stupidest thing you've ever read about the band in a newspaper? Can you think of any good examples?

CN: Oh, God . . . the stupidest thing . . . we were "a cross between Roxette and Slayer," yeah . . .

JS: [*Laughs.*] That's an interesting one . . .

CN: And uhhh, our antics—oh yeah, that we burned down our tour bus. That's it.

JS: Excellent. So when are you expected to tour here again? Do you know?

CN: We'll probably come over and do Reading . . . do some shows . . .

JS: Yeah, I've heard a rumor that you're going to headline the Saturday night—is that sort of confirmed or—

CN: Not really, I haven't heard it. We'll probably be a lot higher on the bill this year.

JS: Yeah, 'cause I've heard you're going to be headlining on the Saturday night—you'll be the top band.

CN: Won't that be great?

JS: Yeah, it'll be excellent. Do you enjoy the Reading Festival?

CN: Oh yeah, we had so much fun last year! I like playing early just so you can get it over with and hang out with all my friends and meet people and just have a good time. Like the rest of the bands—we're done!

JS: Are you just going to come over for the one Reading gig or do a few more, do you know?

CN: I have no idea. I know that Reading's a big possibility.

JS: Alright, well, that'll do for me. I'll just see you when you come over! Thanks a lot!

CN: Well, thanks a lot, dude.

"WELL THIS IS
AS PUNK ROCK AS ELVIS"

Jessica Adams | January 23, 1992 | *Select* **(UK)**

Talking to Kurt Cobain on the phone was a complete fluke. I was supposed to be interviewing Dave Grohl, but at the last minute I heard Kurt's rather croaky voice in my ear. It is a total joy to be able to share the transcript after all these years. I always wanted to give the cassette tape to his daughter, Frances, to prove to her that he had a dry sense of humor and a good heart and that he wasn't a tormented creature as shown in the media. Kurt was very kind to me in the interview, and I feel bad about the photograph they used on the front cover of *Select* and the way the piece was written up. Writers can't control editors or art directors. The piece sensationalized his illness, and to this day I feel guilty about the fact that he trusted me enough to share his memories of recording *Nevermind*, only to have those memories misrepresented in the published piece, which bore my name in the byline. Just another small letdown in what must have been a sea of letdowns for him, at a time when he was so vulnerable. I was very lucky to see Nirvana in Sydney, and the band was so powerful and so affecting, I have to admit I have not been able to listen to *Nevermind* since. I literally have not heard it since that year. Wherever you are now, Kurt, know how loved you are and how important you are—especially to women, for whom you always took a stand. —Jessica Adams

At the first stroke it will be 11:03 precisely [*Pips of the speaking clock.*]
At the first stroke it will be 11:03 and ten seconds . . .
Operator: Go ahead, please; you're connected—go ahead . . .

Jessica Adams: Thanks—bye! Kurt?

Kurt Cobain: Yes.

JA: Yeah, how are you? Good morning.

KC: Good morning to you.

JA: I wanted to ask you first, I've just been reading a story on *Spinal Tap*—are you a *Spinal Tap* fan at all?

KC: At all? Yeah, sure, it's a great movie.

JA: They're claiming to have driven through Seattle about five years ago on a tour and, er, [*chuckles*] heavily influenced most of the Sub Pop bands. I don't know if you'd go along with that?

KC: Well, that's a pretty egotistical thing to say [*sounding similarly amused*] . . .

JA: Yeah, it is, isn't it? I guess they're a pretty egotistical band. They're re-forming, did you know that?

KC: Yeah, I did.

JA: It should be good.

KC: I'm pretty excited about that. They played their last performance in Seattle a few years ago; some friends of mine found the skull that they had as a prop in an old warehouse, and now they have it in their room.

JA: That's great [*laughing*]—it would have been great to get that little Stonehenge there as well.

KC: Yeah, very nice!

JA: Do Nirvana use stage props?

KC: No, we don't, but we intend to. On the next American tour we're going to have a twenty-foot movie doll, hypnotic wheel, you know what kind I'm talking about? Psychiatrists would use them.

JA: Fantastic.

KC: And we're also going to have a projection, a very large projection behind the drums of a *Pong* game playing—you know what that is?

JA: A what game . . . ?

KC: *Pong*, it was the first home video game, which was kinda just a little dot going back and forth on a screen, and you had two paddles opposite each other that would bat the ball back and forth.

JA: Was that a big game in Aberdeen?

KC: Well, it was a big game everywhere in America; you might have it here too 'cause it was the first home version of a video game, before Atari—I mean, it was an Atari actually, a sort of Atari, yeah, that's what it was. The first game that came out on Atari was *Pong*.

JA: It sounds so primitive!

KC: Yeah, it's very primitive.

JA: We had another one here that was about a frog that lasted for about three years; I can't remember. They probably had it in America also. Just a very basic frog game.

KC: Yeah, where you tried to go across the street, cars would hit him, that was called *Frogger*—that was on Atari also.

JA: What else are we going to get when we see Nirvana? Everybody here is incredibly excited about it but a little bit unsure as well.

KC: Why is that?

JA: I think because we've heard so many different things—"Well, they're not into too much hype," and "They're not going to put on a big performance," "It's not very theatrical . . . "

KC: Well, ummm . . . There's really nothing theatrical that we could do, that we could think of. I mean, I don't understand what you mean besides using props and dancers or something like that. We could throw in a brass section to liven things up, but, no, we basically just come out on stage, wave to everyone, and start playing.

JA: It should be good, actually, but I can understand from your angle there would be a lot of pressure on you at the moment, a lot of expectation right 'round the world. Is that the case?

KC: I suppose there is, but I'm so far beyond worrying about those things because we've been on tour for, like, seven months that I can only just try to get by, day by day. We're all pretty fatigued. So I think that probably the most exciting thing that someone might see at a live performance is watching us collapse in front of their eyes.

JA: Go cross-eyed and fall over . . .

KC: Yeah . . .

JA: Somebody said once, and I thought it was a good quote: "The proportion of bullshit increases in proportion to the success rate of a band. Bullshit, coming from the outside world." Is that something you would agree with having lived through the last few months?

KC: Well, that's a pretty broad term . . .

JA: Maybe it should be confined a bit. Have you—

KC: Bullshit. What IS "bullshit"?

JA: OK, Australian, so let's translate . . . Hype, kind of, people who . . . maybe fake people, I don't know—hype basically.

KC: I don't really understand hype at this point. There really is no, there's never any . . . collective conspiracy involved with us, or between us and our label. We didn't pay off MTV to promote the hell out of us—it just happened. It's been very organic even though it happened really fast. It's really not our fault, we can't end it—I'm sorry! But . . .

JA: It's OK, we don't blame you.

KC: We really didn't try very hard.

JA: I heard that you were actually signed to Geffen for two hundred and fifty thousand dollars, is that correct?

KC: Yeah, something around that amount. Maybe two hundred.

JA: It's interesting also that they seem not to have realized, early on, what they actually had—is that something that struck you? Were you confident in the album and were surprised at Geffen underplaying it like that?

KC: Well, that was our intention to underplay it; we just wanted to put out a record and please the people who had heard it already. Geffen was always aware of how . . . at least of our potential, and I'm sure that there's always been a lot of excitement among the people who work there. They just felt there was really no need to really put a lot of hype behind it—just let it go by itself.

JA: It's an incredibly special record to listen to, and I wondered if you also had a special feeling when you were in the studio—did you have a buzz? Did you think this was going to be something really great? Did it occur to you when you were doing it?

KC: Ummm . . . No? [*Jessica laughs.*]

JA: You sorta . . . you had no idea that this was going to be something different?

KC: Well, no, not really. I mean, it didn't seem that much different than the *Bleach* album other than that we were recording every day. We went into the studio every day and tried our best.

JA: Some of the vocal performances on that record are incredible. How do you get that in the studio? Did they leave you to go off to your own devices and go crazy or . . . how do you get that performance?

KC: I usually did them in the vocal room by myself with the lights out and close my eyes and scream.

JA: I love it, it's incredible. It reminds me a lot of . . . that are just like some British punk from about ten years ago—I was wondering if English punk music was something that the band listened to or that you listened to?

KC: Oh, definitely.

JA: What kind of bands were the most important?

KC: Oh, Sex Pistols, the Buzzcocks—any '77 punk rock band . . . from mid- to late 1970s . . . was totally influential on my music—it's still our favorite form of music. Punk. Even though we grew up in the hardcore generation of the early 1980s and were subjected to a lot of—I guess I should say "bullshit" underground music like hardcore, something I've never really liked, the Straight Edge/hardcore scene. So we, at the time, while pretending to be punk rockers at our youthful age, we were listening to anti-hardcore bands like Flipper and the Butthole Surfers and Scratch Acid. We weren't necessarily into all these real heavy political ideals.

JA: It would have been funny, I think; from what I can gather Aberdeen is quite a small town, kind of a small country-type town? (KC: Yeah.) That's right. How do you get exposed to English punk in a town like that?

KC: It's almost impossible.

JA: Did your local radio station play it at all?

KC: Oh boy, absolutely not! I remember, well, there's only one radio station, and it's AM, it's a soft rock station, and they play Tony Orlando and stuff like that. I remember being about fourteen and wanting to hear some punk rock music because I had a subscription to *Creem* magazine and I would read about the Sex Pistols, and I finally got a hold of *Sandinista* at the library—but *Sandinista* isn't a good introduction to punk rock!

JA: No, you should have had *Give 'Em Enough Rope*—that would have been better.

KC: Anything besides *Sandinista*! I thought, "Well this is as punk rock as Elvis . . ."

JA: And you got it from the library, that's great!

KC: And so for the next year or so I decided to try to create my own punk rock just at home on my electric guitar. And then finally I met this guy named Buzz Osborne, who's in the Melvins, and he's been going back and forth from Aberdeen to Seattle buying punk rock records, so he made a compilation tape for me. I was instantly converted—within a day I shaved my head, got some combat boots . . .

JA: That's great! It's amazing that it's stayed with you—that you haven't tired of it, 'cause it's fifteen years since '77.

KC: Yeah, well, there's still people who like Jimi Hendrix, too.

JA: Tell me about the American reaction. I've never been to America—I have no idea what the music industry there is like. But do they tend to catch on to things very, very quickly right around the country, or has it taken you a very long time to break over there?

KC: On an independent level it takes a long time because it's such a big country that communications are real trouble. But major labels have the power to get your record in any store, so it's a lot easier once you're on a major label, to expose yourself.

JA: Have Geffen been talking to you about the difficult second album yet?

KC: Have they been talking to us about it? No, I don't expect to ever have a conversation with them about it. We'll start recording when we feel like it, put it out whenever we want—I'd like to put it out by September . . .

JA: Really?

KC: But our touring schedule is still getting in the way of being able to finish the songs that we're writing right now. It'll be a very tight squeeze to get it in by September.

JA: Are we in for a lot of "on the road" songs?

KC: No, not at all. We've probably written about one, or two, songs on the road—it's almost impossible.

JA: Do you have a tour bus?

KC: I don't know what we're touring in . . .

JA: I was about to inquire about the comfort of bands because I feel sorry for them on the road. It must be a horrible business.

KC: Oh, it is, definitely. If you're driving, especially in the States. United States tours are the worst because they're, on the average of at least ten-hour drives a day to do each city, and we've always been in a very small, compact van, cramming like seven people into a van with your equipment. So it was pretty rough. On our last tour in Europe we had a bit larger van with a stereo so, you know, that was pretty luxury.

JA: Sounds like luxury. Tell us about the cover photograph that Kirk Weddle took for you. Was that the band's concept or was that Kirk's?

KC: No, that was my idea.

JA: That was your idea? It turned out really, really well.

KC: Yeah, it did; it turned out a lot better than I expected it to, more than I envisioned it would.

JA: Was the baby really underwater?

KC: Yeah, he was.

JA: That's incredible. He looks so happy. I love that shot. And I suppose it kind of sums up where the band is now because there's people waving money at you, I guess?

KC: Waving money at us?

JA: Well, maybe not dangling it on a hook, but . . . I guess a lot of money would be part of your world now where it wasn't two years ago?

KC: I suppose it is, but it takes a long time, it takes many months to recoup the amount of money that you put into the making of the album, so we really haven't seen very much money yet. We're expecting to within the next few months. But we basically just live off of credit.

JA: Way to go. Do you have any plans to do anything major with the money that's going to come, like do you have plans for your own studio and stuff?

KC: We'd like to . . . I think, we'd like to buy a house and live in a house, actually have a place to live—before we put money into a recording studio—but I'd like to invest my money into some bands that I like to help promote them whatever way I can. Might toss a few bills into labels to help them out so they don't go under.

JA: I guess it's important in America because you're really fighting against such a huge corporate—I hear it's amazing over there.

KC: They're buying anyone, they're stealing every independent band there is right now. They're signing the most abrasive, subversive bands you can think of.

JA: Great, I think all the abrasive Australian bands should get on a plane! [*Kurt chuckles and agrees.*] Now tell me how are we going for time? I'm not wearing a watch—are we running out of time?

KC: Yeah, actually we are; I'm meant to be doing another interview right now.

JA: Ah hell, I always do this—I'm sorry.

KC: That's no problem.

JA: Thanks for your time, and I look forward to the gig on Saturday. See ya!

KC: Alright, take care.

"ROCK STILL HAS GREAT STORIES TO TELL"

Youri Lenquette | January 23–25, 1992 | *Best* (France)

Joining Nirvana's Australian tour in 1992 was the start of friendships with the band I still cherish, and one with Kurt Cobain I think back on fondly but with obvious sadness. I'd met the band once before, but now they were reeling from the force they'd unleashed. While Dave tried to enjoy himself and Krist played tourist in a new land, Kurt spent the tour sheltering from the endless attention. We bonded after a night when he couldn't sleep and knocked on my door and asked if he might join me. We spent time listening to my cassettes of 1960s garage rock—I was a bit of a specialist, and people forgot what a deep interest in music Kurt possessed. —Youri Lenquette

Translated by Carly Lapotre.

Rock still has great stories to tell. Like the story of Nirvana, a pure underground band stealing the spotlight from Hollywood goliaths like Guns N' Roses, seizing No. 1 on the charts with an album recorded on a shoestring budget. Within a few months, the whole world was talking about Nirvana. Youri Lenquette went to the ends of the earth to track down Kurt Cobain and his band.

You could call it a small world, or a wake-up call. Nirvana is on the pages of magazines at Roissy airport and a little further at Heathrow; they're in Singapore and even on the cover of newspapers in Sydney where their first Australian tour was starting. The goal of this trip would have been difficult to forget, even intentionally. The promoter's smile is beaming. Steve [*Pavlovic* —*Ed.*], barely twenty years old and specializing in independent band tours, had booked Nirvana before the explosion of *Nevermind*. Despite more lucrative proposals in the States, the trio kept their engagement, agreeing to play in a venue that could never accommodate the kind of crowds that Nirvana attracts today. Regardless of their album sales (certainly one of the best of this past year) and the pleasure of seeing rock 'n' roll, mean, dirty, noisy, and iconoclast, push Michael Jackson and Guns N' Roses out of the No. 1 spot on the charts, there's a lot of excitement around the speed of Nirvana's rise. Things happen so quickly the ink doesn't have time to dry. Today the industry, the media, and other opinion leaders know all too well the unbelievable story of the ascent of a band that, six months ago, was in the realm of the hardcore underground.

Half businessman, half provocateur, John Silva looks like he's having fun. Managing Sonic Youth at the same time, he's not crazy about seeing what a small world it is for his protégés. On the contrary, he plays the system, happily telling the story of how he dissuaded Guns N' Roses from having Nirvana as the opening act on their tour, or his plans for an enormous concert in Washington to which other bands from the independent scene will be invited.

John Silva: We were offered the top spot on the bill for the next Lollapalooza. I preferred to decline. In the span of nine months, going from nothing at all to being the headliner for such a huge concert, what can you do after that? Nothing!

Dave Grohl: Hey, Kurt, look what they wrote about us in the gossip column. For once it's kinda funny.

His face hidden behind dark sunglasses and long strands of pink and blue dyed hair, Kurt Cobain doesn't even bother looking at the newspaper the drummer holds out to him.

Kurt Cobain: No, forget it, I don't want to read that shit. Yesterday I told the guy at the record company that from now on I only want to talk to fanzines. He asked me what a fanzine is. Can you believe that?

Covered in sunscreen, crushed by the heat and the time change, the band travels by yacht around Sydney's port and seems as at home as an ashtray full of cigarette butts on the table of a macrobiotic restaurant. Chris Novoselic, the unrelenting bassist of the group, is having fun with the camcorder he just bought, as if the electronic eye could help him understand how he could have got here.

His parents came to the United States from Yugoslavia not long after he was born. More precisely from Croatia, he insists, with the intensity of someone touched by the current conflict. It's a country in which he lived for a year as a teen after having grown up in Los Angeles and before having settled in the little northwestern city where he met Cobain and started Nirvana. At twenty-three, Dave Grohl is the youngest of the group, but he still has an impressive résumé. He's played professionally for five years, and before joining Nirvana he was the drummer of Scream, another band from the hardcore scene in Seattle.

DG: We weren't very well known, but we toured all over in the States and in Europe. I remember our French tour. It was in 1990. We shared the bill with some good French groups. I remember Treponem Pal, that's it, right? And also those crazy psychobillies, the . . . Wampas, yeah, that's it.

Turn It Up

Cobain, the only one who hasn't opened up, quietly shrinks back into the shadows, an extra more than a leading role in this maritime escapade.

KC: Could you turn it up a little?

The reasonable volume of the audio hits nearly unbearable levels. Some of their favorites are on Chris's compilation: Fugazi, Melvins, Pixies, Mudhoney, Hüsker Dü . . . When we ask whether or not success has changed them, the question falls flat. Maybe in three or four years. For the moment the three Nirvana members are still as they've always been: music fans. And not only of their own, as the EP released exclusively in Australia demonstrates, featuring two known titles ("Smells Like Teen

Spirit," "Aneurysm"), and also four never before heard tracks recorded for the Peel Sessions: a cover of a song by Devo; two covers of the Vaselines, a little Scottish group that Nirvana seems to particularly appreciate; and an homage to the Wipers, who ten years ago were playing the sound that has exploded onto the scene today as the sound of the northwest. Fifteen thousand copies of the EP were released and sold out in less than a day.

Settled in the middle of his messy hotel room, Kurt Cobain looks more alive. A few hours earlier he was on the verge of fainting after he left the stage of a particularly furious concert that ended with him kneeling among pieces of a destroyed drum set and mic feedback. Small and frail like many great rockers often are, Kurt Cobain emits something feminine and childlike. He needed to be around us for a few days before accepting the idea of being interviewed, but once we're one-on-one he's more adorable than he is in public. The pressure of these last few months has clearly taken its toll on him. Thin compared to the photos on the album, he has a paleness that can't be attributed to an excessive use of illicit substances. When he speaks, his voice is as stable as it can be, strained to the extreme on stage. Anyone would find it difficult to imagine him doing anything other than music.

KC: I knew I wanted to make music since I was five years old. It seems unbelievable, but it's the truth. My aunt who babysat me always listened to the Beatles. I grew up with it. For a long time I wanted to be a drummer. Until I was thirteen and I started to play in a band in middle school and was forced to admit that I wasn't made for the instrument. I didn't have that innate thing you need to have to be a good drummer. Take Dave, for example, no matter how much time he spends rehearsing, he was a drummer before he started to play. I know it contradicts my idea that being a musician doesn't really matter when making music, but the drums are like that: you either have it or you don't. My uncle gave me the choice between a guitar and a bike. I chose the guitar.

YL: Did you start writing songs right away?

KC: Yeah. The first song I learned to play was "My Best Friend's Girl" by the Cars. You know, with its three notes, like "Louie Louie." I took classes for a week. Once the instructor showed me the power and bar chords, I realized that it was possible to play any note by going down the neck, and I said to myself, "To hell with guitar lessons." I started to write songs. I had this intuition that it was better to try to find your own style than to learn technique. It's what I like best in punk: the theory that technique isn't important. What counts is that you have fun in the basement with your friends. Everything else—making an album, touring, doing your job—is secondary.

YL: I noticed that you often play on Japanese copies. Is there a reason?

KC: I like cheap guitars because they're light. Because they have a corrupt feel. They aren't perfect. I find it liberates you from the instrument. It leaves room for accidents, for surprises. There's more chance of stumbling upon an original sound with these guitars precisely because they don't sound like they should. The problem is that on stage it can get out of tune very easily. I'm happy with this Japanese Telecaster I'm using now. It has a little bit of a dirty sound, and it doesn't get out of tune.

YL: Until the day you destroy it.

KC: I'm going to try to keep this one, but it would be a lie to say that it won't ever be destroyed. I've already broke three guitars that I liked a lot, and I regretted it the minute I left the stage, but whatever, I can't do anything about it. It's out of my control.

YL: Where did you pick up this habit?

KC: I guess it's linked to a feeling of insecurity. In the beginning of Nirvana, we had a drummer that wasn't very good in my opinion. Out of rage and disgust, I sometimes left the stage throwing material. I realized that people liked it. And me, too, I loved doing it at the climax of the show. It compensated for not having a light show. I really don't know why I do that. I think it's the typical attitude of a frustrated little white guy. It also makes me feel alive. A couple times it put me in a bad situation. I wondered how I was going to play the next day. Since I'm a lefty and we were broke, you can imagine what a problem that could be in a little town in the middle of nowhere.

Drinkers

YL: You seem to listen to a lot of music.

KC: Yes, but I'm sure that there are hundreds of bands that I need to know that I haven't listened to yet. Actually, I don't have a choice. Since I don't like to watch TV and I only read a little, there isn't much left other than listen to and play music. I don't know the 1960s and the punk from that era. I'm a fan of the Sonics. These guys were incredibly violent. No one played as hard as they did in 1965. You had to do it at the time: write songs about taking strychnine.

YL: Since you live in the Northwest, how to you explain the region's tendency to make aggressive rock?

KC: It's an industrial region. When you live among workers, drinkers, people not generally happy with their lives, you have a tendency to listen to music that gets straight to the point. I don't see any other explanation.

YL: How do you feel being at the center of a big business today?

KC: Before, I had a tendency to reason in terms of "us" against "them." Since we've been a part of a big business, I realize that unfortunately things aren't that simple. We meet people in huge companies that sincerely love music and are trying to make things evolve. That being said, I understand how kids who like underground think we're sellouts. I used to reason exactly like them.

YL: Were you confident in your chances of success in the beginning?

KC: I don't think we really believed it. No money, getting ripped off, sleeping here and there, it all seemed natural to us. It was only after three years that the idea of wondering how we were going to buy a new battery or a new distortion pedal started to weigh on us. These types of problems wear you down. But we were lucky. Things started to go better for us with the release of *Bleach*. We were always poor, but we had the minimum needed to get us to the next concert.

YL: Do you have a lot of songs that have never been released?

KC: A few, but in general all the ones we thought were good came out. You know what, speaking of that! Iggy Pop asked me to write him a song. It shocked me a little. Writing for the godfather. I would have liked to write something in the style of the Stooges. And I wanted to be able to play it. It's incredible that he's still interested in what's happening with us. He came to see us for the first time two years ago, and ever since, we see him from time to time at our concerts. I've never met anybody with his charisma.

Relax

YL: In a song on *Nevermind*, there's a line, "And the animals I've trapped have all become my pets." What were you talking about?

KC: When I say "I," I don't mean me. I'm not autobiographical. My lyrics are often just bits of sentences put together without any particular meaning. I use ideas that come to my head, and I write them down as I go along in a notebook like this one. "Smells Like Teen Spirit" doesn't have a particular meaning. I have nothing against lyrics with a message, like those of the Dead Kennedys, but it's just not at all the way I write.

YL: Do you still live in Seattle?

KC: No. I've lived in Los Angeles for a few months, but I plan on moving back to Seattle. Right now I can't because my girlfriend (Note: for gossip lovers, Courtney Love, singer of Hole) is about to have her group signed by a big label, but once that's taken care of we're going to leave this city. I don't like having to be on guard all the time so I don't get robbed or held up or murdered. Life is more relaxed in Seattle.

YL: You've lived through the struggle; do you think you can survive success?

KC: OK, we're under a lot of pressure. OK, we've toured too much, and that has certainly had a negative affect on our ability to create. But it would be insulting after what we've been through and what's still to come to whine about it today. I think that along with success we're going to be able to set a certain number of conditions. Not touring as much or refusing a promotion that we don't want to do. It's sure that we need to slow down a little. If only to write a few songs for the next album.

———————

The Violent Femmes, getting ready to go on stage, are going to be hurting. It's not easy to go on after such a barrage of adrenaline and fury. In an hour Nirvana just demonstrated that they were as capable of raising the roof of a ten-thousand-person venue as the tiny club they played in last night—a performance that rendered the half-failure of their first scheduled show in Rennes this past winter all the more regrettable. As if Kurt were dislocated by the effort he just made, he sought refuge behind an amplifier. He's waiting for someone to take him back to the hotel, far from the fans and the vampires. He's no longer the master of a flood of metal, but a young man who would like us to forget him, his talent, and his millions of albums sold.

If stories starting on a laugh aren't the most lasting, they still leave indelible marks.

Note: "It's Revolting when unattractive people try to be sexy or say vile things — it's uncouth, uncultured, air pollution, Noise pollution, They should be fined, or taxed or penalized."

"THE ANSWER IS NO"

Jen Oldershaw | January 24, 1992 | Triple J *The Jen Oldershaw Show* (Australia)

It was midafternoon sometime in late January 1992. By a stroke of lucky timing Nirvana was in Australia when *Nevermind* broke worldwide, and within weeks the band had gone from an indie favorite to a full-fledged phenomenon. I was twenty-two and presenting the afternoon music shift on Triple J, a national youth network that was giving *Nevermind* a lot of love on air. Everyone was crazy about the band and the album. Their incredible performance a few days later at the inaugural Big Day Out festival in Sydney is still remembered as one of those "I was there" gigs. To be honest, I was never a huge fan of doing band chats, but Nirvana's one interview with the station was to be live, and with sound checks to work around, it was scheduled during my shift. All three members. Live. In hindsight, that should have rung huge alarm bells. Previous interviews around this time had demonstrated that the band were reluctant participants in the media frenzy surrounding them. True to form, they were uncooperative and difficult from the start. Kurt was very ill and spent most of the interview with his head on the desk; I remember Dave taking to our brand-new mic socks with scissors; and Chris said little of use, playing class clown. I recall cutting to a song early to regroup and see if I could get the interview back on track. No such luck. In the end I just gave up, outfoxed, out of my depth, and completely defeated. I bid them a tense good-bye, turned the speakers up loud, and looked away as they shuffled out. It wasn't much but a small attempt to rescue some of my dignity. I burst into tears after everyone had gone. I'm now a lecturer in radio, and while I haven't listened to the interview in years, my students find it on the Internet every year and we talk about it. It's been more than twenty years now, and Triple J broadcasts it occasionally, much to the amusement of my friends. It was lost for a long time until a fan gave Triple J a copy he'd recorded on cassette at the time. Quietly, I preferred it when it was lost. —Jen Oldershaw

Jen Oldershaw: You're on Triple J right around the country, and just before that track—we'll get to that in a moment—we heard from Pearl Jam and the track from the LP *Ten* and "Alive." And just then "Turnaround"—

Chris Novoselic: [*Interrupting*] The Rolling Stones.

Kurt Cobain: I thought it was the Rolling Stones?

JO: Aw, it was, too, thank you, guys. The Rolling Stones and "Sad Sad Sad."

KC: It's very hard to confuse.

JO: I didn't write it down, that's the problem. In the studio telling me what I've played over the last five minutes is Nirvana, and the track just then we heard was "Turnaround" from their brand-new tour souvenir EP *Hormoaning.* Welcome, guys. Thank you for coming in.

Dave Grohl: You're welcome. [*Muffled acknowledgment from Chris.*]

JO: How y'all doing?

DG: Fine, thank you.

KC: Good, good.

JO: Well, welcome to Australia for the first time and congrats on the way the LP has gone. Has it surprised you? Are you blown away?

CN: No. [*Laughter.*]

KC: Yes. Yeah.

DG: I would have expected it to do well.

JO: Two no's and a one.

CN: It would had better gone gold or . . . heads would have rolled. [*Coughing and laughter from Kurt.*]

JO: Well, it's also kicking in for you in a big way overseas; was there much pressure on you to stay back home and consolidate that?

CN: No!

JO: No?

KC: No.

CN: No.

KC: The answer is no.

JO: Fine! OK. [*Laughs.*] We might get another track . . . we seem to be having some technical problems with this one, so if you guys can just hang in there, we'll hear another track from *Hormoaning*.

CN: Hey Snoopy, Snoopy hang on.
[*Breaks to a Nirvana song —Ed.*]

JO: Another track there from Nirvana's *Hormoaning* tour EP, track called "Aneurysm." What's the story behind the EP? Where was that recorded?

CN: Oh, it was recorded here and there . . . part of it was recorded in—

KC: Well, that last song was recorded in Seattle. And then some of the other ones were taken from a Peel session we did about a year ago.

JO: And is that likely to be released? As a Peel session?

KC: I don't know. I don't think that we're . . . we . . . we've never heard anything about it.

JO: Right, you'd think they'd be quite interested in doing that. Kurt, you sound in quite fine voice on that one, but we've heard some stories about you having some voice problems over the last couple of months. How's the voice holding up now?

CN: [*Putting on the huskiest croak he can manage*] Well, let me tell ya, I gargle glass and eat kerosene. [*Laughter.*] I smoke Camel Filters.

JO: How is the voice, Kurt?

KC: It's fine now, I've had a month rest, and I've been babying it and gargling milk of magnesia. It's fine.

CN: You did that, ah, Luciano Pavarotti apprenticeship in Rome last month (KC: Yeah . . .), and that helped a lot.

DG: Had a lot of cheese.

CN: What are all those rumors about the sex and, uhh . . .

KC: What? Me and Luciano, hey, let's have a party? [*Laughter.*]

JO: I'm sure we'll hear about those in *Melody Maker* one of these coming days. [*Trying to hold it together amid the ongoing guffaws.*] You toured pretty extensively over the end of last year. How did they get to you? Do you get really tired toward the end? I know your voice sort of suffered from it.

CN: [*Shouting*] People were saying that we were getting uptight and pissed off and cranky but they—

KC: To heck with them!

CN: To heck with them! P'fooey! [*Laughter.*]

JO: Can't imagine you boys getting uptight or cranky. What did y—

CN: [*Interjecting*] Whadya mean by that?!

JO: I said that I can't imagine that at all. [*Kurt laughing.*]

KC: Oh crikey, yoinks . . .

JO: What did you do over your month break?

KC: What?

JO: What did you do over your month break?

KC: I slept. The whole time.

DG: I ate.

JO: Chris, what did you do apart from making noises under your arm?

(DG in the background: He made new armpit jokes.)

CN: I made new armpit jokes.

JO: Oh. That's good.

CN: I perfected my, ah, magician act. Magic act.

KC: You're supposed to be a musician, not a magician!

CN: Magician, that's not right . . . I'm a championship diver and a professional photographer. And in my spare time I do horseback riding and cake decorating.

JO: And you like meeting fun people, I'm sure. Now your LP has done amazing things . . .

CN: I make fun of people like I make funny faces at 'em like "nyah-ne-nyah-ne," and I stick my tongue out at 'em and . . .

KC: Really gets on the nerves . . .

JO: Now the LP has done exceedingly well for you. Did you ever sort of sit back when you were recording it and think, "My God, we're onto something pretty amazing here . . ." or is it—has the thing completely surprised you?

CN: I sit back sometimes and think, "When are we gonna get outta here?" [*Laughter.*] I'm hungry.

JO: You didn't think that? It didn't sort of, when you were in the process of making it, think . . .

CN: Well, back to taunting people, I think that's a very intense part of a human being, when they're on the edge and they're . . . you're bugging the hell out of 'em and . . . and doing that . . .

JO: And just waiting for them to pop, huh?

CN: And doing a study on human reactions to petty type, ah . . . distractions. Like giving somebody a flat tire or flicking their ear . . . it's very interesting.

JO: Yeah?

KC: Putting your finger, your index finger, to their chest and saying, "What's that?" then poking them in the neck.

CN: Yeah! Yeah! Or you can walk up to somebody and say, "Hey, who won the race?" And they go, "I dunno, who?" And you go "Charlie Horse!" And you knee them right in the . . . in the thigh.

KC: And then there's prank phone calls . . .

CN: Oh yeah!

DG: That's true.

KC: That's another story . . .

JO: And destroying furniture? Destroying hotel rooms? Equipment?

KC: It's all a bunch of . . . oh, you can't cuss can you?

Background voice: You can't cuss, yeah.

JO: I think we get the gist—rubbish? Not true?

DG: Rubbish.

KC: Not true. Not Everett True.

JO: Now Kurt, um . . .

KC: If it's not true, it's Everett True.

JO: You talk a lot about, um, your uhhh . . . other bands like Mudhoney and Sonic Youth. Can you see yourself opening up—and bands like Sonic Youth—opening up the field for a lot of other bands who are perhaps just starting out?

KC: Oh, absolutely. One hundred percent.

JO: What other bands have you, sort of, seen along the months that you would like to see sort of, y'know, might have advantages out of your success?

KC: Well, a lot of bands who have gone on tour with us, like Shonen Knife and Captain America and Melvins, Jesus Lizard, Urge Overkill, all those bands—I'd love to see them become the Top Hot 100. Great.

JO: And do you think that the climate is right for that kind of stuff to happen?

KC: Very much. Major labels are signing every underground band there is.

DG: Flipper got signed! If Flipper's getting signed then you know that something's happened.

KC: The Melvins, Hole, Urge Overkill are all getting signed to major labels. Mudhoney, Urge Overkill . . .

CN: There's bands that practiced in their garage a couple of times . . .

KC: Yep, then "Let's go to a major . . ."

JO: Is there any danger that it's a, it's a thing that majors are into doing at the moment, but they're not really thinking about the long term, like five years down the track and supporting these bands?

KC: Well, most independent bands don't last more than five years anyhow, so who cares? May as well get some money out of it instead of getting ripped off by SST for five years, y'know?

DG: Exactly. And who wants to end up like the Rolling Stones' Fortieth Anniversary thing anyway? [*Kurt laughs.*] You don't want to make it seem like a career.

CN: [*Stutters repeatedly*] And the good stuff will just rise to the top, y'know?

JO: Yeah . . .

KC: Float.

CN: Like a turd.

JO: Well, if you're talking about independent bands, I think a lot of people would have thought you started out as an independent band . . . [*Band talking among themselves.*] Can you see yourselves combusting in a couple of years and saying that you're not going to last that long?

DG: Who cares?

KC: That can happen, that can happen, as soon as you start writing bad songs—you know, you've got to be prepared for it.

CN: [*Putting on snooty voice*] Well you've got to have security in a career . . . See?

DG: It's just not fair.

JO: What about Nirvana in the near future? Are you going to be going into the studio soon?

KC: Not soon, no . . .

CN: This fall.

JO: For a new album?

DG: A new CD.

CN: A photo album.

KC: We're going to record with Steve Albini, aren't we, guys?

DG: Yes, we are.

CN: Aren't we, John Silva [*Nirvana's manager —Ed.*]? Proud dad.

JO: And have you got any new songs that you might be showing us on this tour?

KC: Um, yeah . . .

DG: Maybe.

KC: "Aneurysm."

CN: No, no, there's even newer songs we've been playing—you'll probably hear them on a bootleg somewhere.

DG: Yeah . . .

KC: Well, we don't play brand-new songs, songs that aren't even written yet all the way anymore . . .

DG: We might, though. There's a few.

KC: Why don't we just make up a buncha' songs in a twenty-minute psychedelic jam.

CN: Unless we start going into the repertoire . . . if you play it.

DG: Yeahhhhh . . .

JO: Well, I might leave you guys to work that one out for yourselves. I hope the tour goes well for you.

CN: We're fishing for your advice.

JO: Um, I'll give that to you off-air, guys. Kurt, Chris, and Dave—

CN: [*Interrupting*] Yeah, go take a hike, jerks!

KC: We geddit, don't stand up in boats—

JO: Another track from the *Hormoaning* EP, this is "Son of a Gun." See ya later.

"IT'S GOING TO MOVE OVER AND KNOCK IT OFF THE PRECIPICE. INTO OBLIVION."

January 25, 1992 | SBS *The Noise* (Australia)

Sandwiched between the Chills' "Heavenly Pop Hit," a quick word from host Annette Shun Wah, then "Rush" by Big Audio Dynamite, Chris Novoselic was collared for a few words at Sydney's Big Day Out festival (which was headlined by the Violent Femmes). The only surviving material from the interview consists of what was broadcast on the Australian music program *The Noise*. —Ed.

Annette Shun Wah: Another of New Zealand's finest, the Chills. And I believe that their countrymen, the Headless Chickens, are planning another visit here soon to promote their next single. We'll have an interview with them in a few weeks' time. For now, a chat with Chris Novoselic, bass player with Nirvana, considered—by some—to be the hottest band around at the moment, as evidenced by their feat of knocking Michael Jackson off the top of the charts.
[*Cuts to rendition of "Smells Like Teen Spirit" recorded on January 25, 1992 —Ed.*]

Chris Novoselic: Just to see all those people there is pretty amazing. It's a big collective energy.
[*Cuts back to "Smells Like Teen Spirit" —Ed.*]

CN: I think it's . . . dangerous, an insane situation to have eight thousand people in this . . . just crammed into a hall like sardines, I mean, it's unnatural.
[*Cuts to live rendition of "Floyd the Barber" —Ed.*]

CN: Everything just happened by itself; there was no marketing scheme or plan or anything. It just took off and they just kinda let it go by . . .
[*Cuts to live rendition of "Floyd the Barber" —Ed.*]

CN: Y'know, we were worried about a child's penis on the cover of our album. Some retailers wouldn't stock it just because of that, y'know? That's how . . . that's the way people think in America, the "moralists," y'know? Some morals, right?
[*Cuts to live rendition of "School" with Chris speaking over the top —Ed.*]

CN: But uh . . . We just do our thing, and if—if they don't want to sell our record, that's fine 'cause we don't really want to compromise. That's not what it's about.
[*Sound cuts to "School" —Ed.*]

CN: 'Cause we've been really busy touring and making videos, so it's kinda distracted us away from the creative process but um, after this Australian, New Zealand . . . uhh . . . Japanese and Hawaiian tour we're gonna, um, take a couple months off, just write songs.
[*Cuts back to "School" —Ed.*]

CN: It's kind of a sick system. Just, they came up with this tag "alternative music," y'know? Because traditionally in rock 'n' roll, new movements would come up and knock the old guys off the top, y'know? And it would just be the new, happening thing 'cause rock 'n' roll is constantly re-creating itself. Well, this new movement was coming up and so instead of knocking the old guard off, they just labeled it "alternative" and did a . . . just kinda moved to the side. Well, now it's starting to run parallel with the old stuff, so I think it's going to move over and knock it off the precipice. Into oblivion.
[*Cuts to "Smells Like Teen Spirit" video —Ed.*]

ASW: Obviously "Teen Spirit" has a lot to do with elevating Nirvana to a position far beyond anything reached by their heroes Sonic Youth. And if you have any doubts about their international success, Nirvana and fellow Americans Public Enemy will be headlining at the massive Reading Festival in England later this year.

THANK HEAVEN FOR NIRVANA

Patrick Chng | February 12, 1992 | *BigO* **(Singapore)**

BigO was a monthly rock magazine in Singapore that started out as a photocopied fanzine in the mid-1980s. It became a full-fledged magazine in 1990 and was the only serious local rock publication around that championed Singapore original music as well as the indie/alternative rock scene. In early 1992, Nirvana was in Singapore to do media interviews, and *BigO* was offered an exclusive one-on-one with Kurt. I attended the press conference, which was held at the Glass Hotel (now the Holiday Inn), where the band was staying. After that, I was introduced to Kurt and we took the elevator to his hotel room. *BigO* photographer Jacque Chong, Kurt, and I were the only people in the room. Kurt was friendly, forthcoming, and soft-spoken. We talked for more than half an hour. I had a bag of stuff that friends had passed on to me for him to sign. I asked if he would sign them, and he obliged willingly. After the interview, I discovered, to my utter horror, that my tape recorder didn't record the interview. It was a portable cassette recorder where you had to press the Play and Rec buttons at the same time, but apparently I hadn't pressed the Rec button. Fortunately, I had taken notes too, so I had to rush home to write the interview while it was still fresh in my head. Later that night, I followed the band to the airport to see them off. Kurt was suffering from stomach pains on the bus, but he was kind enough to sign and write on my guitar strap Strap On Dildo. —Patrick Chng

In the age of massive corporate rock and mindless consumerism, Nirvana represent and uphold the soul of rock 'n' roll high and mighty. The band with the teen spirit and refreshing individuality is getting a whole new generation excited about the music again. Those who fear that rock is getting too safe in the '90s, thank heaven for Nirvana.

KURT COBAIN (there are many variations like Curt/Kurdt or Kobain/Kohbeine, etc.) was still pissed off that the band won't be playing in Singapore. He knew that BigO and BMG Singapore had wanted to organise a gig but his Asian tour manager didn't do anything about it. "Chris Dalston. Put his name in your mag. Chris Dalston!" He swore to get to the bottom of this.

We entered his hotel room and the first thing he did was to offer us drinks. He flipped through the photocopied BigO issue which featured the Sub-Pop label (BigO #52, March 1990) and exclaimed: "You mentioned The Melvins! That's cool. If not for The Melvins, we wouldn't be here. They started the grunge scene. They're a really incredible band!"

I pointed to the write-up on Nirvana which read, "Sadly, another band who is not going to make it to the charts. This is the stuff which cults are made of." I said: "We were wrong! We'd never expected it (mass acceptance)."

Cobain let out a rare laugh. "Me either!"

We sat on the bed and he took off his shades. I could tell he was tired. To his credit, Cobain was still sharp and very forthcoming with his answers.

Our conversation inevitably turned to the Seattle grunge scene and the Sub-Pop label.

"The guys who set up Sub-Pop basically wanted to promote the music but it grew too big. The accounting was screwed up and we didn't get paid for a long time. The distribution was inadequate too. We had kids coming up to us saying they couldn't find our records anywhere. That's when we decided that we should leave Sub-Pop."

"We wanted to get out of the contract but we had signed a seven-record deal. For another label to sign us up would mean that that label would have to pay Sub Pop some money to get us out. Another independent label would not be able to afford that so we decided to go with a major."

There were a number of major labels which showed an interest in Nirvana after the long-awaited release of Bleach in 1989. However, DGC (David Geffen Company) won them over.

"One way to judge a label is to walk into their office and see how they work, shake their hands and then you look around and see what kind of posters they have on their walls and try to figure out what kind of persons they are. That's basically how we judge these labels.

"DGC (David Geffen Company) was obviously more underground than any of the other labels. They knew everything about punk rock and they have about five or six employees who have worked on other independent labels previously."

What's the current state of the Seattle grunge scene? Is it thriving?

"No, it's not thriving anymore. I haven't been to Seattle for a long time now because of the touring. And we actually grew up about 60 miles away from Seattle but the past year, there hasn't been a band which started out, which really caught my attention at all.

"All the Seattle bands like Tad, Mudhoney, Soundgarden are leaving Seattle to tour and they are getting signed up by the majors too."

With the majors "stealing" bands from the independent companies, what is the future for these small labels?

"You could say 'stealing' and it's not exactly good for the small labels. But there are a number of independent labels in the States which are doing great.

"For bands starting out, they would need the independent labels to put out their first album or singles to build up a fan base. I mean you can get signed to a major for your first record, you can be really good, grungy like us, but the band would not seem real. It just doesn't look right."

Since Elvis Presley in the '50s, each generation of rockers has taken rebellion to an extreme more decadent than the previous one. In the '90s, how extreme is the rebellion?

"Compared to the '50s, it's extreme. But it seems to revert back every few years. It seems to go back and forth between the corporate ogres swallowing up the music industry and keeping it safe and commercial. And then somehow, an independent band would infiltrate that and shake things up a little bit.

"And at that time it makes everyone feel like there might be a new awakening on the horizon but then all of a sudden, the corporate ogre comes bashing and rapes these bands and it turns back to the '50s again."

It happens all the time. I mean, The Ramones had a movie at the height of their success. Sire Records put a lot of promotion into them. They had the world in their pocket, and still the general public didn't swallow it.

"It's all a matter of timing and social conditioning. It takes a long time for people to develop an open mind. It takes generations and it takes a lot of education to solidify it.

It looks like Nirvana's success has a lot to do with timing. As Cobain pointed out: "We came at a time when the music was getting a bit too safe. I think the kids are tired of listening to Vanilla Ice."

"I just think the '90s has a new generation of kids and teenagers who are more aware and they're generally more intelligent than the last generation of kids about 10 years ago when punk rock had all the right in the world to become really popular because The Sex Pistols, The Clash and The Ramones had a big push behind. There's a lot of attention and promotion and it still didn't work because socially the public wasn't ready for it."

Then again, a lot of people caught onto punk rock more because it was a hip thing and a fashion trend rather than because they were really into it.

Cobain thought for a moment and agreed: "Yeah, that's probably true too."

As the group becomes more successful, there will likely be poseurs who would jump onto the bandwagon and claim to be grungy, cool and rebellious like them.

"Yeah and it's happening already! There are some bands that I absolutely despise and I'm not afraid to name them. They are The Nymphs, Alice In Chains and especially Pearl Jam. They are just career-minded bands out to make big bucks and we've been unfairly lumped together with them. But ultimately it's the music and the kids will know what's crap."

But doesn't this run against Smells Like Teen Spirit, their hit single about kids not having opinions about anything? Or is it more of an observation than a derogatory statement?

"I'm not pointing the finger at the kids, it'll make me look like a father figure. It's not meant to say who's right and who's wrong. There's a line that goes, 'it's fun to lose and to pretend,' which is about trying even though you know you're gonna lose. Because the fun part is the trying part and when you lose, you can pretend."

Music critics generally label Nirvana as "rebels." Is Cobain comfortable with the tag?

"Well, I do not take offense to it. I think it's cool but we have our commercial side too. Some of our songs are really accessible, so accessible even grandmothers can listen and enjoy. On one hand, we have the really loud and noisy stuff, and then we also have the melodic stuff."

Cobain picks up a recent issue of BigO as an example. "Look at this mag. It's a commercial product. It's glossy and has an attractive cover to lure the customer. But look inside (flips through several pages), hidden between are good stuff that the reader might chance upon and be curious about. You've got to balance up. We've sold lots of records and made some money but there's nothing wrong in that. We need the money to carry on the crusade, don't want to sound pretentious, but it's a crusade to me."

What if critics cry "sell out?" "We deserved it. Bands like Sonic Youth deserve to make it big and earn some money. They are definitely a better band than Poison."

In the press conference the day before, Cobain mentioned that Axl Rose not turning up for a gig or making the fans wait for two hours just because "he's got diarrhea or something" is plain rock star attitude. How would he draw the line between responsibility and rebellion?

"When you're a popular figure, you owe a certain responsibility to your fans. I think Guns N' Roses are promoting the wrong values like sexism and the way they do drugs. I mean, what are they rebelling against? I don't think this is rebellion. Rebellion is standing up to people like Guns N' Roses."

It is a known fact that Cobain is a firm and vocal advocate of women's rights. At the recent Headbangers' Ball in the United States, Cobain attended the Ball in a dress.

"I think there's too much sexism in the world. About 90 per cent of the women I know have been raped one way or another. It's crazy. I find women to be very compassionate human beings. Polly is a song about a girl who was raped.

"You know, I listen to rap and it's got a nice beat and rhythm and all that, but when I listen to the words, they really put me off because some of them are bloody sexist."

Cobain is also known for disliking to talk to the press. I pressed for his reasons.

"I don't like the press generally, especially the English press. The weeklies are the worst. They put you on the cover and feature you but they've really got nothing new to say. So they cook up stories of us bashing our hotel rooms and stuff like that.

"I mean, we do break things at parties when we are drunk like some other bands do when they're drunk. But there's no violence. It's amongst friends and we did it for fun. The press just blow things out of proportion. I prefer talking to fanzines 'cause they know the music. They know what they are talking about."

Well then, which media broke Nirvana? Is it MTV? "Definitely. I've met a few guys in MTV who really care about the music. They are really into our music and other underground bands and are trying to break these bands too."

And does he [*Kurt —Ed.*] like making videos?

"Yeah. I like making videos. I love to act, but I wouldn't want to make a clichéd video. I came up with the idea for the Smells Like Teen Spirit video but the director had different ideas and what emerged wasn't what I had in mind.

"I had to go in to the editing room in the last days of postproduction to salvage whatever I could, like inserting certain scenes which the director had left out, to salvage it and make it tolerable. It was our mistake to go in with a commercial director. But I really like our next video, Come as You Are."

What about Nevermind's producer Butch Vig?

"He's great. I heard the Killdozer's album produced by Butch Vig and thought it was really well-produced. Really heavy-duty production."

Vig also produced The Young Fresh Fellows.

"Yeah, that's right. I've heard of them though I haven't really sat down and listened to their music. I love the sound on Nevermind. But for the next album, I would like to work with Steve Albini but I've heard he's not easy to get along with."

Where do you see Nirvana heading after this success? "Down! All the way down." And judging by his grin, I know it makes no difference to Kurt Cobain.

WHAT HAPPENED TO THE OTHER EX-MEMBERS OF NIRVANA?

Kurt Cobain says: "Jason Everman actually didn't play on Bleach. He was a good friend who contributed money to pay for the recording of Bleach. In return, we credited him as a guitarist and put him in the picture in the album.

"Nirvana has always been a three-piece band even on Bleach. Chad Channing just wanted to leave although I'm not sure why. But we're still friends even though we don't keep in contact very frequent these days. When Chad left, we looked for a drummer and found Dave Grohl whom I think is the best drummer I could ever find. He was playing in a hardcore band called Scream and he's simply the best, the most incredible drummer I've ever seen!"

ENLIGHTENING TRIO

Sujesh Pavithran | February 13, 1992 | *Star* **(Malaysia)**

It was before the age of the Internet. Whatever information I gathered on new bands, music, and the industry was from magazines like *NME*, *Melody Maker*, *Rolling Stone*, *Billboard*, and *Smash Hits*. Which meant I was as updated as I could be on popular music trends in the United States and United Kingdom. I had read a few articles about Nirvana when the band began making waves in 1991—someone called them the "next big thing."

It was in early February 1992 when the band's album distributor in Malaysia called me to ask if I would be interested in interviewing Nirvana in Singapore, as they were promoting their new album, *Nevermind*, in the region. Other Malaysian journalists weren't interested, but I jumped at the opportunity. I made one condition: I wanted a face-to-face interview. And got it!

So, after the afternoon press conference in an upmarket Singapore hotel, I was set up with the three guys at the hotel's first-floor café. The session lasted an hour, including a few minutes for photos, which I took myself. My one regret is that I didn't pose with them for a photo.

My impressions: Kurt Cobain was very intense and wore his dark glasses throughout the interview. He was matter-of-fact, no airs but not effusive. I got the feeling he would rather be playing on stage than doing interviews, but he never showed any impatience. And he was passionate each time he spoke about the music.

Krist Novoselic was more interested in the camera I was carrying; he kept asking questions about it every few minutes. But that's not to say he wasn't paying attention. He just knew it was Kurt from whom the quotes would be taken. I got the impression he was more the thinking guy in the band.

As for Dave Grohl, apart from clowning around a bit, making faces for the photo session, and answering a couple of questions, he didn't say much. He had just joined the band on *Nevermind*, so I guess he was still "fitting in." Kurt and Krist were, after all, Nirvana's founders. I believe my interview captures the mood of that hour quite definitively. —Sujesh Pavithran

Rock music's hottest property at the moment is Nirvana. You may not have heard of the band yet, but its second album *Nevermind* recently peaked at the top of the Billboard charts, displacing Michael Jackson's *Dangerous* and chalking up a sales figure of 1½ million copies.

The Seattle-based trio's music blends the raw aggression of punk-rock with melodic pop sensibilities. Right now, Nirvana is bigger than U2, more talked about than Guns 'N Roses, and as outrageous as any self-respecting rock band anywhere else in the world—these lads have reportedly indulged in the usual quantum of excesses, from wreaking havoc on stage to physically abusing journalists.

SUJESH PAVITHRAN, nervously aware of this reputation, met the trio in Singapore last week (the band was between tours of Australia and Japan) and emerged unscathed from an hour-long exclusive.

You're sitting in the coffeehouse of Singapore's Concorde Hotel with three hungry Americans who are giving the waitress the strangest orders she's ever taken.

Tuna cornbread sandwich (at which the puzzled lass enquires if wholemeal will do), chocolate mousse cake (she looks momentarily relieved), *mee siam* (pronounced "sah-yem" and leaving her in total confusion), yoghurt with chocolate milk (she drops her scribbling pad in anxiety) and . . . "call me frank," smiles one of the trio, which she, in a flash of inspiration, accurately interprets as a hotdog.

Orders taken, she scrambles hurriedly away to relate this to the chef; she is blissfully unaware of her customers' identities.

"We had hardly heard of Singapore and had no idea we had a following here . . . I kept signing autographs at the airport until my arm grew tired," says one, a thin, extremely pale and intense-looking chap with massive black shades permanently fixed across his eyes. He looks like he'll either explode into frenzied activity or fall into a psychedelic stupor any moment.

This is Kurt Cobain, guitarist, singer and songwriter, who, with bassist Chris Novoselic, formed Nirvana in 1987. When he talks, those shades seem to drill into you like searchlights, harsh and inscrutable, daring you to ask him a sensitive question and spark the fireworks.

Carefully, you dip your toe in the water, wording your questions so as not to offend, like . . . *er, you guys, seem to come across as a band that takes great pleasure in parodying the rock star lifestyle thing . . . ?*

"Yeah, we've definitely made fun of what rock stars are supposed to do, in retrospect, it's so ridiculous. We've got drunk and destroyed backstage areas after concerts, just to have fun, just like any other band," Cobain scowls.

"We don't do such things consciously, when these things happen, we're just doing what the average rock star is supposed to do . . . we just don't subscribe to the average rock star lifestyle!"

Novoselic, a towering two metres tall, and drummer Dave Grohl, the band's effervescent funnyman, nod their heads absently. Clearly, Grohl would rather be seeing the island's sights, but Novoselic is fascinated by the camera and getting a closer look at it—he took up photography six months ago.

Cobain and Novoselic come from Aberdeen, Washington. When they met, both were art students in a college near Seattle. Grohl only joined the band a year and a half ago, its fifth and most-likely-to-stay drummer.

"The other drummers were just bad drummers," Cobain explains.

Nirvana graduated from the underground punk circuit to bigger venues; then a recording deal with the Seattle-based independent Sub Pop label followed. The year 1989 saw the release of Nirvana's debut effort, *Bleach*.

A year later, the band received a substantial offer from DGC Records and its passport to the big time.

So what difference has success made to you? One moment, you guys were hardly known, a year later you're hopping across the globe . . .

"Actually, we had been touring Europe and America long before we became well-known all over the world," Cobain corrects, "so things are exactly the same now as they were then."

But when Nirvana entered the studios for *Nevermind*, it was different, he admits: "Well, DGC is a bigger label and we had a bigger budget and more time in the studio. We took about a month, as opposed to our first album which we did in a week.

"Our idea was to get in there, record the album and get out as fast as possible. We work relatively fast."

As the food arrives and Cobain digs in, he generously allows that the label's reaction to *Nevermind* was unexpected.

"We were surprised at DGC's reaction, although we were very sure of what we had done. We had total freedom to do as we pleased on the album."

The album has received rave reviews on both sides of the Atlantic, and wherever else it has been released. Ranging from thrashy punk-rock to melodic acoustic rock, it tackles a variety of subjects including teen angst, religion, relationships, social injustices and rape.

Politics, however, was and is still strictly off-limits to Cobain, who writes the band's lyrics—the very mention of the word gets him into a white rage.

"We're politically aware as individuals, but we don't like to force our opinions down people's throats. Political bands haven't been very effective, you can't expect a rock 'n' roll band to have a lot of impact politically.

"First and foremost, we're all entertainers. The politically confrontational attitude may be fine for other bands, but it's not for us because it seems to overpower the music."

And that's not the only subject that turns the normally reclusive Cobain into a fiery orator—do not ever mention the Grammies (for which the band was recently nominated)!

"I don't give a sh*t about it! We're not in the least bit honoured to be associated with it. The Grammies are just another part of the promotion machinery, I've always thought it was a load of sh*t!"

It must be the food that's keeping him good-tempered, you think; one wouldn't like to catch him on a bad day. Having established this, you broach another volatile subject.

How do you react to the success of Nevermind, *which many rock crit-ics think significantly surpasses Guns 'N Roses' recent albums in terms of redefining the boundaries of rock music?* (Nirvana has professed a distaste for GNR and other chart-topping rock bands.)

"We never expected to be able to sell the album—and now that it's sold over a million copies, the feeling is great. We don't ever keep track of the charts, so all we know of our album's or singles' progress in the Billboards (charts) is when someone tells us.

"It's flattering to know that so many people like our music."

And then Cobain warms up, fired no doubt by the chocolate cake, most of which he has put away.

"If you think of the competition we're up against, I don't feel sorry for the other bands. Look at Poison—they've sold 20 million records and they suck and they just can't write a song!"

And what about the band's reputation for causing mayhem on stage, and playing on even when guitars drift out of tune? (Oops . . . you get ready to flee here, but Cobain smiles briefly, a rare event.)

"We're pretty unprofessional on stage," he admits.

"We don't have a lot of roadies to keep our instruments in tune all the time, so we just keep playing. But I've never been very keen on people who go overboard on the professional thing . . . if the song feels right, we just play on."

And as for wrecking instruments on stage, Cobain has just signed an endorsement deal with Fender. This means he gets to buy inexpen-sive Japanese-made Stratocasters—his preferred make of guitar—at even cheaper prices.

One foresees more guitars being ripped apart during Nirvana's cur-rent four-city tour of Japan and, later, America.

(For the record, Novoselic uses Ibanez and Gibson basses, Grohl pounds a set of Tama skins.)

Wherever it is that the band performs, the adrenalin keeps pumping fast, from gigs like the Reading Festival in England where the audience numbered around 40,000 to less than a thousand in Belgium's Ghent.

"Every place has its own identity, but people are the same everywhere. They just want to see the band, they get excited and then we get excited! It's a good feeling."

Although the trio format has not restricted his songwriting, Cobain plans to expand the band.

"We've managed to pull it off as a trio, but in future, we would like to experiment with more layers of guitar sounds. We'll be looking out for a new guitar player."

And Nirvana fans need not expect a new album too soon, even if Cobain already has about five songs written.

"We're going to take our time, there's no date set for the album's release. We've got to make sure the product is good."

The hour's about up, and Alex (just Alex) [*McLeod* —*Ed.*], the band's touring manager, politely hovers around . . . the guys have radio and television interviews to do, more fans to meet.

Cobain gets a doggie-bag for the uneaten food, photographs are taken (Novoselic is still eyeing the camera), there are amicable handshakes all round (the guys relax when you mention you're a bit of a guitar player yourself), and then they're gone.

For some moments after, you wonder if what had transpired during the past hour had simply been a figment of your imagination or if you had actually been in the company of the soon-to-be biggest and most unglamorous rock band in the world.

Your photographs and illegible notes will confirm the latter . . . but just for the moment, you can't help feeling that if rock's new messiahs have arrived, they certainly don't give two hoots about their status.

"THEY'RE JUST IN THEIR SEATS AND IT'S REALLY STRANGE"

Beatriz Pécker | February 22, 1992 | RTVE *Rockopop* (Spain)

Rockopop was a Spanish music show that aired on the main channel, TVE1 (La 1), of Spain's public service broadcaster Radio Televisión Española (RTVE). The show ran from October 1988 through October 1992 under the stewardship of presenter and director Beatriz Pécker. The interview with Chris Novoselic and Dave Grohl was conducted by Beatriz and took place in the aftermath of Nirvana's final show of the Asia/Pacific tour in Honolulu. —Ed.

[Live footage of the band playing "Been a Son" —Ed.]
Dave Grohl: It's strange 'cause in Australia it's sort of like England. And in New Zealand . . . it's just sort of strange. Japan is strange! Japan is really strange! Because, the show . . . when you play in Japan, there's so much security and there's . . . usually we have one barrier in front of the stage so people can't, like, jump up on stage and kill us or whatever. But in Japan, they have barriers, like, it's a barrier for the stage and a barrier here and a barrier here, and it's like in all these sections and it's so weird. And then in other places . . . most places in Japan you have to stay—you can't move out of your seat. So you stay in your seat and just do this [*pumps fist in the air and bobs up and down —Ed.*], and it's strange for us 'cause when we set out there and we look out at all these people standing—I mean, sitting!—they're just in their seats and it's really strange.
[Chris arrives. —Ed.]

Beatriz Pécker: Hello, hi.

Chris Novoselic: Hi.

BP: Do you like to provoke the audience?

CN: [*Totally deadpan*] No. They provoke us. They do!

BP: Really? We must be talking about a different audience from you two.

DG: I was talking about Japan, how they have all these . . .

CN: Oh, Japanese audiences are just like . . . [*purses lips, nods head politely, and gives gentle applause*]

DG: It's weird, though. I mean, if they could ever break out I'm sure they'd go completely insane. They would really go crazy, there's just so much control, it's just . . . (BP: Too much.) too much, wayyyyy too much control.

BP: In these months, you have become a very important group everywhere, also in Spain. Why do you think people can feel your music, for instance in Spain, so easily?

CN: [*Making faces and periodically shaking head throughout*] Music is the international language! Y'know? Rock 'n' roll's been around now for thirty years and people . . . it's just a beat, and it's just got that beat. [*Begins clicking fingers in down strokes.*] It's got that beat.

BP: So it's just the music? Because critics talk about you, your spirit, your influences, but music is just music?

DG: Well, it's also . . . I mean, music, with music comes energy and, I mean, if you see a lot of energy on stage you don't have to say anything, y'know? Usually if there's energy on stage then there's going to be energy in the crowd and if there's energy in the crowd, there's usually going to be energy on stage. It's just a vibe, just a feeling . . .

CN: There's a lot of bands out there, lot of them just . . . take up space. Give something back—I like to really get something across. You've just got to give energy and passion and feeling.

BP: You have a lot of energy . . .

DG: Well, now and for the next couple of years you'll be seeing a lot of new bands, bands like Urge Overkill and the Melvins and Mudhoney and Hole and, y'know, Sonic Youth who are the godfathers of everything . . . you'll see a lot of new bands, honest bands, that have a lot of sincere energy, it's not contrived, it's not like some heavy metal band up on a stage twenty meters away.

BP: You don't like?

DG: No.

BP: Why?

DG: Because it's just false, it's not true. They have the wrong motivation. A lot of heavy metal bands go out and do it for the money and not to make good, honest music and make songs for the sake of writing songs.

BP: In your group, melody is very important. What is the importance of the lyrics for you?

CN: Well, Kurt writes the lyrics, and I have my own interpretation of the lyrics. See, I think a song has to be different for everybody. Like, I have some songs, not by my group, but just, like, old songs and new songs by new bands that have a special meaning to me personally. So to really operate on the lyrics, or what a song means, might rob somebody of their own perception because music should be a personal thing.

BP: Last question and then I leave you . . . [*breaks into laughter*] . . . last question: who chose the cover of your record? The little baby.

DG: We did. Yeah.

BP: Who's the child?

DG: We . . . I don't know!

CN: Some artist got the baby swimming in a pool, got in with a special camera and took pictures underwater. And I guess the parents are going to bother the child by having a huge poster in the living room.

BP: Thank you, and congratulations for the show tonight.
[*Cuts to Nirvana playing "On a Plain" at the show —Ed.*]

COBAIN CLIP

Looking to a Brighter Future

"All I need is a break and my stress will be over with . . . I'm going to get healthy and start over . . ."

—from "Inside the Heart and Mind of Kurt Cobain"
by Michael Azerrad, *Rolling Stone* (US), April 1992

COBAIN CLIP

On Doing It for the Ages

"I'm really into doing it for the kids. It's cool doing these all ages shows. It kinda sucks that the door was so high. But the way I figure it is we've got a lot of expenses. It's not like we're getting rich off of these shows. We totally do them for kids and shit. But there's a lot of people we have to pay now."

—from "Nirvana" by Lance Hahn, *Maximum Rock 'n' Roll*, April 1992

COBAIN CLIP

Embracing Love and Change

"My songs have always been frustrating themes, relationships that I've had. And now that I'm in love, I expect it to be really happy, or at least there won't be half as much anger as there was. I'm just so overwhelmed by the fact that I'm in love on this scale, I don't know how my music's going to change. But I'm looking forward to it. I love change. All the bands I respect the most have changed with every album."

—from "Kurt and Courtney Sitting in a Tree"
by Christina Kelly, *Sassy* (US), April 1992

PART VIII

March to September 1992—Rest and Resuscitation

THERE ARE JUST EIGHT KNOWN INTERVIEWS WITH NIRVANA DURING the three months after the band finished its tour. Cobain turns up in only one—a *Rolling Stone* encounter in which he denies any drug use. Nirvana has only just reached superstardom, and already the band is the subject of speculation and lies. When Nirvana returns to Europe in the summer, the bandmates are selective regarding their media entanglements, compared to the madness of late 1991. It barely counts as a break in their withdrawal.

Krist Novoselic steps up as the public face of Nirvana. Encountered alone, his maturity begins to outshine the surreal humor with which he draws attention away from the group when they're all together. His willingness to open the door to kids with a community access show and his burgeoning interest in using the platform of fame are parts of a visible effort to find the good in Nirvana's situation. It's the focus of his conversations throughout the summer.

Already famous musicians, the band members are now becoming something else: famous celebrities. The April/May interview with Novoselic and the September piece with Cobain no longer emphasize the music, the scene, the backstory—the pieces mark the beginning of the press's focus on understanding the bandmates as personalities, their origins, their mind-sets. Increasingly, the questions turn to: "Who are you? Where do you come from?"

Alongside this comes a quest for novelty that the band is happy enough to indulge. The Reading Festival on August 30, 1992, is Nirvana's most high-profile show ever, and they've chosen or agreed to stage an ad-libbed comedy segment in a bathroom. It shows their mood that day: they want to shed their albatross by simultaneously making fun of their own tarnished reputation and the British media's sensationalism and seriousness. The extent to which the famous arrival on stage in a wheelchair was all about taking direct aim at the UK press is underrated. Nirvana is using humor aggressively, as we've seen before.

The year 1992 sees the members of Nirvana claiming they haven't changed while simultaneously losing their naïveté when faced with a microphone. Cobain's full retreat is one approach, but even Novoselic is learning. Already, in Hawaii, Novoselic and Grohl are unwilling to answer a question discussing Cobain's activities. In July, Rafa Cevera openly tells Novoselic, "Kurt said . . . to preserve the good relationship between you, he's decided to keep his personal life a little more separate from you two," and Novoselic responds by talking around the point rather than revealing that anything has changed in the band's relationship. But in the interview with Cyrus Aman, Novoselic mentions Cobain is living in Los Angeles and working on the video for Nirvana's next single. It's the first time there's been a true divide within Nirvana—the first time that the members haven't been working together as a band on something intended to emerge under their name. The months of relative silence conceal a turning of the tide.

AN INTERVIEW WITH . . .
KURT COBAIN

Carlos "Cake" Nunez | March 1992 | *Flipside* **(US)**

How lucky was I to interview Kurt Cobain? Al Flipside and I didn't even have to call Nirvana's publicity department to interview Kurt. I had Kurt and Courtney's Los Angeles phone number and just called him up and we started the interview. Kurt was a bit upset because he had told me that he thought that Al Flipside and I were coming over to his apartment in the Fairfax District to interview him. "That sucks, man! I bought all this food for us! I had no idea it was going to be a phone interview," Kurt said to me. I was upset, too, because Courtney had told me it was going to be only a phoner in a prior conversation earlier in the week. Oh well. I just remember being twenty-six at the time and how everyone in the L.A. scene was still astonished at Nirvana's worldwide success with *Nevermind*. Al Flipside was making an exception by allowing his fellow writers to interview bands that were signed to major labels because so many "indie" bands were getting huge contracts at the time—following the success of *Nevermind*. Sadly, the interview microcassette was either taped over or was stolen from the Flipside office, according to Al. I hope, if it wasn't erased, it will someday resurface for all of us to cherish and enjoy. Twenty-two years after this interview, I can say that I still very much miss Kurt as a friend and as a human being. He was more than a songwriter and a musician. Seeing his face on T-shirts around the world is still pretty damn surreal to me. —Carlos "Cake" Nunez

(Excerpt from the full *Flipside* interview)

Carlos "Cake" Nunez: The English press seem to write a lot of stuff about you, like they said you had OD'd, which obviously isn't true. One minute they love you and the next they attack you.

Kurt Cobain: Oh, has the backlash begun now? I haven't been keeping up on the English press.

CCN: I just read one "on page three, Kurt OD's in Australia." I'm like, what? I called Courtney, and she goes, "He's right here!"

KC: God! They announced on MTV in Europe that Courtney and I had both died in a drug overdose. We had friends calling up for days, really upset, thinking we were dead. I don't know. I'm just now learning to accept all the rumors and all the lies that are involved in being a big rock star. It bugs the shit out of me, but I just have to deal with it. I don't take drugs. I have taken drugs in my life and every once in a while I may dabble in drug-taking, but I am definitely not a drug addict and I don't like to condone anyone using any kind of drugs. They're a waste of time.

CCN: The media is your worst enemy when you're in the spotlight. They look in every nook and cranny. Any move you make, if you look sick, "Oh, he's on drugs."

KC: Yeah, right. I was almost dead from touring. My body wouldn't allow me to take drugs on tour even if I wanted to. I'd die in a day.

CCN: Don't you have a condition that makes you fall asleep or something?

KC: I've got narcolepsy, and I can see how someone would think I was nodding off when I'm just falling asleep. Just being on the road is stressful enough physically—there's no way I could ever take drugs. I just couldn't do it.

Al "Flipside" Kowalewski: Being a band of your size, is there more of that offered?

KC: No, not at all! Backstage at our shows is pretty sedate, I mean, it's really boring—there's no groupies, there's no drugs, and we haven't even drank for a long time! I haven't drank for months, and Chris quit drinking.

We wanted to survive this tour so we even quit doing that. It really bugs me a lot to be accused of being a drug addict—there's constantly articles being written about it. It sucks because I kinda feel a responsibility to kids who might want to start taking drugs. In a few interviews Chris and I have talked about smoking marijuana, and we read it back and thought, "Jeez, that probably influenced someone." I've done enough pot in my life where I don't need to do it anymore. I learned too late that it destroys your memory, and now I'm suffering for it. I think it's really lame for journalists to write and accuse me of taking drugs because kids are going to read that article and then they're going to do drugs because I do. That's really lame. [*Interview continues with discussion of "Endless Nameless" and of bands jumping on the grunge bandwagon —Ed.*]

KC: When you're in the public eye, you have no choice but to be raped over and over again—they'll take every ounce of blood out of you until you're exhausted. Weird Al Yankovic is . . . his whole album is devoted to us! In the beginning I talked to him on the phone and he's like, "Hey Kurt, how ya doing? I'd like to record your song 'Teen Spirit' for my next album." I thought, "OK, that's fine," I liked "Another One Rides the Bus," I thought that was kinda clever. Then all of a sudden he's done a video in mockery of our video, and the album has a picture of him naked in the water with a dollar bill. I think it's gone a bit too far! We weren't prepared for something like that. Legally he can do stuff like that, but at the time I thought he was just going to record our song, but he's trying to revive his career based on us. I don't know . . . I guess it's no more offensive than a bootleg. Journalists are groveling for any kind of article about us, like they're going down to Aberdeen and talking to kids that look to be in my age range and they look like they could be my friend, and these guys in tractor hats and moustaches are claiming to be my friends. They're saying, "Yeah, Kurt slept on my couch for six months, it was great!" "I sold him his first amplifier!"

CCN: Then you'll have all these people writing books on you!

KC: Well . . . it won't last. I'm looking forward to the future. It'll only be another year and then everyone will forget about it.

"HE LIKES TO KEEP THINGS CRYPTIC AND OPEN-ENDED"

Cyrus Aman | April 3/May 1, 1992 | *Cyrus . . . The TV Show* **(US)**

I grew up in Olympia and was in high school when alternative bands were truly alternative. My best friend was obsessed with the local scene and professed the greatness of bands like Nirvana and Soundgarden. I would mock him, saying, "If they were any good, they'd be on a major label," and touting the genius of Kiss and Iron Maiden. At the time, there was a public affairs television show, filmed in Seattle, called *Town Meeting*. My family used to request free tickets for the tapings. We'd watch "experts" debate current affairs relevant to Washington State, with the only thrill being that later I'd see my seventeen-year-old face on TV.

One time, though, I was surprised to find that Krist Novoselic was appearing on the show. This was right around the time "Smells Like Teen Spirit" exploded and Nirvana was becoming a sensation. The topic was music censorship, and Krist was a highly articulate contributor. After the show I walked up to him. "Hi, Krist, my name's Cyrus. I write for my school paper and produce a community access TV show. Would you do an interview?" He said yes right away and gave me his phone number, adding, "Just don't give it out to anyone."

The next day in school I gloated to my Nirvana-obsessed friend before having him and another friend come up with questions to ask Krist because I knew next to nothing about the band. My mom drove us to Seattle, and we conducted the interview at Krist's house. There were many cool aspects to the visit: we were at a rock star's house, he offered us wine, he gave us radio promo CDs that were never released commercially, and he let me play his Kiss pinball machine.

In my naïveté as a first-time interviewer, I failed to see the benefit of miking my subject and relied solely on the camera's microphone. When the manager of the community access station reviewed my footage, she said, "We can't air this! The audio is terrible. If you want it aired, you'll have to do it again, properly miked." I was devastated. I had the rare opportunity to interview a member of one of the hottest bands in the world, and I blew it. But being naive also contributed to my fearlessness. I called Krist, told him the story, and asked if we could come back and do it again. Being the nice guy that he is, he didn't hesitate.

Both interviews are reproduced here. The first one is only a portion, while the second interview is transcribed here for the first time. However, if you want to see both in living color, both videos are on my website. —Cyrus Aman

April 3, 1992

Cyrus Aman: What nationality are you?

Chris Novoselic: I'm not a nationalist; I do have an ethnic background. It's Croatian, Southern European. I speak Croatian. I guess you could say I'm an American citizen, right? Technically. But we're all on the planet, and—due to the miracle of modern communication—satellites, radio, TV make the world a lot smaller. So the whole idea of nationality is kind of outdated. You have an ethnic background, but I'm an earthling.

CA: Where were you born and raised?

CN: I was born in Compton, California. I'm from straight out of Compton! My family moved from there, and I moved to San Pedro, California—there in Los Angeles. I moved to Aberdeen, Washington, in 1979. I freaked out on the move west, so they sent me to Croatia for a year. I lived there, and I moved back to Aberdeen. Spent some wasteful years there. Decadent. Teenage drug haze. Moved out when I was eighteen.

CA: Do you have any funny childhood stories?

CN: Oh, man. My brother was always a troublemaker. He'd always break his glasses and stuff like that. I got in trouble in the schoolyard once. "What's your phone number so we can call your parents?" I just started rattling off these phone numbers. Like, who knows what the prefix was, not even any local prefix. "Hey, that's only six numbers!" "Uhhh . . . 2!"

CA: Where did you go to school?

CN: Well, I graduated from Aberdeen High School in 1984, and I never went to school after that. I always wanted to go to college, but I never got around to it; I had all these jobs. Just starved and stayed in a band. I went through the school of hard knocks.

CA: Still have your yearbooks?

CN: Well, going back to teenage debauchery, and kind of a weird haze, whenever it was picture time I would skip. "Let those guys take their pictures. I won't go. Alright! I've got a whole period off!" Smoke some cigarettes.

CA: What bands did you listen to in high school?

CN: Didn't have access to a lot of music in Aberdeen, kind of isolated. Started off listening to older Scorpions, like *Lovedrive, Animal Magnetism*. Ozzy Osbourne, *Blizzard of Oz*. Just teenage cock rock. Beatles, Devo, B-52s; prog rock. Still held on to bands like Zeppelin and Sabbath.

CA: Give us a status on your personal life right now.

CN: Oh, well, very happy. So much has happened to me in the past year, it's like winning the lottery. Go buy a house, indulge in materialistic acquisitions. Still found out that all my friends are with me. My wife and I have been getting along really well, financial pressures are off us, because we were always poor. The end of the month it would always be stress time. Gotta keep the lights on, gotta pay the rent. I wasn't working. I'd just bring home whatever I could from the band, and she was working, and there's all this car insurance, take the cat to the vet, and now I've been alleviated of those financial burdens. It's been said before, though, the only good thing about having money is that you don't have to worry about it anymore. So I guess I'm pretty happy. If I don't lose it all tomorrow, hard to say. But, if I was the antimaterialist that I claim to be, I'd be happy living in a wood hut in the woods.

CA: What can fans look for in your next album?

CN: A lot more diversity, experimental. That's about all I can say, but that's a standard answer: "We're going to try to be 'experimental.'"

CA: What were some former band names?

CN: Pen Cap Chew, Bliss. We were called Ted Ed Fred for this one show, by this one person, 'cause he made the fliers for it. So I guess we were called Ted Ed Fred at one point . . . uhhhh . . . Oh, Skid Row. [*Laughter.*] Yeah, it never stuck.

May 1, 1992

CA: Welcome to *Cyrus . . . The TV Show*, episode number ten, with Chris Novoselic of Nirvana. We did previously have an interview with him, and the sound quality turned out to be null and void, so we are repeating it. So, I've got some questions to ask you, and we made up some new ones, so you'd have more of a lively response to them instead of repeating old ones.

CN: Certainly.

CA: I'll start off with some questions about the band. What is the band doing now, and what are some future plans?

CN: Well, right now, we're just kind of taking it easy. Laying around. Sleeping in. Trying to acquire the patent for the shovel.

CA: Can we expect more videos or singles from *Nevermind*?

CN: Oh yeah, I just saw a rough cut of the "Lithium" video. Kurt's been working with a guy named Kevin Kerslake, who did "Come as You Are." He's been working with him down in L.A. on this video. It's a compilation of live shots taken from a show we did at the Paramount on Halloween of 1991. It's pretty neat.

CA: Would that be different than the original production of it that was used for local access television channels?

CN: Oh yeah, not that I watch a lot of that stuff, you know. I mean, any kind of productions, whether it's a video or audio, has its own merit. I mean, it just depends on what kind of perspective you put on it. You could put on a very elitist-type audio, videophile perspective on it. Say, you know, you're into the latest technology, but a lot of times you can look at things with a Super 8 camera, and it'll have a quality of its own. It just depends on the perspective you put on it.

CA: This is something I've been wondering, because I bought *Nevermind* recently. Many people say the lyrics are questionable as to what they mean. Do all your songs have some underlying meaning?

CN: Well, I don't want to talk about the lyrics, because they're Kurt's lyrics, but I've heard him express that he likes to keep things cryptic and open-ended. But I think he knows what the song means. The songs have meanings for me too. They affect me personally and probably different than, say, maybe they affect you.

CA: Even maybe, "Smells Like Teen Spirit" would have its own underlying meaning?

CN: Yeah, yeah. There's a meaning behind "Teen Spirit." I think all the songs have meanings. I don't think they're really mindless or anything. I mean, I've read the lyrics off the lyric sheet, and I've got a hint of what they mean. I think they're really good. I think there are plans for a lyric sheet to surface one of these days. I haven't paid much attention, so I don't know.

CA: Are there actually printed ones for the band?

CN: Yeah, yeah. We have to print some for the publishing company, so they can be copyrighted and all that. They're out there somewhere.

CA: But you're planning to release them as an official thing for your fans or for records or something?

CN: Yeah, maybe our next single is going to come with a lyric sheet for the album. [*The "Lithium" CD single insert —Ed.*]

CA: What are some ideas the band has for the next album?

CN: Well, we're kicking around a lot of ideas, you know. Nothing's really concrete. I mean, there's some songs we got and some production. We have some perspectives on production, but nothing's really concrete. Never mind, I don't know. Right now, we're just kind of kicking back and not doing anything. Next month, we're all going to get together and start writing songs. There's some songs already written. We're just going to start making some noise and see what comes out of it.

CA: Is there any symbolism in your videos? For example, "Come as You Are?"

CN: Yeah, yeah. There's symbolism in there, but that's also . . .

CA: Open-ended?

CN: Yeah, I mean, it's the old artistic cliché, "It's open for interpretation." But I remember coming up with the imagery for, say, "Teen Spirit," as an anarchist high school, with the cheerleaders dressed in black and with anarchy A's on their costumes. It's kind of a weird image, since high school is so regimented and controlled, you know. And then, you have a concept of anarchy where there's really no control and no rules because in high school there's unwritten rules of social behavior and accepting people. There's written rules, of course. You know, school rules. You've got to be in class on time. You can't be tardy. To have an image like that, with the anarchy symbols, was just a statement, really. We can divulge into it, you know.

CA: The lyrics themselves, it's hard to match them with the video. Would you say that maybe the lyrics and the videos would be two separate things, or do they coincide?

CN: They can be, in every case, yeah. A lot of times, maybe a song has a feel to it. I don't write the lyrics, so a lot of times I feel like the lyrics accent the feel of the song, as maybe a video should, too. "Come as You Are" is kind of a laid-back tune. It's got a lot of weird chorus on the guitar. Maybe you get . . .

CA: Sort of a haunting effect.

CN: Yeah, haunting. You see colors like purple and magenta and what are used in the video.

CA: Like a very dark atmosphere.

CN: Yeah, yeah.

CA: Do you consider yourselves above playing parties and college dorms?

CN: No, never ever. I mean, we don't consider ourselves above anything, because once you start doing that, you're not really thinking clearly. You're being wrapped up and swept away in something that's probably not that healthy for yourself or for other people.

CA: Have you or will you play small gigs or whatever, since you're signed up with . . .

CN: Yeah, because those are the best. You get to share more things with people than just being isolated from them. Being behind a barrier or somebody else is in the back of the stadium. It's pretty far away and seems kind of impersonal. But if we were to announce that we were going to play at the Vogue . . .

CA: Big riot, probably.

CN: It'd be insane, so it's really not our fault that we can't play small places. We kind of have to just sneak in and do it.

CA: Have you done that? Have you shown up unexpectedly into some club?

CN: Not yet, but I'd like to, sure. [*In late 1992 Nirvana did in fact play several unannounced guest slots at shows in Washington State —Ed.*]

CA: What's the deal with that nameless song at the end of *Nevermind*?

CN: Oh, that song. Well, that song, the guitar got smashed in the recording of that song. We were just screwing around with that. There's really no name for that song. CDs are kind of a new format, and we thought we'd screw around with it, like the Beatles put an extra groove at the end of their record with some gibberish or something. We thought we'd put ten minutes of gibberish or a song. There's something to be said for songs like that, too, because it is a song even though it was improvisational, but there was some structure to it. There was some parameters we worked in, but we just kind of got on it like a roller coaster and just saw where it took us.

CA: What do you think about Tori Amos and Weird Al Yankovic doing covers of your songs?

CN: Well, Tori Amos is pretty funny.

CA: I haven't heard that, but I've seen a video for her style of music.

CN: I'll play it for you.

CA: I can't picture her playing "Teen Spirit."

CN: It's a lot like Kate Bush. I don't know. It just sounds pretty funny. Sounds like it'd be a parody, a better parody than Weird Al.

CA: Did she do it as a joke?

CN: No, she's really serious about it. She wants to express herself in that way. I mean, that's fine.

CA: You guys gave her the permission to use that song?

CN: No, she just did it. I mean, she did it legally. There's certain ways you do it legally. You just have to pay what's prescribed legally. You have to pay the publishing and list the writers and publishing company and all that, or credit the writers. I don't know. She just did it, and whatever.

CA: What about—

CN: Weird Al's hilarious.

CA: Yeah, I saw the video a day or two after it premiered. It was a really great parody.

CN: I was really freaked out because a friend saw them film it down in L.A. He goes, "Man, they're having these cows and these sheep around there." And I go, "Oh, man, they're going to make us look like just total jerks. I mean, they're going to take the piss out of us."

CA: I saw it. It was hysterical. It was really good. It was really, really, really good.

CN: The thing I like about it as a video is it's like watching "Eat It" for the first time or "Fat." It's a perfect parody. It exaggerates upon some of the things that most would take seriously.

CA: Yeah, it was hilarious. All right, that's all the questions we could think of about the band. Here's some about your own personal opinions. Current events: What do you think of the Rodney King trial and the protest related to it?

CN: Oh, wow. Well, the protest is fine, and all that rioting. The riot has always been with us. It's been within our minds, and it's been within the minds of the African American community in Los Angeles. It just took something like that for it to materialize. I mean, the emotions are going to subside. The emotions of rage and the reactions that came along with it, but the deeper things of racism and economic injustices, I mean, these are real problems, and I don't think that elected representatives have really been addressing it. They've just been kind of sweeping it under the rug. For something like this to surface, it's not really a surprise.

CA: Do you think the looting of stores and the damaging of property is a result of the riots, the protests, or the verdict itself?

CN: Well, it grew out of a protest, but, I mean, there's so many implications. The people are poor. They've just been having all these hard times economically. Especially if you live in a city like Los Angeles, where you walk down the streets poor and there's all these Mercedes and Jaguars driving by and you look up all in the hills all around town, and there's multimillionaires living up there. And a lot of the people who have millions of dollars worked really hard for that. A lot happened, and a lot of the people that perpetuated all that violence and looting were nothing short of thieves and thugs taking advantage of that situation. Because it was just a reaction. What were they thinking about accomplishing by smashing in a fellow black person's business and cleaning them out and ruining their lives? Korean people just grabbing innocent white people and beating them like that. That's just reactionary. It's not really thinking. It was an insurrection, but it was so unorganized. There was no vision or focus. It was asinine and stupid. It was a waste of time, and it was really detrimental to anything positive that's going to come out of it.

CA: This is quite off the subject and a divisive issue. How do you feel about abortion?

CN: Well, if I was really confronted with the option, I'm not going to say what I'd do, but I've seen what's become of abortions. It seems like a pretty gruesome thing. There's so many variations to consider in other people's situations. A woman's situation, I think a woman, it's her body and she—and the person responsible for the pregnancy—they should weigh their options. I believe in a lot of civil liberties, like gun control. I don't really think people should be like, "People shouldn't be allowed to own guns, even though I don't own a gun and I never will because I don't like them." But I think people should be responsible for their own actions. I hope you understand how I relate that to the whole abortion thing. It's like a person's own choice. A lot of these girls are just confused, and they're getting pregnant in high school. I guess they can give up the kid for adoption, but most of them don't. Most of them keep the child. My brother had a kid. He's having a lot of problems now. It could have been an abortion. The problem could have been over, but then again—I like that little kid. He's a neat, neat baby. The government's just putting their fingers in so many things, and they're completely ignoring other things. I don't have the capacity to carry around a child for nine months, so I don't think my opinion is as relevant as 50 percent of the human race's is.

CA: Yeah. Last time I talked to you, I found out that you are of Croatian descent and that you lived in Croatia for a year. How old were you at that time?

CN: I was fifteen or sixteen years old.

CA: What was life like in Croatia?

CN: Oh, it was very nice. People were really down to earth. School was a real experience. School was really serious there. Education, you have to study a lot. You have a lot more courses you have to take. It was economically not as advanced as the West. It was more third-world-like, but there were inklings of Western culture all over. It was a pretty neat place. People seemed like they had a pretty cool disposition. Then, economically, things went down the tubes. People started grabbing for things and pointing fingers. Lines were drawn along ethnic lines, just like we've seen in Los Angeles and around the country in the last few days. People started reacting instead of acting. Next thing you know, ten thousand people were killed and countless others injured and maimed. Injured emotionally from the loss of their previous lives and loved ones. It gets pretty discouraging what's going on. I've always believed in the saying "What's the value of preaching if man isn't redeemable?" That's always kept me going.

CA: This is kind of back to the band: Do you think success has or will change you?

CN: Well, it's changed things, but I don't know if it's changed me. I don't think it has, because I've been ignoring it and denying it so much. People coming up and asking for autographs, or pointing at me, or staring at me, or whispering about me in a safe way. I'm getting used to that, but I think me going out there instead of hiding away will kind of dispel all that cult of celebrity.

CA: Like Elvis secluding himself in Graceland.

CN: Yeah, yeah, I mean, I don't want to participate in that. I mean, financially it's changed things for me, but I just kind of deal with it, really. I don't want it to change me to where I have to hide out or be like Michael Jackson or wear a disguise. Because I'll just out and go anywhere, go skateboarding around, walking around.

CA: Would the band go on if either you or Kurt decided to leave?

CN: Just depends on what terms we left on. Because you see a certain chemistry there in some bands where just a few of the members happen to be the center of the group because they're usually the founders of the group. No, yeah, I don't know. Kurt's kind of the main guru of the band, but he's the last one to admit that. We all have a stake in the band. I think if Dave was to leave the band, I think the band would break up because we'd never go through that thing of finding another drummer. Yeah, I mean, it's hard to say. Depends on the situation because that's such a broad question.

CA: Do you like my mom's baklava?

CN: Yeah, it's really good. It's nice. Nice flaky crust. It's really good.

CA: That was basically my last question.

CN: Oh, OK.

CA: Also, can we take a tour of your house?

CN: OK. What do you want to see?

CA: *Cyrus . . . The TV Show* watchers don't care what they see, really.

CN: I don't want to show people my house, man. They'll come rip it off!

"WE WERE THE CHOSEN REJECTS"

Kenan Seeberg | June 26, 1992 | Danmarks Radio (Denmark)

In the summer of 1992 I was asked to cohost Danmarks Radio's coverage of that year's Roskilde Festival and do most of the interviews with the international and local bands attending. Among them was Nirvana, the main attraction on Friday night, June 26. Earlier that night Denmark's soccer team played against Germany in the European Championship final. Just before the interview took place, Denmark won sensationally by 2-0—hence the crowd singing soccer chants in the background. The interview had been postponed twice before it took place. Kurt Cobain wasn't ready and needed "to rest," we were told. Many years later I was told that he needed a fix of heroin, which was apparently secured somewhere backstage at the Roskilde Festival.

I arrived with my crew and met Krist Novoselic and Dave Grohl, and we sat at the back of the main Canopy stage, at which they performed later that evening. They were quite forthcoming and relaxed, and told me that Kurt would be there soon. As he arrived I noticed that his hair was shorter, which I mentioned in my first question to him. I had been warned that the band members could be "difficult" and even hostile to reporters, but although I detected a slight skepticism in the beginning, they soon did their best to answer my questions during the interview, which unfortunately wasn't the most well-prepared one of my career. I recall the meeting as a most pleasant experience with three honest guys really trying to do their best and be polite to this Danish guy, who clearly was on a high because Denmark had won the European soccer final. This fortunately spawned the questions about their own relationship—or lack of one—with sports, and their depiction of themselves as the "chosen rejects" who never strived to be part of the "popular crowd" at school. Today I am proud of the fact that I'm the only Danish reporter to ever have interviewed these guys who changed the landscape of rock, and that I met a sorely missed legend who burned so strong, gave so much, and still shines so bright. —Kenan Seeberg

Everyone in Roskilde wanted to watch Denmark in the European Championship final on the big screens set up on the stage, so Nirvana agreed to go on one or two hours late. I was commissioned by Geffen's Danish subsidiary to photograph the band receiving gold records for *Nevermind*'s Danish sales. They arranged for a handover ceremony right before the concert. Backstage, however, I was told nobody from the company or management could promise who would turn up. I think they were afraid that the delay meant the band had too much time to get drunk or stoned; at the last minute I was told Kurt wouldn't be coming. Imagine, though, in the meantime the final ended and Denmark had won! The crowds were going crazy by the main stage! When the time came for the gold record ceremony, everyone stood around nervously . . . and suddenly Nirvana appeared. Kurt came straight up to me, shook my hand, and congratulated me on Denmark's victory—he even made some comments about the game, which the band obviously had watched. I've always liked the idea that I received Kurt's greeting on behalf of all Danes. —Søren Rud, Geffen's photographer at the Roskilde Festival

Kurt Cobain: Morning.

Dave Grohl: [*Humorous voice*] Good morning to you.

Kenan Seeberg: Good morning to you, man, hello. My name is Kenan.

KC: Hi Kenan, I'm Kurt.

KS: Hi Kurt. I hardly recognized you because you've had a haircut since I've seen you last.

KC: Yeah? It's summertime; I like to shed my skin in the summer.

KS: Why don't you shave it all, then?

KC: I don't know. I really don't know. I'm not into sculpting my head like a hedge . . .

DG: Like Right Said Fred.

KC: Right Said Fred! [*Chuckles.*]

KS: I hear you've been sleeping until now?

KC: [*Nods vigorously*] I've slept all day. I was up very late last night with my friend Roddy Bottum from Faith No More. He was showing me some new keyboard maneuvers.
[*Interview breaks to video clip of Nirvana performing "Lithium" and cuts back as Krist joins them —Ed.*]

KC: Most people usually don't sit down and have a discussion on how their band should be before they start playing. They usually get together with whatever equipment they can muster up and play, and whatever comes out comes out. You can't decide on exactly what you want to be before you play—it's usually a natural thing.

KS: So when you write a song, do you write a song on an acoustic guitar or piano, or do you meet in the rehearsal room?

KC: No, sometimes we write it on an acoustic guitar, sometimes we write it on a flute or an electric guitar. It doesn't really matter—any instrument that's laying around.

KS: Do you do it together or . . . separate?

KC: I come up with the basic idea of the song usually, the guitar part. Then we get together and play it over and over again. We decide on how long it should be played and all that stuff.

KS: And what about the lyrics, then?

KC: I usually come up with all the lyrics.

KS: Do you do it before or after the music? [*Drowned out by panpipes and bongos on the stage over the band's shoulders.*]

KC: Pardon?

KS: Do you do it before or after the music?

KC: Usually after.

KS: After the music?

KC: Yep.
[*Breaks to Nirvana performing "On a Plain" —Ed.*]

KC: We were the chosen rejects; we chose not to be part of the popular crowd. I mean, I can remember a lot of times when the more [*using air quotes*] popular people, the jock-type of people who were into sports and staying clean and brushing their teeth all the time and doing what their parents were asking them to do, they always asked me if I wanted to join their little club, and I decided not to. I would rather hang out with the people who didn't get picked for the baseball team and who smoked cigarettes and listened to rock 'n' roll music.

Krist Novoselic: Skipped class, y'know . . .

KS: Why did you go to school anyway at the first time?

KN: Because you have to.

DG: For lunch.

KC: Yeah, the hot lunch.
[*Breaks to Nirvana performing "Sliver" —Ed.*]

KN: There was kind of a little scene, and just all the people who just kind of didn't fit in and liked punk rock music kind of congregated, and we just had our parties and we wore, like, thrift store clothes, and we did our own thing and . . . That's when we discovered punk rock, and I know that's when I discovered there was nothing wrong with me, it was the majority of people in town; there's something wrong with them, they were really closed-minded, and I just could not get along with them. They were just so rigid in their perspective [*imitates horse blinders to emphasize point*], just totally closed minds. It was stuffy.

KS: So all three of you are the ones who the other kids didn't want to play with? Forbidden by the parents or . . . ?

KC: Well, we didn't want to play with those kids either. Really. We could have if we wanted to. And stayed well groomed.

KN: It was impossible because we had a different perspective than them, and a lot of times we would meet somebody, like, try to turn them on to, "Here man, this is the Dead Kennedys!" or "This is Black Flag!" [*proffers hands in a vinyl-wide gesture*], and it was just "Oh, ugh, you're weird!" They were just so closed-minded that we were just dismissed as freaks, y'know?

[*Breaks to Nirvana performing the finale of "Lithium"* —*Ed.*]

"RAW, WILD, AND CONFUSING"

Lars Aldman | June 30, 1992 | SVT *PM Intensiven* (Sweden)

I had actually met Krist Novoselic a couple of days before, at the Roskilde Festival, and found him really cool and social. We had a few laughs and beers and said farewell with a "See you in Stockholm!" But up until the minute my cameraman had mounted his gear and we stood waiting by a beautiful canal in the Stockholm park Djurgården, I was unsure about whether the interview would take place at all. I was especially unsure about who would show up for the interview. Krist, probably; Dave, possibly. Kurt? I couldn't hope for it. Rumors said he was unstable and unreliable. I was the only journalist granted an interview that day.

But when at last they came strolling under the park trees to the canal, there were—yes!—three of them! Kurt was hiding his face under a hood attached to a jacket with a sort of map pattern. It looked like a ski jacket. We shook hands and sat down.

Suddenly, I was extremely nervous, which seldom happened to me. I had been a music journalist for more than ten years and had met quite a few weird and reputedly difficult guys, like Blixa Bargeld, Nick Cave, Greg Dulli, and Bobby Gillespie. My respect for Kurt Cobain was so intense that I felt like a school magazine reporter. However, the warm gentleness that Krist radiated soon calmed my nerves, and we got along really well in the sunshine by the oily water of the canal. Kurt revealed a sincere and thoughtful side that day, but there was a bit of sadness and pain in his voice too.

Afterward I had this great feeling of having been part of something unique and spectacular. I phoned Swedish Television's news desk and told them I could supply them with a fresh interview with the band that sold more records than Michael Jackson. They didn't believe me and said no thanks. And with that reaction I felt like a rebel, fighting a rebel's cause. —Lars Aldman

Translation of Lars's voiceovers by Jonas Sorensson.

Lars Aldman: [*Voiceover*] Heroes, Nirvana, from the super-hip city of Seattle in the United States, have had a tough and exhausting summer that resulted in Cobain losing his voice due to exhaustion. By now he's collapsed on another couple of occasions and has a bleeding ulcer after having toured every festival in Europe. This means no more jumping around on the stage smashing instruments—from now on it will be about the music. They may feel a little tired and disillusioned by all the hysteria and attention now.

Krist Novoselic: We got a lot of attention, y'know what I mean? Lot of . . . "Teen Spirit" was kind of played into the ground. Kinda made me feel a little self-conscious, y'know? [*Turns to Kurt and Dave.*] What do you guys think of the hysteria?

Kurt Cobain: [*Hums dramatically*] Ohhhhhh . . . It's a load of shit. I think, I think there are at least ten to fifteen other bands who are just as good, if not better, than us—and they deserve just as much attention as we do . . . if they choose to take that attention, if they want it. [*Breaks to Nirvana's "Lithium" video —Ed.*]

KN: I wish we would have thrown a bomb in the music business, and they all would have been at least dismembered but, I dunno, it was more like a firecracker, Ladyfinger—"POP!" [*Breaks to the "Lithium" clip —Ed.*]

KN: What we're doing is nothing new; it's just that our band happened to penetrate into the mainstream.

KC: Yeah. So mainstream kids now are realizing the fact that they can start bands. I think that's very good; it's very nice and flattering that we helped aid something like that. But, um, I dunno, that ideal has always been around in the underground. [*Breaks to Nirvana's "Come as You Are" video —Ed.*]

LA: Is it fun to be famous?

KN: Uhh . . . not if . . . not if you're walking down the street.

Dave Grohl: Not when people recognize you, and you can't have a moment's . . . the people are waiting in the lobby of your hotel and constantly asking you for your signature, which still baffles me; I don't understand the autograph concept at all.

KN: It can be a burden, y'know? To be . . . to be wanting to be famous, y'know? Kind of vain, really, when you think about it: "Everybody look at me!" Y'know? It's like "Yeugh." It'll pass someday, y'know?

KC: Most people who are really famous end up staying in their hotel rooms all the time. [*Krist shakes head: "Yeah."*] Total reclusives and they don't do anything. That sucks.
[*Breaks to Nirvana's "Smells Like Teen Spirit" video —Ed.*]

LA: There's all sorts of rumors going on about how your next album will sound. Some people say it's going to be really wild, raw, and confusing; some say it's going to be really quiet and acoustic and pretty.

KC: Both. A mixture of both.

LA: Yeah?

KC: Yeah. [*Nods emphatically, smiles.*] It won't be as clean as the last album—that's for sure.

KN: That's a good album cover [*shakes head*] or name. Our next album, [*Dave talks at the same time: "Raw, Wild, and Confusing". . .*] "Raw Wild!" Now if our next record is that name you're gonna go, "Shiiiiiiit . . ." You're gonna go, "Those guys, man . . . " Raw, Wild, and Confusing— we're going to be on the cover going [*flexes right bicep while pretending to roar*] . . . No! One of us is gonna look raw, he's gonna be naked. One of us is gonna look wild with a loincloth and like a wild man. One of us is gonna look really confused. Raw, Wild, and Confusing . . .

LA: [*Voiceover on footage of Nirvana performing in Stockholm —Ed.*] That's right. Nirvana is in the studio working on the follow-up album to *Nevermind*, which they themselves find too polished and easygoing. The new album will blow away all speculations that Nirvana is finished. It will bite.

KC: I have a feeling with the next record we're gonna lose a lot of our audience.

"THERE ARE THINGS THAT YOU CAN'T TURN DOWN"

Rafa Cervera | July 2, 1992 | *Ruta 66* (Spain)

The backlash had begun. Cobain's notable absence, his mercurial pronouncements, the visible evidence that he was "challenged pharmaceutically"—it all led to a change in the media's perspective for the simple reason that they were doing their jobs and trying to find out what was true. The tour of the summer festivals had to go ahead; the money was too big to turn down, and they formed the only major interruption in many months of silence. Rumors of rifts and relationship issues within the group are tackled head-on in this piece catching the band in Spain. —Ed.

Translated by Kaye Soulsby and Javier Lahuerta.

She's a Bonus

Dave and Krist do the soundcheck in the square by themselves shortly before lunchtime. Dave has rented a motorbike so he can run around the arena to kill time. There's no news of Kurt until late afternoon. That's when we see him on stage, playing drums while Courtney tests out the guitar. Once everything is ready for the concert, and before dinner, they jam together.

Lennon had Yoko; Lou Reed had Sylvia Morales. Kurt Cobain, spokesman for Nirvana, the Beatles of Punk, has Courtney Love, and she sure has him. I don't know how to say it without feeling like a punk

Jesús Mariñas [*a famed Spanish gossip columnist —Ed.*], but there's the slight impression that this woman controls the singer and that the estrangement between the two parts of the group has something to do with this.

But Kurt Cobain is no moron. Shortly before the concert he can be seen in the backstage area, appearing to be fighting confusion, looking slightly crushed by a weight that haunts him but that he must master. As he wanders around looking for the bathroom, maybe there's a chance to engage with him. Then the words of a journalist from *NME* come to mind; he said that "Kurt Cobain pounced on the next person to ask for a photo." Uh, well, let's allow him to piss quietly. The night before, as he was the only one around, I'd asked Novoselic—who also doesn't like these things—if he would give me a few minutes the next day (his record label had categorically ruled out any possibility of this), and the lanky one said "sure."

When I approach Krist to remind him of our commitment, he's eating a plate of salad while visually savoring some records—Stiv Bators and Dead Boys mostly—which he discovered in a nearby store. "Sure," he answers. Smells like a joke, I know, but he points to a row of chairs suggesting we talk there in about an hour. In case he forgets, I agree and grab a chair standing near there. After this game, I turn my head to where the bassist sits. He understands the gesture and motions for me to go with him.

We climb to the highest tier above the square and sit on the floor with a view over the tame bulls' enclosure, Krist with a cup of hot tea and me with the tape recorder. The lowing of cattle and the church bells add their chorus to his words.

A Mystical Talk with Mr. Novoselic

He is tall, very thin with an endearing face, and behaves shyly. He's wearing frayed pants and a grubby shirt. He looks comfortable, however, to be interviewed by someone who isn't dying to launch ignorant attacks on modern rock's latest sensation, nor will be asking if he's buddies with Guns N' Roses. When he finishes talking over the last point of our conversation, he stands up, slaps his butt to shake off the dust from the ground, and says, "Great!"

Rafa Cervera: Nirvana was one of the favored underground bands; now suddenly you become an overwhelming sensation selling millions of records. This leads to tremendous pressure, right?

Chris Novoselic: Yeah, it's been a huge pressure on us . . . but there comes a time when suddenly you decide to move on. The root of all this is the music we do, and that is still something that comes exclusively from inside us. Once we'd got our heads together and gotten our positions straight it was different. Personally, I think I feel much better now. I can be a lot more relaxed about things, you know? [*Laughs.*] The truth is that there are certain things I give a damn about and, on the other hand, situations emerge whether I like it or not. I'm not willing to get involved in everything that's happening around us; that side of rock 'n' roll is pretty stupid anyway.

RC: Perhaps that's the result of mental and physical exhaustion, tours, interviews . . .

CN: Uuuuuuhhh. No, I'm not tired at all, I simply have to . . . everything you do has to be satisfying; you have to manage to bring out the best in yourself. We always have to give the best of ourselves. It's a challenge and that's that. I'm grateful for everything that has happened to us over these past few months, as well as the position I'm in personally thanks to these events.

RC: Well, being in a rock band with punk ethics who have also become millionaires must have a bright side . . .

CN: There are things that you can't turn down. Touring, giving interviews, doing promotion. What I appreciate most of all is that this time we've had direct and privileged access to the media. Our music is still the same, but the media are introducing us to a lot of people now; that allows us to expose our ideas and views to a huge audience. Today I can communicate with a lot of people on a lot of topics, something that was impossible before.

RC: As an individual, to what extent has your life changed?

CN: As I didn't want to be a celebrity, my private life hasn't changed, at least not greatly. Materially I have a much more comfortable existence. I can see other places; I can do things that a year ago I would never have imagined. Look, I'm here now, in a square by the bullring in Valencia. It's incredible—and also I don't have to work!

RC: What do you recall about the days of Sub Pop, the time of *Bleach*?

CN: For a long time we were stuck in a corner, about to take off, but never did. We had a lot of promise. Now our fans have quintupled. A very big thing happened to Nirvana, the biggest thing that can happen to a rock band. We're like buds that have blossomed; we've grown, things have become more grounded. All that's left is to find out where we'll go after all this.

RC: Then, when you abandoned Sub Pop, you became convinced you had to get rid of all that?

CN: No, not at all. When we were on Sub Pop we got used to the lack of options on an independent label. All these challenges, the lack of cash, being independent and small, can strangle your infrastructure, you know what I mean? There was no future, so we looked for a major label because we were fed up with the poor distribution of our albums; we wanted stability. The whole world around us told us that what we were going to do was dumb; but now we have absolute control over what we do.

RC: What's clear is that this has encouraged many multinationals to bring alternative rock bands onboard.

CN: Yeah, it seems there's a lot of change in that area. Large companies are getting out their checkbooks to catch the independent bands. It's inevitable; certain things contribute to other things happening. They've reflected on the state of music, and they've made a great discovery. At last they're aware of what's been cooking for years on independent labels; now they want to bring that music to the surface. As a result, the independent or alternative label is meaningless.

RC: But that perhaps has paved the way for a number of groups who make good music.

CN: Perhaps. It's too early to judge what's going on with all these changes. You need some perspective to know if this will help change something, some value, or some market rule. What I do know is that all these bands are different to the conventional pop product; they've got nothing to do with the prototype of album-oriented rock, or with all those heavy metal bands. People want genuine rock 'n' roll, which reinvents itself all the time. It's natural with any art form. It's the fate of the planet, the forces that make the continents drift, day become night, people getting older, sea change. Everything's got to change.

RC: Do you believe that rock music has any tangible existence after Sonic Youth?

CN: Sure. It comes down to how record executives begin to change their methods, their way of seeing things. They wonder, What the hell are all these new bands? What the hell is happening? It's hard to retrain that kind of thinking. It takes a long time. You and I have always known who Sonic Youth were, even five or six years ago when they were an underground band. In the prestigious mainstream circuit, nobody had the slightest idea they existed. There's always been that part of the market throughout rock history. Everyone knew who the Rolling Stones were, but at the same time ignored the Stooges, Seeds, New York Dolls. There were no alternative bands. Something similar happens each time something new and different starts to slowly enter the mainstream pop circuit. It was unthinkable just three or four years ago.

RC: What will the next Nirvana album sound like?

CN: It'll be different from *Nevermind*—it's a kind of small challenge for us. *Nevermind* has been a success because of the circumstances; we delivered it to DGC and told them to take it or leave it. I'm hoping the next LP doesn't have quite the same success. You may not like it compared to *Nevermind*; it'll be harder, rockier, wilder . . .

RC: It seems that you've found the ideal drummer with Dave Grohl.

CN: We had many drummers before Dave. It's true that they came and went, but . . . Dave is perfect. He's totally tuned into Nirvana. He has it all: the energy, the style, the mind-set.

RC: Kurt said in an interview that, to preserve the good relationship between you, he's decided to keep his personal life a little more separate from you two . . .

CN: Success has had a negative influence on us, but not in that sense. We're stressed; it's made us all anxious. But our ethics meant we could see that we'd become a part of the mainstream. We're just working-class guys, though, and we're not suddenly going to start loving the people who ignored us before all this happened. Fuck that. We're not going to become materialistic and screwed up. Nothing will change my mind. I'm really sure about that.

RC: Are you going to carry on with this policy of supporting bands you like?

CN: We always do what we like, and presenting new bands to the public is part of it. I don't think the bands that we love the most are the ones best positioned to achieve success, but if you notice, they're groups with songs that are easy to listen to. I'm talking about people like Shonen Knife or Captain America. But every time I see the Top Ten on MTV I still see the same old shit. No, I don't think it's that easy to make an impact.

RC: How is your relationship with DGC?

CN: We sell a lot of records so they leave us alone; we can do whatever we want. I just couldn't give a shit about anything related to the business; I'm just not interested in the corporate executives, or their politics, or their campaigns. It's crap, I don't like it, but it's not my business. At first I worried about it, but as it made me feel so bad, I decided to step away from it.

RC: What do you think about the sociopolitical situation in the United States, the race riots, Bush . . . ?

CN: The Rodney King case was the straw that broke the camel's back. That's the incident that made it happen, but these riots have been going on for years in people's minds. Anger, hatred, and fear are there, they still exist, but they've gone back inside the bottle. American values are too reliant on materialism. From children who are obsessed with TV, purchasing power, and taking themselves too seriously. We're not on this planet very long, not long enough to let us wrap everything in plastic, glass, steel, and all that consumerist materialism. People are ignorant, insecure, living by these dogmatic ideologies, hairstyles, clothes. Any change scares them. And changes are natural, continents change, night becomes day . . . that's just a normal transition because it's a fact that we never have the same face.

RC: And do you feel you are being sucked into the cycle of consumption?

CN: Imagine it: six or seven million of your records worldwide. It's amazing; I don't know what to think. Everyone has their own way to approach it, everyone has a natural inclination toward the melodies . . . I could be cynical and say that I don't care, but it's not true.

RC: What about all the lawsuits that have come raining down on you recently?

CN: Rubbish, crap, parasites . . . the karmic wheel always moves on, thankfully.

"EVERY BATH IS . . . AN EXPERIENCE IN ITSELF. LIFE OR DEATH."

August 30, 1992 | ITV *Raw Power* (UK)

Raw Power was a UK music show that aired from 1990 to 1993 (then from 1994 to 1995 as *Noisy Mothers*). The show was developed by Music Box (now a part of Sunset + Vine) for the British network ITV. The interview with Nirvana took place on the day of the band's performance at the Reading Festival in the incongruous setting of a bathroom, with Dave Grohl soaping himself down in the tub while Krist Novoselic sat comfortably on the toilet and Kurt Cobain perched on the side of the tub. It's safe to say this was one of the band's more offbeat interviews but very much in line with their more humorous outings.

Even in this strange setting the band's regular traits are on display: Krist leads the band's contributions with his usual cheery humor. Kurt sits back and lets his friend take the strain, choosing when he feels like interjecting. Dave remains in the background; then, when speaking, he barely pauses. His sentences run together, and he blurts out everything rapidly as if he fears interruption. This was the band at the peak of their fame, laughing at it. —Ed.

[*Studio introduction*] **Ann Kirk:** Next up, one of the weirdest, shortest, and cleanest interviews we've ever done—it's Nirvana in the bath, and don't expect any sense from them at all.
[*Clip of the "Smells Like Teen Spirit" video —Ed.*]

Krist Novoselic: Hi! Welcome to Bathrooms Today. Today I'm sitting on a beautiful porcelain can . . . [*Dave while scrubbing himself: "American*

Standard . . ."] American Standard! With matching bathtub. Notice the lovely brown and white striped decor in today's most modern, appealing type . . . furnishings.

Kurt Cobain: [*Interrupting, handing over a cigarette butt*] Could you give up furnishings to dispose of this? [*Krist takes a drag.*]

Dave Grohl: You can throw it in the bath.
[*Clip of "Smells Like Teen Spirit" —Ed.*]

DG: Well! You know, one time, a band I was in before Nirvana played in Spain. I had a fever, and upstairs at the club right after we got done playing, I went up and I drew this really hot bath, and it was so steaming hot and I had such a high fever that I took this bath and then I got out of the bath and I had welts on my forehead I was so hot. And that was it. [*Krist pours water over Dave's head and "Smells Like Teen Spirit" returns —Ed.*]

DG: I teeter a radio right there, right on the edge, and I put like two-ounce weights here and an ounce weight there, and I sort of make it so [*balancing weights on an imaginary radio with his hands*] every bath is . . . an experience in itself. Life or death.

KN: Living on the edge, the edge of the bathtub.

DG: Kinda like having all this electrical equipment in the bath . . . [*Indicating the TV recording equipment out of shot.*]
[*Clip of "Come as You Are" video —Ed.*]

KN: This rock 'n' roll is an international language.

KC: Ooo! [*Chuckles.*]

KN: Being the age of communication. (DG: Ding-ding-ding-ding-ding . . .)

KC: [*To Dave*] Are these the socks you got on the airplane? [*Krist busies himself simulating an uncomfortable toilet experience.*]

DG: Yeah, I've been wearing them ever since.

KC: [*Sniffs sock and passes it to Krist.*] Hey, you want to wipe with this?

DG: No—not my sock! [*Krist mops his brow with it before tossing it on the floor.*]

COBAIN CLIP

Courtney Love Gets Herself into Trouble in *Vanity Fair*

"I heard a rumor that Madonna and I were shooting heroin together," she says rather gleefully, lighting up a cigarette. "I've heard I had live sex onstage and that I'm HIV-positive."

Courtney laughs. None of these statements is true, although the live-sex thing is a very persistent rumor. "Now," she continues, balancing her cigarette on the edge of the ashtray, "I get a chance to prove myself. And if I do, I do. If I don't—hey, I married a rich man!"

She drags for dramatic effect. She's joking and, then again, she isn't. Audacity is one of the keys to her charm. "You know, I just can't find makeup that stays on in the summer," she says, abruptly changing the subject. Courtney stamps out her cigarette. . . .

"Just call me Yoko Love," she says. "KU'-RT." Kurt curls up with the phone, and Courtney plops down on a legless sofa. She is wearing a green flowered dress that's ripped along the bodice so that her bra is exposed. "They all hate me," she says. "Everyone just fucking hates my guts."

—from "Strange Love" by Lynn Hirschberg, *Vanity Fair* (US), September 1992

GRUNGE IS DEAD

Jim Crotty and Michael Lane | September 11, 1992 | *Monk* (US)

September 11, 1992—Kurt Cobain is deep inside his "hiding from the press" phase. It's only Nirvana's third show on the US mainland that year, and journalists are knocking down the door to get access to the man at the center of it all. He doesn't care. He's alone in a dressing room with his three-week-old daughter, and the one interview request he accepts is *Monk* magazine. It's fair to say we were surprised and honored. Mike and I joined Kurt for a long and cheerful chat in which he moved effortlessly between truth and myth-making about his life. It summed up the guy. We enjoyed his company, but it was always clear this was someone riven with contradictions—the anticelebrity who enjoyed using the power fame gave; the man cussing and praising his fortune simultaneously. The show itself was . . . uncomfortable. The band looked static—devoid of their sparky luster. Backstage, though, we enjoyed the glorious sight of Courtney holding court to all and sundry about "that bitch" Lynn Hirschberg and her (essentially true) report about the couple's lives and habits—while regularly demanding psilocybin 'shrooms from Novoselic. That fragile man in the dressing room was cocooned somewhere inside this weird world. —Jim Crotty and Michael Lane

In a quiet room off of Eban Ritchie's Suite at the Hotel Sorrento, Kurt Cobain lovingly holds his baby, Frances Bean Cobain. He sits on a couch, sweat beading on his face. He looks fragile, sensitive and intense. He stares right at me when I talk. It's the Kurt Cobain stare that is checking out my authenticity.

Jim Crotty: Tell me about Aberdeen. That's where you grew up, right?

Kurt Cobain: Aberdeen, it's a coastal town about 100 miles away from Seattle. It's a really small place. A very small community with a lot of people who have very small minds. Basically if you're not prepared to join the logging industry, you're going to be beaten up or run out of town.

JC: And that's what happened to you?

KC: Yea, I was run out of town. They chased me up to the castle of Aberdeen with torches. Just like the Frankenstein monster. And I got away in a hot air balloon. And I came here to Seattle.

JC: Is this metaphor or literal reality?

KC: It's a wet dream.

JC: Was there an incident that really pushed the button that got you and the town at loggerheads, as it were?

KC: Well, what started the witch hunt was I decided to take some acid one evening and spray paint "queer" on the side of four by four trucks, the local rednecks' trucks. And so one of them saw me from his window and started chasing me and started screaming "there's a queer vandal!" I'd been doing it for a while. But that night I decided to really go for it and do a lot, a *lot* of vandalism. So they caught me and chased me around.

JC: The cops caught you or just some of the local toughs?

KC: The locals. The local toughs, right. *He laughs.*

JC: And did they know who you were?

KC: No. Just that crazy skinny kid who never went to school. Who was probably *gay*.

JC: Well, are you?

KC: If I wasn't attracted to Courtney, I'd be a bisexual.

Courtney Love: Faggot!! *Laughter.*

JC: So they ran you out of town?

KC: Yea.

JC: Did you ever go back?

KC: Well, um, every time I've gone to Aberdeen lately I've felt a real big threat. Actually, Chris was beaten up at a Denny's one night. Some locals were giving him the eye and I don't think it was sexual. They started beating him up in the men's room saying "some local hero you are." Next thing he remembers he was dancing on a table.

JC: So you got run out of town because you went up against the logging interests, the logging mentality, of your local town.

KC: I was the guy who screamed "save the spotted owl!" *Kurt smiles.*

JC: You actually did say it one time somewhere?

KC: Yea I did, at school.

JC: At school? And the loggers' sons and daughters came after you with chainsaws?

KC: No, chisels. They weren't advanced.

JC: Okay, so they ran you out, where'd you go first?

KC: I went to Olympia and became a hippie.

JC: You didn't go to Evergreen.

KC: No, I didn't, but I hung out with a lot of friends from there . . .

CL: He couldn't afford it.

KC: I couldn't afford it. I was a janitor.

JC: Where were you a janitor at?

KC: I was a janitor at Lemons Janitorial Service.

JC: Wonderful, wonderful. Looking back at Aberdeen do you have a place that was the quintessential Aberdeen place for you?

KC: The bridge of Aberdeen going over to the south side of Aberdeen. I used to hang out with the bums and share Thunderbird wine with them underneath the bridge.

JC: Would they recognize you if you went back today?

KC: Oh absolutely, if they're still alive. There's a little tent bum community there. They live in tents and just drink wine and roast marshmallows.

JC: And hang out under the bridge.

KC: Yea.

JC: Is there a Seattle scene or is this all a myth?

KC: Yea, but it's in Portland.

JC: The Seattle scene's in Portland?

KC: Yea. *Laughter from Kurt and Jim.* It started with The Wipers in 1977. It's a real dirty, grungy place.

CL: Seattle is one of America's cleanest cities.

KC: Right, there's nothing grungy about it at all. But Portland is extremely grungy. It's a real industrial, grey, dark town.

JC: What do you want to be when you grow up?

KC: A janitor.

JC: Achieve nirvana through janitorial services?

KC: The power of Lysol.

JC: From a janitorial perspective what is grunge?

KC: It's a fine mixture of cleaning solvents, not to be used in the toilet. It doesn't go well with porcelain. When I was a janitor I used to work with these guys Rocky and Bullwinkle. They'd clean the toilet bowls with their bare hands and then eat their lunch without washing their hands. They were very grungy.

JC: From a Kurt Cobain *musical* perspective what is grunge?

KC: A fine mixture of hygiene paraphernalia—bleach, Lysol, bubblegum flavored toothpaste, isopropyl rubbing alcohol 90 percent, hand and body lotion, and conditioning shampoo.

JC: What's your favorite food?

KC: My favorite food is water and rice.

JC: Heard of this band called Nirvana?

KC: Yea, they're English, they're British. They were a hot group from the 60s and we recently had to give them about $200,000 for using their name. And we recently gave a $100,000 to a local Christian band named Nirvana in Orange County. We had to go to court over it. Now we have to call ourselves Nirvana UK anytime we play in LA.

JC: How would you describe Dave Grohl?

KC: Dave is in really good shape although he smokes two packs of cigarettes a day.

JC: Chris Novoselic?

KC: Chris is the horror of the stars. He has no shame whatsoever in carousing with the likes of Winona Ryder and Johnny Depp.

JC: And Kurt Cobain?

KC: Fuck him, he complains too much.

JC: Do you believe in reincarnation?

KC: If you're really a mean person you're going to come back as a fly and eat poop. You'll come back as a fly or Matt Lukin.

JC: What would you title your autobiography?

KC: *I Was Not Thinking*, by Kurt Cobain.

JC: Final messages for the youth of America?

KC: I'm bowing down gracefully and taking off my crown and I'm giving it over to Eddie Vedder of Pearl Jam. He's now the representative of the youth of America.

JC: Is there a changing of the guard now?

KC: Yea.

JC: What caused this, because you're a family man and you're embracing family values?

KC: Because he stole my look . . . And he uses it better than I.

COBAIN CLIP

Defending His Family

"If anything comes out in this book . . . that hurts my wife—I'll fucking hurt you . . . never been more fucking serious in my life . . . I suppose I could throw out a few thousand dollars to, er . . . have you snuffed. But maybe I'll try it the legal way first."
—Voice mails left by Cobain for Victoria Mary Clarke, October 1992, in relation to a planned biography of Nirvana

---

PART IX

October 1992 to January 1993–Nadir

TO SAY THE ARGENTINA EXPERIENCE "strained our humor," as Nirvana does in Buenos Aires, is an understatement. The show is notorious for the band's antagonism toward the audience. On the day of the performance, the bandmates' limited encounters with the media are "business as usual," with Cobain nowhere to be seen. There's no obvious tension, just a relaxed desire to simply perform and head on home. October 31, however, is a different tale. Having upset the local audience and confused the media in attendance, Cobain suddenly is wheeled out for a pair of interviews. A dance occurs. The journalists cautiously query the reasons behind the poor show; Cobain, in turn, downplays it and won't insult his hosts. Cobain displays something close to passive-aggression: polite and courteous, he's clearly perturbed by the show when speaking to *Monk* magazine in November but then spouts bile at the Argentine crowd in the liner notes to *Incesticide* in December.

The *Monk* recording from November captures Cobain still bruised from Argentina; embarrassed about the furor over the leaking of Nirvana's interest in Steve Albini (a man whose name was mentioned in interviews all the way back to April 1989) as producer soon after his collaboration with William S. Burroughs; and quietly mentioning his first encounter with his father in more than half a decade ("I don't know his birthday"). He can't even recall his father's age. Cobain is still generally welcoming company, but all the difficulties of 1992 are piling up and he's opening up his relationship with the press precisely because he needs the support in print.

There are still pleasures, though. He's clearly comfortable and enjoying himself with Jim Crotty and Michael Lane as they goofily run through ideas for the photo shoot–dangling off the Space Needle wins. Cobain finds time to recount a ghost story from a former tour, he accepts the quiet ribbing about his image, he doesn't object to anything he's asked to do. It's a good moment amid bad ones.

In January it starts again. There's a set of questions, all about bad news circulating around the band. Cobain does the lion's share of the press work on this trip, and Nirvana hasn't done a group interview in months. Not one. Grohl and Novoselic might handle things as a pair sometimes, but they've not been joined by their front man since September.

"A LITTLE TRIP DOWN HERE FOR THE WEEKEND"

Jorge Aedo | October 30, 1992 | TVN *Sábado Taquilla* (Chile)

In October 1992, we were invited to cover the Nirvana concert in Buenos Aires, Argentina. We were told we would be permitted to interview the band just before the concert while they were still at their hotel. Ultimately, however, only Krist Novoselic and Dave Grohl joined us—they told us Kurt was sleeping. Still, the result was an enjoyable interview talking about the band and the context of their presence in South America—they even teased me gently. We were then permitted to record the band on stage; we were just a few meters from them as they performed. The results were broadcast in a special episode of *Sábado Taquilla* that fans remember to this day—the ratings were great! Curiously, Nirvana never played "Smells Like Teen Spirit" because of Kurt's anger toward the public for their dismissal of the band Calamity Jane, which he was sponsoring. —Jorge Aedo

Translated by Elitsa Teodarova.

Jorge Aedo: Here is what we have promised you. We will interview two of Nirvana's members while Kurt is off getting ready for his concert here in Buenos Aires. Here are Krist and Dave, two of Nirvana's members joining us tonight for *Sábado Taquilla* on TVN. Hey, how are you?

Dave Grohl: Fine, how are you?

Krist Novoselic: Bien . . .

JA: At what moment is Nirvana right now?

DG: The actual "moment" of Nirvana? Wow, I don't know . . .

KN: Well, it depends on what kind of stimulation we're about to achieve, whether it's through artificial stimulation or genuine orgasmic sensations.

JA: This visit to Buenos Aires is part of Nirvana's tour of South America—is it part of the '92 tour?

DG: No, this is kind of just a little trip down here for the weekend. We're going to do the show, then we're going straight back. It's not really a part of the tour.

JA: After this stay, where are you heading?

KN: Gonna go back home and work in the garden and clean up—vacuum the house.

JA: What's going on with the new album being released in Chile next week—Nirvana's first album, named *Bleach*? Why is this 1992 album proving more popular than the one from 1989?

KN: It's more popular? Oh, well I'm glad to hear that; that record's been out three years, and I'm glad that people enjoy it. It's a different record, it's kind of a . . . *Nevermind* is more of a glossy, mainstream, or more accessible—it's easy to listen to, to where *Bleach* is more dirty . . .

JA: Why do you think Seattle has been the birthplace of a lot of groups like yours? Is there anything special in Seattle that made this happen?

DG: Quite a city, I guess . . . there's a lot of bands and some of them suck, but some of them are really great. It's just another city, really.

JA: How would you like to be remembered: more as a rock band or as a group that made a real contribution to music as a whole?

DG: Our epitaph!

KN: Will read . . . "A bunch of schmucks that cashed in."

JA: We will have three songs from the Nirvana mini festival and then we'll close this set.

"THREE COMMON GUYS WHO MADE MUSIC THEY COULD HUM"

César Fuentes Rodríguez | October 31, 1992 | *Madhouse* (Argentina)

Nirvana played the Vélez Sarsfield stadium in Capital Federal, Buenos Aires, Argentina, on October 30, 1992, with Los Brujos and Calamity Jane as supporting acts. The band played reluctantly to the hungry audience because the entire stadium despised and booed Nirvana's protégées, Calamity Jane. In the end Nirvana refused to play "Smells Like Teen Spirit" to punish the crowd that had paid to see their show. In the liner notes to *Incesticide*, Kurt Cobain lied about the incident, describing it as a gender conflict and affirming that the women were "Heckled by twenty thousand macho boys in Argentina." In fact, this is utterly outrageous because Calamity Jane was totally unprofessional and one of the most untalented bands that ever performed in the country; they were rightly booed by men and women alike. No gender conflict was involved, just a genuine reaction to poor artistic output. We can say virtually the same about Nirvana, whose performance that night was pretty lame and impolite. Everyone referred to the show as one big disappointment. The interview took place the morning after the show and appeared in issue 27 of *Madhouse* under the title "Our Music Appealed to Common People." —César Fuentes Rodríguez

Translated by César Fuentes Rodríguez.

Nirvana gave few interviews in Argentina. In a small room of the Sheraton Hotel, Chris Novoselic and a ghostly Kurt Cobain shared the first round while Dave Grohl attended our table to speak about success, contradictions, and the future of three guys who could easily pass unnoticed everywhere if fortune hadn't singled them out.

César Fuentes Rodríguez: Did the local audience's reception of Calamity Jane influence your mood last night?

Nirvana: It's weird because when you go to a country for the first time, you don't know what to expect. We were kinda annoyed to see people not appreciating the kind of music that we do appreciate, that underground punk rock. I mean, I don't think, it didn't matter when we went out to play. We didn't expect so many people and such a big show either. We don't do these kinds of shows at home, but it's OK.

CFR: Why did you do a show in a stadium here then?

Nirvana: Uh . . . I don't know what to say. I always get kinda nervous and get infected with the atmosphere of the place, and in this case with what happened with Calamity Jane. It did strain our mood a bit. Probably it wouldn't happen to us in a smaller place.

CFR: Nirvana was a small underground band and suddenly . . . what happened?

Nirvana: I don't know, really. When *Bleach* came out there were a lot of comments in the underground. We started to have followers; college radio stations broadcast our music. There was a lot of talk about Nirvana in the punk scene and even in the indie record industry. When we were recording *Nevermind* we simply thought it was one more record. Two years passed between one and the other. Nobody could give a proper explanation or expect that something like that would have happened. I think people were sick and tired of dance music, of bad heavy metal, of everything . . . and discovered three common guys who made music they could hum.

CFR: The fact that the music was back to basics had something to do with it?

Nirvana: Well, usually songs that stick in your mind are the simpler ones, like children's songs that help you to remember things. None of us are great musicians. I can play drums, Chris can play bass, and Kurt the guitar, but I don't do drum solos, and Kurt can't do guitar solos. We're not skilled musicians so we can't play complex music; our thing is so simple that anybody can get it. Our music appealed to common people.

CFR: Aren't you planning to improve as musicians?

Nirvana: Not really. Sometimes when you concentrate on skill, you lose feeling. It's easier to capture an emotion if you keep yourself at a minimalist level. A lot of technique can ruin a band, make you lose spontaneity. Nah, I don't think we'll ever become accomplished musicians.

CFR: All that Seattle fuss—isn't it a little bit out of control?

Nirvana: In the States, a city explodes every three years. It was New York before, or Los Angeles. Today it's Seattle, tomorrow it'll be Boston or Texas. There are good bands and good music everywhere; it's only that the focus is set on Seattle right now. I think people don't know exactly what's going on there. A huge punk scene was happening, a lot of friends that got together to drink some beers, and some of them put together Sub Pop, the record label.

CFR: You see yourselves more as part of the punk scene, so why do you think that metal magazines took such an interest in Nirvana?

Nirvana: It was weird at first. None of us really likes heavy metal. We're against the poses, the macho stuff, and all that. When we saw ourselves in all these magazines, we felt it wasn't bad at all because we could show what we thought about it to all those sort of people.

CFR: But not everything in Seattle emerged from punk . . .

Nirvana: No, of course, there are bands like Soundgarden, Alice in Chains, or Pearl Jam whose roots are in 1970s hard rock, and they're doing great because their music is closer to mainstream rock, the kind of rock you hear everywhere.

CFR: What do you think about the tongue-in-cheek clip Weird Al Yankovic did based on "Smells Like Teen Spirit"?

Nirvana: It's funny. He called us to comment on the idea and, since there's a sense of humor in the band, it was OK with us. Funny.

CFR: Will the next record be in the same vein as *Nevermind*?

Nirvana: No, I think it'll be more like *Bleach*. Without the big production and so on.

"I USED TO PRACTICE WHEN I FIRST GRABBED THE GUITAR"

Sergio Marchi | October 31, 1992 | *Clarin* **(Argentina)**

When I interviewed Kurt Cobain, he was a rising star. Nirvana was seen as something new, something good, something different. And because of the anxiety that's characteristic of Argentinian entrepreneurs, the band was hired to play in a football stadium; this setting isn't recommended for music, but it's good for business. For Nirvana it was an unnatural situation that the band aggravated by including Calamity Jane—a band that wasn't ready to face an audience that didn't speak English, that didn't want to see them, and that was vastly greater in number than any crowd the band had played for.

Kurt watched the show from one side of the stage and saw the audience booing his friends and throwing things at them. "That's why I started 'Smells Like Teen Spirit' three times and didn't play it—the audience didn't deserve us playing it," Kurt told me when we discussed it the following day. He showed himself to be kind, relaxed, and in good humor even though his face didn't betray many emotions. When someone wanted to cut our interview short, he asked them to leave us alone. I certainly couldn't imagine that I was interviewing someone who, with the passage of time, would become a legend. Through the years this report would also become legendary, to the point that when people see the picture we took with Kurt, they ask if it's a montage. Of course, it's not; Photoshop wasn't invented until long after our meeting. —Sergio Marchi

Translated by Kaye Soulsby and Javier Lahuerta.

Sergio Marchi: Do you feel comfortable doing shows in stadiums?

Kurt Cobain: Not really. We're more accustomed to clubs; I've not even been to many shows in stadiums. I went to two in my whole life; Sammy Hagar when I was twelve and Aerosmith at twenty. I started going to clubs at age fourteen to see underground punk rock bands in places where there would be at most a hundred people, but most of the time there'd only be twenty. It was a very closed environment, where things were always the same. Being on a stage in front of thousands of people is very odd for me. I feel like a martian. I'm not used to it. It's not something that's very inspiring for me, nor do I want to be in that position; it's very strange. Over time I've learned to accept it, but I still prefer to play for a small audience; it's a lot more stimulating.

SM: [*An aside*] Water is better. You want some lights? Now, "Lithium"?

KC: We play it a lot. It's fun to play that song because the verse is real quiet, and it all erupts in the chorus.

SM: You have a very unique style of playing the guitar.

KC: It's because I don't practice, rather than through practice . . . I never took classes or tried to copy the style of other guitarists. I really don't care, to be honest. I play the wrong notes all the time in different keys to the others. I find it more fun to improvise what I play and whatever happens, happens. I'm sure you may have noticed in the show last night that when I play my solos they don't even fit the song. I don't care; I prefer that to trying to be a guitarist with an efficient technique. I find those kinds of guitar players boring. I really don't believe in solos, but there are songs that require them, so I assume that I can play one. I played a long one last night in the last song. It was fun. Lots of noise.

SM: So, how did you learn to play guitar?

KC: I used to practice when I first grabbed the guitar, but not now. I don't like polishing my technique and stuff. When I began playing guitar I began writing songs immediately. I learned a couple: "My Best Friend's Girl" by the Cars and "Back in Black" by AC/DC. After that I started to write songs, so when I had my first band I already had material to play. It's better to do that than to play covers; otherwise you end up sounding like them.

SM: I take it you were surprised by the success of *Nevermind*?

KC: Sure, we didn't plan this. It was released, and it wasn't even an important promotion. It wasn't in our company's plans to have this great plan, to spend a lot of money and try to sell it that way. We gave copies to some radio stations, and it started being played. We became popular that way. After, it caught on with MTV. In the United States, MTV is like God; it's very powerful. Everyone watches and listens to that channel.

SM: Here it is different; we don't have MTV, and we only have one rock station. The rest of the way things spread is when people hear something they like and the rumor passes from mouth to mouth.

KC: That's great; I like it a lot more that way. It's better that way than corporations telling you what to listen to. A lot of kids are naive and don't know where to look for music; the corporations have the control, and the monopolies grab crap bands and put in so much money that in the end the kids end up listening. I prefer word of mouth; it is much better.

SM: What degree of contact do you maintain with other Seattle bands, such as Mudhoney, Pearl Jam, etc.?

KC: We were close friends of Mudhoney for a long time. Pearl Jam I don't like at all. I cannot stand them. They started after us. The scene in Seattle was good three or four years ago, when we were all friends and we played in clubs. Some of the bands, like Soundgarden, have been playing a long time. Now everything is different. Sub Pop, the label, is really good; it really helps bands. I always liked punk rock, grunge, or things like Mudhoney, Tad, the Fluid, which makes it seem, to me, that Pearl Jam are like the 1990s version of Lynyrd Skynyrd or Genesis. They're very clean and nice, very radio-friendly. The singer is a good guy.

SM: Eddie Vedder?

KC: Yeah, Eddie Vedder. Wait for a second, I have to go to the bathroom. [*Settles back down.*]

SM: From Buenos Aires, where are you flying to?

KC: I'm going back to Seattle for a few days.

SM: Are you going back to vote in the elections?

KC: Yeah, I'll vote for Clinton.

SM: Do you think he's the true change that he says he is?

KC: No, he's a Democrat, and the Democrats are not close either morally or philosophically to what I think. The Democrats are very conservative, but at least they're not as conservative as the Republicans. Republicans are the incarnation of Satan. I hate them. For me the word *Republican* is a bad word; when someone says *Republican* they are saying "cheat." It's the most offensive term you can say to someone. But in America there's nothing beyond these options.

SM: Ross Perot?

KC: Nah, the guy sucks. He's rich; I don't trust him as president. In the end, though, I would risk it with someone who is not a professional politician, someone who does not follow the guidelines for being a certified politician. I'd prefer to vote for Perot, but he's not going to win; he is well behind. I don't want to waste my vote, and I prefer to make sure Bush doesn't continue. Obviously, the way the guy is doing things doesn't work.

SM: You once said you were not happy with the people of your generation, because the kids are very apathetic.

KC: I wouldn't want to project that image of disappointment with people because they could think I don't like them, and that's not the case. It's like saying I don't respect people who come to our shows because they're very apathetic or very lazy. But I don't think our generation has done too much to get people like Bush out of government. But it's not like if I wanted . . . to instruct people, to make them think in political terms, but I think there are other things people can do to promote their views and make people listen. I don't think our generation has staged a sufficient challenge to the old guard; they've left it so they have to be told what to do. In the United States they give the impression that, as this is an election year, everyone is more concerned with what will happen, but I don't know. I was always a very nihilistic person, so I do not have many good thoughts about people, but it seems that very slowly people are becoming more conscious. I think my generation is the last generation in America that has enjoyed having its innocence. When I was a kid, there were TV shows that were not very violent, and there was no cable, and the kids had no access to banned films; I had no awareness of murderers and rapists. But kids at six years old know about sex, realize that there's a lot of violence in the world, and it spreads more because there are better communications. It is sad to know that the next generation is going to be fucked from such a young age, because there's no chance of having innocence. And for a boy it is absolutely necessary that you can have a period of innocence in your life that will last for a few years.

[*Interview breaks —Ed.*]

KC: Obviously it's a tragedy, something terrible. A lot of artists are sick and don't think the government cares a fuck. In twelve years, the Republicans have preferred to see people with AIDS, homosexuals, as people of a lower class and have preferred to see the genocide of these people. Imagine if we still put people in gas chambers; they still have that shit working. They ignore it and haven't contributed funds to stop the disease. It's very sad. There was so much promotion that you would have to be an idiot not to know that today you've got to use condoms or not share a needle. That promotion had the effect of slowing AIDS. You attempted to lower the number of patients by means of promotion. After that, they talk about conspiracies and stuff. I don't know enough to just give an opinion.

SM: While you now live in Seattle, you spent your childhood and adolescence in Aberdeen. How is that place?

KC: It's a very small town. See, here is a great city and here is Aberdeen, which is miles from anywhere else. And there are plenty of even smaller places far outside the cities. All it's got is the ocean, and the rest is flat. There's the sea, some mountains, and very little else. In the big cities they were listening to punk rock or knew of all the new-wave cultures, or news. But only a lot of years later have things come to Aberdeen.

SM: Just like Argentina.

KC: Sure, sure, Aberdeen too. It's really dumb.

SM: The people?

KC: A small town creates a small-town mentality. There are very ignorant people, and they don't believe in anything very different. They frown on anything that's different from what they know. They did not like the idea that my friends and I were punk rockers. But it is understandable, and we don't hold grudges.

SM: And when you were growing up, what kind of music did you listen to?

KC: The Beatles, mostly. The Monkees. Hendrix—not really. Black Sabbath, Aerosmith.

SM: New bands?

KC: The Breeders. R.E.M. Have you listened to them? They're really good.

SM: I guess you're going back to visit your family in Seattle . . .

KC: No, the only reason I'm going back is to see my little daughter. I miss her so much—she's only nine weeks. I can't wait to go back home with her.

"THE PROBLEM IS YOU'RE NOW A CARICATURE"

Jim Crotty and Michael Lane | November 1992 | *Monk* (US)

The tape of *Monk*'s September interview with Kurt Cobain has long since disappeared. While searching for it, however, Jim Crotty and Mike Lane uncovered the existence of a second, previously unknown tape. This documented their meeting with Cobain in November 1992 to shoot the photographs that would accompany the final article. Caught in casual conversation, Cobain roams through topics—a rare mention of continued awkwardness with his father, his recently initiated contact with William S. Burroughs, the commencement of Nirvana's work on *In Utero*. It also captures his annoyance with the treatment meted out to Nirvana's support band in South America—something he would express furiously when provided the forum of Nirvana's December compilation release, *Incesticide*. —Ed.

We headed back to Seattle in November to catch up with the 1990s' very own James Dean (minimal output, the right look, an eternal sense of all that could have been). He arrived alone at Charlie Hoselton's photo studio and, from the start, was a courteous and exceptionally cooperative presence. It said a lot about him and the selflessness he could often display toward the needs of others—he told us, "I'll stay as long as you want, I'll do whatever you want. You just have to do two things for me: turn off your phone and don't answer the door if anyone knocks." After that we had fun dressing him as a logger, posing him with a chainsaw, persuading a barista to let Kurt pose with the espresso machine—at which point Kurt took over and made a coffee. Our ultimate idea was to shoot him hanging from a mock-up of Seattle's Space Needle. It was intended to show Cobain on the edge and point to Seattle's rep as Smack City, USA. Maybe we were too darkly honest for our own good. After the shoot Cobain asked for a ride home. I ended up driving him around downtown Seattle, taking his orders about where to go, where to stop. He'd vanish, return, tell me where next. Eventually he returned with a visible tranquility. It was finally time to take him home. But then, maybe home was that comfy cloud floating inside his mind at that moment. Maybe that was the only place this guy really lived. —Jim Crotty and Michael Lane

Jim Crotty: You were down in Argentina? Buenos Aires? It's a cool city, I understand.

Kurt Cobain: It's not like "cool"—high-rises everywhere.

JC: I was in Brazil for summer.

Mike Lane: Sort of like New York?

JC: Brazil's like that—São Paulo's like that.

KC: No, I mean Buenos Aires.

JC: Is it?

ML: Sort of like Manhattan?

KC: I don't think so. I didn't see a lot of real high-rises while I was . . . not really. Really scummy, like, shanty towns.

JC: That's the thing about South America. It's fucking weird—it's like the rich are really rich and the poor are just dirt poor. Have you been to Rio?

KC: No.

JC: See, it's like that—the favelas. It's a beautiful town. These gorgeous little mountains, little hills, they're phenomenal. But, like, all the poor live on there—it's like major crack trade . . . it's OK, but they gotta get a middle class.

KC: We brought this all-girl band, Calamity Jane, with us. I dunno . . . the whole audience—it was mostly young boys anyhow—and they were screaming "Puta!" at them the whole time.

JC: "Puta madre!" [*Laughs.*]

KC: Guys screaming it at them the whole time. Throwing dirt and pieces of paper at them . . . yeah . . . it was awful. It was just the girls got treated so badly.

JC: It's that old macho South American dudes—that's the thing . . .

KC: It was terrible. But at least we got to pay the girls really well, so who's working that out?

JC: So you brought them—where're they from?

KC: They're from Portland.

JC: Oh, good, man. How long were you down there?

KC: Three days.

JC: I say, you just flew down for three days? What you take, Varig—what airline? PWA or sumthin'?

KC: Something like that, yeah . . . it was a long ride . . . eighteen hours—two layovers. I mean, I'd just barely started to adjust as we were leaving, to the pattern, y'know, by the time I got back. But! It's really helped me! Because now I'm getting up at, like, eleven in the morning—it's really early for me.

JC: Oh, is it?

KC: Yeah, like, even today I had breakfast at seven.

JC: Holy cow. It's starting to sound corporate! I can't handle food in the morning when I'm going to bed at five or four.

KC: No one can eat breakfast at five in the morning. At least. Jeez, I wanna go to Buenos Aires next time and try it.

JC: Yeah . . . What time do you usually get up—two? Three?

KC: Yeah, probably. That's a decent hour.

JC: That's a good hour. What time do I normally get going? Ten-thirty?

ML: You get going around four.

JC: I'm cooking at four, man. At four-thirty I'm rolling now. I'm ready, this is it. This is the time. So you're just here for another night—that's it, you guys go back to L.A. or . . . ?

KC: We haven't decided. We'll probably just stay another day.

JC: And you're gonna . . . you're recording stuff, or . . . you're not recording yet, you're just practicing?

KC: Not really. I just recorded some guitar feedback for a William Burroughs record I'm doing.

ML: William Burroughs? What are you doing with him?

JC: Great fucking idea!

KC: He wrote—he read "Junkie's Last Christmas," and I'm doing some feedback noise over the top of it.

ML: Are you kidding?

KC: And then I get to play feedback for another twenty-five minutes. So, his piece is only as long as that story is, which is like five minutes maybe, and mine is gonna be about another twenty minutes, twenty-five minutes.

ML: Who's producing this?

KC: This guy Thor [*Lindsay —Ed.*] from Portland. He runs T/K Records. He's put out a couple of Burroughs's records—Gus Van Sant did some stuff with him too.

ML: Have you hung out with him?

KC: No, uh-uh.

JC: Oh, so you didn't get to meet Bill? Oh, too bad. He's in Lawrence, Kansas.

KC: I know. But I get to meet him, though, 'cause Thor's a pretty good friend of his so . . . yeah, he's flying me down to Kansas sometime.

JC: Oh, you'd have a riot!

KC: Yeah, I wanna go really bad. Last time I was in Kansas I wanted to try to just knock on his door, but I was too nervous. I had a Lead Belly record in my arm; I was ready to go.

JC: That's too bad. Well, you'll just have to go there, yeah. I'm from Nebraska, so I know that whole area pretty well . . . nothing much happening there. They vote Republican pretty much.

KC: Actually Burroughs gave me a first edition of *Naked Lunch,* signed . . .

JC: That's groovy, that's cool.

KC: But I still mean to meet him.

JC: So you guys gonna put out a new album soon?

KC: Well, we'd like to, we pretty much have enough material, but we're trying to decide where we want to record. We tried to record at Reciprocal, but the neighbors sort of complain by ten at night. Then I was only here for a couple of days, so we got about three tracks done. It's in Ballard. It's where we recorded our first record. And we did it with Jack Endino—the guy who did our record.

JC: What's his name again?

KC: Jack Endino.

JC: Oh right, he's from Seattle, isn't he?

KC: Yeah . . .

JC: Actually, a friend of mine . . . I was telling this to your drummer, Dave, that I went to school with a pretty cool producer—Steve Albini. I was in a band with him, actually.

KC: What was that?

JC: Well, it wasn't anything; it was, like, he was really just wanting to start this punk band—it was like '79. And there's, like, two people in the whole school—Northwestern—that were any way into this music. So he grabbed me, but I didn't know how to do shit. It was pretty pathetic, so we wasted no time at all—I was out of there. But I guess he's a pretty good producer.

KC: Oh yeah, he's my favorite, actually. I really want him to do this next record, but I don't think he really likes us. We haven't officially asked him, but the rumor mill came out in the papers and so everyone was saying that he was going to do it already. So he sent a fax to, like, three of the papers in England—like *Melody Maker* and *NME*—and said that there's no way he's associated with us in any way, and he's not doing our next record because we haven't asked him. So I don't know . . .

JC: Well then ask him!

KC: Well, I will, I will. But . . . it was just . . . I dunno . . . it just kinda made me feel like a dork, y'know?

JC: Oh yeah . . . well, see, his whole thing is he's a real confrontational kinda person.

KC: Yeah, I know. That'd be, that's kinda half the reason I wanna use him.

JC: He's very confrontational. I mean, he'll just say stuff just to say it, and it doesn't mean he doesn't want to work with ya. I mean, he may say you suck! He'd say that to an interviewer . . . but he would still do it. He used to light fires in the dorms and stuff; he's just that kinda person—just for the hell of it.

KC: Oh yeah, I don't care about that stuff, I really don't. I've heard a lot of Albini stories . . .

ML: So what's this new sound you're looking for?

JC: Perry Como, I think . . .

KC: I dunno . . . yeah, Perry Como, and Kojak . . .

JC: Get back to the roots—the Seattle roots.

KC: I've got so many effects pedals that I'm just overwhelmed by them and just making so much noise. It's really not music! It's just—actually it sounds a lot like Big Black, Steve Albini's band . . . it's definitely different.

JC: [*To the photographer*] Well, let's figure out something here—what do you wanna do in terms of . . . do you want to get Kurt first so he can get on?

ML: Well, that's fine, basically . . .

JC: So turn the backdrop so you can do him—or no? OK, good . . . let me ask him, ask him.

ML: Did you work in, like, a movie theater ever, when you were really young?

JC: No, he was a janitor. The power—of Ajax.

KC: Yeah, I was a janitor. Nope, I never actually worked in Aberdeen—I worked in Ocean Shores.

JC: A subtle difference—between the two towns?

KC: Yep. Subtle.

JC: I'm going to go to Aberdeen—I wanna go to Maria's Hair Shop.

KC: Oh, you'll love Maria!

JC: I love Maria. I met her at your show, man! She's a sweetie-pie, I really liked her! She definitely talks. I mean, I talk a lot . . .

KC: [*Kurt puts on high-pitched voice.*] Chris! Your hair's too long! You should have a crown!

JC: Chris would have gone, "Right."

KC: I know, yeah, he's kinda blocked her out . . .

JC: I thought she was a trip. Her whole family—it was such a family affair. They were just, like, this nice family coming there. Maria's just too fun.

KC: Yeah, my dad, for the first time in six or seven years got back there.

JC: Oh, that's right! How was that? God . . .

KC: It was kind of a weird thing. I dunno . . .

JC: You hadn't seen him in six or seven years. Oh wow . . .

KC: It was just like . . .

JC: He's a big fan of your music now.

KC: That's what I hear.

JC: No he's not!

KC: Sure he is!

JC: Seriously?

KC: Well, yeah, of course! I mean . . .

JC: How old is he?

KC: Uhh . . . I don't know.

JC: In his forties? Fifties?

KC: Probably late forties.

JC: Good for him.

KC: I don't know his birthday—and he hated what I used to do.

JC: My parents hate what I do.

ML: My mom likes your stuff!

KC: Everybody's mom likes our stuff—we're not doing it right, are we? [*Laughs.*]

JC: Yeah, that's true—what's going wrong here? Put out another album like R.E.M. put out. Their recent album? It's just not melodic, it's just down . . . There's no "Happy Shiny People"–type lyrics or anything. Really, it's just like they just sort of went the other direction. Nah, but then . . . so you've got to milk that rock 'n' roll thing, man, as long as you can . . .

KC: Oh sure . . .

JC: You've got maybe three years. You've got to get rich off it and then go back to being a janitor.

KC: Oh, in just a few years because, I mean, Garth Brooks milks it like a mother! He puts out like two albums every year—last year he had two albums out and this year he has two albums out.

ML: And the last three are in the charts at any given time. All at the same time.

KC: That's why we're putting out this throwaway, B-side record out really soon with just demo stuff we did a few years ago. They'll eat it up right now, so . . .

JC: Just feed 'em! How much time do you have, y'know? There's not going to be any more Beatles, Rolling Stones things any more. People last about five years max, at most.

KC: Oh yeah . . .

Courtney Love: Really? You don't think there's going to be any more?

JC: No, man, nobody lasts twenty years—twenty-five years! Have you seen a group in the last fifteen years that's lasted . . .

KC: REO Speedwagon.

JC: Actually, I want to see you play OREO Speedwagon . . . that'd be great—you should do covers of Bachman-Turner Overdrive, OREO Speedwagon, Kansas . . . So, question for you: what do you want to do, that you've never done, in a photo, that expresses who you are or what your music is? I mean, really seriously, think about that, 'cause we have ideas, but . . .
[*Interview break —Ed.*]

JC: We're going to have you hang off the Space Needle. Here's our mock-up, see? Here's what the cover's going to look like: SEATTLE SUCKS. Alright? I'm going to change in a second, but I'm basically sawing the Space Needle, OK? Michael's hanging off it, and he's stolen your song title, "Stay Away," so the whole idea is it sucks, don't come here. OK?

KC: Good idea! Californians—stay away.

JC: Except it won't be big enough to do that. So we were going to have you hanging with him, or we were going to have you in the shape of the *K*, or we're going to have you playing on—actually we're just gonna try different things. But that's the concept we're working with.

KC: OK.

JC: Also, we want to get one shot with Kurt at an espresso cart. I want to use that inside. I want you to be like "Mr. Espresso"—just pull on the lever, OK? Actually, we could do that right away while she's outside, or shall we have her bring the cart in here?

ML: Actually, I don't know if I can talk her into bringing it in.

JC: Let's do it out there. Let me talk to her right now, then. We'll do that first so we can get that out of the way. 'Cause it'll get dark out there, see.

KC: Hi, Chris! We're going to do a shot out here, OK?

JC: Is there a lever?

ML: No, there's not a lever. There's buttons and shit. It'll be cool.

JC: Yeah. Let's do that. It'll be cool. We'll have the monks buying a cookie from Kurt . . . Right, I gotta get dressed here, shit. You didn't bring a guitar, did you, Mr. Cobain? You gave up on that, right? Fuck the guitar. You're playing an accordion now, I hear?

KC: I have wah-wah pedal shoes . . . that's my thing now.

JC: Fuck guitar, man! You should do bassoon. That's your look, man; you've got to milk it.

KC: Yeah, that's what I talked about yesterday. You know what? This image that I have, I should be able to write off my stage clothes because these are my stage clothes. But I can't do that now—I guess they changed the IRS laws. You can't write off under five dollars.
[*Photos continue —Ed.*]

JC: We're trying to do this lampoon of this "grunge look" . . . See, what we were going to do on the inside was have you—we're gonna open it up—and it's going to be you, holding your baby, and Courtney's right there and it's sort of like *American Gothic,* like happy family look, and it's gonna say "Grunge Is Dead."

KC: Uh-huh.

JC: But we thought it's a little too negative, people might not get too . . . "didn't get the joke," and they might take it too literally.

JC: Kurt, you wanna wear a chain wallet? Have wallet, will travel.

KC: I have a hippie purse; I don't even carry a wallet. Well, I do, in my hippie purse.

JC: Oh, that's right, you've got a hippie purse. See, now kids all over America are going to be buying those hippie purses. See, the problem is you're now a caricature.

KC: Yeah!

JC: See? I can imitate you right here, and it's not you I'm imitating, it's the caricature. It's why I say you've got to start playing Perry Como because . . . OK, here we go—Mr. Espresso. Here we go! He wants an espresso, Kurt, fix him up!
[*Interview break —Ed.*]

JC: See, we have a book coming out next June, and hopefully we're going to make it into a movie—it's a big deal. So maybe that's what we'll do! Maybe as part of the promotion in L.A. we'll just put Courtney, Kurt, and the kid in an RV. We'll go and have the book signing at an RV park—wouldn't that be great? We'll get a bunch of people to come . . . we should have a barbecue.

ML: We're pretty white trash, though, Kurt.

JC: We are—we're very white trash.

KC: I'm not. [*Chuckles.*]

JC: See, you're like bourgeois—we're *Monk* white trash . . .

KC: What's that place in Kansas? Starts with a *Y*; it's supposed to be the eighth wonder of the universe; it's supposed to be a satanic place . . . Yull? There's a church—there's an old burned-out church there, it's in this really small town, outskirts of like—somewhere in Kansas, it's not too far away from Lawrence, I don't think. And all this weirdness keeps going on about it, happened for years, a lot of people have seen ghosts . . . Urge Overkill put out an EP—oh, Stull—that's what it's called. We went there one night.

JC: Oh shit, I've heard of this place. How was it? I think I've seen Stull on an album cover.

KC: Yeah, that was Urge Overkill. I swear to God there is some kind of scary stuff going on. I just remember walking toward it, and it seemed to be getting further and further away—it was really pitch black. And, like, the Urge Overkill guys saw dogs—and there were all these dogs barking like real violently from the neighbors. It just wasn't normal at all—and we all felt this weird presence, this weird, evil presence. We just ran back to the van. They were so scared they wrote a record about it.
[*Final photos take place —Ed.*]

ML: Before we leave, can we have you sign something? Will you sign my leg here?

JC: Oh, you're gonna sign that? I love you, you're so cute! I don't believe in this sort of thing, but maybe I should—should we try and profit off of rock 'n' roll? Do you think they'll be worth something?

KC: Sure! Anything with my name on it . . . I don't know how to write professional autographs . . .

COBAIN CLIP

Novoselic on THAT Buenos Aires Performance

"We were playing with the passion of a cold fish. It's not that I blame it on the few misguided Argentineans who gave Calamity Jane a hard time; it's mainly that the novelty of playing these 30,000 capacity stadiums has worn thin."

—from "Nirvana: Nevermind the Bollocks"
by Krist Novoselic, *RAW*, December 1992

INCESTICIDE

Kurt Cobain | December 1992 | Nirvana *Incesticide* Compilation Liner Notes

A while ago, I found myself in bloody exhaust grease London again with an all-consuming urge to hunt for two rare things: back issues of NME rumored to be secretly hidden in glass casings and submerged in the fry vats of every kebab machine in the U.K. and the very-out-of-print first Raincoats LP.

The NME search was a clever, saucy upstart of an attempt to be, uh, nasty. However, the Lord and Julian Cope himself know how we need, need, need the NME to embrace the unifying hands of our children across this big blue marble and NIRVANA's tarty musical career. So please bless us again—we'll forever feed off of your high-calorie boggy turbinates.

In an attempt to satisfy the second part of my quest, I went to the Rough Trade shop and, of course, found no Raincoats record in the bin. I then asked the woman behind the counter about it and she said "well, it happens that I'm neighbors with Anna (member of The Raincoats) and she works at an antique shop just a few miles from here." So she drew me a map and I started on my way to Anna's.

Sometime later, I arrived at this elfin shop filled with something else I've compulsively searched for over the past few years—really old fucked up marionette-like wood carved dolls (quite a few hundred years old). Lots of them . . . I've fantasized about finding a ship filled with so many. They wouldn't accept my credit card but the dolls were really way too expensive anyway. Anna was there, however, so I politely introduced myself with a fever-red face and explained the reason for my intrusion.

I can remember her mean boss almost setting me on fire with his glares. She said "well, I may have a few lying around so, if I find one, I'll send it to you (very polite, very English)." I left feeling like a dork, like I had violated her space, like she probably thought my band was tacky.

A few weeks later I received a vinyl copy of that wonderfully classic scripture with a personalized dust sleeve covered with xeroxed lyrics, pictures, and all the members' signatures. There was also a touching letter from Anna. It made me happier than playing in front of thousands of people each night, rock-god idolization from fans, music industry plankton kissing my ass, and the million dollars I made last year. It was one of the few really important things that I've been blessed with since becoming an untouchable boy genius.

It was as rewarding as touring with Shonen Knife and watching people practically cry with joy at their honesty. It made people happy and it made me happy knowing that I had helped bring them to the U.K.

It was as rewarding as the last Vaselines show in Edinburgh. They reformed just to play with us in their home town, probably having no idea how exciting and flattering it was for us (and how nervous we were to meet them).

It was as rewarding as being asked to support Sonic Youth on two tours, totally being taken under their wing and being showed what dignity really means.

It was as rewarding as the drawings Daniel Johnston sent me, or the Stinky Puffs single from Jad Fair's son, or playing on the same bill as Greg Sage in L.A., or being asked to help produce the next Melvins record, or being on the Wipers' compilation, or Thor from T.K. giving me a signed first edition of *Naked Lunch*, or making a friend like Stephen Pavlovic—our Australian tour promoter who sent me a Mazzy Star LP on vinyl, or playing "The Money Will Roll Right In" with Mudhoney, or having the power to insist on bringing Bjorn Again to the Reading Festival, or being able to afford to bring my friend Ian along on tour just to have a good time, or paying Calamity Jane five-thousand dollars to be heckled by twenty thousand macho boys in Argentina, or asking my friends Fitz Of Depression to play with us at The Seattle Coliseum, or playing with Poison Idea at a No On Nine benefit in Portland organized by Gus Van Zandt, or being a part of one of L7's pro-choice benefits in L.A., or kissing Chris and Dave on *Saturday Night Live* just to spite homophobes, or meeting Iggy Pop, or playing with The Breeders, Urge Overkill, The T.V. Personalities, The Jesus Lizard, Hole, Dinosaur Jr., etc.

While all these things were very special, none were half as rewarding as having a baby with a person who is the supreme example of dignity, ethics and honesty. My wife challenges injustice and the reason her character has been so severely attacked is because she chooses not to function the way the white corporate man insists. His rules for women involve her being submissive, quiet, and non-challenging. When she doesn't follow his rules, the threatened man (who, incidentally, owns an army of devoted traitor women) gets scared.

A big "fuck you" to those of you who have the audacity to claim that I'm so naive and stupid that I would allow myself to be taken advantage of and manipulated.

I don't feel the least bit guilty for commercially exploiting a completely exhausted Rock youth Culture because, at this point in rock history, Punk Rock (while still sacred to some) is, to me, dead and gone. We just wanted to pay tribute to something that helped us to feel as though we had crawled out of the dung heap of conformity. To pay tribute like an Elvis or Jimi Hendrix impersonator in the tradition of a bar band. I'll be the first to admit that we're the 90's version of Cheap Trick or The Knack but the last to admit that it hasn't been rewarding.

At this point I have a request for our fans. If any of you in any way hate homosexuals, people of different color, or women, please do this one favor for us—leave us the fuck alone! Don't come to our shows and don't buy our records.

Last year, a girl was raped by two wastes of sperm and eggs while they sang the lyrics to our song "Polly." I have a hard time carrying on knowing there are plankton like that in our audience. Sorry to be so anally P.C. but that's the way I feel.

Love,

Kurdt (the blond one)

THE DARK SIDE OF NIRVANA'S KURT COBAIN

Kevin Allman | December 1992 | *Advocate* (US)

The interview cassettes went missing in the days after Hurricane Katrina and the levee collapses in New Orleans, but 99 percent of the interview ended up on the page. It came about when a mutual acquaintance of Cobain's contacted me and said Kurt was interested in an interview—the intermediary said Kurt wanted to get some personal things off his chest. I flew to Seattle, where he was staying in a downtown hotel (not a suite, but a regular hotel room). A couple of planned meetings didn't materialize, but when we finally met, I found him smart and funny and sarcastic, and not at all impressed with his stats as the world's biggest rock star. In fact, he was rather horrified—not only at being a corporate commodity but also at being idolized by the same sort of meatheads he couldn't stand. He identified more with the misfits and the kids who were bullied. Kurt was nervous, but he put no preconditions on the interview and answered every question honestly and thoughtfully. I do remember that before the tape recorder went on, Kurt and Courtney wanted to know if I was a "Beatles person" or a "Rolling Stones person." They said they were "Beatles people."

Nirvana's record label wasn't aware that we'd done this interview until weeks later. A publicist called me and asked to see it before it went to print. I said no. I got a glimpse of what Kurt's life must be like right before the piece was published, when the syndicated columnist Liz Smith printed an item saying that he and Courtney were both coming out of the closet and talking about their multiple sex partners in a soon-to-be-published interview. Smith never called me to fact-check. My first thought was that they'd think I planted the item, so I tracked them down, prepared for what I thought would be a difficult conversation.

Courtney answered the phone. I explained the situation to her, and she just laughed and put Kurt on the phone. To my relief, he believed me. "Don't worry about it," he told me. "This kind of thing happens to us all the time."

I never spoke to either of them again, but a decade later I picked up a copy of Cobain's *Journals* in a bookstore and, in a weird coincidence, opened it to the page where he'd written a note citing the interview and saying it was his favorite. I like to think it was his favorite not because it was a puff piece but because it was a chance for him to talk intelligently and speak the truth as he saw it at the time. I liked him, very much. And I still love his music. Nirvana never put out a bad album. —Kevin Allman

It's 4 o'clock on a cold Seattle afternoon, and Kurt Cobain, the lyricist-guitarist-lead singer of Nirvana, is sitting in a downtown hotel room, playing with his 5-month-old daughter, Frances, while his wife, Courtney Love—lead singer of her own band, Hole—applies her makeup. At the moment, the Cobains (including baby) are on the cover of *Spin* magazine—which has named Nirvana as Artist of the Year—and the band's new album, *Incesticide*, is due out within the week. The Nirvana media machine should be in high gear.

But, no.

What's surprising is what's not in the Cobains' room: no entourage, no groupies, no publicists, and no signs of the high life—in any sense of the term. Cobain, in fact, is wearing a pair of fuzzy green pajamas. And he and Love are in Seattle for the sole reason of trying to speed the deal on a modest house they've been trying to buy. The only concession to Cobain's being what he mockingly calls "a rock icon" is the pseudonym under which he has registered, Simon Ritchie.

It's a joke—Ritchie was the real name of Sid Vicious, the Sex Pistol who died from a heroin overdose—and it shows that the Cobains have a sense of humor about being tagged by the press as a modern-day Sid and Nancy. If the Cobains are being reclusive these days, they explain, it's not because they're strung out but because they feel they've been strung up—by the media, which they feel have painted them as a pair of junkies without a cause. "Everyone thinks we're on drugs again, even people we work with," says Cobain resignedly as Love paints on a perfect baby-doll mouth. "I guess I'll have to get used to that for the rest of my life."

While Cobain, 24, is quiet and thoughtful, Love is tailor-made for the media attention, blessed and cursed with what seems as an almost genetic inability to censor herself. Within the first five minutes of *The ADVOCATE*'s arrival, she is spinning a story about an ex-flame and his lingerie fetish: "He had to wear nylons to have sex—not just any nylons but flesh-colored nylons. And he couldn't buy them, he had to *find* them." Listening, Cobain smiles, holding Frances by her arms, walking her across his lap. He is—at least for the moment—not feeling beaten up.

Getting beaten up, though, is a recurring theme in Cobain's life. In his hometown of Aberdeen in rural Washington, he was branded a "faggot" from an early age. It was a title he eventually embraced and threw back in his tormentors' faces—just for the hell of it. In 1985 he was even arrested when he and friend Chris Novoselic spray-painted HOMOSEXUAL SEX RULES on the side of a bank.

Four years later, Cobain, Novoselic, and drummer Dave Grohl released the first Nirvana album, *Bleach*, on the small Seattle label Sub Pop Records. Recorded for $606.15, it was a blast of pure punk rock that earned them a reputation in Seattle and drew the interest of several major labels. Their major-label debut, *Nevermind*, was released by DGC in September 1991—and by the end of the year, *Nevermind* (fueled by the inescapably catchy "Smells Like Teen Spirit") had come from far left field to sell 3 million copies and top critics' best-of-the-year lists. Last January cellular phones all over the record industry were crackling when Nirvana hit number one—toppling U2, Metallica, and Michael Jackson from the top of the charts. Punk rock was suddenly a commodity, and the term *grunge*, denoting flannel shirts, ripped jeans, dirty hair, and especially anything Seattle-based, entered the lexicon. Soon record executives were spending weekends in Seattle, trying to find the "next Nirvana," and models cropped up on Paris runways sporting haute grungewear.

But even as Nirvana went from playing club dates to selling out 40,000-seat arenas, the band still didn't play by the rules. They spurned an offer to tour with Guns N' Roses, further fueling already rampant industry rumors that Cobain and his then pregnant wife had a big problem with heroin. Last April, when *Rolling Stone* put the band on its cover, Cobain showed up for the photo session in a T-shirt that read CORPORATE MAGAZINES STILL SUCK. And an unflattering profile of the Cobains in September's *Vanity Fair* dropped the two into the world of glossy journalism with a jolt when Love confirmed to writer Lynn Hirschberg that she and Cobain were indeed using heroin in the early stages of her pregnancy.

While not denying the heroin use, both Cobain and Love insist that they have been misquoted and misunderstood. They maintain that the interview was given early in the year, and at the time the article appeared (the same month Love gave birth to Frances), both had been clean for months. "When I first talked to her [Hirschberg], I had just found out I was pregnant, and I had done some drugs in the beginning of my pregnancy, and that's what I told her," says Love.

Equally misunderstood, to Cobain, is Nirvana itself—particularly the fact that the band appeals to many of the same hard rock fans who pack Guns N' Roses concerts. But while Axl Rose sang derisively of "immigrants and faggots" in his song "One in a Million," Cobain closed his song "Stay Away" by howling "God is gay!" and Nirvana defiantly cavorted in dresses in the video of their hit single "In Bloom." Last year Nirvana traveled to Oregon to perform at a benefit opposing Measure 9, a statewide ordinance that would have amended the state constitution to prohibit protections for gays and lesbians. And when they appeared on *Saturday Night Live*, Cobain and Novoselic made a point of kissing on-camera.

In person, Cobain is the antithesis of a preening guitar cocksman: He's small, pale, soft-spoken, and articulate. Prejudice infuriates him; he spits out the words "homophobe" and "sexist" with the same venom he reserves for the word "spandex." Particularly upsetting to him was an incident last year in Reno, when two men raped a woman while chanting a Nirvana song. On the liner notes for *Incesticide*, he vented his frustration in a blunt statement to Nirvana fans: "If any of you in any way hate homosexuals, people of different color, or women, please do this one favor for us—leave us the fuck alone! Don't come to our shows and don't buy our records."

Despite Cobain's wish that people "leave us the fuck alone," both he and Love seem determined not to surround themselves with a glass bubble of security precautions and stereotypical rock-star trappings. Before this interview—the only one the band's lead singer says he plans to do for *Incesticide*—Cobain set down no conditions regarding the questions that could be asked, nor did he bother to notify his record company that the interview would be taking place. (Love, in fact, insisted that the mutual friend who arranged the meeting put *The ADVOCATE* in direct contact with the couple: "Gay people can have our phone number!")

Back in the hotel room, Love goes out and leaves Cobain to his interview, but she's wary enough to come back twice: "I'm worried about what they're going to write," she finally blurts. Still, her need to trust overwhelms her protectiveness. When she leaves for the third time, she says, "It's a gay publication, Kurt, so don't forget to tell them about the time you stole your tights out of your mother's drawer." Cobain smiles; she laughs and sighs. "I guess I have that effect on men. Bye." And then she's gone for good, pushing Frances's stroller out the door.

Kevin Allman: You two don't seem like Sid and Nancy.

Kurt Cobain: It's just amazing that at this point in rock-and-roll history, people are still expecting their rock icons to live out these classic rock archetypes, like Sid and Nancy. To assume that we're just the same because we come from the underground and we did heroin for a while— it's pretty offensive to be expected to be like that.

KA: Does it hurt worse when they say bad things about Courtney?

KC: Oh, absolutely. What they said about me is not half as strange as what they've said about her. She doesn't deserve that. She sold 60,000 records, and all of a sudden she's found herself as commercially popular as me, and she's just in a punk rock band. Just because she married me, she's subjected to being as popular as an actress or something.

KA: Who do you trust now?

KC: Uh—no one? [*Laughs*] I've always kind of kept myself purposely naive and optimistic, and now I've been forced to be really paranoid. Judgmental. Really defensive all the time. It's been hard for me to change my attitude.

KA: You're here in this hotel room. Can you go out?

KC: Yeah. The other night we went shopping at a second-hand store and bought some fuzzy sweaters and some grungewear.

KA: Real grungewear, not the designer kind?

KC: Not Perry Ellis. [*Laughs*] We were driving around in our Volvo, after buying some grungewear, and we realized that we're not necessarily as big as Guns N' Roses, but we're as popular as them, and we still don't have bodyguards. We still go shopping; we still go to movies and carry on with our lives.

I've always been a paranoid person by nature anyhow, and now I have these people so concerned with what I say and what I do at all times that it's really hard for me to deal with that. I'm dealing with it a lot better than I would have expected. If I could have predicted what was going to happen to me a few years ago, I definitely wouldn't have opted for this kind of a life-style.

KA: Would it be cooler to have stayed in Seattle and not been on the cover of *Rolling Stone*?

KC: Yeah. Well, I *chose* to do that—although it was a hell of a fight. We were on tour in Australia, and I had completely forgotten that I had promised to do the *Rolling Stone* piece. And that day, they called and said, "Are you ready to do the photo shoot?" And it was like, "No, I really don't want to do this." I had so much pressure from my management and the band members—they wanted to do it, and I just agreed. On my way there I just decided, "I'm going to write something on my shirt that's offensive enough to stop getting our picture on the cover." This way I could say that I actually played along with it and still didn't get picked to be on the cover. I wasn't necessarily challenging *Rolling*

Stone, saying, "You suck" and "We don't want to have anything to do with you, but we'll still use you for our exposure."

Rolling Stone sucks, has always sucked, and still sucks just because they have a hip band on their cover. We're not as cool and hip as everyone thinks. Having us on the cover isn't going to make *Rolling Stone* any cooler. Ever since this band has been popular, I've always thought of us as just a '90s version of Cheap Trick or the Knack. They had the two sides of appeal that made them kind of a cool band—a commercial side and kind of a new-wave side. We have that.

KA: Everything you do seems to get analyzed. You can't even say or do anything off-the-cuff.

KC: Yeah. I still have the same views I've always had. When I used to say things to my friends, I didn't expect to be taken so seriously. Now I have to learn to detour my thoughts and what I say in order to stop someone from saying I'm a hypocrite. That was the *Rolling Stone* debate: "Corporate magazines suck, but you're still on the cover." Well, of course! It's a joke. Get over it.

People should take things rock stars say with a grain of salt because there's no one in rock and roll right now who's a relevant example or a spokesperson for anything. They do have an influence on people, and I think there's a new consciousness that's really positive among rock stars, like Rock the Vote. They're trying to make people aware, but I really can't think of anyone who's really schooled enough to be political to the point that would be required for a rock star. If Jello Biafra [former lead singer of the Dead Kennedys] was a big international star, it would be really cool. But he's not on a major label, and he doesn't write commercial enough music to use that as a tool.

KA: Does it make you laugh when people take apart all your songs and try to figure out what you're saying?

KC: Oh, yeah. At the time I was writing those songs, I really didn't know what I was trying to say. There's no point in my even trying to analyze or explain it. That used to be the biggest subject in an interview: "What are your lyrics about?" [*Laughs*] I haven't written any new lyrics, that's for sure. We have about 12 songs for our new album we're scheduled to record in February, and I don't have any lyrics at all. Within the past year, notebooks and poetry books I've had lying around have either been destroyed or stolen. So I don't have anything to go back on at all. It sucks.

The past year I haven't been very prolific at all. A few months ago we went on tour to Europe, and before we went I took two of my favorite guitars and all my poetry books and writings and two tapes that had guitar parts I was going to use for the next record, and I put all this really important stuff in our shower, because we've never really used our shower before. And the roommates upstairs had a plumbing problem, so when we came back, everything was destroyed. I don't have anything to go back on at all. It's pretty scary.

KA: I read the liner notes you wrote on *Incesticide*. I've never seen somebody on a major label say, "If you're a racist, a sexist, a homophobe, we don't want you to buy our records."

KC: That's been the biggest problem that I've had being in this band. I know there are those people out in the audience, and there's not much I can do about it. I can talk about those issues in interviews—I think it's pretty obvious that we're against the homophobes and the sexists and the racists, but when "Teen Spirit" first came out, mainstream audiences were under the assumption that we were just like Guns N' Roses.

Then our opinions started showing up in interviews. And then things like Chris and I kissing on *Saturday Night Live*. We weren't trying to be subversive or punk rock; we were just doing something insane and stupid at the last minute. I think now that our opinions are out in the open, a lot of kids who bought our record regret knowing anything about us. [*Laughs*]

There is a war going on in the high schools now between Nirvana kids and Guns N' Roses kids. It's really cool. I'm really proud to be a part of that, because when I was in high school, I dressed like a punk rocker and people would scream "Devo!" at me—because Devo infiltrated the mainstream. Out of all the bands who came from the underground and actually made it in the mainstream, Devo is the most subversive and challenging of all. They're just awesome. I love them.

KA: Maybe there'll be a Devo revival soon, like the Village People revival.

KC: I saw the Village People two years ago in Seattle! They were so cool. They still have the same costumes.

KA: Is there anything about Guns N' Roses' music you like?

KC: I can't think of a damn thing. I can't even waste my time on that band, because they're so obviously pathetic and untalented. I used to think that everything in the mainstream pop world was crap, but now that some underground bands have been signed with majors, I take Guns N' Roses as more of an offense. I have to look into it more: They're really talentless people, and they write crap music, and they're the most popular rock band on the earth right now. I can't believe it.

KA: Didn't Axl Rose say something nasty to you at the MTV Video Music Awards in September?

KC: They actually tried to beat us up. Courtney and I were with the baby in the eating area backstage, and Axl walked by. So Courtney yelled, "Axl! Axl, come over here!" We just wanted to say hi to him—we think he's a joke, but we just wanted to say something to him. So I said, "Will you be the godfather of our child?" I don't know what had happened before that to piss him off, but he took his aggressions out on us and began screaming bloody murder.

These were his words: "You shut your bitch up, or I'm taking you down to the pavement." [*Laughs*] Everyone around us just burst out into tears of laughter. She wasn't even saying anything mean, you know? So I turned to Courtney and said, "Shut up, bitch!" And everyone laughed and he left. So I guess I did what he wanted me to do—be a man. [*Laughs*]

KA: Does he remind you of guys you went to high school with?

KC: Absolutely. Really confused, fucked-up guys. There's not much hope for them.

KA: When he was singing about "immigrants and faggots," people were excusing it by saying, "Well, he's from Indiana—"

KC: Oh, well, that's OK then. [*Laughs*] Insane. Later, after we played our show and were walking back to our trailer, the Guns N' Roses entourage came walking toward us. They have at least 50 bodyguards apiece: huge, gigantic brain-dead oafs ready to kill for Axl at all times. [*Laughs*] They didn't see me, but they surrounded Chris, and Duff [McKagan of Guns N' Roses] wanted to beat Chris up, and the bodyguards started pushing Chris around. He finally escaped, but throughout the rest of the evening, there was a big threat of either Guns N' Roses themselves or their goons beating us up. We had to hide out.

Since then, every time Axl has played a show he's said some comment about me and Courtney. When he was in Seattle, he said, "Nirvana would rather stay home and shoot drugs with their bitch wives than tour with us." [*Laughs*] That's why there's this big feud in most of the high schools. It's hilarious. He is insane, though. I was scared. I couldn't possibly beat him up; I know he would beat me up if he had the chance.

KA: How do you feel about Guns N' Roses fans coming to see you?

KC: Well, when we played that No on 9 benefit in Portland, I said something about Guns N' Roses. Nothing real nasty—I think I said, "And now, for our next song, 'Sweet Child o' Mine.'" But some kid jumped onstage and said, "Hey, man, Guns N' Roses plays awesome music, and Nirvana plays awesome music. Let's just get along and work this out, man!"

And I just couldn't help but say, "No, kid, you're really wrong. Those people are total sexist jerks, and the reason we're playing this show is to fight homophobia in a real small way. The guy is a fucking sexist and a racist and a homophobe, and you can't be on his side and be on our side. I'm sorry that I have to divide this up like this, but it's something you can't ignore. And besides they can't write good music." [*Laughs*]

KA: You know, you were probably taking money from people who were voting yes on 9—but they really wanted to see Nirvana.

KC: [*Laughs*] Right! Chris went to a Guns N' Roses concert when they played here with Metallica a couple of months ago, and he went back-stage, and there were these two bimbo girls who looked like they walked out of a Warrant video. They were sitting on the couch in hopes of sucking Axl's dick or something, and one of them said, "Chris, we saw you at that No on 9 benefit! We're voting yes on 9! You kissed Kurt on the lips! That was disgusting!" [*Laughs*] To know that we affect people like that—it's kind of funny. The sad thing is that there's no penetrating them. After all that, after all the things those girls had seen us do, that was the one thing that sticks in their mind.

KA: You used to push people's buttons like that in high school, didn't you?

KC: Oh, absolutely. I used to pretend I was gay just to fuck with people. I've had the reputation of being a homosexual ever since I was 14. It was really cool, because I found a couple of gay friends in Aberdeen—which is almost impossible. How I could ever come across a gay person in Aberdeen is amazing! But I had some really good friends that way. I got beat up a lot, of course, because of my association with them.

People just thought I was weird at first, just some fucked-up kid. But once I got the gay tag, it gave me the freedom to be able to be a freak and let people know that they should just stay away from me. Instead of having to explain to someone that they should just stay the fuck away from me—I'm gay, so I can't even be touched. It made for quite a few scary experiences in alleys walking home from school, though.

KA: You actually got beat up?

KC: Oh, yeah. Quite a few times.

KA: And you used to spray-paint GOD IS GAY on people's trucks?

KC: That was a lot of fun. The funnest thing about that was not actually the act but the next morning. I'd get up early in the morning to walk through the neighborhood that I'd terrorized to see the aftermath. That was the worst thing I could have spray-painted on their cars. Nothing would have been more effective.

Aberdeen was depressing, and there were a lot of negative things about it, but it was really fun to fuck with people all the time. I loved to go to parties—jock keggers—and just run around drunk and obnoxious, smoking cigars and spitting on the backs of these big redneck jocks and them not realizing it. By the end of the evening, usually I'd end up offending a girl, and she'd get her boyfriend to come beat me up. [*Laughs*]

KA: Because people thought you were gay and you had gay friends, did you ever wonder if you might be gay?

KC: Yeah, absolutely. See, I've always wanted male friends that I could be real intimate with and talk about important things with and be as affectionate with that person as I would be with a girl. Throughout my life I've always been really close with girls and made friends with girls. And I've always been a really sickly, feminine person anyhow, so I thought I was gay for a while because I didn't find any of the girls in my high school attractive at all. They had really awful haircuts and fucked-up attitudes. So I thought I would try to be gay for a while, but I'm just more sexually attracted to women. But I'm really glad that I found a few gay friends, because it totally saved me from becoming a monk or something.

I mean, I'm definitely gay in spirit, and I probably could be bisexual. But I'm married, and I'm more attracted to Courtney than I ever have been toward a person, so there's no point in trying to sow my oats at this point. [*Laughs*] If I wouldn't have found Courtney, I probably would have carried on with a bisexual life-style. But I just find her totally attractive in all ways.

KA: She has been described as a fag hag—

KC: Oh, she is. That was all she did for about five or six years of her life—hang out in gay clubs. She learned everything about perfume and fashion from her friends.

KA: Now that you've got a baby, how are you going to teach her about sexism and homophobia and things like that?

KC: I think that just growing up with Courtney and I will be a good enough example that, hopefully, she won't be prejudiced. You have to admit that most of the reasons a person grows up hating the isms is because their parents taught them. She might get confused, but I'm not worried about it at all.

KA: With the state the world is in, do you ever feel scared for her?

KC: Well, I have apocalyptic dreams all the time. Two years ago, I wouldn't even have considered having a child. I used to say that a person who would bring a child into this life now is selfish. But I try to be optimistic, and things do look like they're getting a little bit better—just the way communication has progressed in the past ten years. MTV, whether they're the evil corporate ogre or not, has played a part in raising consciousness.

It seems tacky almost, but rock and roll and our generation are not going to put up with the same Reaganite bullshit we were subjected to when we were younger. I was helpless when I was 12, when Reagan got elected, and there was nothing I could do about that. But now this generation is growing up, and they're in their mid 20s; they're not putting up with it.

I know there's still Republicans all over the place, but don't you feel that it's getting a little bit better? Not just because Clinton is in office now but—look at the first thing he did. He tried to take away the ban on gays in the military, and I think that's a pretty positive thing. I don't expect a lot of change, but I think in the last five years our generation's gotten a lot more positive. I know that by reading *Sassy* magazine, you know? As tacky and stupid as that seems, I can tell that the average 14-year-old kid is a lot more sensitive—or trying to be—than they were ten years ago.

KA: Are you pro Clinton?

KC: Oh, yeah. I voted for him. I would have rather had Jerry Brown. I contributed my hundred dollars. But I'm definitely happy that Clinton's in.

KA: Would you play at the White House if they asked you to?

KC: [*Laughs*] If we could have some kind of influence on something, yeah. I know that Chelsea likes us a lot, so maybe Chelsea could say, "Dad, do this and do that! Nirvana says so!" [*Laughs*] Sure, I'd play for the president. And Chelsea seems like a pretty neat person—Birkenstock-wearing kid. Amy Carter's pretty cool too, from what I've heard. She's been seen at Butthole Surfers concerts!

KA: You guys aren't preachy about your opinions. It's a sensible approach.

KC: Gee. That's pretty flattering, but out of all the people I know, I'm about the least qualified to be talking politically. I hope I come across more personal than political. About a year ago, when we realized the impact that we have, we thought it was a great opportunity to have some kind of influence on people. I've been called a hypocrite and an idiot and unqualified, but I can't help it. It's just my nature. I have to talk about things that piss me off, and if that's negative or that's preachy, then that's too bad. No one's gonna shut me up. I'm still the same person I was. Actually, I used to be way more of a radical than I am now.

KA: In thought or in deed?

KC: Both, really. Mostly in deed; I can't really go around vandalizing anymore. But I have—actually, I just did a while ago.

KA: What?

KC: I can't say! [*Laughs*] I can't even say! I have people checking up on me all the time—especially because of the heroin rumors. That's been blown out of proportion so severely that I'm constantly harassed at airports and immigration all the time. And the cops—I get pulled over whenever they recognize me, and they search my car.

It all started with just one fucking article in *Bam* magazine. This guy—I wasn't even high that night, and he just assumed I was and wrote a piece on how sunken in my cheeks were and how pinholed my eyes were and that I wasn't able to cope with the success and everything that was going on with the band. It was very embarrassing. It didn't bother me at first, but then once one article is written about a person that's negative, it just spreads like wildfire, and everyone just assumes it's true.

KA: You're talking about Lynn Hirschberg's profile of Courtney in *Vanity Fair*.

KC: I've never read an article that was more convincing yet more ridiculous in my life. Everybody from our record label to our management to our closest friends believed that shit.

She [Hirschberg] did a really good job of taking a piece of what Courtney had said and turning it into something completely different. I've seen that happen before—it's happened with me a lot of times—but this was such an extreme and done so well that I have to give her credit. She's a master at being catty.

KA: What about the drug use?

KC: Courtney was honest about the heroin excursion we went on for a few months. Then Courtney found herself pregnant, realized she was pregnant and had a drug problem, and got off of drugs. It's as simple as that. But it made it look like eight months after the fact, Courtney was nine months pregnant and still doing drugs and everyone was really concerned. Like there was some awful den of iniquity going on in our apartment. I looked really skinny. Well, I am a skinny person, and I gain ten pounds every time I'm photographed, so people assume I'm this chunky, normal-weight person.

I'm just so tired of thinking about this. We have to live with the results of this one article every fucking day. It's something we have to deal with all the time.

KA: How did you feel when you read it?

KC: I was totally pissed off. My first thoughts were to have her fucking snuffed out. I wanted to personally beat the shit out of her, and I've never wanted to do that to anybody, especially a woman. But I just had so much anger in me. It was done so well. We were just helpless to combat something like that. We've had to do fluff pieces to try to fight this thing. It's embarrassing to have to do that: to pose with your family on the cover of a magazine, to hope that some people at least question the validity of [*Vanity Fair*].

KA: You're talking about posing for the December *Spin* cover?

KC: Yeah, and we've done a couple of other things. It pissed me off to the point of . . . not even wanting to hate that much. We could have filed a lawsuit with Condé Nast, but they have so many millions of dollars, they could have filibustered for ten years, and we wouldn't have come up with anything except losing most of our money.

KA: What's the funniest thing you've ever seen written about you?

KC: Practically all of it. [*Laughs*] Most of the time I come across as just this redneck little rocker kid who basically can't put a sentence together, you know? I come across a lot of times as just a stupid rock-and-roll kid.

KA: Courtney comes across in the press as the Nancy Reagan of this relationship.

KC: It's just sick. God! I don't want to say something like "Well, if anything, I wear the pants in the house." It's completely divided. We have influence on each other. It's totally 50-50. Courtney insists on this: She has a tab when she borrows money from me that she has to pay back. She's only up to $6,000. We're millionaires, and she goes to Jet Rag [a Los Angeles vintage-clothing shop] and buys clothes—$5 dresses. Big deal! I'll gladly buy her some $5 dresses. We don't require much at all.

Our personal expenses over the last year—we made a million dollars, of which $380,000 went to taxes, $300,000 went to a house, the rest went to doctors and lawyers, and our personal expenses were like $80,000. That's including car rentals, food, everything. That's not very much; that's definitely not what Axl spends a year. She insisted on a prenuptial agreement; no one knows that. So there's definitely not manipulation going on in this relationship at all.

It really sickens me to think that everyone assumes this. It makes me feel even stupider. I'm not the most secure person in the world, and I don't need to know that every time I go outside and someone recognizes me, they think of me as this defenseless little rocker idiot that's being manipulated by his wife. It's a little bit more complex than that.

Courtney's had misconceptions about herself all her life. I talk to people who knew Courtney five years ago, and she was way more of a volatile, fucked-up person than she is now. She was insane at times. People would see her at parties just begging for attention. I never could have predicted a successful marriage with this person a few years ago. It just couldn't have happened.

KA: How does all this affect the other members of Nirvana?

KC: Definitely not as severe as everyone thinks or what has been written. There was an article in the [British music magazine] *NME* that was nothing but an "exposé" on Courtney fucking up Nirvana and making us come close to breaking up. It's pretty frightening to find that an article like that can be written by a friend of yours. It makes it hard to trust anybody.

Chris and Dave liked Courtney before I even liked Courtney. During that time, I knew that I liked her a lot, but I wouldn't admit it. She and Dave were really good friends—I shouldn't say this, but they almost wanted to get together for a time. When we were on tour in Europe, some of our shows collided with Hole shows, and Courtney would hang out on the bus with us, and Chris and Courtney were really good friends. And it hasn't changed at all. There hasn't been any bad blood except after the *Vanity Fair* piece.

For a few days, even Chris was convinced that Courtney had said those things. Courtney had said, "Why don't you kick Chris out of the band?" She said that, but it was a total joke. That's the biggest problem with articles—context. The word *sarcastic* needs to be in parentheses 90% of the time in an interview with us. Dave and Chris are dealing with this fine, and they're defending us as much as they can, but we can't expect them to go on a defense crusade, because it doesn't affect them like it affects us.

KA: Have there been times in the last year when you've just wanted to quit?

KC: Oh, yeah. The other night. I called up Chris late at night; I was really drunk, and I said, "I don't want to be in this band anymore. I'll call you tomorrow." I was dead serious. For a couple of hours. [*Laughs*]

KA: How is it dealing with a big label?

KC: We haven't had any complications. In our contract we have 100% artistic control. What that means in fine print, I don't know. All the evil corporateness that I've heard about since I've been into underground rock probably is true with other bands, but we have a good lawyer and a great contract. And we sell a lot of records for them, so we have the upper hand.

KA: Courtney's band got a good contract too?

KC: It's actually better than ours. This is the first decade major labels have even dealt with a contract like this. They're so used to having bands that don't even know what they want to do that they have to be in control. There are a lot of bands that don't have any artistic direction at all, so they need to dress up in spandex.

KA: So you can turn on mainstream radio and hear some music you like these days.

KC: That's part of the reason I'm a little bit more optimistic this year— Clinton and because the Screaming Trees are on heavy rotation right now. It's commercial, but it's good music. I don't like Pearl Jam's music at all, but at least they have good attitudes; they're not another Van Halen, who totally refuse to address anything.

The only sad thing about it is that the innocence of underground music has been lumped in with the corporate idea of what underground is. There are no boundaries. Pearl Jam's a good example. I don't mean to harp on them; I'm tired of talking shit about them, but they're a real commercial rock band.

KA: What do you do when you're not playing music?

KC: Well, I'm reading *Perfume* for the second time. It's about a perfume apprentice in the 1700s. And I really like Camille Paglia a lot; it's really entertaining, even though I don't necessarily agree with what she says. I still paint once in a while—I painted the cover of *Incesticide*.

And I make dolls. I like the style of things from the 1700s and 1800s from Yugoslavia and that area. I copy from these doll-collector magazines. They're clay. I bake them, and then I make them look really old and put old clothes on them. They look like I actually came across a real antique, because I don't know where to find the dolls that are in those magazines. I could go to a doll-collectors show, but they're so expensive. I don't want to indulge in things like that—"Now that I'm a rock star, I buy antiques," you know? [*Laughs*] Some of those things are, like, $50,000.

I can't find anything I want. I go shopping, and I buy food, and that's about it. Now that I have all this money, I just can't spend it on anything. Everything that I appreciate is old but not necessarily an antique, so I can get it really cheap.

KA: So you're not falling into the trap of spending money on things just because you can?

KC: Sometimes I wish I could. I've noticed there are specialty shops for the rich and famous that have basically the same things you can find at Kmart, but they have a ridiculous price tag, and people buy it just because they don't have anything else to do with their money. There are a lot of things like that on Rodeo Drive. We went into Gucci just to see what a Gucci bag cost. [*Laughs*] Just this leather bag, and because it had a Gucci name on it, it was, like, $10,000!

KA: Do you like L.A.?

KC: I *hate* L.A. I love the weather, but I can't stand being there. I absolutely hate it. A lot of it has to do with having the responsibility of driving around with the baby. People are so rude there. I'm not that bad a driver, and I get in a wreck almost every day.

We were there for the riots. That decision was the most asinine thing I'd ever seen. If they were going to riot, I just wish they could have rioted in the middle of Beverly Hills. Got all the Gucci bags. [*Laughs*]

KA: Now's your chance to say anything you'd like to say.

KC: I always clam up when that question is asked. Maybe I'll just fumble and stutter and end up saying, "Don't believe everything you read." I

THE TRUE PICTURE OF THE NINETIES ROCK ICON THAT COURTNEY SAYS SHE LIKES TO FIGHT

Antonio Carlos Miguel and Eva Joory | January 19, 1993 | *O Globo* (Brazil)

O Globo's photographer Marcia Foletto and I arrived at the hotel where the band was staying around noon—six hours before we entered Kurt Cobain's room. His two Brazilian bodyguards helped me get the interview by acting as messengers. I argued that I wasn't an ordinary journalist, that I was someone who really loved music and that I had enjoyed the anarchic concert that Nirvana gave three days earlier in São Paulo, one that most of my colleagues in the Brazilian press didn't understand. I also gave the bodyguards a copy of Brazil's top rock magazine, *Bizz* (where I had previously worked), with a cover shot of Cobain. Two hours later, I saw Courtney Love leaving the elevator and seating herself at the coffee bar in the lobby. So I introduced myself as the guy who was being so persistent. She looked me over and asked me to wait just a little longer. Thirty minutes later, Marcia and I were invited up.

It was a sunny summer day, but Kurt was wearing very warm clothing because he liked the "carioca" pattern, a shirt over a T-shirt. He also claimed he was in pain from strong colic; he held his belly many times during our meeting. He told me about his passion for Jimi Hendrix's music—"We used to sit near his grave to play some music and drink beer"—and one of his goals as a composer: "To blend the punk urgency of the Sex Pistols with the Beatles melodies!" Kurt also talked about some problems with his bandmates ("I don't understand why their names have to be in the credits; I wrote 99 percent of Nirvana's music.") and a strong disillusionment with all the buzz around the grunge scene ("I'm tired of all this; my fifteen minutes of fame are over. I wish that a lot of unknown bands I adore could have their doses too.").

Kurt said he'd like to come back, incognito, to Brazil to say hello. He seemed sincere and gave us strong farewell hugs. I still regret not giving him the joint I had in my pocket. It might have helped his symptoms. I loved the conversation, but my editor chose to put a piece on the front page exploring similarities between Kurt and Courtney and Sid and Nancy. I really hated that decision. My interview with Kurt was mixed with Eva Joory's interview with Courtney for the front-page story. —Antonio Carlos Miguel

In 1993 I was writing for *O Globo* as a music, cinema, and culture reporter. My job was mainly to interview people and review records. At that time, Rio de Janeiro and São Paulo had big music festivals, and Nirvana came to perform. The band was at its peak—a huge worldwide success story.

I managed to secure a phone interview with Krist Novoselic, and once the band members had arrived in Rio, our editor decided we had to talk to Cobain. He sent Antonio and me to the band's hotel to try to speak with him casually, with no manager or press agents present.

We sat there for six hours, doing nothing, until we saw Kurt alone in the lobby. He was so tiny and skinny, and was walking barefoot, talking to himself. We approached him, but he wouldn't talk to us. That same night, we met Krist, and he invited us to his room for a drink and to chat for a while. It was the coolest sensation, being there with one of the leaders of this amazing band that we loved, along with his girlfriend, talking about politics and music. It was a great article to write—not just an interview but a profile of a truly great band.

The next day, Antonio and I decided to go to the hotel one more time to try Kurt again. While waiting for Kurt, I saw Courtney Love leaving the hotel. I approached her and asked if I could interview her. She told me she was going shopping alone, because Kurt hated shopping. Then she declared that she would talk only if I told her where to get drugs. I told her it was a dangerous thing to do, but she insisted, so I showed her the Rocinha, one of the biggest favelas in Rio, which was close to the hotel.

During our short interview, she was in a very good mood. She spoke about her relationship with Kurt, confessing that they were a boring, everyday couple. She showed me a photo of her baby daughter, Frances Bean, telling me she loved her, and she confirmed the rumors that she fought with Kurt every day: "That's the fun of a wedding," she replied.

The front-page article legitimately compared the couple to Sid and Nancy because of the similarities in their behavior, their fights, and their difficult relationship. —Eva Joory

Translated by Sophie-Claire Soulsby.

After six hours of waiting and negotiating, our reporter from *O Globo* is allowed to go to Kurt Cobain's room in the Intercontinental. Courtney Love passes through the hotel lobby, apparently to see if the team is confident enough to do the first exclusive interview with the front man of Nirvana in Brazil. Half an hour later, security takes the reporter to Kurt's room. Fresh out of the bathroom and with a sickly appearance, he confirms he isn't doing well; "I have terrible diarrhea." The topics of conversation have to be restricted to the field of music—hence the reporter isn't able to check if Cobain's problems are a result of the heroin detoxification treatment which, according to the US press, he was undergoing. Kurt was friendly, chatting about the typical debauchery of rock stars. The picture that remains is of a fragile and honest person who at age twenty-five was stunned by resounding success. An underground band from Seattle until the end of 1991, after the album *Nevermind*, Nirvana became the center of attraction of the global media and the first rock icon of the 1990s.

Antonio Carlos Miguel: You and Courtney are being called the "Sid and Nancy" of grunge; what do you think of this?

Kurt Cobain: It's nothing. I don't want to talk about it, and I don't like it at all.

ACM: Then let's talk about a curiosity in the introduction to "Territorial Pissings." You guys sing an excerpt from an old hippie song, "Get Together." A joke or a tribute?

KC: Both those things. The idea came moments before we recorded the track. We didn't want to be offensive to the guy who wrote the music. The song speaks of people who join together and be cool and try something new, the ideal contrast to the macho men I'm portraying in "Territorial Pissings"—the title is a reference to the habit of certain animals to urinate to mark their territories, and we thought it would be good for Chris to sing "Get Together" in the opening.

ACM: Do you like the rock of the 1960s and the ideals of the hippie movement?

KC: Yes, very. I, as a teenager, lived through a bit of it in the 1970s and it was fantastic. The idea of being positive and causing change in society and the world was appropriated by the media, who turned it into something ridiculous, a caricature. The hippie movement actually happened in San Francisco in 1967, but American society still lived this hippie ideology for another ten years, even in a superficial way.

ACM: Do you think it's possible to draw parallels between Nirvana's music and the music of the hippie era?

KC: The biggest point of contact might be the manipulation by the media, already leading to the ridiculous things my generation believes. Fashion, designers, people who do clothes, begin to market shirts like this one that I'm wearing for thousands of dollars.

––––––––––––––

Courtney Love finally proved to be in love with her husband Kurt Cobain. After starring in several scandals in Brazil and fighting Cobain on the day of his arrival in Rio, on Thursday afternoon in the hotel lobby she didn't stop to embrace her husband. Courtney is beautiful; her white skin and bleached hair emphasize her big, blue eyes. Despite having left the lobby at high speed with her security people without stopping to sign autographs, she agrees to answer some questions from *O Globo* about her troubles and even made a point of proudly showing off a Polaroid photo of her daughter, little Frances Bean Cobain; "Isn't she so cute? She's already six months!"

Eva Joory: Is it true that you love fighting with Kurt, as reported by the press?

Courtney Love: I never read the press; what else are they saying? That I fight with Kurt? Of course, we fight every day. That's all the beauty of a marriage.

EJ: So you think you have a normal relationship with Kurt?

CL: We're so normal that we become boring. We're a typical couple, quite normal. There's not any news about it, why talk about it?

EJ: Why are you out alone?

CL: Doing a bit of shopping. Kurt doesn't do that stuff.

Beer at the Tomb of Hendrix

Cobain recounts that he was a fan of Jimi Hendrix—who also played guitar left-handed—and punk rock. As for his name and the correct spelling, it's *Kurt*, but lately he's been signing *Kurdt* more and has already used *Curt*; "Choose which you prefer."

ACM: With so many different styles, is it possible to speak of a sound of Seattle?

KC: Everybody enjoying the music already knows these bands don't sound the same.

ACM: Is Nirvana influenced by punk?

KC: I always wanted to be close to punk rock, and it's my favorite type of music.

ACM: Do you agree that Nirvana, like Hendrix, mix noise and weight with great songs and beautiful melodies?

KC: Hendrix really had a lot of melody. It was noisy, great music, and he was a great composer. I have a lot of respect for him, and I visit his grave every year and drink a few beers.

ACM: The majority of your songs are credited to you and Chris Novoselic . . .

KC: Well, I don't understand why they're credited to both. I write 99 percent of the music at home and then work it up in the studio.

ACM: What happened on stage in São Paulo?

KC: Having to play the same songs every night turns into a job. Perhaps speaking another language means the public didn't understand the joke.

We exchanged instruments and played old, favorite songs—very badly, obviously, because we hadn't rehearsed anything.

ACM: And what should we expect from the show in Rio?

KC: I think it'll be better, not so much nonsense. Maybe we'll invite everyone in the audience to take the stage.

ACM: Recalling Andy Warhol, that in the future everyone would be famous for fifteen minutes, would you like a second turn at it?

KC: Oh, my fifteen minutes are up. I hope that a lot of bands I love have their turn. I'd give up my fifteen minutes to anyone, with pleasure.

"SO MANY BRIGHT LIGHTS IN MY EYES"

Rodrigo Lariú | January 23, 1993 | *College Radio* **and** *Midsummer Madness* **Fanzine (Brazil)**

Three friends and I ran a show called *College Radio* that aired every Saturday at Fluminense FM in Niterói. I was in charge of journalism and was granted two passes for the Hollywood Rock Festival in January 1993. I've always liked Mudhoney and Love Battery more than Nirvana or L7, but still, it wasn't a bad festival at all. That morning we went to Sambodromo, where Nirvana was sound checking, and it was easy to convince the bouncers that we were allowed in with our passes. My friend Dodô Azevedo and I, wearing handmade T-shirts and clutching fanzines, watched the sound check, then headed to the backstage door, shouting that we were from *College Radio*. Krist Novoselic showed us mercy and told us to go to the band's hotel while he tried to arrange an interview.

Flocks of fans were crowded outside the Hotel Intercontinental. Krist headed past the entrance and noticed us. By this time Dodô and I had hooked up with our friends Livia Lazzaro, Rogério Goulart, and Leandro Ferreira. We were told to wait. Minutes later the elevator opened, and a huge guy, Kurt's personal Brazilian bodyguard, leaned out and shouted, "Where are the guys from the radio program?!" We hollered back, "Here! We're here!" He looked at these five youngsters—I was twenty, Livia was still seventeen or so, the others were all around twenty. He gave us a funny look. "ALL of you?" But he took us up to the room, made us wait, and then told us Kurt wanted to talk to us. We were stunned. Kurt? We were happy enough to talk to anyone from Nirvana, but Kurt himself? Wow. Just two minutes later Kurt entered. He greeted each one of us, we explained who we were, and he sat on the sofa so we could chat. He asked us to record sound only—no image—on our VHS camcorder. There are no photos of our meeting.

For thirty minutes we sat together, chatting about all kinds of things—smashing guitars, fanzines, Brazilian bands, the set list for that evening's show. Eventually, Courtney walked in and told Kurt they should go paragliding. We were invited to leave—someone else was waiting. Kurt gave me John Silva's address so I could send him demos of local bands, but in the end I didn't send anything. We didn't even use the tape on our show; our show was really alternative, and maybe we felt Nirvana was too pop for us. It took another year and a half for us to realize we'd been given a unique opportunity. We met a super-friendly and truly interested Kurt Cobain who wanted to hear all about the scene in Rio de Janeiro. He was a very fine man, and I'd never have imagined he would . . . y'know? —Rodrigo Lariú

Livia Lazzaro: Did you like the concert in São Paolo?

Kurt Cobain: Yeah, a lot.

LL: How were the people?

KC: A lot of times, when we play bigger shows, there's so many bright lights in my eyes that I can't really see anybody. It's blinding. And I asked about five times if they would turn the lights off that were out in the audience in my face—but they wouldn't do it so . . . I imagined, I sense that they were having fun! Yeah.

Rodrigo Lariú: When you give a big concert, do people have less fun than in a small place with a lot of feedback?

KC: Well . . . I have more fun. I know that. I know the rest of the band members have a lot more fun in smaller places; they're always more enjoyable. Because I've never really enjoyed going to a large show and watching bands—the sound is bad, and the band is so far away that it's really like watching television. There's not much I can do about it, really. Hopefully, if our next record is even noisier, we will lose some people in the audience who won't appreciate that and we can start playing smaller clubs.

LL: What about American bands? Which do you like the most?

KC: I like Pavement . . .

LL: Sonic Youth?

KC: Yeah, of course! Do you like their new record?

LL: Sure, I like, but I think I prefer their last album. *Dirty* is OK. They had the same producer as you, Butch Vig.

KC: I like Pavement and Sebadoh and the Breeders, Pixies—I love the Pixies. They broke up . . .

Leandro Ferreira: And what about the other bands playing with you here—Alice in Chains, Red Hot Chili Peppers—what do you think about them?

KC: Hmm . . . Well, Red Hot Chili Peppers are entertaining—I like to watch them. I don't own any of their records. They're a fun band, but I prefer more noisy, raunchy punk rock kinda stuff. I like old funk music, like Funkadelic and old black stuff.

LF: Don't you have any plans to combat this mainstream music, to get out of the mainstream?

LL: To go back to the underground?

KC: Well, I've racked my brains trying to figure out how the hell I could do that. I've tried to think of many scams, and it's almost impossible. I mean, I've refused to do interviews and stuff . . . I don't want to be a part of it, but I don't know what to do. I don't want to break up my band, because I like to play with them.

LL: You didn't mean that? When you started to say that?

KC: Not at all!

LL: In reality, I don't think it is a shame to be a success. If you do what you want—if you do good music—in fact the media wanted you to be successful. Then it's not a question of popularity; it's a question of authenticity. So if you are successful, it doesn't mean that you're not good.

KC: That's good. I'm noticing that that's the feeling of a lot of people.

LL: Yeah, they say Nirvana now is known by everyone, so it's not good anymore.

KC: Yeah, well, that means that those people don't like music. They're the kind of people who are really into feeding their egos by pretending that they're discovering new bands that no one knows about so they can feel cool. Those people are just as stupid as people who only listen to commercial music, as far as I'm concerned.

Dodô Azevedo: Is it true that Pavement and PJ Harvey have signed to major record companies?

KC: Well, Pavement is on Matador, and they just got bought out by Atlantic, and PJ Harvey . . . I think she did too. But one good thing about it, there are a few bands who are still very raw and still very punk rock who are getting signed to major labels and they're not changing their sound at all. And the major labels are letting them do this. Like Flipper, they're a San Francisco band from the early 1980s—well, actually, they started in the late 1970s—very noisy, very influential for my band, one of my favorite bands; they're very slow and noisy and fucked up. Punk rock attitude, and they've just been signed to Def American and their new album sounds just like their old albums. And Hole has been signed to DGC, and they sound just like they used to, really noisy and raunchy. They have a few more pop songs now . . .

Rogério Goulart: Don't you ever think about producing anything?

KC: Yeah, I have, actually. I helped Hole produce their demos that they've been doing, and I'm producing the Melvins' new record. That's going pretty well—we've done about six songs so far.

LL: What about the concert tonight—do you think that there is a great difference between São Paolo and Rio, in terms of the public?

KC: I don't know. I have no idea because I don't know the country.

LL: People always say that the public, the audience in São Paolo, that they're cooler. That in Rio they dance, that they're a bit easier to deal with. You'll learn tonight.

KC: I guess I will.

RG: It was great, the finale of the São Paolo concert—I liked it so much. But people didn't understand it.

KC: Oh, you liked it? Yeah, I didn't expect them to really understand what we were doing. I didn't care; we had fun. I knew there were some people in the audience that, like you guys, would understand and enjoy it. We like to do stuff like that sometimes.

LF: A lot of people don't have a voice, so they can't say that they enjoyed the show as much as the others. The next day the newspapers said that the end of the Nirvana show was a mess, but the people who liked it can say nothing because they don't have the media.

RG: We liked it because it's a way to play with the mainstream. You're up there, you can do whatever you like.

KC: Yeah, because they just expect a very professional, slick production—they expect for us to say some chanting thing before a song and get everyone to scream and then play the song perfectly and end it perfectly. We just like to play noise sometimes . . .

RG: Any surprise tonight? [*All laugh.*] Surprises?

KC: I dunno, I wouldn't expect much. We're just going to play our songs.

LL: Do you play songs from *Bleach* and *Nevermind*, that's the set list—*Incesticide* too?

KC: Yeah, maybe a couple from that too. That's the set list, *Bleach* and *Nevermind*, and some new . . .

LL: Do you still play "Love Buzz" in shows? I love that song.

KC: Yeah, sometimes; we didn't write that song, though. That's Shocking Blue.

LF: I used to have a band and we wanted to cover the last song—"Send Me a Postcard"?

KC: Oh yeah, that's a great song! That's my second favorite Shocking Blue song.

LF: What about new songs from the next album?

KC: Yes, we're going to play some—we're going to play about three maybe.

LF: I have a friend who says you're going to record it on an eight-track.

KC: No, it's a change—we're going to do it on a twenty-four-track, but we're going to do it with Steve Albini so it'll be really pretty raw. There's going to be a lot more guitar noise. I'm not going to try and play any solos with notes that go along with the songs, just a lot of noise, and I have a lot of new guitar effect pedals, old 1960s ones that make weird noises. I use a lot of Electro-Harmonix effects—Echoplex and Phaser. Small Clone . . . just a lot of different crazy names, but they make great sounds.

LF: I use a Fuzz Face . . .

KC: Oh yeah, those Jimi Hendrix ones? Yeah, they're cool.

RG: Do you have any creative art activity other than Nirvana?

KC: Yeah, I painted the *Incesticide* album cover. I paint a lot. I was supposed to go to art school, but I just didn't enroll; I wanted to be in a band.

RL: Once a friend of mine played me a demo tape of you from 1987–1988; it had five tracks, six tracks, but the first song didn't have a name. I would like to remember the name . . .

KC: Were any of them on *Incesticide*? You don't think so . . . ?

RL: It was an instrumental.

KC: Ah, well, I don't know what that could be. That could be a board tape from a rehearsal—it could be a sound check or something.

LF: About the guitars, sometimes you break them on stage, but now I've seen you're playing with Jaguars—you don't break them, do you?

KC: Oh, I've broken a Jaguar before—actually, I've broken two . . . Well, I like to use older Fenders, old vintage ones. I always regret breaking them after I do it, but in the middle, when I'm doing it, I really don't have much rational thought, so . . .

LL: What about fanzines? Do you have any contact with American fanzines?

KC: Oh sure, we do fanzine interviews all the time—that's just about all I ever do myself. We don't do the mainstream stuff anymore. Right before *Nevermind* came out, we went on tour to Europe and the United States and we were just freshly on a major label and we had a publicist who we weren't familiar with and she just set up these interviews. And we would have interview days that would last for eight hours sometimes—and just sit there and talk about ourselves for eight hours with different people coming in and having no idea what magazines we were doing. We didn't even know what magazines we were doing them for, we just did 'em. Then months later when they come out, we go, "Oh my God! We did [*inaudible amid laughter*] and stuff." And so now we try to have some discretion and we try to find out what the magazine is like first, and I just offer to make sure we do the fanzines. And a lot of times, someone from the record label will say, "We have a fanzine interview for you," and they come and it's nothing like this at all—it's a glossy magazine, so, well, it's like, fuck that . . .

RL: My view is that the fanzines talk about the human bands that haven't got any magazine coverage yet. And it's better when we can interview and you can talk with the guy who is playing in those bands, not translated into platitudes. But now there are just a couple of fanzines that are trying to write about Brazilian bands. Most of them are making compilation tapes of these bands, because in Brazil it's difficult for bands to have an LP. You must have received a record from a Brazilian band?

KC: Gash and Second Come and that's it, just those two, that's all I've got so far.
[*Long discussion among the interviewers regarding the difficulty of singing in the Portuguese language.*]

LL: Kurt, there's someone knocking at the door.

KC: We're supposed to go flying at 5:30 . . . It's a little past. I think if it's good music, it's good music. But I understand what you're saying—the English language is simpler, so the paraphrasing is easier to use because there are more rhyming words and there aren't as many syllables, and so in other languages it is a little bit harder—I find it a little bit harder to comprehend. But if the music itself is good, you can tell, you can always tell. And I can't explain why . . . There are a lot of bands that I've heard . . . I've not heard a lot of bands from other countries—I just don't have access to finding that kinda stuff. If I looked really hard, I could. I have no excuse for that. But I can't explain why I don't find very many Japanese bands, besides Shonen Knife, because they sing in English but they also sing in Japanese too, and they have a charm with those songs as much—and they're just as good. But I just don't understand why, from other countries, there aren't as many good bands as there are from bands who choose to use the English language.

PART X

May to December 1993—Damage Control

"IT'S NOT ON MY MIND ALL THE TIME. What I say is scrutinized to the point where I'm afraid to say things." The media make the story as much as they report it, understandably reading one another's articles and marking things to be asked. If Cobain or his colleagues answer, then it adds to the weight of comment on those issues—but reflects what the media are asking, not necessarily what Nirvana is thinking about.

Phil Sutcliffe's interview is remarkable in its momentum: a relatively upbeat Cobain recounts the recording of Nirvana's *In Utero* album, his excitement, the attempts to revisit Nirvana's live show. He tackles the most recent controversies casually and honestly. But then the door opens, he leaves for a moment, and he returns with two different voices: one claiming things are better than they've ever been, the other declaring he's "back into the state of mind I'm in every few months or so." And there's still concealment. Cobain is only one day away from an overdose incident—he's living day by day with an elevated risk of accidental death; it's no normal life, nor are his interviews full disclosure.

But then the positives are warming, such as the desire he expresses to keep playing with Novoselic and Grohl. A month later, the *In Utero* press interviews are a show of the continued solidarity within the reconnected group. The bandmates' anger toward certain media intrusions flares up, their tiredness with the press in general is aired several times over from different angles, they pick over *In Utero*, and they'll even consider explaining a song. However, it's apparent that this isn't the playful Nirvana of 1991, or the slightly manic jesters of 1992—they've sobered up significantly. It's perhaps only with Youri Lenquette—an old friend they've met several times before—that there's a wider air of entertainment, not work.

Amid it all Cobain reiterates where his interest lies, and it's not in music: "I feel I've achieved fantastic things, much more beautiful than in my dreams as a kid. Darn it! I'm married, I have a kid." But look back over earlier interviews in light of what he says now about how depressed he was in the past; try to see it—can you? The band members were wrong all those years ago; interviews are not a visit to the psychiatrist. One attends therapy to seek help, to find answers—no one attends a journalistic interview for self-revelation.

Come December, Nirvana is touring, the controversy has receded—it's an almost placid spell for the band with Cobain semi-invisible, focused on his family and his privacy, while Novoselic once again acts as the voice of Nirvana. And despite all we've learned in these pages, it amounts to no more than what a person speaking to an audience was willing to say in public. There's nothing that anyone could point to that suggests what the future might be, because every word spoken, however honest, was only what someone would say to a stranger knowing it would be broadcast.

RE: "YOU CALL THIS NIRVANA?"

Kurt Cobain, Dave Grohl, and Krist Novoselic | May 1993 | *Billboard*

The May 22, 1993, edition of *Billboard* magazine featured an intriguing full-page ad in the form of a letter from Nirvana to the editors of *Newsweek*. By May—barely three months after *In Utero*'s recording session—the band had spent weeks trying to head off speculation surrounding the album's release. There were tabloid tales of widespread dissatisfaction with the management at Geffen Records; that the label was refusing to release the album; that the album was undergoing extensive remixing; that Steve Albini, with whom the band had produced the album, was objecting to the remixing, and so on.

Nirvana had tried in 1992 to simply ignore rumors about the band, but that approach had failed to quell the stories. Now, sensitive to the merry-go-round of rumor, the band couldn't help but respond. However, Kurt Cobain, Krist Novoselic, and Dave Grohl now distrusted the media so deeply that instead of the usual approach of statements via representatives or personal interviews—each of which seemed only to fuel more stories and misrepresentations—they wrote their own statement, feeling that it was the only way they could ensure their views were relayed directly and without editorial interference.

The resulting ad politely and formally states *Newsweek* was lying. It says everything about the situation the bandmates were in that one of the biggest advertisements for their next album would consist of an accusation directed at the media, via the media, and having nothing to do with the music at all. —Ed.

Re: "You Call This Nirvana?" May 17, 1993
Editors:
Jeff Giles has written an article on our band, Nirvana, which was not based on the band's view nor on information provided by our representatives.

Rather, he pulled together quotes from unnamed sources and "music industry insiders," and misled others into believing the story was on Steve Albini, the producer we recently worked with, and not the record that we worked on together. He quotes Albini at length and never approached our management company to speak to us at all. After stating that Albini will not speak about "the Nirvana fracas," Giles quotes him ranting about Geffen Records (our label) in the very same paragraph. How balanced can any reporting be if the center of "the fracas" cannot respond?

Further, though Giles did speak with representatives at Geffen Records and Gold Mountain Entertainment (our management), their quotes were rendered invalid in his piece by other quotes from unnamed sources. He chose to cite these same sources as more factual than a release sent to him and four editors at Newsweek that completely explained the status of our upcoming album.

Most damaging to us is that Giles ridiculed our relationship with our label based on totally erroneous information. Geffen Records has supported our efforts all along in making this record.

We hope, in the future, information provided by us will be taken literally and gossip will be taken for what it is.

Kurt Cobain
Dave Grohl
Krist Novoselic

FROM A STOWAWAY IN AN ATTIC

Kurt Cobain | June 1993 | *The Raincoats* Album Reissue

Cobain helped arrange the reissue of the Raincoats' discography and, as a further use of his star power and an additional favor to a band he adored, agreed to contribute a liner note to hopefully gain them further attention. This was one of just four occasions on which Kurt would write a statement intended for public consumption. —Ed.

I know a lot of coolies who suck and feed off the fact that they know about and (supposedly) enjoy unknown, obscure bands of present and past. These coolies thrive on their own little discoveries like those tiny fish who attach themselves to bigger fish and parasitically feed off the hosts' droppings and burnt coffee.

The Raincoats were not very well known in the States—I don't know about the U.K. and Europe. In fact, I don't really know anything about The Raincoats except that they recorded some music that has affected me so much that, whenever I hear it I'm reminded of a particular time in my life when I was (shall we say) *extremely* unhappy, lonely, and bored. If it weren't for the luxury of putting on that scratchy copy of The Raincoats' first record, I would have had very few moments of peace. I suppose I could have researched a bit of history about the band but I feel it's more important to delineate the way I feel and how they sound.

When I listen to The Raincoats I feel as if I'm a stowaway in an attic, violating and in the dark. Rather than listening to them I feel like I'm listening in on them. We're together in the same old house and I have to be completely still or they will hear me spying from above and, if I get caught—everything will be ruined because it's their thing.

They're playing their music for themselves. It's not as sacred as wire-tapping a Buddhist monk's telephone or something because if The Raincoats really did catch me, they would probably just ask me if I wanted some tea. I would comply, then they would finish playing their songs and I would say thank you very much for making me feel good.

Kurt Cobain 'Nirvana' June 1993

"BACK INTO THE STATE OF MIND I'M IN EVERY FEW MONTHS"

Phil Sutcliffe | July 24, 1993 | *Q* (UK)

My night . . . and day . . . and another night . . . with Nirvana. On Friday, July 23, 1993, I saw them play the Roseland Ballroom. I heard not a whisper of the story that emerged later: that at the Omni Berkshire Hotel that morning, Courtney Love and daughter Frances's nanny Michael DeWitt had found Cobain on the bathroom floor, overdosed and all but dead. DeWitt knew the correct first-aid routines and revived him. By evening, no outsider looking in could tell that anything beyond Kurt's abnormal normal had occurred.

My interviews for *Q* magazine—separate sessions with each band member—were scheduled for the following day. Along with photographer Hugo Dixon, I arrived at the hotel on East 52nd Street around lunchtime. We settled into the foyer's extensive sofas alongside the *Melody Maker* team and, for a couple of hours, consumed all the coffee, puff pastries, and interminable ennui we could eat, until the arrival of Krist Novoselic ("cranky, hungover," he called himself) and Dave Grohl ("clad informally like a naff Superman, boxer shorts over white, saggy long-johns . . . Juddering with drummer energy and feeling a bit irritable," I noted).

They promptly offered themselves for talk with anyone who cared to. So I got those interviews done—animated, fine, no hints of the previous day's near-catastrophe, although one can only presume they were worried sick. Kindly, Krist even invited me to join him and his wife in their room for a glass of wine "after you've spoken to Kurt" and stuck to it, although that turned out to be at 2 AM.

Oh aye. Two hours later, Kurt appeared wearing a woolly cardigan and that sheepskin-lined, leather, flying-helmet-style hat he often sported. We all decamped to Central Park for Hugo's quick-fire picture session. (Courtney said hello thus: "You from *Q*?" "We are." "Fuck *Q*"—unless it was just "Fuck you.") Then back to the hotel sofas. For another seven hours. Until "Kurt will see you now," or similar. I entered the sterile sanctum hired for the occasion. Kurt rose from his chair behind a bare table, shook my hand, and apologized for keeping me waiting. —Phil Sutcliffe

The interview below is taken from Phil Sutcliffe's 1993 transcript of the original (now long-gone) tape. His original sidenotes, written while his impressions were still fresh, are retained where they capture the environment and atmosphere in which the encounter took place. —Ed.

Phil Sutcliffe: Can we start on the concert? It was different for you and for any band, the way you presented the acoustic set. What was the thinking behind that?

Kurt Cobain: It was a very last-minute idea. Last week. We'd been toying with the idea for a month or so. But we finally found the cellist two days before we were scheduled to leave for here and she was only available to practice with us for about three hours, so we ran through the four or five songs in that three hours—which gave me quite a heavy bit of nervous tension before the show because I'd never done anything like this at all. I didn't know what to expect. It was like, I didn't want it to seem like . . . For years I've always loathed the idea of acoustic sets because of the indulgence aspect with Zeppelin making a big production out of it, sit down for an hour or so, which seems to take away the whole energy that's given off by the electric part of the set.

The sound check turned out really good, but once the venue filled up and we got on stage, it made the monitors sound completely different—the guitar sounded like a banjo, and I couldn't hear the cello. I could hear people talking louder than I could hear our band. That's a New York audience for you. Very rude.

PS: Around me people were talking all through, very loudly about the music, then at the finish of the number saying, "Hey, that was really good!" (Phil Note: Kurt crunching his sweet loudly; note he has the remnants of red varnish on all his nails.)

KC: God! At first I was really pissed off about it, then I realized it's New York and the New Music Seminar is on. You can't expect an audience in this kind of environment to pay a lot of attention to you and accept something as different as Nirvana doing an acoustic set. Although we've had a couple of acoustic songs on both our records, it's not what's expected from us. Then there's the particular effect of finishing the set with it . . . Wha?

PS: It emphasizes it, places more of a burden on it.

KC: That's true. I think it wouldn't have gone over so well if we hadn't have come back out on stage and played a couple more songs.

PS: What did you think of the reaction when you went off after the acoustic set and there was more or less silence?

KC: I didn't notice that; it didn't even cross my mind. Maybe they hated us. (Phil Note: Laughs mildly—voice generally is a low, drawly murmur.)

PS: Well, it shows you were different and you provoked a different response. Maybe they couldn't come out of the acoustic set into themselves making a load of noise. "Is this a rock show" sort of puzzlement. Then, when you came back on and played "Teen Spirit" they knew what to do again. So would you do it again?

KC: I'll do it again if I can make sure that the monitors will sound better next time. I've tried to play acoustic guitar live a few times, and it's just never worked. It's never sounded like an acoustic guitar by the time it's been put through the PA and monitors. It's really hard to mic an acoustic guitar and get the same sound out of it as when you play it in a room. So maybe we'll leave it to surprise shows, when we play small pubs and so on. I'd rather do that; I didn't enjoy it as much as I thought I would.

PS: How did you feel about it in relation to your previous reservations about it being an indulgence?

KC: We knew it wouldn't be as indulgent as a Led Zeppelin acoustic set. We made sure we'd only play four or five songs, go off the stage, and then play some more electrically.

PS: What about the Lead Belly song [*"Where Did You Sleep Last Night"* a.k.a. *"Black Girl"* a.k.a. *"In the Pines"* —Ed.]—was that the first time you'd played it?

KC: I've been playing it for years myself, but that was the first time the band's played it. It was thrown together at the last minute, so we weren't tight enough; it didn't seem familiar enough to relax and enjoy it. I should still be able to enjoy it whether or not my guitar sounds good to me. I should know it's going to at least sound good in the audience—which I've been told by at least ten people it did last night.

PS: Uh, you lost the volume up toward the back, I think, which is where I was. I've been very puzzled in recent years about why people come to concerts to talk. There was somebody politely asking, "Would you mind not talking?" and the answer he got was, "Fuck off!" (with two fingers).

KC: That's New York for you. Maybe it'll go over better in Idaho. There's been times when we've played "Polly"—that's with an electric guitar—and people talk through that as well.

PS: I guess you discover what a concert's about. A lot of it seems to be about socializing.

KC: It does. I was hoping because it was such a spontaneous event our truest fans would be in the audience, the ones who I would expect to have enough respect to be quiet during the acoustic part. Very odd! [*Laughs.*]

PS: In a few articles I've read you seem to be having an unusual time in that all of you seem to express reservations about your own audience as if you'd prefer not to be liked by some of them—such as "jocks."

KC: Yeah, there are quite a few of them in our audience. At this point if they haven't realized our opinions about certain things, then there's no hope, there's no point in us talking about certain things. They're still going to show up, they're still going to cause problems and carry on the tradition of being macho and disrespectful towards women. I'd rather talk about other things than try to change their attitudes and opinions about lifestyles. Last night was a good testament to that.

I've been realizing for a long time that there's no changing people with what we say in interviews. It doesn't do any good. I'd rather play music with Chris and Dave and concentrate on that. I'd rather please ourselves. I still like playing live shows. I still like playing with Chris and Dave, so who is in the audience is not going to bother me anymore.

PS: That's something from experience that's made you decide you have to set it aside?

KC: Yeah, I don't want to react in such an extreme way as maybe U2 has by turning their show into a kitsch vaudeville act by being so sarcastic about the whole idea of being a rock 'n' roll star that it becomes a sick joke. I'm still a serious music fan. Even if I don't like a band that much, I'd still have enough respect not to yell and scream or talk during an acoustic part; there's one point of the show where this girl was hoisted above everyone's heads and all these men in the audience started catcalling her and yelling—that really upset me, but what am I supposed to do? Throw my guitar down and start yelling at them about it? It doesn't do any good. All you do is get ridiculed for it. Fugazi do that all the time and they get nothing but shit for it.

PS: So these things are going through your head while you're playing?

KC: Yeah, it's pretty distracting. Especially when I'm trying to remember the songs. That was enough pressure right there; remember the songs and hopefully do a good job.

PS: The album . . . why did you choose Steve Albini, and did it work as planned?

KC: Yeah, it did. We got the sound that we wanted. Exactly the same sound that I have been carrying in my head since the beginning of this band. I always had wanted to record a record which has a very personal ambience to it—that sounded as though you were standing next to a band in a room, that you're hearing all the reflections off the walls. We recorded in a studio a little bit bigger than this room, and that's exactly how it transferred onto tape. The reason for that is we used a lot of microphones. The theory that I came across one night when I was thinking about how to get a band across on record was I realized microphones are directional and they only pick up the surface of whatever the microphone's pointed at and within a radius of a few inches. I thought if you pointed three or four microphones at the snare drum you'd be able to get the real sound of the snare drum. It sounds ridiculous to 99 percent of producers because that's not the way they've been taught; it's not the standard way. But I've always liked to experiment, so I thought I would like to do something like that. Ever since we started recording I've suggested it to producers—Jack Endino, Butch Vig—and they weren't willing to do it. They just said it isn't the way to record. But listening to *Surfer Rosa* and *Pod* I sensed that was what Steve was doing, though I didn't know—I'd never read any interview where he explained his recording process, but I just felt he might be doing it. And I'd heard he was very much into experimenting, so I thought if he didn't do it this way then he might be willing to try it. But it turned out that's exactly what his trick is. We used maybe thirty microphones taped to the walls, the ceiling, the floor, all over the place.

PS: And then the whole band played live?

KC: Yeah, that's exactly how it was recorded. I had five or six microphones in front of my amplifier. A few up close, a few a couple of feet away, and that's how we recorded; that's how the vocals were recorded—with five microphones.

PS: You recorded vocals with the band?

KC: No, I did vocals and guitar separately. We used a ridiculous number of microphones; they play a big part in his theory of recording. He uses a lot of old German microphones from the 1930s and other brands I can't name, but very specific ones. I never really wanted to become this much of a tech-head. I always figured if you just played passionately it would come out that way, but it's not like that. It's a very strict and meticulous job, something I've had a hard time with ever since I've started recording. It's mathematics, and I've always been terrible at math. It's a very long, tedious process which just goes on for hours and days and days. Mind-boggling! It's like trying to cram for an exam the night before; it's definitely not as easy as a lot of people think—put up a few microphones and play, that's not it.

PS: Mixing, if anything, is even worse. That can take days on just one song. But you recorded in a couple of weeks?

KC: Yeah, which is very fast for a lot of bands on major labels and really into their art form. Metallica spend months just doing the drums. I've heard stories—I've heard it enough times to believe it, from people who've worked with Metallica, to believe it. I've heard that James Hetfield and Lars Ulrich, the drummer, will record each drum hit—he'll hit his snare and they'll cut that piece of tape out, paste it to another piece of tape with another snare hit on it, to layer this drum beat, then they'll run it through a computer to make sure the timing is exact. By that time, to me, it seems all the energy, all the human elements, must have gone and you might as well play with a drum machine. For a band like us to record in three weeks is a ridiculous amount of time. We recorded our first record in two days.

PS: Like the Beatles recorded their first album in twelve hours.

KC: Really? Wow. Then as the years went on they started getting into the technical side of it. Well, I don't plan to go any further than a few weeks with every record—unless we decide to use a completely different . . . like samples, sounds which require a lot of samples.

PS: You're not averse to samples?

KC: Probably not, because I'm always looking for new ideas, experiments. But if I were to sample, I would sample from obscure things. I wouldn't base a song on a guitar riff from someone else's song. (Phil Note: Room service brings Diet Coke for me and mineral water for Kurt.) It's real easy to take a dance beat and take well-known guitar parts from well-known songs. If I was to do it, I'd do it from children's records and sound effects' records, things like that. (Phil Note: His drawl has an oddly English upper-class air to it.)

PS: The singing on this album—you're famous for your screaming, so to speak, but on one or two tracks it seems about as far as a human being could go in letting something rip vocally.

KC: I didn't notice I was screaming any more violently or louder than on other recordings.

PS: "Scentless Apprentice" was one I thought . . .

KC: I dunno. I did all the vocal tracks in about six hours for the whole record, kept knocking them off one after the other. It just happened to be a good day. Sometimes my voice will go out within a couple of hours. That happened a lot on the *Nevermind* sessions.

PS: Are you still doing this thing of the darkened room and closing your eyes to sing?

KC: Yeah, I think the lights were dimmed. (Phil Note: Anton Brookes— PR representative—brings in a tuna sandwich from the deli, not room service. Kurt unwraps it noisily.)

PS: There's some kind of abandonment in your vocals. What is it?

KC: I dunno. If I'm to sing on a really aggressive song, I just scream as hard as I can.

PS: Is it an emotional thing for you or a technical thing?

KC: Probably both equally as much.

PS: "Scentless Apprentice" is one of several songs on the new album where it seems to be very personal. It seems to relate to you having a baby?

KC: Not at all! [*Laughs.*] It's based on this book called *Perfume* by Patrick Süskind. Amazing story. One of my favorite books. I've read it six times, I can't stop. Every time we're on a trip, on a plane, it's always in my bag so I end up reading that instead of new stuff. It's about this perfume apprentice in France—I think it's in the late 1700s—he has this incredible disgust for human beings. He's been an apprentice for so many years that he feels his life is pretty much useless. He knew he could be a perfume master—I can't remember what they're called—he knew he had the talent to be one of the best in the world, but he hated the idea of producing this substance that was mainly used to cover up the smell of human sweat, the smell of human flesh. The way it's written is just so detailed it makes you want to cut your nose off; you feel and smell so much while you're reading this book. It really attacks your senses. And I've felt that way at times, like, quite a few years ago, I was so disgusted by human beings that, I've felt that, how do you get away from everybody?

PS: So it's personal in a way?

KC: Yes, though I've never been as extreme as the person in the book.

PS: Well, you always associate what happens in people's lives with their work, and there's quite a lot of images about babies and births in this album. Is that coincidental?

KC: It is coincidental (Phil Note: A gentle emphasis), because I've been fascinated with reproduction, birth, death, and life—but especially birth—for years. I've collected paintings and books that deal with that subject. I've been painting fetuses for years; I've been making fetus dolls out of clay forever. There's just something really glorious about pregnancy and just supporting the woman. I just can't imagine what it would be like to be pregnant, you know? It just fascinates me. I've got so much respect for women because they not only—not only because I love them—but because they give birth and so they seem more sacred to me, they seem the more sacred of humans. (Phil Note: Is it Robert Redford his accent reminds me of?) I'm also kind of interested in sea horses' reproduction. There's a male and a female, the male impregnates the female, and the female grows the babies, then transfers them to the male, who carries them until they're developed enough that he gives birth. I think it's the only being on this planet that does it that way.

PS: A sort of shared pregnancy? You think we should work on it?

KC: I think so. I think we'll get there. [*Laughing gently.*]

PS: I'm sure women would wish for it. It may be connected in some sense, but I want to focus on "Rape Me." I think it's going to disturb some people.

KC: Yeah, I know. I have to admit it's a bad choice for a title; I didn't think about it hard enough. (Phil Note: He says through his sandwich.) In a way I was trying to make a point that in order to get a point across, you have to make things as obvious and bold as you possibly can. Like if we wanted our audience to at least question whether they were homophobic or sexist or racist, we'd have to give out leaflets or flyers to each person at the door with some little manifesto written down—very simple. That was my way of putting a twist on an anti-rape song. Instead of trying to be really artistic about it or in any way cryptic, I decided to do it in a very bold in-your-face way. At the time it didn't even seem as though it would affect it, because at different times of my life I've felt that people are so jaded that they wouldn't even question the topic, you know? I titled that song about two years ago, and since then, since I've supposedly become a lot more optimistic and had a lot better attitude than I did before, I should have thought about it more. But we've always known that song by that title and we haven't questioned it. I should have, actually. I kind of regret it—and in a way I don't.

I mean, I just don't like the idea of a woman walking around in her apartment humming "Rape Me." It's kind of an offensive thing to do because it's kind of a catchy song too, and some people have found themselves doing that, so I've gotten a bit of flak for it.

PS: When you're singing it, I mean, are you thinking as a man or as a woman, saying "rape me"?

KC: As a man.

PS: So it's most directly about homophobia?

KC: Yeah, I mean, men get raped as well. I really don't have any answer for it. I really was thinking at the time that I wanted to write an anti-rape song but I wanted it almost to be about me or other males, although the most important thing would be to address rape against women in the first place, get that out of the way, and address other kinds of rape—not only physical but media rape and everything else. Since . . . after I wrote the song, the bridge where it says "My favorite inside source," is . . . whatever it says after that, I threw that in six months ago. It's my way of bitching and complaining about the media, the way they treated us . . . There's all different kinds of elements to it.

PS: A lot of the time with your lyrics—although that was one that was supposed to hit you right between the eyes—a lot of the time it seems to be you use images within the one song which are very different. Not obviously connected.

KC: Right.

PS: I wondered if that had anything to do with your painting and sculpting approach to things at all?

KC: Yeah, it does. I've always painted abstracts; I've always thought abstract. I love dreams that don't make sense; I'd much rather watch a film that doesn't have a plot. For me, the reason why most of my lyrics don't connect is that they're all pieces of my poetry. I've used lines from all of these different poems—and in the first place none of the poems are about anything, they're not thematic, and then I take lines out of each of them, put them together—and I make up a theme to the lyric well after the fact, oftentimes as I'm being interviewed. Or someone will suggest something and I'll think, "Hmm . . . That's a good idea!"

PS: And the point is you think that's OK?

KC: Yeah, that's the way people should interpret most of our music. Which is why this album is a bit different, because there are a few obvious subjects in the songs on this album, a few themes. It's the first one I've ever written where the lyric's based on a book or a story. I might have been inspired to write a poem where one of the lines was from a book, but this is the first time I've used it in its full context.

PS: So the whole song is one context?

KC: Right. And that's how most people want songs to be. They need it. That's pretty much my reasoning for writing more that way, because people need things thrown right in their face.

PS: You're adapting to listener reaction, then?

KC: I didn't have the audience reaction in mind at all when I was writing these songs. I've thought about it since. Although I know that's what needed to be done and that's what people expect, I still wanted to do something different for myself in the first place.

PS: You mentioned you've had a hard time off the media. Do you want to say anything about that?

KC: No, if I say one quote about it in the article, that'll be used in twenty more articles and people will notice some connection with something I said in another interview and people will come to the conclusion that I'm complaining about it all the time, that I'm always bitching about it. I'm not. It's not on my mind all the time. What I say is scrutinized to the point where I'm afraid to say things. But anyone in their right mind would know that we'd be upset and offended by many of the things that have been written about us. So I really can't anymore . . . I started to when I was doing interviews three weeks ago; I was trying to defend myself and straighten out a lot of myths, but it isn't going to do any good because people are going to think I'm a complainer—they already think that now, so . . .

PS: One factual thing, in England there was the story about you leaving messages on these authoresses' answerphone—is that real or fake or what?

KC: That's me. I've never denied it. (Phil Note: Though management did.)

PS: On the album there's been another whole legend about Geffen blocking it and so on. What's the truth?

KC: The truth is Steve Albini is very paranoid, and I've never worked with so many people who I respect ever. I've had a lot of coworkers who do their jobs—and at this point I do have to consider that this is my job, it's how I create my income—everyone at DGC has been nothing but supportive and truthful to us; they tell us what they feel. We could disprove the myth about them wanting to not put the album out by making copies of the contract we have with DGC, because we have 100 percent artistic freedom and control. We can do anything we want. I know there are a lot of major labels who put a lot of pressure on their artists to do something different with what they've recorded. I can understand that paranoia, but honestly . . . some of the people at DGC didn't like the record; they didn't think it was a very good record. Our A&R man, for one, didn't like the record and he called me up personally, as a friend, to tell me he didn't think it was a good record. The only thing I felt was kind of sad because I wanted everyone to like it, of course. But some of them don't. Some of them love it.

But that had absolutely no bearing on our decision to remix two songs. And the mastering was a very important part of what happened, which I hadn't realized before, because when we brought the tapes home from the studio and put the tape in our home studios, it sounded very different to what we'd heard in the studio. For about three weeks we were baffled ourselves—we didn't know what was wrong. So I wasn't looking forward to hearing it, when usually I'll listen to what we've just recorded a lot to scrutinize it. I just could not put my finger on it at all. I couldn't tell what was wrong. Then after about three weeks we all realized the vocals weren't loud enough. We just hadn't spent enough time on the mixes. The mixing we did with Steve Albini was on the average of one an hour. It was so fast it was ridiculous. We haven't recorded that way for a long time. That's not the way we want to mix anymore. It's not a matter of money, because we've spent a lot of money and the actual recording of this album cost seventeen thousand dollars, which is nothing for a major label release—it just took a long time to figure out exactly what was wrong.

We decided to take a chance on remixing two of our favorite songs to make sure the vocals would be loud enough. They're two of our favorite songs, "Heart-Shaped Box" and "Scentless Apprentice." The rest of them we thought we'd take the chance of improving them during the mastering. Mastering is an amazing thing. You can really change a lot of things. You can take the vocals completely out or turn them up four or five more decibels. That took care of it. We'd realized the bass wasn't audible enough and the vocals were way too quiet and that's about it. But that's all we changed and now we're a hundred percent satisfied. I wouldn't change anything now—though there was that three weeks when it's true we didn't know what the fuck we were going to do.

PS: You sound very friendly with your corporation. Have you changed your views on "corporate rock whores" and so on?

KC: (Phil Note: Small laugh, just the expulsion of air through the nose, not actually voiced, which is his usual way of expressing merriment with severe reservations.) I've always liked DGC and I've always liked the people there. That's why we chose to sign with them. That slogan was just a joke, no more than our way of telling everyone to back off on that retarded punk rock idea that all corporate labels are evil. Because they're not. We know there are some evil ones out there because we met them during our wining and dining stage. You could tell how controlling they would be. But DGC is really different because it's practically an independent label. It's really small, a subsidiary of Geffen. I know the names of all the people who work at DGC, and I know them on a personal level. It's not like walking into the tower of MCA.

PS: Was it a joke that went too far, then? Didn't you have a big row with Pearl Jam about the corporate whore argument to the extent that Eddie Vedder wrote you a letter begging you to lay off?

KC: No, he never wrote me a letter . . .

Courtney Love: Kurt! (Phil Note: I look around and Courtney Love stands there in jeans and a short top rubbing her bare tummy, looking oddly meek and beaten down.)

KC: Yeah?

CL: Where are you?

KC: I'm right here. (Phil Note: She gestures for him to come out, he gestures no, she gestures insistence, he goes. He returns, obviously distracted, and gets settled.)

KC: Um, I just don't like Pearl Jam. It's as simple as that. They suck. Eddie happens to be a nice guy. I am good friends with some people who are in really bad bands. Eddie is a friend of mine who I have respect for because he's a nice person. Probably all the other guys in Pearl Jam are nice people, but I don't like their music. But . . . it's just one negative thing said about one band, you know? For some reason English bands can get away with slagging off everybody and their mother all the time, but I can't.

PS: You've been in the middle of one of the most extraordinary explosions of success, fame, that's happened in the last ten years—I have a feeling that the success of Nirvana may well not have changed you very much, you may have sidestepped it, but that being a husband and a father has been a much more changing experience. Is there anything to that?

KC: Yeah. How do we really know that the majority of people who become famous, or rock stars, really do change as much as it seems?

PS: It's a perceived expectation.

KC: I don't understand why.

PS: I suppose it seems such an extraordinary thing to happen to people that it must affect their characters immensely. Especially if someone has gone out of their way to become famous, it seems people frown upon that more and will accuse them of wallowing in everything that goes along with fame. The more I've read about you, you seem to have been doing whatever it was, including drugs, before you got famous. You were leading your own life and you carried on leading your own life, it appears . . .

KC: Actually, I'm carrying on with a life that's very different than what I had before—my attitudes and opinions have only got better. I've become more optimistic.

PS: Oh, that's what you mean by "better"?

KC: Yeah, about eight years ago I was an extremely negative person.

PS: As in "Negative Creep"?

KC: Yeah. Having a child and being in love with someone is something that everyone wants. It doesn't happen very often. It's the only thing I feel I've been blessed with. I could give up everything for that, and I've often wanted to in the last two years. Almost every other day I want to quit this band. It has nothing to do with Chris and Dave, the way we get along, or my lack of creativity; it has nothing to do with our music. It's only because of everything that goes along with it . . . it's a nuisance. I dunno, I'm really naive about what happens with people when they become famous. I never paid attention to . . . Uh, when I used to buy *Creem* magazine I never read about Van Halen or any of those bands; I just used to look at the pictures, maybe skim through a little of the article. Then I started to look into it a bit more closely, and when I was in a punk rock band I used to buy *NME* and *Melody Maker,* and still do to this day, and it's probably because I haven't paid attention to mainstream press, but I don't know of any other band that's been picked apart as much as this band. I'm sure that perception has a lot to do with it affecting me personally. I'd love to see some old Led Zeppelin interviews, because I've heard that they were completely crucified by the press all the time; their lives were blown totally out of proportion. It's really surprising that they could survive that—because I barely have. When I talk about surviving, I don't mean dying over it, I mean quitting your band and giving it all up. I can't compare the two. I can't decide whether I like playing music enough to put up with the shit that's written about us all the time, especially the shit that's written about somebody who I totally love more than anyone I ever have. It's hard to decide whether it's really worth it all, and it's pretty pathetic that you have to make a decision on something that's as simple as music, a thing you enjoyed as a pastime when you first started, to give up because of that. I dunno . . . I've quit this band well over thirty times in the last two years.

PS: In your head, you mean?

KC: In my head. And I've got to the point of calling up my manager and calling up Chris and leaving messages at four in the morning saying, "This is it!" It's always been after reading yet another article . . . There's a few weeks' resting period to recover in, then they bring in another one. The whole Britt and Victoria thing. [*Victoria Clarke and Britt Collins had been attempting to prepare a biography of Nirvana, which Cobain and Courtney Love would subsequently manage to halt, having objected to certain lines of inquiry made by the two journalists —Ed.*] I wish I would have known about that. I wish I could have prepared for it. I wish I could have taken a class on becoming a rock star. People dig through your garbage and they fester in their minds. They get these ridiculous ideas of what you're like, a lot of the time based on one article. These two women have gone out of their way literally to try to destroy two other people's lives. They're either so coldhearted or so numb that they thought it wouldn't bother us if that's what they did . . .

PS: The real issue is heroin and the baby, I presume . . . ?

KC: That and everything else they've written. We're just now reading the book. Their publishers are so afraid of us suing them because there are so many obvious misquotes and whole made-up chapters that they've given us the option to edit whatever we want out of the book, or write a little essay at the beginning of the book—or something else, there's three options. They're so afraid to go to court over this that it's not worth it because it's a badly written book—these women have shown their publishers that they're not the people they thought they were in the first place. They've dealt with them over the last few months and realized it's a very touchy situation.

I've been reading it tonight; Courtney was reading it, that's what she came down for, she was really upset—it's the *Vanity Fair* article magnified a hundred times worse. They really went out of their way to find people who it's obvious are enemies of ours, people who never really knew us or who claim they met us before—it's amazing. Courtney was just telling me some of the people who spoke to them, who I thought were friends of mine. I'm just in a haze right now. I'm really upset about it. It's just amazing. For the last six months or so, there have actually been a few positive articles written about Courtney, defending her, and we thought our curse was finally over—but then there was the DGC thing, and now there's this. If this book comes out, there's no point in trying to defend myself. I've vowed never to do another interview before. But I thought I could say something to defend myself, and I also have something to say about this record because I really like this record. I have an excitement about it; I actually want to promote this record, for the sake of promoting it. I dunno, it sounds to me if this book comes out, then there won't be any more interviews; there probably won't be a band. It's impossible. It's not worth it. I didn't enjoy myself that much that it's worth dealing with this. If I'm going to have to deal with this all the time, fuck it. I'm not going to spend the rest of my life numbing my brain with drugs to avoid the pressures of it. I'd rather just give up, start another band, play anonymously when I feel like it, put out records—probably with Chris and Dave but with a different name. Don't promote it. Who knows? It's not worth it. I adore my wife and my baby. That's the life I want. That's the life that I was searching for for years. I wanted a partner, I wanted security, I wanted a family, stuff like that. It's more important than anything else. Everything else is totally irrelevant.

You see, I'm back into the state of mind I'm in every few months or so. Within the last two years, the negative articles have been coming out, but more and more I've been learning to ignore it, and then since the baby was born there were a few positive articles counteracting this stuff. It looked like I would be able to deal with it. But it sounds like this book is too much. I shouldn't even be saying anything, but . . .

COBAIN CLIP

On the Domestic Abuse Incident

"Total bullshit. That's another thing that has made me want to just give up. I never choked my wife, but every report, even *Rolling Stone*, said that I did. Courtney was wearing a choker. I ripped it off her, and it turned out in the police report that I choked her. We weren't even fighting. We weren't even arguing, we were playing music too loud, and the neighbors complained and called the police to us. It was the first time they'd ever complained. . . . There's a new law, which was passed that month in Seattle, that says that when there's a domestic violence call, they have to take one party or the other to jail. So the only argument Courtney and I got into was who was going to go to jail for a few hours. And they asked us, out of the blue, "Are there any guns in the house?" I said no because I didn't want them to know there were two guns in the house. I have an M16 and two handguns. They're put away, there are no bullets in them, they're up in the closet, and they took them away. I can get them back now. I haven't bothered to get them back yet, but it was all just a ridiculous little situation. It was nothing. And it's been blown up out of proportion. It's just like I feel like people don't believe me. Like I'm a pathological liar. I'm constantly defending myself."

—from "Sounds Dirty: The Truth About Nirvana"
by Jon Savage, *Observer* (UK), August 1993

COBAIN CLIP

On His Youthful Depression

"I was a seriously depressed kid. . . . Every night at one point I'd go to bed bawling my head off. I used to try to make my head explode by holding my breath, thinking if I blew up my head, they'd be sorry. There was a time when I never thought I'd live to see twenty-one."

—from "Storming Back from the Brink" by Robert Hilburn,
Los Angeles Times (US), August 1993

"I HAVE NO DESIRE TO BECOME ANY BETTER OF A GUITAR PLAYER"

Edgar Klüsener | August 1993 | *RTL2* (Germany)

In the early 1990s, I worked as a freelance writer and, at the time, I had no experience with TV at all. The interview was arranged with Nirvana's record company for print only. However, when a German TV show approached me and asked if I would mind if they filmed the interview and used parts of the footage in one or more of their broadcasts, I agreed to that. I met the cameraman for the first time minutes before the interview. What followed was a bit bizarre, at least for me. As a print journalist I was used to informal interview settings where you meet the artists in a room and sit very relaxed around a table, on a couch, or even on a bed. As a warm-up and to develop a feel for each other, you engage in a bit of small talk, which then slowly leads into the interview. In a setting like this, the interview is less of a question/answer exercise and more a free-flowing conversation that often—though not always—breaks free from well-rehearsed promo routines. The presence of a cameraman and the particular needs of the medium prevented all of this to some degree. The cameraman needed an "interesting" setting and more light than was available in the room. So we finally ended up on the balcony. Because of the very limited space, I had to position myself behind the cameraman, which made the situation even more uncomfortable for everybody. To their credit, Kurt and Krist dealt with the whole thing in a rather relaxed manner. On that day they had already given a few interviews, and not all of them had gone well, so I was a bit nervous. However, once the first few awkward moments had passed, everything went fine. I was surprised at how much Kurt talked on this occasion and how he seemingly did not mind the setting. Of course, the only reason this interview had been arranged was to promote *In Utero*, but they were perfectly happy to leave the promo trail and to discuss other topics. Kurt Cobain appeared calm and collected. The one I was most impressed with, though, was Krist. Off the record we had briefly spoken about the situation in the former Yugoslavia that was on the brink of a full-blown civil war, and he was very well informed about the course of events in the Balkans. His assessment of developments was spot on. He also showed a keen interest in social affairs and in politics in general.

Interestingly, a few hours later I met them again—at an Aerosmith concert, of all places. —Edgar Klüsener

Transcribed by Emily Jones.

Edgar Klüsener: I think the bonus track on the CD, "Gallons of Rubbing Alcohol Flow Through the Strip," it sounds very spontaneous; did you quote that on the spot?

Krist Novoselic: Which song is it?

Kurt Cobain: We just made that up on the spot. I just started playing the guitar part and then Krist and Dave started playing and then, as we were recording, I just made up the lyrics.

KN: We recorded the song in Rio de Janeiro at this tiny BMG B studio that hasn't been used for like six years, and they had this, like, Neve board and they blew the dust off it and we just plugged in and just started screwing around, and we did that song and it was totally spontaneous, you know, just one of those things.

EK: Yeah, it gives that feeling.

KN: It was free association.

EK: What the hell does the title mean anyway?

KN: *In Utero* is, like, I think an in vitro pregnancy, then there's . . .

EK: No, I mean of that song.

KN: Oh, "Gallons of Rubbing Alcohol . . . Will Cleanse the Strip"? Well . . . ?

KC: I guess it's a contempt for the hairspray, Guns N' Roses–poisoned scene that was going on in L.A. a few years ago.

EK: Something else I found out. Oh no—one question beforehand. The way you recorded this on an eight-track machine. Is that true?

KC: No, that's not true.

Dave Grohl: It was a twenty-four track.

KC: It's the same board that recorded *Back in Black* by AC/DC.

EK: And what was the story that some of the songs have been remixed?

KC: Two songs were remixed.

EK: Which were?

KC: "Heart-Shaped Box" and "All Apologies." Because the vocals weren't loud enough and I wanted to put some harmony vocals in the background that I failed to do when we recorded at Steve's, so we asked Scott Litt to come down and do it. It took about a day or two.

EK: But I noticed this, not only on this record but on the records before too, there are some very fine harmonies and melodies on it; it makes me wonder, does one of you have a sort of musical education?

Various: No, no . . .

DG: I don't think any of us did . . .

KC: I have no concept of knowing how to be a musician at all, whatsoever, I mean, I don't know the names of chords to play, I don't know how to do major and minor chords on a guitar at all. I mean, I couldn't even pass, you know, Guitar 101—full Guitar 101. Everyone knows more than I do.

KN: I took accordion lessons when I was a little kid.

DG: I played the trombone, I think, when I was about eight. (KN: Really?) For real.

KC: I was in a band and I played snare drum during junior high at grade school, and I never learned how to read music; I just copied the other people who took the time to learn how to read, you know. It was just so simple, boom tap boom tap boom tap tap tap tap, and I just copied them, you know, just to pass. I didn't see any reason to—even at that age I didn't see any reason to learn anything that someone else has written, you know; if you go by the text you're pretty limited.

EK: Do you consider yourself more of a songwriter or a guitar player?

KC: Oh, songwriter. I have no desire to become any better of a guitar player. I just don't. I'm not into musicianship at all. I don't have any respect for it. I just hate it—you know, to learn how to read music or to understand arpeggios and Dorian modes and all that stuff, it's just a waste of time, it just gets in the way of originality.

EK: Do you like Leonard Cohen?

KC: Hmm?

EK: Are there other writers who you could name as sort of an influence or people who impressed you in what they were doing?

KC: Well, yes, mostly, you know, early-to-late-1980s punk rock, you know, American punk rock, and late 1970s English punk rock have a lot to do with stuff that I was into. I was just pretty much consumed with that whole scene for so long that . . . I never really denied any of the other influences that I had before . . . [*Interrupted by someone blowing a raspberry—tunefully*] which was like the Beatles and stuff like that, dinosaur rock, but . . .

EK: What about writers, like lyricists or poetists?

KC: Ummmm . . . probably Beckett's my favorite. I like him a lot . . .

EK: Because sometimes when I read or listen to the lyrics, it sounds to me as if you are sort of inspired by the Beat writers too, especially Burroughs.

KC: Yeah, yeah, Burroughs, the king, yeah! Actually, I got to do a record with him, a ten-inch record.

EK: You are doing one?

KC: Uh, we, it's already out, yeah. He did a passage from a poem called "The Priest They Called Him," and I played guitar in the background and just made a bunch of noise.

EK: What is this guy like?

KC: I don't know, I never met him. [*Laughs.*] I could have talked to him the other day; I was supposed to, there was a set-up meeting for him to call me because we wanted him to be in our next video because of the—mostly not because of our association with him or to exploit anything like that, maybe because, I don't want anyone to think I want to have a relationship with William Burroughs because of like, y'know, my past drug use or my respect for him or anything. We mainly wanted him to be in our video because he's an odd-looking character, you know; we wanted an older gentleman to be in our video and to do a few things, but we realized that the things that we wanted this older person to do, it was a bit degrading to have William Burroughs himself do it, you know. We wanted a person to be on a cross and in a hospital bed and stuff like that, and it was just too insulting to ask him, so I canceled the call. I mean, that was my chance of actually meeting him, and we've exchanged a letter through fax and we have respect for what each other does, but I've never really had the opportunity . . . I mean, other than that I haven't bothered to meet him yet, but I still want to.

EK: Yeah, he must be a great guy; I would love to meet him one day.

KC: Yeah. His letter was really nice.

EK: On one or two songs you hear a cello or some string arrangement . . . is that played live?

KC: No, we had her come in after the basic tracks were down—we had her play along with it.

EK: This was the cello player you had in New York . . . ?

KC: No, this cello player was Steve Albini's girlfriend at the time. It was just a really—it was just a matter of convenience; she happened to play cello and we needed one, so she was there. She turned out great; she did a really good job.

EK: Another question, for Kurt again, are you left-handed? Do you find it hard to get the right guitar?

KC: Usually, yeah. It's a bit easier now because I have an endorsement with Fender Guitars now, so they are making me left-handed Mustangs, so it's a lot easier. It used to be a total pain in the ass. I mean, when we were on our first couple of tours, you know, I'd only have one guitar and it had to be cheap, you know, a thirty-dollar guitar from a pawn shop, and I'd end up breaking it after the show and then the next day was, was consumed with trying to find a pawn shop and the few dollars that we had to buy a guitar, and then we'd have to turn the strings around and try to intonate it ourselves, and it just made for a really out-of-tune, raunchy experience, you know, during those first few years.

KN: It was a pain in the ass trying to find a guitar.

KC: Yeah, it was like the biggest dilemma of the day.

KN: This one will work left-handed, yeah, it's cut—this part's notched a little bit . . .

KC: It was a big hassle.

KN: . . . The electronics are in the top . . .

KC: In fact, we even built a bunch of Mustangs one time. We bought some necks and took pieces of wood and cut out the bodies and put the necks on, and they were completely out of tune all the time—but we did a pretty good job at it.

KN: We had this little assembly line in the garage and we hung them up and painted them and stuff, yeah. [*Laughs.*]

EK: You used some kinda neat-looking guitars on stage anyway. Were those the ones you built yourselves?

KC: Ummm, I don't think so. Those were all just destroyed on one tour. That was about, like, four years ago probably. At least. But the ones I use now are just—I use this same Jaguar a lot . . . mostly Mustangs. And I'm having Fender build me a special guitar, which is like a mixture of a Mustang and a Jaguar, which might be interesting.

EK: Did you give them the directions of what you wanted?

KC: Yeah, I took a picture of a Jaguar with a Polaroid and a picture of a Mustang, and then I cut them down the middle [*laughs*] and glued them together and said, "Build this."

EK: This record, *In Utero*, is getting more back towards *Bleach*, and you said, like, months ago, that you want to get rid of some of the fans who just came from the pop side. Do you think you will achieve that? Or is the name Nirvana already gone so big that the fans will buy anything, it doesn't matter what it sounds like?

KC: I don't know. I don't think so, because when we put out *Incesticide* it didn't sell very well at all. It didn't even sell, like, a few hundred thousand copies. You know.

KN: We don't, don't wanna exclude anybody or anything, you know.

KC: No, we're not as concerned with that as we used to be, you know. It's not—

KN: I think I was being a little reactionary, like, going through the whole fame and fortune thing and just making statements like that, you know.

KC: There's nothing you can do about it, you know. You can put on a cabaret show and, you know, just make a total mockery out of your success or you just deal with it, you know.

EK: I guess, especially at the beginning, it must have been pretty hard to deal with that.

KC: Yeah, it was, because we were really concerned with losing the audience that was into us before, you know, we still wanted those people because, you know, I suppose we feel like we relate to them in a way, y'know? I mean, those are the kind of people that we share common interests with and those are the people that we're friends with, so we were really worried about that. I don't think we've lost very many of them, so it doesn't matter anymore. As long as they're there, we can, you know, just forget about the idiots at the back so long as they don't cause any trouble. That was another concern we had, is that if we were to have this massively mainstream audience, that we were going to come across a lot of problems in live shows with macho guys beating up on girls and, you know, starting fights and things like that. You know, the typical things that you see at a Van Halen show or something. We just didn't want to have to deal with something like that.

EK: I guess you must have found it pretty hard too, like, getting that intensity with them because . . . Do you ever feel like you lose intensity at these big arenas or big places?

KC: Yeah. I don't find myself having as much fun as I did when we played in clubs or theaters. The biggest example of that is when we played in Europe, and we played all these outdoor festivals. I had a terrible time. I hated it. Like, Krist and Dave were like thirty feet away from me, you know. It was like "Hi-ii!" It just didn't seem right. So, we're gonna make a few changes in our stage setup to alleviate some of those problems, you know. We're gonna squeeze closer together on these big stages. And whether that fucks with the visuals for people out in the audience, oh well, at least we'll play better and enjoy ourselves.

KN: We played in front of, like, a hundred thousand people down in São Paulo, Brazil, and I just saw the video from the back of the stadium, and we were just like little ants on stage and I was just, God . . . Who was standing there? Y'know, and how do they feel about that?

DG: I don't think our music translates in that kind of situation. Those people can't appreciate the energy that's on stage at least because they're so far away.

KC: It's almost understandable why a lot of lead singers in arena rock bands have this kind of rapport with the audience where they're going, "Hey! How's everybody doing? How are you at the back, people?" and stuff like that—"Are you feeling alright?" Because that's pretty much all you can understand when someone's saying something like that over a PA in front of a hundred thousand people. It's just, it's hard for us to adapt to that because we just can't do that; we can't bring ourselves to be that ridiculous.

KN: And there are live shows, like, you know, you try to experience this thing with the audience, kind of reciprocate this feeling, this energy, and I don't know how this translates from three people to a hundred thousand people. It's mathematically pretty wild.

KC: We need to get a horn section. [*Chorus of "Yeahs" from the others.*]

EK: Are you thinking of employing a second guitar player again?

KC: Yeah.

EK: Will it be Big John?

KC: No. We've hired Pat Smear, who was in the Germs. It's working out great.

KN: He's got good energy. So I think he'll add that to the band live. If one of us is kinda slacking that night, I think we can count on him to keep the energy going, you know.

KC: He's the backup engine.

EK: It's, er, I guess it must make your job a lot easier too?

KC: Yeah. It does. It totally relieves me of a lot of unnecessary things that I have to think about.

EK: Looking back, do you sometimes sort of regret the major success of *Nevermind*?

KN: I don't.

KC: No, because—

DG: Not really.

KC: For the most part, I'm pretty convinced that most people liked that record, so you know, the more, the merrier. I mean the more people who can listen to your music and enjoy it, the better it is.

DG: If it was some big marketing scheme, then I think I'd probably feel guilty about that . . . if it was just, like, a contract thing . . .

KC: It was just like it happened organically—more organically than anything has in a long time. So, you know, it's flattering . . .

EK: You know, especially in the beginning, you sometimes had this feeling that even the record company was completely overwhelmed by it, they didn't expect it.

KN: They shifted like forty thousand copies and they, like, sold out in a day or two, then you couldn't get the record for, like, a week until they . . .

KC: It's nice to know that you can sell your music on the music alone. I mean, the time that it took off, a lot of radio stations were playing it before we had a video, which is . . . that's an uncommon thing in this day and age.

DG: So it's not our pretty faces that are selling the records, it's the music.

KN: And it's so neat . . .

KC: Our skilled musicianship.

DG: That's right.

KN: I walk into the Fred Meyer department store down in Longview, Washington, this tiny town, and I look and I go, "Oh, there's Mudhoney, there's Sebadoh, there's Sonic Youth!" I go, "This is really great!" And before . . .

KC: Just a couple of years ago that was impossible. Totally uncalled for.

KN: Yeah. And then kids down there are exposed to that. I think it's really positive.

EK: You obviously helped a lot of other bands too.

KN: Well, what happened to us has kinda opened a lot of doors. I think we were in the right place at the right time for, like, rock 'n' roll because all those old rock stars, all those poof-di-doo hairspray bands, were just hanging on and doing the same thing, basically emulating Hanoi Rocks, like, over and over again and it stagnated, like the Soviet economy or something—you know what I mean?

KC: Yeah, it got just as boring as grunge will within a year.

DG: We did a photo shoot with someone for a cover of a magazine, and he was telling us a story about how Bon Jovi came in and said, "Make me . . . "—he came in with like a flannel shirt on and he wanted, he said, "Make me look like Nirvana" and . . .

KC: Wow. That's pretty flattering.

DG: If Bon Jovi wants to look like us, you know, something's wrong.

KC: Well, that just proves he's a desperate, untalented piece of shit.

EK: Do you have yourselves an explanation for your success?

KN: Explanation . . . it's all in the cards. It's a roll of the dice.

KC: It's a lot of luck.

KN: Timing.

KC: Being in the right place at the right time.

KN: I think this whole . . . that the old dinosaurs were just, like, holding on for as long as possible and we had this really strong song and there were, like, no No. 1 rock records, maybe R.E.M. was No. 1. And Metallica came out with good stuff, but um . . . just, change has to happen, you know, just part of the whole human experience is change, so

I think that next we're probably gonna be these old hacks and there'll be this young, happening band going on and probably slagging us off or something for being dinosaurs and being defensive and we'll be sort of established and . . .

KC: Make me look like this new band! [*Chuckles.*]

KN: Yeah, yeah! And we would have, like, just totally consolidated our relationships with people in MTV, the music labels, different magazines . . .

KC: We'd apologize to everybody!

KN: We're gonna be like the establishment and hopefully someone will come by and . . . kill us . . .

KC: We'll be on the cover of the *Rolling Stone*: "Please! I'm sorry!"

KN: No, 'cause we're so in, we're so established . . . "Cover of *Rolling Stone*, when do you guys want it?" We're just, like, totally, totally terrible, we're doing . . . we're hanging out with Arnold Schwarzenegger . . .

KC: Bruce Willis at the New Club . . .

KN: Bruce Willis, yeah, of the New Club . . .

KC: "Hey, I'm a Republican now, Krist!" "Hey, me too, what do you say?"

KN: "Well, it was cool until we had to pay 38 percent or 36 percent in taxes, gee, you know, we got the shot and we lived under Reagan and now we're getting a shock under Clinton. I say we vote for Pat Buchanan!"

KC: Rush Limbaugh!

DG: Rush Limbaugh!

KN: Rush Limbaugh, yeah. Those femi-Nazis, huh.

EK: I guess that must be a strength for you anyways, suddenly being involved in real big business, like, on the promotional side giving you the tax . . .

KC: I'm happy to fucking suffer for, you know, I'll be glad to throw out more of the money that I've made if it's gonna be put in the right places, if it's going to help the economy. I mean, everybody should suffer, y'know? Everyone should start wearing sweaters and turning their heaters down . . . I didn't mind standing in gas lines when I was a little kid during Carter. I mean, I had to sit in the car and wait in line with my dad, and he would just curse Carter all the time, you know, "What a bastard!" The convenience of America is ruining—

KN: Everybody had it bad during that time.

KC: Yeah, you know, everybody has to swallow a little bit of bad medicine to make things better, so, fuck it.

KN: They're kicking Clinton around, but it's like, remember Nixon? And Iran-Contra, Reagan S&L scandals? No one ever brings that up; it's, like, crazy.

EK: Do you ever . . . do you think as a band you have to try to move something in people's mind to make them think or at least get a message across?

KC: Well, it's not, like, a real conscious goal of ours, or something that we prepared to do, it just emulates the personalities that we have, you know, we've always been conscious of political things as much as our, you know, mental capacity can hold and, and we—

KN: We've just been aware of things and it just kinda surfaces and comes out, just because, that's what happens. I mean, we don't have, like, this angle like we're in a political band or—

KC: We've always tried really hard to not put out too much of an image of being too politically conscious, you know, so it gets in the way of the music, 'cause, you know, that's more important.

KN: And I think, too, that in this country that people are so apathetic and, like, they're so unconscious in front of their TV sets, and then somebody like us who has somewhat awareness, it makes us look like we're really aware, and we're not. Y'know what I mean? This is just things we're concerned about and we just talk about. Just 'cause we talk about them at home or we talk about it with friends and just having a talk about things in interviews.

EK: Have you ever had the experience of the groups that are, like, political, or other social groups, try to use you or the success you have with the name or . . . ?

KC: No, I wouldn't say they've used us. We've had a few offers from some political organizations like the FAIR organization, who've been working for years to expose a lot of injustices and try to promote real truths in a lot of things that have happened politically. It's, like, an underground leftist organization that tries to expose the truths, and they're totally masked over by *USA Today* and magazines like that, right-wing magazines that, a lot of time, the truth and the details of the story aren't ever reported, and that's what this organization does. So, they came to us and of course we're going to want to do something with them to help them out, because I wouldn't say anyone's trying to take advantage of us in that way at all.

KN: FAIR is an acronym for Fairness and Accuracy in Reporting. I think I've been really conscious of what's been going on in the media with being part of the media, and then I just look at the way, you know, the press responds, and it's like being all over the press . . . being all over Waco, Texas, or Amy Fisher. It's really interesting; there are a lot of bozos out there, who they form public opinion and, you know, people really don't think for themselves, so they have a big responsibility and they're basically just exploiting it, and this just . . . it's into, like, truth, reality, you know. Just like these bad dema . . . demagogues, demagoguery politicians manipulating people and spreading their lies for their own personal gain. Former ex-Communists, or ex-Communists, or, like, former ex-Communists. [*Kurt interrupts—half singing—"I can't get into you . . ."*] Help people out, not just putting Band-Aids on the situation. [*Woman laughs.*] Totally dispose of the regimes over there, you know, but there's not going to be any change, you know? They don't even recognize the Serbian opposition; the guy's languishing in prison, they beat the hell out of him, they don't even help the guy out. There were elections in Serbia, the guy Milan Paroški, it was a sham election; they didn't do anything about it. Anyway, getting back—where were we? Rock 'n' roll!

EK: After all your experience—you've met with media all over the world—do you still believe what you read or see on television? (Various—"Never. Never!")

KC: I never did before, but I don't believe even more now. I know that I don't even have the right—it's the only thing I've learned—I don't have the right to make an opinion on anything that I read or see, you know, on television until I go to the fucking source myself personally. My attitude has changed so much in the last couple of years, mainly because of the crap that's been written about us that I don't know, I don't even find myself having many opinions on, like, bands anymore or putting them down or going out of my way to, like, to have any kind of expression about them at all because I don't know these people. Bon Jovi could be one of the nicest people in the world, their music sucks, but, like, I don't even want to bother with even expressing those kind of opinions anymore. I just don't wanna, because I know that there are people probably in this town right now talking about us. So I heard that, y'know, Krist Novoselic, blah blah blah . . .

KN: With his dog . . .

KC: With his grandmother's dog. And it has AIDS.

KN: Which is not true, by the way.

EK: I was just wondering, does that sometimes affect your private life too? I mean, your friends or your family are reading these stories about you?

KC: Mmm-hmm.

KN: Yeah. It's weird to talk with your wife's great-grandparents and they bring up something like that, you're just, like, "Man . . . that's not true at all!" And you have to explain to them how people have different agendas, each writer has their own perspective, and maybe the magazine editor has an agenda, y'know what I mean? And you're just at their mercy, basically, so all you can do is be as honest as possible, put on a happy face, roll with the punches.

EK: I mean, frankly it appears to me, even though I'm working in the media, there are certain magazines where I thought, OK, whatever they've printed is at least, like, well-researched, like *Newsweek* in America, which we get in Germany, I found it quite confusing that even they made up stories.

KC: Oh yeah.

KN: I was surprised about *Newsweek*. I thought they were of a different caliber.

KC: I'm not surprised at all. No magazine has any ethics at all. There isn't any magazine—

KN: [*Interrupts*] Mainstream magazine.

KC: Yeah, mainstream magazine that would ever stop a good story. They wanna sell magazines. They're in the entertainment business.

KN: Yeah, that's a good point.

KC: And they use politics as some kind of fucking fake tool to sell their magazines.

KN: Right, right.

EK: But in this case, I thought this is the sort of magazine that has to lose a real reputation as well.

KN: I think we're going to have to get Dave in . . . David Gergen.

KC: No, there is no one that is challenging these magazines, though; there are no protection laws against false things that are written about celebrities. Libel suits are a complete farce. Basically, a libel suit is just a challenge between two people that have a lot of money, and you know whoever has the most money will win it. And if you go up against Condé Nast or some major corporation that runs a whole bunch of magazines and owns this one magazine that wrote shit about you, they'll just fili-buster for years and you'll spend hundreds of thousands of dollars in challenging them and you'll end up losing, so there's really . . . you can't even get to that first stage of even filing for a libel law, a libel suit—it's just a waste of time.

KN: It's pretty wild, like, all the relationships between people and the bands and the labels and between magazines and all that stuff, you know. You've got so much, like, Bill Clinton had a bad time so he hired David Gergen, who started throwing parties for the press corps and started smoothing people over because he had relationships, and whaddya know, we have news coming out, "Washington for Clinton," and it's manufac-tured perception; it's like it's not real, it's all just a charade, you know, and the bottom line is Stoli vodka ads on the back page, you know, Marlboro ads; they just get that money and, you know, everything in between is just not that important . . . Television, the same way . . . So we're gonna start our own magazine. It's gonna be called the *Nervewracker.*

EK: The *Nervewracker.* It's a good name, anyway.

KN: Full of character assassinations left and right. We're gonna schmooze with all the people. Whoever greases our palm the most is getting a full cover story, you know what I mean? Step one, take the guys out for dinner—"I'll have lobster, thank you." Step two—(KC: "Get me in the show for free!") Yeah! "Get me in the show for free." Step three, "Uh, I've got this niece, she needs a new, I wanna get her a Mustang . . ." "Car? Done. You're on the cover of *Nervewracker.*" Unscrupulous maga-zine—go ahead.

EK: How seriously do you take all these clichés and standards of the business and the roles people play?

KN: Uh. Well, I just think of, like, the wrestling industry, like WWF World Whatever Federation Wrestling, where there's like Hulk Hogan and all those Rowdy Roddy Piper, and . . . Can you imagine all the poli-tics going on in there, you know—he's gonna win this match but, see, he has to lose this match, and well, they're gonna be on this TV show, and it's, like, wow, all the drama and all the egos, personalities . . . World Federation Wrestling, it's like—get me out of here.

KC: Yeah . . .

EK: Getting back to the records, is it incidental that the opening of the track "Rape Me" sounds a bit like some part in *Nevermind*?

KN: What part of *Nevermind*?

DG: "Smells Like Teen Spirit." [*Aside to Kurt and Krist*] I read the question!

EK: I'm just trying to remember that.

KN: What was the hit song off the second Knack record?

KC: It's an obvious inside joke.

KN: If you play that hit song of the second Knack record, if you play it backwards it sounds like "My Sharona."

DG: Really?

KN: I recommend playing *In Utero* backwards, and that's—ooh, I let it slip, oh, I shouldn't have said that. There's all kinds of "Kurt Is Dead" stuff, you know, but it's total devil worship . . . of the worst kind . . . altars, virgins . . .

KC: Those white-trash mothers are gonna sue us after they beat their children for a few years and then they kill themselves and blame it on us! And then blow their faces off; "I gave them a good Christian upbringing . . ."

KN: Don't, man . . . And what happened?

KC: "I tanned his ass every day, he should have turned out just fine, if it weren't for that record . . ." [*Laughter.*]

DG: Tanned his ass!

EK: Because no kid's committed suicide yet listening to a Nirvana song.

KN: Let's hope. Let's hope.

KC: They're committing social suicide.

EK: This is so typical American; you never get that in Europe or Germany.

KN: Well. This is, I dunno, there's a lot of symptoms out there, like, I don't know, kids killing themselves or people walking into McDonald's and blowing people away.

KC: They're always killing people who don't deserve it, though, you know what I mean? If you're going to kill a bunch of people, why not assassinate someone who deserves it?

KN: But they don't, they don't show that as, like, a symptom. They just say that's a problem. "Random act of violence!" But maybe that's a symptom of what kind of a country you live in and people's values, you see what I mean? I say they're all just fucked! I'll answer that question by first off saying that everybody's fucked. If you ask me. And then why don't we take it from there? We're all fucked. Alright, well, we've established something. Some kind of criteria. Like a base to where to go on to. Maybe we're all . . .

KC: And how are they fucked?

KN: How are they fucked? Well, I don't wanna think about that because that just involves effort.

KC: Because then if I just waste my time thinking about it and we create some kind of dialogue about it for a while, then we'll just come back to the conclusion that everybody's fucked.

KN: Everybody's fucked, you know, so you just have to take up smoking and, you know, live a leisurely lifestyle and, you know, bomb some third-world countries, walk into McDonald's and shopping malls with automatic weapons readily available and . . .

KC: Hey, if life gets too tough, just buy an AK-47 and walk into McDonald's. You'll feel better.

KN: Yeah. 'Cause you hate Mondays. [*This was the reason provided by a sixteen-year-old killer at a 1979 school shooting in San Diego —Ed.*] What's your favorite day of the week?

EK: Pardon?

KN: What's your favorite day of the week?

EK: I guess Wednesday?

KC: Wednesday?

EK: Yeah . . .

KN: 'Cause you're in the middle of the week? Mine's Friday, man. TGIF. Thank God It's Friday! [*Laughter.*] Or Sunday. Because it's the Sabbath, the day of the Lord. But if you're a Seventh-Day Adventist, your Sabbath is on a Saturday, and they don't eat meat, by the way, and they seem like nice people and I don't know how preachy they get, so if I was to subscribe to a, any sort of Christian dogma, it would be a Seventh-Day Adventist . . . I'd be a Jehovah's Witness.

KC: You'd be a Hobo Witness, Krist, walking around peddling *Watchtowers.*

DG: Hobo Witness, huh?

KC: I'd be a Moron Mormon, moron.

EK: By the way, who's that Frances Farmer who's gonna have her revenge on Seattle?

KC: What about it?

KN: What denomination was she? [*Laughter*] Baptist or . . .

KC: You should read *Dreamland* [*actual title is* Shadowland *—Ed.*] by this PI reporter who wrote this book about her. It's really good [*Now widely debunked —Ed.*]. You know her story, don't you? She was an actress; she was kind of a foul-mouthed person and she hated the whole Hollywood scene and she expressed her hatred for them publicly. And she also, when she was, like . . . I think she was fifteen—she entered this essay contest when she was living here in Seattle entitled "God Is Dead," and a lot of people accused her of being a Communist. And then she went to New York and was a part of this acting troupe and it supposedly had Communist ties too. So then there's this big conspiracy amongst this judge, a very well-known, prominent judge here in Seattle, and a bunch of other people who had ties with Hollywood, and they basically just set her up and ruined her life. They had some pictures taken of her when she was arrested for drunk driving, and it was just a big huge scandal. And she eventually was sent to a mental institution and given a lobotomy and raped every day for years and just totally abused and ended up working at a Four Seasons restaurant and dying by herself.

KN: It was Bainbridge Island. That's where she was institutionalized. Right over there. It was this old broken-down infirmary there.

KC: For years, every night, there would be lines of custodians, friends, and people, part of the staff who would wait in line to rape her every day. She went through a lot of shit. And it just disgusts me to know that some of the people that were part of that conspiracy were living here in Seattle in their comfortable, cushy little homes and their families and . . . this is twenty, this is forty years after the fact, and it just makes me want to kill them.

KN: It's a just God, not a fair one, you know, that's what the Christians say. "God! Why was there Auschwitz?" "Well, I'm a just God, not a fair one." "Oh, OK." You know?

EK: Yeah.

KN: Why is there . . . oh, I, uh, ask Saint Paul, he'll tell you all about it. We'll just call the Bible. Find the little Jew that wrote the Bible.

EK: Do you already have a tour set?

KC: Not for Europe. Just for the States. We're gonna take it one tour at a time. I mean, we definitely want to and plan to go over to Europe and Japan, Australia.

KN: It'll probably be early, probably January or something like that, you know, we'll be in Europe.

EK: I mean, touring must have changed for you quite a lot too, suddenly being confronted with this giant machinery; I mean, when you play big venues and you don't have a lot of people and equipment, and the real organization required—

KN: Yeah, we used to drive around just three guys in a van.

KC: But you know, for, compared to a lot of other bands that are on our scale, like, we only have like a handful of roadies, people, and a tour manager and a helper for him, you know? It's like a lot of bands that are bigger than us or as big as us, you know, have like fifty people on the road with them; it's this big, confusing, stupid thing that happens. We're still really down to earth in that area, and we may suffer for it a lot of times because we don't get things done, but oh well . . .

KN: We save a lot of money. [*Laughter.*]

KC: It's just funner and simpler that way.

EK: Kurt, did having a family change your attitudes towards music at all?

KC: Mmmm, not towards music.

EK: But towards the life combined with it?

KC: Mmmm, it doesn't seem that much more optimistic; I mean, I totally, I like having a family, it's fun, it's great, but . . . you know, I'm still angry about a lot of other things, you know, in life, so it doesn't really, you know, stop me from being angry in music. It hasn't changed us very much.

EK: Do you sometimes write together with your wife?

KC: Sometimes. We usually . . . I wouldn't say it's really writing, it's jamming, playing together.

EK: I think "Royal Penny Tea" . . . ?

KC: "Pennyroyal Tea"?

EK: "Pennyroyal Tea," yes.

KC: Yeah. Well they're [*Hole —Ed.*] covering that song. It's mostly my song, you know, but um, we just jammed on it together and they wanna record a version of it.

EK: OK, I'm gonna finish. Thanks a lot. How many more do you have to do today?

KN: I don't know . . .

UTERINE FURY

Youri Lenquette | August 1993 | *Best* **(France)**

I'd caught up with Kurt when Nirvana played the Zenith in Paris the previous summer, but August 1993 was a formal engagement. *Best* sent me over to cover the band's promotion of *In Utero*. I was accompanied by a young kid who had won a Nirvana competition—his prize was to meet the band in Seattle, so out we went, this sixteen-year-old and I, to spend three days in the city. We conducted a photo session in the garden of Dave Grohl's house after a pleasant day hanging out with the band. I have only happy memories of that day: we went go-carting, we sat around at the house chatting, the weather was good, and we were all pleased to see one another. There were so many jokes—at one point Kurt saw a miniature toy M16, grabbed it, and put it in his mouth. It was just another joke, though I would come to regret the existence of those photos a year later when they were everywhere and I spent my time explaining to anyone who would listen that the only intention had been humorous. —Youri Lenquette

Translated by Carly Lapotre.

Some people are lucky, but unlike lottery winners, the winner of the *Best*/Nirvana contest got to spend a well-deserved weekend in Seattle to interview and spark a friendship with the holy trinity of grunge.

VvvvVVVRRROOOMmmmm!

The echo of small motors at full throttle bounces off the supermarket walls next to the deserted parking lot where we stand. The surrounding suburb looks like the set of a Spielberg film: cozy, discrete houses between trees, people who recognize and greet each other. A white America, nice and neat, where everyone gives each other the right to be a kid on the weekends as long as they rake in the cash during the week. Two of the very well-known rock stars are driving go-carts across the street, and it seems to provoke little more than amused smiles reserved for unruly neighbors. Currently we're in the process of finishing the interview that led us to Seattle.

Things never happen as planned with Nirvana; it's basically obligatory and part of their charm. First surprise, they were right on time for the interview and we were late. No problem, they waited patiently for us on the porch of Chris's house, enjoying the sun between the sound of lawn mowers and the back-and-forth of birds making a home under one of the wood beams of the veranda. There's a familial, easygoing atmosphere that we wouldn't expect to be part of the life of one of the hottest bands of the moment with more than nine million albums sold worldwide.

In the wake of the blitzkrieg of *Nevermind*, and at the end of their exhausting world tour, each of the three bought himself a house in a nice neighborhood. Their standard of living followed an ever-ascending curve, but there isn't any of the luxurious debauchery and flashiness that often surround those for whom success comes quickly and on a significant scale.

Chris owns three cars today. There's an all-terrain four-by-four, a 1960s Volkswagen stripped of all its glamour and dignity, and a Dauphine that he's trying to restore whose original charm prevents it from looking like it's on its last legs in America. Without his beard and with his short hair, Chris Novoselic still has the allure of a friendly giant.

"I also found a piece of land in the mountains," he says while we drive in the direction of a neighborhood restaurant. "There's a house above it, but it's completely isolated. Very difficult to reach. There isn't even a telephone. But it's exactly what I was looking for. There was a time last year when I felt like it would be better to disappear for a little while. Isolate myself from everything that was surrounding me. After the tour I needed to put things back in perspective and accept what had changed."

Nirvana's story is quite dizzying. A lot of others would have suffered. A lot of others would have lost track of their lives and their dreams. They seem to have known how to maneuver the fast lane that brutally propelled them from precarious yet reassuring anonymity to an international glory for which they weren't prepared: its rewards, its tricks, and the difficulty of recognizing the difference between the two. Money, public attention, their image projected everywhere: it didn't make them lose their human dimension and their taste for the real. It's without a doubt the reason they can continue to live almost normally.

The restaurant we go to seems to stand on grease and decrepitude. The place is more or less run by an association that takes care of troubled youth. In fact, none of the clients are over twenty-five years old. It's obvious that everyone recognizes the people who just walked in, but no one even thinks of bothering them.

Serial Killer

At the end of the table, Kurt Cobain eats a cheeseburger dripping with grease and surrounded by fries. I mention that it's probably not the best way to cure the frequent stomachaches he would complain about when we first met, almost two years ago, during their Australian tour. The pain was later diagnosed as a stomach ulcer that required a few hospitalizations.

"It's over." He hesitates. "Well, I think. It was due to the way I sing. I use my stomach, and since I scream a lot, it ended up causing an irritation. The tour was really long; we played almost every night, so it couldn't heal. I ended up with a hole in my stomach. It was also linked to a lot of stress . . . too many things were happening at the same time. I went through a very negative period. I felt like music was moving into the background. For a while I wanted to stop everything. I think what happens in your head ends up coming out in your body. Well, now it's healed."

He looks carefully at his burger.

"In any case, try to find something better on the menu, if you can. Any suggestions are welcome."

Of the three, Kurt Cobain is certainly the hardest to connect with, but also the most endearing. In contrast with the six-foot-tall Chris and the athletic build of Dave Grohl, he still looks, at twenty-seven years old, like a fragile, sensitive child. His face is partly hidden behind long hair separated by a center parting; he speaks in a soft voice, barely audible. A calm that must be there, but only when you catch in his glance a glimpse of the whirlwinds of energy that inhabit him. If one day someone makes a film where the Little Prince turns into a serial killer, Kurt could easily play the lead role. Because he's the band's leader, but also because of his nature, he has suffered the most from the succession of events provoked by the success of *Nevermind*. He who spoke so little found himself suddenly bombarded as the spokesperson for a generation. He who had found in music a mode of expression saw himself obliged to explain with words what was actually his only mode of communication. For a few months things almost turned bad. Rumors that he had started a bad heroin habit became more and more persistent. Certain people speculated on his death. And his relationship with Courtney Love, the singer of Hole, served as the lifeblood of gutter press looking for a scandalous couple. The intrusion into his private life culminated with the announcement of the release of a particularly "shit-stirring" book, written by two journalists whom the band had accepted into their entourage before realizing what type of book they were in the process of writing. Kurt, at the end of his rope, left a threatening message on the answering machine of one of the journalists, who then, of course, hurried with it to the newspapers.

Dave Grohl: "I don't think the book will ever come out, and if it does it'll be as thick as that." He indicates the space of a few pages with a smile of vengeful satisfaction. "They'll send it to our lawyers, who will take out all the passages that aren't true. Not only is it filled with completely unbelievable information, but the style is so bad, even grade-school kids wouldn't write like that."

Today Kurt seems to have overcome his auto-destructive demons. And you'd really have to know nothing about all of these things to go question someone on such an intimate subject. He's not ready to replace Schwarzenegger, but today he has a positive energy that he attributes to his marriage with Courtney and the birth of their daughter, Frances Bean, last year.

Jokes and anecdotes turn around the table. Time does, too. Chris and Dave talk about motorcycles. They recommend excursions around Seattle. This meeting is turning into an old friends' reunion. The three share the same distaste for interviews. Not to mention photo sessions! Not because they judge their time more valuable than ours (we wouldn't have been here for such a long time if it were the case) but because they seem to dread the artificial nature and self-consciousness that the process entails. As a result, they lag behind.

Finally, we decide that we're going to do it at Dave's house. We meet his fiancée and his mom, who have come to spend a couple days. With some cookies and cola it could have been a regular after-school playdate. We had to stop in the garage, where Dave stores his two motorcycles. A remote control airplane, a snowboard, a skateboard, an all-terrain bike . . . the place seems like a teenaged Ali Baba's cave. The highlight of his collection, though, is the two go-carts he just acquired. And before we had time to look around, the motors started . . .

That's how we found ourselves in the parking lot. The cans on the ground demarcate a vague track. The little improvised race between Kurt and Dave is quickly in the drummer's favor. They were giving us a try when bad weather came along to put some seriousness back into the afternoon. It's the middle of August, but Seattle still lives up to its reputation of being rainy and chilly. We end up in the basement of the multilevel house that Dave built. The new carpet, paintings, and unopened crates suggest a recent move-in. We sit down on the floor amid piles of vinyl records. Among them is the single, "The Priest They Called Him," released under two names, William Burroughs and Kurt Cobain.

Kurt Cobain: It was the idea of a friend who had a label in Portland. I actually never met Burroughs. We never even talked on the telephone. We each did our thing on our own side. At first that wasn't supposed to be a single; it seemed like we were going to maybe make an entire album. For a while we were thinking about asking him to have a part in our next video. There's an old man character. But after thinking about it, we thought that it could be degrading for him and we forgot about it.

Did he have an influence on me? I don't know if what I write compares with Burroughs, but his books were certainly among the ones that had the biggest impact on me. I'm not in a hurry to meet him. I think those kinds of meetings shouldn't be forced. It will happen when it happens.

Even with the re-release of *Bleach*, that many now discovered, and the compilation *Incesticide* that gathered the rare and unknown titles, we have to admit that we haven't heard much new material from the trio since *Nevermind*, with the exception of a title on a single shared with their friends Jesus Lizard. On the other hand, they're going strong. We've heard they were in the studio with Steve Albini, and that the record company refused to release an "unlistenable" record, that the band started over entirely with Scott Litt. Even the title seemed to not want to stabilize. The album was first called, *I Hate Myself and Want to Die* and then *Verse Chorus Verse*, but finally they settled on *In Utero*.

Fetus

Chris Novoselic: They were just titles we were having fun with. Nothing was set. But the littlest factoid was blown out of proportion by the media. It's totally ridiculous. There are enough crazy things in the world: what's so important about a rock band recording their album?

DG: We quickly forgot about *Verse Chorus Verse*. It was giving a mediocre connotation to the album. As for *I Hate Myself and I Want to Die*, it's the title of a song that was supposed to be on the album but that we decided not to include. It sounded too much like others on the disc. It will come out on a *Beavis & Butthead* compilation (Youri Lenquette: Two characters from a cartoon made popular by MTV, a sort of caustic cross between *The Simpsons* and *Wayne's World*).

CN: And with a title like that, it would have only taken one kid to commit suicide for us to find ourselves in the courtroom next to Judas Priest.

YL: Did this title reflect your state of mind at the time?

CN: Yes, ha ha . . . [*He laughs sarcastically.*] We must have been playing Russian roulette with loaded pistols that day.

Kurt is suddenly interested in the sole of his shoe, a way to avoid having to explain this line he authored.

CN: All three of us have a penchant for the second-degree and dark humor. The problem is that what makes us laugh in private could be taken badly or distorted when you're talking to people you don't know or who don't know you.

KC: *In Utero* is one of the last titles that came to mind. There isn't a big meaning or message to find. It went with the cover art on the sleeve where you see pregnant women and fetuses.

YL: Was it difficult to make a follow-up to *Nevermind*?

KC: I know there was a time when I wanted to fuck it all up. I wanted to make an album that no one would want to buy . . . We eventually got over this sort of attitude motivated by despair. We decided to make the album we wanted to make without thinking about what it could mean to the public, the media, the industry, or anything.

Listening to the pre-cassette of the album confirmed the legitimacy of this self-seeking approach. Less polite and clean than *Nevermind*, *In Utero* captures Nirvana raw. A little as if Cobain and his band had combined the fanatic incandescence of *Bleach* and the obvious pop sensibility of *Nevermind*. The album was recorded in record time: two weeks in a studio near Minneapolis, last winter.

KC: Honestly, it's not very hard to make a rock 'n' roll album. The songs were ready. All we had to do was agree on the details. If we put a solo there or not . . . We did the entire foundation in three days. Three or four more for the vocals or guitar add-ons, and the rest for mixing. We always took very little time to record. There was snow everywhere. We booked the studio under a pseudonym: the Simon Ritchie Band; Simon Ritchie was the real name of Sid Vicious. No one knew we were there; even the manager of the studio didn't find out about it until afterwards.

YL: Why did you choose Steve Albini?

KC: We liked the type of sound he got on previous productions. He records sound in a very natural way. We didn't really need a producer. The sound of our albums is primarily our own. It's not like certain bands from the 1960s, or today, productions like Whitney Houston, where the producer chooses the songs, the musicians, arranges the tracks . . . We really needed a sound engineer, someone who takes care of technical problems. Steve's attitude was right for us. He's anti-establishment, he's ready to try new things.

CN: He has a particular way of recording the sound. He uses a bunch of microphones. Weird microphones. Old machines, machines that he got in West Germany . . . He doesn't want to do a standard installation. It let us play with the reverberation of the room, the sound bouncing off the walls.

YL: Contrary to rumors, your relationship with Albini seems pretty good even if two of the album tracks were remade with Scott Litt.

KC: Honestly, if Albini hadn't been able to make this album, it would have been a real dilemma. We would have spent months searching for the sound we wanted. With another producer and another studio, we would have had a hard time not getting stuck with a sequel to *Nevermind*.

YL: On top of the tracks on the album, the band recorded four titles seemingly to feed the B-sides of the singles, and Dave wrote one of them.

DG: Actually, it's an old title. It goes back to the days when Kurt and me shared the same apartment. We bought a four-track recorder and wrote some songs to try it. "Pennyroyal Tea," which is on the album, was composed at that time. We thought that it deserved to be re-recorded. I don't compose often. It's a hobby for me more than something serious.

YL: *In Utero*, like *Nevermind*, ends with a trick. After twenty-three minutes of silence, a completely unbelievable surprise title emerges from the speakers.

CN: When *Nevermind* came out, the CD was still a pretty new format. We were just looking to have some fun with its possibilities. It was a way to annoy people with multidisc CD players.

Ashtray

If we're only talking about numbers, *Nevermind*'s sales were significantly inferior to those of Garth Brooks, Michael Jackson, and other driving forces in the industry. On the other hand, its impact and its repercussions exceed everything that has been done since. When has a real rock 'n' roll band, a real punk band, succeeded to the point of making itself heard? The Sex Pistols and Clash were certainly proud patrons of an aesthetic, of a consciousness, of a movement. The Stooges and the Velvet revolutionized their era. But their sales were never sufficient enough to be even a grain of sand in the machine. By imposing this type of music today, Nirvana created a magnet effect, the full importance of which won't be clear until later. For now, their success has already allowed a slew of bands to sign, when two years earlier they would have been happy if their demo served as an ashtray. As for the nine million albums sold, from now on they're there to remind the industry that the era of all that 1980s marketing is over. Without wanting to be, Nirvana is the source of the grunge look that is every fashion magazine's delight.

Diet Grunge

CN: What can I say? It's grotesque. But I don't think it's going to last, for the simple and good reason that there isn't a lot to exploit. Grunge isn't just a branch of rock 'n' roll. And OK, even if there are still some posers, there aren't thirty-six different ways to wear a plaid T-shirt with frayed jeans. You'll probably find a few people who will go buy a three-hundred-dollar designer plaid T-shirt, but most will continue to go find them for five dollars in a thrift store. If there isn't money to make, the industry will always move on to something else.

Inevitably, Nirvana can no longer rest peacefully in the Manichean divide opposing mainstream and alternative. Whether they like it or not, their story represents a big business. However, they never cease to exhibit a taste for shaking things up, and their desire to see things change has remained intact.

"If any of you in any way hate homosexuals, people of different color, or women, please do this one favor for us—leave us the fuck alone! Don't come to our shows and don't buy our records." This advisory in the sleeve notes of *Incesticide* summarizes their state of mind pretty clearly. There's an almost frighteningly urgent anger on certain tracks of *In Utero*. "Frances Farmer" is Kurt's homage to the actress and Seattle native, broken by the establishment because she didn't want to conform to American laws for young girls, a victim of McCarthyism but more broadly of reactionary stupidity and bureaucracy. As for "Rape Me," the hostility and disgust that transpired in Kurt's way of singing gives you the chills.

YL: Aren't you afraid that the message is misunderstood?

CN: Maybe if this song had been on *Nevermind*, there would have been the risk of confusion. But I think that we've done enough interviews for everyone to know our opinion on it.

One of the best ways to see Cobain withdraw into himself is to question him on the precise meaning of his words. When we ask him what he meant by "I wish I could eat your cancer when you turn black," a line from "Heart-Shaped Box," it's Chris who neutralizes any idea of going further.

CN: Let's see, what is the answer to that question today? Oh yeah, it's a song dedicated to people born in July.

YL: And who is this Tourettes, whose name is one of the titles of the songs?

KC: He's French, I think. A doctor who studied this mental illness that makes you suddenly lose control in the middle of a sentence and start saying horrible things. I didn't feel like writing the words for the song. I went in front of the mic and I aligned all the curses that came to my head.

Dave's girlfriend can't stand cigarette smoke, so we move to the terrace so the tobacco addicts can satisfy their vice.

Cyril [the contest winner] talks about what Chris Isaak said about their music, that he found it calming. The reaction wasn't predictable:

KC: That's exactly what I think of his. No, really. I like his music a lot. And he's a really pleasant person.

I tell them that Paul McCartney had said that "Lithium" was the song he liked the most recently.

CN: That's funny, because when I made the bass line for that song, my goal was actually to give it a Beatles vibe.

KC: I think that if John Lennon had said that I would have peed myself in joy. But Paul, what a dickhead. OK, that's unfair. I'm sure he contributed largely to a lot of things I like about the Beatles. But I hate his solo albums. And I have trouble with his persona. His innocent, clean vibe . . . I was flattered when I heard that his wife, Linda Eastman, wanted to take photos of us.

Contrary to what I presumed, the three Nirvana members appreciate and know rap well. The GOAT [*Greatest of All Time, a reference to LL Cool J —Ed.*], Arrested Development, Public Enemy, they know nearly everything interesting about what the genre has to offer.

CN: I have trouble with rap when it sinks into male chauvinism. This obsession with gold chains and huge cars and a world where all women are whores . . . it's hard to believe. That and the glorification of guns. I don't see what's cool about having one. Guns are scary. They kill people in this country. Wait, you don't know the best. I read that a gun store in, I don't remember what city, had put a sign in their window that said "Back-to-School Special." That says a lot about the mentality of people who sell them and the age of those who want to get their hands on them!

Night is starting to fall. Everyone remembers that they have plans for tonight, more or less. Kurt needs to finish a bio that he promised to finish last week. Dave has his mom over for her birthday and needs to help prepare the meal. Chris has roughly the same plans with an uncle from Croatia, the country that his parents left to emigrate to the US not long after his birth, and to which the bassist of Nirvana has returned regularly ever since his childhood. While we exchange phone numbers, Dave goes to look for one of the platinum albums that he got for *Nevermind* and gives it to Cyril as a gift.

Before we leave, we ask them if they plan to renew the experience attempted at their New Music Seminar concert for the next tour that starts in the fall by including an intermission where they'll perform a few songs acoustically.

CN: Why not? It's always fun to see guys in the front groan and mosh while you try to play a slow song. And melodies attract girls, right. Wait, maybe we should launch a new concept. We'll call it Diet Grunge!

IN THE WOMB WITH THE NEW LP

Marcus Koehler | August 3, 1993 | *No Trend Press* (Germany)

At the time of this interview almost everything about Nirvana seemed to have been said. The media circus had built a glass house around the life of each band member. Minimal privacy. No secrets. Just new rumors that were sort of an everyday business. Kurt Cobain had become the idol for a whole generation, and most of the media attention was focused on him and his excessive existence as a rock star. When I hung out with Sub Pop band Seaweed in Tacoma, Washington, back in 1992, I got in touch with Tracy Marander, who at that time was engaged to their guitar player, Wade Neal. Tracy was responsible for the cover of *Bleach*, which features a photo she took at an early Nirvana gig during the period she dated Kurt Cobain. It was Tracy who, a year later, hooked me up with Krist Novoselic, with whom she had remained friends. *In Utero*, Nirvana's new album, was at the starting gates. But the suspense I experienced at the Roxy two years before had gone. Everything seemed to have been replaced by mere routine. Of course, Krist still was nice and funny. But the carefree vibe of their early days was lacking. —Marcus Koehler

Translated by Inga Owczors and Jon Darch.

There had been a lot said ahead of the release of the new LP: Albini is producing/not producing it; it wasn't commercial enough; Geffen didn't want to release it; plus week after week a new album title, etc., etc. The rumor mill was really bubbling again, and in no small way. Being assiduous Nirvana researchers, *NT* naturally wanted to get to the bottom of it all, and fortunately, thanks to long-standing relationships, we managed to do so. At practically the last minute, the telephone interview with Krist Novoselic that we'd had planned for two weeks finally took place. Nirvana's most popular member had repeatedly agreed to it but then kept having to put it off again at short notice, until on August 3, not much more than five minutes before our absolute deadline, we finally got there. At approximately 10:30 PM Central European Time, the tall Croat spared us half an hour of his time for a chat—between lunch and going for a swim. As ever, he was a nice, witty person to talk to, although over the course of the conversation you could definitely detect that he'd gained a certain distance and objectivity toward the media in recent years.

Marcus Koehler: Let's briefly go back, first of all, to *Nevermind*. Lyrically it deals, doesn't it, primarily with blind consumption and the manipulation of the masses by the ruling classes. Now, however, it itself has become a mass product, with its six million units sold. What do you make of that development?

Krist Novoselic: I do have to agree with you up to a point, but I don't feel wholly comfortable commenting on the lyrics, as it wasn't me who wrote them. I'm sure there were lots of different reasons for people buying the album. At the time it came out, there were practically no other hard rock releases having any success. There'd already been no rock album up near the top of the *Billboard* charts for a year or so.

MK: What about Skid Row, Guns N' Roses, and all the other tripe?

KN: People probably just wanted to hear something different, and we had it ready and waiting for them.

MK: Do you think that through the lyrics for *Nevermind*, your punk attitude, and the way you present yourself in the media, you've been able to change something in people's consciousness as well?

KN: As I've said, I don't want to comment on the lyrics themselves. I think it was time that some band or other from the underground/alternative scene made it big, and sooner or later it would've happened anyway. It had been bubbling away for a long time, and we ultimately had the right songs to do it. I actually always saw us as a band whose music is accessible. We now had good songs, and they simply appealed to people. Of course, a lot has changed in the music industry as a result of *Nevermind*. They see now that bands who make this kind of music do sell. I think everybody knows that rock 'n' roll constantly reinvents itself, and now the industry seems to have grasped that as well.

MK: Would you describe yourselves in a way as trendsetters?

KN: No, I wouldn't say that. We were just in the right place at the right time. That's all. You're asking the wrong person in any case, as I've tended more to downplay things the whole time. I take a backseat in that regard.

MK: I've heard that a lot of people tried to exploit your success financially. Is that right?

KN: Yeah, there were a few wiseguys who wanted to take a big slice of the cake, too. They'd work on the basis that everyone else pays a hundred dollars, but Nirvana has to pay ten thousand. That sort of thing.

MK: Wade from Seaweed also told me that some distant cousins of yours, who you'd also not seen for ages, suddenly declared they'd like a new car and such like from you.

KN: Yeah, that's true.

MK: I hope I'm not now being indiscreet, but what have you in fact done with all your money?

KN: I bought two houses with it. One is an old junky house, which I'm currently renovating. It had previously been empty for about twelve years, and it's in the countryside. The house I live in is in Seattle. The one out in the country, by the way, is part of a proper farm from the 1950s. I'm practically the Bob Vila of rock 'n' roll!

MK: The who?

KN: Bob Vila. He's the guy on TV who shows you how to get old buildings back into shape. Apart from that, I've used the money to buy a whole load of junk.

MK: I also read somewhere that you guys don't have any flashy wheels either—no Ferrari, Cadillac, or the like. Is that right?

KN: Yes, I drive a 1997 VW Class 3. Plus I bought a small truck for my farm. And a jukebox. And that's probably about all. Oh, I bought a computer as well, and some records, of course.

MK: How much has the financial success changed your life in general?

KN: Quite simply to the extent that it makes life more agreeable and that I'm not such a wretch anymore as I used to be. When we go on tour, I also no longer need to have any concerns about losing my job. It is simply easier to live this way. But don't get me wrong, I had just as much fun back then as I have today. In many respects, however, the (financial) success has also made me wiser and more mature, I've got to say.

MK: I heard that you and the rest of the band became involved in campaigning against some law and also took part in a demonstration against it. I just don't remember what it was . . .

KN: You probably mean the Erotic Music Law.

MK: Yes, I think that was it. You also wrote an article for *Spin* about the situation after the war in your home country, Croatia. How did that come about?

KN: The publisher of *Spin* was evidently impressed by my knowledge of the war in the country. He asked me, anyway, if I'd like to go there and write a report about it. They then covered the flight and expenses and paid me a fee for it, which I then donated to this particular charity that helps raped women. It was around three thousand, two hundred dollars.

MK: But you didn't make the trip for charitable reasons.

KN: No, I took the job mainly because I wanted to see what exactly is going on over there and reflect upon it.

MK: A friend of mine [*Boris —Ed.*] is sitting here next to me. He's also a Croatian and would like to know what you think of the way things are going there.

KN: That's something we could certainly talk about for hours.

MK: Do you have any relatives in Croatia yourself?

KN: Yes, quite a few. It's all in *Spin* and the English magazine *The Face*. Haven't you read the article?

MK: I've not yet had the chance. But the German *Kerrang!* also had something about it along with a really god-awful picture of you. It looked extremely sleazy and styled. I was shocked when I saw it. Why would you do that?

KN: Don't know. Maybe I just had a bad hair day, who knows?

MK: But let's stay with more critical matters. It's clearly no bad thing if you as a now famous person use this position to exert a positive influence. But what's the situation with Kurt? I get the impression that all the responsibility that he's trying to prove he's taken on through his marriage and especially fatherhood is only covering up his drug problem. How do you see that?

KN: I think you can see it however you want; there are always different ways of viewing things. He might well have really been in love with Courtney, don't you think? However, I don't want to talk here now about my friends and their supposed problems.

MK: But it seems pretty clear that he did have these problems, doesn't it? People who have had a close relationship with him for many years have confirmed it. So why doesn't he do the honest thing, admit it, and say he's changed his life, rather than continuously hiding with his lies behind his baby?

KN: Nobody's perfect. Let me put it that way. We're just a rock 'n' roll band, after all, just very ordinary people making music. Everybody has times in their lives when things go badly. And as we were just speaking about babies—in some way we're all babies trying to make the best of ourselves and our lives, aren't we?

MK: I agree, it's just that people also ought to be able to admit their mistakes. I'm sure a lot was exaggerated by the media, which Kurt indeed tried to set straight at the MTV Awards.

KN: Of course. There are a lot of very capable and honest writers out there, but also a lot of really evil muckrakers. You just have to see what a load of crap gets written in the tabloids. The minute they pick up anything at all, they bandy it about right away.

MK: I am fully aware that a lot of it isn't true. That's indeed why I'm asking you.

KN: I'm not able to speak for Kurt. Nor do I have the right to. He, after all, is the one who's responsible for what he says. I know what he said and how he intended to come across, and I know he's not a liar, making out things are different to how they actually are.

MK: Sometimes, however, it also seems as though rumors are getting spread on purpose to help with promotion, especially now with the new record imminent. I remember a news item not long ago that said Kurt had beat up his wife and been thrown in jail for it.

KN: Just like the rumor was spread that Geffen didn't want to bring out the new record.

MK: Exactly. Is it true that Albini is responsible for it?

KN: Up to a certain point, yes. But, you see, that's a mountain being made out of a molehill right there, just because everybody wants to know what we're up to right now. And that's the thing, too, that has fundamentally changed for us. Everything Nirvana now does or gets involved in gets minutely scrutinized. People have also now frequently used that to try to drive a wedge between us. During the recording of our new album, for instance, there was this one minor disagreement and immediately somebody was trumpeting that Geffen didn't want to bring it out, that it would be commercial suicide and bullshit like that. And yet it's all no big deal. We're three people making music together who want to bring out a record that we like, that's all. We really don't care a jot what other people think about it, whoever they may be. But when people are putting rubbish around like "Geffen hates the album" or that our management is putting us under pressure, we do have to react to it and set the record straight.

MK: Judging by what I've heard so far about the new record, it seems as though you're planning to consciously change your audience by producing a less commercially oriented record. Is that true?

KN: No, that's not the case. We don't want to get rid of people; quite the opposite—we want to attract new ones by saying, "OK, so you liked *Nevermind.* Here's something that's different, primarily through being more raw and noisy." In this way, hopefully people who already liked *Nevermind* will be alerted to the new record too and thus in turn to other music with this sound, like Jesus Lizard, for example. We don't want to exclude anybody through our music; that's happened already as a reaction to *Nevermind* and for no other reason than we've become famous. In the beginning, that was a real problem for us, especially for me. We'd achieved the breakthrough, you see, practically overnight. Now we can deal with it perfectly OK. We're really proud of the new record and intrigued to see how it'll be received. And we definitely don't want to exclude anybody by releasing it. We want people to listen to it, we want to go on tour, give interviews, and continue to appear on TV. We're not trying to say "Fuck off!" to anyone; that's not true.

MK: What you're talking about there is effectively another musical revolution that you're aiming at. Trying to make a completely different sound accessible to people.

KN: Yeah, that's basically it. Perhaps that way we can attract people to rawer music as well. Just look at what happened after *Nevermind.* All those hairspray and lipstick bands like Poison, Skid Row, and so on changed after that, discarded their outfits, and from then on paid more attention to attitude than to their band members' looks. There, too, you could definitely see a certain amount of progress.

MK: What's the name of the new record going to be? The definitive one!

KN: *In Utero.*

MK: Why not *I Hate Myself and I Want to Die*?

KN: We seriously considered using it; we thought it was kind of funny. In the end we decided against it, as we feared that the same could happen to us as befell Ozzy Osbourne and Judas Priest. That's to say some poor kid kills himself, and as a result we get taken to court or something of that sort. People know, you see, where there's money to be had, and it's already happened to us so often in the past that someone's tried to sue us that we've become more careful now in that regard.

MK: So, what happened exactly?

KN: Well, for example, there were some bands with the same name that tried it on, but without success. "Nirvana" from L.A., from the United Kingdom, and so on and so forth.

MK: There was once a review of Nirvana live in *Your Flesh* in which it said that Kurt smashed his guitar over someone's head and got prosecuted for it . . .

KN: No, that was a bouncer who had hit him first. We've got it all on video. He'd pulled him towards him by his hair and tried to beat him up. So again you see here how things get completely twisted and exaggerated. That's also how all the rumors start.

MK: Let's come back to the title of the album. After *I Hate Myself . . .* the word was it was going to be called *Verse Chorus Verse*.

KN: Yeah, but in retrospect we thought that sounded too tame.

MK: To me that sounded as though you wanted to express the exact opposite of the way the structure of the new songs looks.

KN: The song structure still does follow that pattern, as it did on *Nevermind*. Nothing about that has changed.

MK: Will there also be some older songs on *In Utero*, such as "Everything and Nothing," for example?

KN: We never had a song with that title. It was probably named wrongly on a bootleg. Yes, there are some older songs on it as well—"Pennyroyal Tea," for example.

MK: What about other song titles?

KN: Other ones are called "Rape Me," "Serve the Servants," and "Heart-Shaped Box."

MK: Why have you not done any proper touring since the *Nevermind* breakthrough? In Europe especially, you've seldom been seen live since then.

KN: We simply weren't prepared to appear in the big arenas and take part in the whole circus. We did a few smaller tours, though. We went on the road in Japan and Australia, played a few times in South America, and performed at the Reading Festival as well. Here and there we also did a few one-off shows on the West Coast.

MK: You also had an offer from Guns N' Roses, didn't you?

KN: Yes, that's right. But we didn't want to put our fans through having to go to that.

MK: So you still don't see yourselves as a heavy metal or hard rock band?

KN: No, definitely not. We're just a popular rock band, nothing more. Maybe the "kings of alternative music." Bullshit, a bunch of assholes is what we are!

MK: What about touring in the future?

KN: We'll be on the road in October, starting in the United States, then in Europe in December/January. Australia and Japan are also being planned.

MK: To finish off, one more thing: for each letter of Nirvana, give me a reason why you are so successful.

KN: *N* stands for *Nevermind, I* for *introverted*—we are all introverts, you see. *R* because we're *ridiculous. V,* that's a difficult one . . . maybe because we are against any *invasion,* give me a moment . . . [*Boris suggests* vagina.] OK, *vagina!* Because it takes nine months for a man to slip out of a vagina and he spends the rest of his life trying to get back into one. *A* because we're *assholes* and *N* because we're from *North America.* No, let's say the *Northwest.* And *A* because we're an *A-class,* number one, simply the BEST. That's the lot.

MK: Krist, thank you for talking to us.

HELL, IT'S OTHER PEOPLE

Emmanuel Tellier | August 10, 1993 | *Les Inrockuptibles* (France)

I treasure a very specific memory when I think back on the day I interviewed Nirvana in Seattle in the autumn of 1993. Just a moment before, I had left a hotel room in the Edgewater having encountered Kurt, Krist, and Dave, but there in the corridor, with a forty-five-minute interview tape in my pocket, all I kept thinking was that it was too short, too little. An idea struck me. I shrugged. It was worth a try. I ran down to the lobby of the hotel, to the Geffen press agent who was coordinating events, and proceeded to tell the biggest lie of my (young) journalistic life. "A catastrophe!" I told her. My tape recorder had screwed up, it hadn't recorded anything—how could I fly home to France with nothing? I ladled on the air of doom, and she bought it. She ran off to find Kurt, to ask him if he might be willing to repeat the interview.

Very graciously, he agreed. Just five minutes later I was back in the room, just Kurt alone this time. "OK," he said, "let's go through those questions again." And, of course, I started with a completely different question. He was half-amused, half-astonished by my little trick—it was so obvious that this was "part two" of the conversation. All he said was, "Hmm . . . a new question . . . Why not? Go ahead!" I made sure not to outstay my welcome but departed half an hour later with two full sides of tape and what I believe is one of the longest interviews Nirvana—and Kurt himself—gave during that spell of the band's all-too-brief existence. —Emmanuel Tellier

Translated by Carly Lapotre.

Emmanuel Tellier: Are the people of Seattle proud of you?

Dave Grohl: They're pretty nice, but I'm sure they're ashamed of us. They see us as the weirdos of the community, not local celebrities. Ever since we got famous, journalists only talk about the "big grunge movement." Throughout the world, the city is associated with this fake, shady image. That doesn't thrill anybody around here. The legend of rock city, it's really just journalist bullshit; people who come here for a week "looking for grunge." You saw Seattle; it's a nice city, not a slum . . . The most depressing thing about this whole media thing is that the music scene hasn't benefited from all the attention Nirvana has got. Before, three out of ten music groups were pathetic and the others were pretty good. Now nine groups out of ten are crap. All the lame East Coast people moved to Seattle, and the old people from the area were scared the city would become like Los Angeles, that the music boom would provoke a kind of negative rush to the city. A few years ago, *Money* magazine voted Seattle the most livable city in the country. No traffic problems, no pollution, a reasonable number of habitants, a beautiful region, productive industry with a lot of huge companies like Boeing and Microsoft. A real American paradise. So people started to move here. You could find a good job easily and buy a cheap house. Then rock came along.

ET: Concretely, what was the impact of your success in the city? Are there more clubs, record labels?

DG: The only noticeable changes are the crowds in the clubs and the number of albums the labels release. When I moved to Seattle in 1990, I met everyone in a few hours. In two nights, Kurt and Chris introduced me to the "inner circle" of the Sub Pop label, about a dozen people maximum. That was Seattle: some friends sitting around a table in a bar. The atmosphere was excellent, very friendly, very student-ish. Today, I don't know anyone anymore. I meet guys every day who claim to belong to the "family," but I've never seen them around. In underground concerts, we cross paths with well-known rock artists, famous bands just passing through. They come to see what's happening in the clubs; they like to have a drink with us. It's pretty healthy, I think. There are always a ton of kids at concerts, little guys who come to the city with their guitar to "make it big." I met a few who were on the road last week. They came from Minnesota, and one ran up to me and said: "My friends didn't want to come with me to Seattle. They said that you moved and lived in the mountains, that there was nothing going on in Seattle. I have to call my friends to tell them to come here. This city is awesome!" [*Laughs.*] But for Kurt, it's a lot harder. For him, everything is different, extreme. For me, life is good: I'm getting married in a few days. I have a new house and enough money to die comfortably. And all that is pretty recent. Just last year, I had no comfort. When *Nevermind* exploded, I was living in a minuscule place, a real closet. I had a bed and a lamp, that's all.

ET: What did you think of the group before being a part of it?

DG: They were pretty good, but not magic. I had just left my best friends, the band Scream, who I'd played with for four years. Suddenly, I had to live at the other end of the continent and work with two strangers who hired me over the phone. So I decided to go all out. I wanted to impress them, play with all my strength. And right away it clicked with us. At fifteen, I played with a group that had an identical structure: three musicians, with a singer-guitarist. Our music sounded like Nirvana's, pop songs played to the max. At the time, every one of our rehearsals started with a long instrumental racket, each of us hammering on our instruments. Then we started to really play. During my first rehearsal with Nirvana, we started like that, a half hour of din. We never abandoned that method; it's perfect for us. We play hard, we laugh, we see the rage in us. I think that all three of us are abnormally sensitive to noise and simplicity. We can spend a lot of time suspended on one damn sound, simple and straight. It's one of our strengths: we know how to stay simple and powerful. The band's most beautiful weapon is its spontaneity. If we want to scream, experiment, nothing's stopping us. The concerts end a lot of times with white noise. Sometimes the din makes no sense. The sound sucks us in, the instruments are free, each of us exploding however we feel. It's the moment that counts. We play as loud as possible for that instant, for that high.

Chris Novoselic: Keep in mind, nothing is calculated. The band comes from the subconscious. We don't go to rehearsals to compose; we play together to experiment. The classic "verse-chorus-verse" structure doesn't interest us. It's a joke to us. In fact, we wanted to call our new album *Verse Chorus Verse* to spit in pop's face.

DG: The structure of punk rock songs is based on the dynamics, not the writing. The song dictates the changes, not the musician on their own. I brought the most to Nirvana in the realm of dynamics. Before, the group was fine just playing in a linear way. I taught Chris and Kurt how to dig the songs, to train the sound to bounce back better. Now, we can be extreme in two directions: softness and noise.

ET: How do you organize work in the band; who makes the decisions?

DG: Little daily decisions escape us; other people decide that for us. Where to rehearse? What technicians to hire for the tour? Where to meet journalists? These choices don't belong to us anymore. Kurt would like to control all of that, but it's impossible. He already takes care of the album covers, posters, visuals: that's his territory. For concert dates, cities, or where we want to play or not play, everyone has an opinion. Most often, it all ends up being a miserable "Ugh, why not?" We're so lazy and stupid that most of our discussions finish by a series of sighs. "Guys, do you want to play in New York for the New Music Seminar?" "Ben, if Chris and Kurt are for it, then I have nothing against it . . ." In the band, "I don't give a shit" is really popular.

ET: You never refuse a proposition?

DG: Yeah, sure. When someone's making a fool out of us. A few weeks ago, our record label wanted us to play a private concert in front of two hundred assholes from show business. In this situation, we stand up for ourselves: "Go fuck yourself!"

ET: Are you close with anyone outside the band?

DG: Our manager is a friend, a fan of punk rock. It's not one of these fat fucks who only talk about ass and money. It's a guy like us. Other trustworthy people—I can count them on one hand: my fiancée, my two friends, my mom. I don't have anything against the people at our record label, Geffen. Some of them are very cool, we can have a drink together, but that's about it.

CN: Two years ago, it was simple. We put our gear in the van and we set out for hours on the road. Get to the club, play a concert, spend the night at a hotel or in a tent, sometimes under the stars in the woods. It was physically very hard, but I miss that time. We had a lot more fun than today. We didn't care about being found in our underwear around a campfire in the middle of the night in a field in Tennessee; nobody knew us. This kind of shit would end up in the papers today.

Kurt Cobain: We recaptured this carefree spirit last week during a concert in Seattle. The poster announced Tad with "special guests." We were the guests. It was so much better to show up on stage five minutes before the concert with all the people hollering.

CN: The place was packed, like at any local concert announcing "special guests!" The people of Seattle always expect us to come out. Now all the local promoters announce "special guests" on their posters, at every concert. What's less fun is that the concert was dedicated to a friend, a singer from the Gits who was found dead on the highway after having been raped. The money raised will go to finding the fucker who did it.

DG: When we talk to people about business, Kurt, Chris, and I know exactly how to behave. All three of us are very natural but suspicious.

ET: Where are you situated on the spectrum between suspicion and paranoia?

DG: So many things happen around us. I have a hard time keeping track, I step aside. I leave all that shit to other people. I never wanted to have a fax machine at my house. That would be the end of my liberty. I'm too sensitive, too fragile to let myself get tangled up in all that. Chris likes to be informed. As for Kurt, he physically needs it. If the fax machine breaks down, he goes crazy. He's so afraid of getting fucked over!

ET: Who suffers the most from the continuous pressure?

DG: Kurt, without hesitation. Anything that has to do with the album or the industry is torture for him. But everyone suffers from it. We've all thought about quitting the group. None of us were predisposed to becoming a rock star. It's too bad, because if we were real fucking rock stars, we wouldn't give a royal shit about all that crap. Real rock stars surf the shit. Real rock stars make videos with girls who show their big tits. Real rock stars can do anything, even insult women in their videos. Fucking rock stars live in another world. All these huge hard rock groups don't give a damn about women's issues, respecting others. I never wanted to be a stupid rock star.

ET: Have anxieties about your condition affected your intimate relationship with the group?

DG: I've never been fed up with Chris and Kurt [*smiling*] . . . but sometimes I'm fed up with Nirvana, by this beast, this machine that's become our band against our will. The group became much more than three friends; it's a fucking phenomenon. And that, I just can't believe it. Things got so crazy and we didn't have the time to adapt. We left on tour and bam! the sky fell on our head. Everyone wanted to meet us, know who we are, what our favorite meal is, the radio started to spew out our music constantly. After eight months of that shit, I couldn't take it anymore. I didn't want to talk about the band anymore, about all the "Smells Like Teen Spirit" crap, but I have to accept it. It's my life; when I'm fifty, they'll still be talking about me as the drummer of Nirvana. But I don't want to be the drummer of Nirvana all my life.

ET: How do you see your future?

DG: I want to go back to school. Be a good husband, have some kids. Be a good dad.

ET: And the band?

DG: We don't have any plans. Without question, there'll be another album from Nirvana, and afterwards, we'll see. As long as all three of us live in Seattle, I think the band will continue to exist. Maybe we won't have a contract, we won't be the mega band that everyone knows, but we'll play for fun because we're three friends who get along well musically. But we already work like that. When we get together to play, we forget the rest. The bullshit stays at the studio door. And if everything falls apart tomorrow, if Nirvana no longer exists for anyone except Chris, Kurt, and me, I would feel freer. Life would be simple. We would play at the neighborhood club. There would be fifty people. That would be good.

ET: Is the band still a daily topic of conversation?

CN: How can you avoid it? We try to understand what's happening around us, how the public sees us. Why us? Have we been particularly lucky? For us, *Nevermind* was a good album, better than all the ones that came out at the time. From there to selling ten million . . . We talk a lot about the industry. Of the effect that *Nevermind* had on the business. Are we accomplices? Or are we resisting from the inside?

KC: We're like African tribes cut off from the world. In Africa, there are some people who don't know what war is. There's one tribe in particular where gender has no value. Men and women do the same tasks, by instinct. Men and women fish; men and women take care of the children. Everything is shared, discussed. If Nirvana was a tribe, we would certainly be like them: free. There's never a problem between us.

ET: After *Nevermind*, have you ever wanted to kill off the band in all its glory, the rock fantasy of "live fast, die young"?

DG: We would keep the essential, the music. All the shit around us would fly away! People would keep hold of the songs. It's an exciting idea, but the love of music has kept us going. Since the release of *Nevermind*, we've been thinking of the next album. If we killed off the group, we would make a legend out of it. Certain people have said that *Nevermind* changed the face of rock. How could three fucking losers have done that? We barely change clothes, so changing the face of the world . . .

KC: It's the love of music that gives me the strength to continue. Nothing else. But I could quit any day. I have enough money to disappear without a trace. Bye-bye, end of story. If I stay, it's only for punk rock.

CN: *In Utero* came very naturally. It's not a reactionary or vengeful album. The songs came on their own. The rage was there, deep rooted in Kurt, from his stomach. There was nothing more to do than let it out. At the beginning we had the fantasy of a huge rock album. The thing that would crush all the existing albums. We wanted to surpass *Nevermind*, surpass everyone. Then, in the studio, things got simpler. And the album made itself. We were incredibly relaxed.

DG: We wanted to test certain songs on stage. But the bootleggers, these fuckers who record concerts to release them on disc, wouldn't give us that opportunity. We had to play the same songs for two years.

CN: We wanted to advance, to give life to new songs, but our managers and the recording label were putting pressure on us: "Whatever you do, don't play a new song!" So the concerts became routine. If I wanted routine, I would get my old job back as an industrial painter. But I wanted to live, to move forward with Nirvana. Without a doubt we're going to find a cruising speed. After a pretty brutal takeoff, we're going to stabilize, chill out.

ET: That's a different kind of future for a rock band.

CN: Everyone likes comfort, no? No one wants to sleep on a bed of nails! Me, I prefer the good old feather mattress. Settled in comfortably, you can easily use your brain and your senses. Comfort allows for work.

DG: We wanted to be more radical in our choices. If Kurt wants to title a song "Rape Me," he can! No one can stop us anymore.

ET: Why, then, did you change the title of the album, which was *I Hate Myself and I Wanna Die*?

CN: I didn't like the sentence and I said to Kurt: "What if a twelve-year-old kid shoots himself in the head on a farm in Nebraska after listening to the album?" That happened to Judas Priest and Ozzy Osbourne, too. These irresponsible idiots had problems because of their stupid songs. But we're not stupid enough for that. I found the title very negative—too predictable, too. We read so many stupid things in the news: "Nirvana wants to kill themselves! Nirvana is preparing a suicide album! Without

Courtney Love, Kurt Cobain would kill himself!" I didn't want the band to add to it. Humor is sometimes taken the wrong way.

DG: Look what success has made of the band: all three of us are completely washed-out, used up by the concerts, the pressure. So now that we are at the top, we want to try everything, benefit from the position that put us through hell. We held on, we resisted the shockwaves. Everyone rushed Kurt, the bastards. Jealous and frustrated people. Now I think they'll finally leave us alone. As humans, we're stronger than ever. Like three guys who just got out of some intense bodybuilding. Look at Kurt: he's much better, he's relaxed.

KC: I'm much happier today than two years ago. Out of torment, I wanted to drop everything. The band became a monster; we weren't controlling it anymore. Suddenly, people we hated, people against whom the band was formed, started to buy our albums. Meatheads, machos, truck drivers loved Nirvana. I was disoriented. But Chris and Dave talked me down. And I met Courtney. I found a woman I love deeply, which seemed totally impossible a few years ago.

ET: Did the incessant attacks against the symbol of "punk-rock success" that you and Courtney incarnate surprise you?

KC: I didn't expect all that shit. The hardest, of course, was the *Vanity Fair* article, a real vendetta against Courtney by some prude journalist. To write that our baby was going to be born on drugs is irresponsible. How could someone hate people so much? That girl didn't have the least bit of proof about what she was putting forward. I really wanted to kill that bitch . . . Luckily, my family brought me a lot of serenity. They gave me the interior strength to dissuade myself from going and crushing the heads of those assholes who wanted to skin us. If I were alone in the world, without any responsibilities towards Courtney and my baby, I would certainly have acted otherwise on multiple occasions. I don't know where I would be today.

ET: In articles appearing in *Vanity Fair* and elsewhere, it's said that drugs were threatening the band's existence.

DG: What drugs? I haven't touched anything in four years. Not even a pathetic little joint.

CN: Nothing in four years, are you kidding me?

DG: I swear. I was addicted to hash. It started to make me stupid and paranoid, so I quit. I never tried anything else. Frankly, I had the impression that the press's attacks on Kurt's so-called addiction hurt him more than the drugs themselves.

KC: I understand why we're questioned on it. Drugs are part of the circus, the rock attitude. But it's still a personal problem. I'm the only one to know the truth of the subject, the only one who's responsible for it. Just drop it.

ET: The book by Clarke and Collins, two journalists who investigated Nirvana for a year, is coming out in the fall.

KC: They aren't journalists. They're just fucking groupies. People who buy the book are getting their money stolen. I read the manuscript of the book—it's the biggest pile of shit I ever held in my hands. But legally, these two girls can publish whatever they want. I can't fight it.

CN: I don't worry about anything. I have so much money today . . . People have a hard time talking about money, but me, I want to stay cool with it. Why hide stuff? When I bought my house in Seattle, an old friend asked me how I was going to pay back the credit. I said: "What credit? I paid cash!" [*Laughs.*] I just bought an old farm, completely run-down, unoccupied for twelve years, in southern Washington State. My wife and I spend all our free time there. We fix it up, we have enough for our entire lives! I feel great there. I don't need anything. I fulfilled all of my dreams: I have a 1971 Volkswagen that'll last forever. I don't need a Rolls; my old car is OK for me. I bought a jukebox and a pinball machine, two of my childhood dreams. That's it. I'm perfectly happy this way. I have a lot of friends, people I've known for years.

KC: I feel like I've done fantastic things, better than what I dreamed about when I was a kid. Damn! I'm married. I have a kid. I never would have thought that was possible. When I was a kid, I imagined myself getting old alone, like a jerk . . . Today, I want to get back into painting. I want to try other things besides punk rock. I was really excited about the 45 project with William Burroughs, who I admire more than anyone else. Unfortunately, we didn't meet; we made the album remotely.

ET: Are you afraid of becoming jaded?

KC: I was much more jaded five years ago, before all this craziness. I was pretty negative. At the time, I was completely infatuated with punk rock. I lived the marginalized ideal: the complete rejection of all commerce, full-out rebellion. Impossible to become famous with punk rock, impossible to go outside the limits of Seattle. I didn't want anything. I was very good the way I was.

ET: What effect did worldwide fame have on your ego?

KC: Actually, I started to feel more confident once *Bleach* came out. The album's relative success and the little concerts we were giving in American clubs helped me overcome my doubts and anxieties. It's thanks to the ten people who applauded us in 1986 or 1987 that I'm here today. I already felt like I shot the moon: I was being paid to play my songs and, what's more, people liked it! For a guy like me, it was already glorious. We were going to little lost towns and the local radio station played our single. I couldn't have dreamed of doing better . . . Today, I feel a little overwhelmed. All these people who pay to see us, I don't understand it.

ET: You've often said that you were afraid of not being able to recognize your fans, that you were afraid of no longer knowing exactly who they were.

KC: That's true; it's my biggest anxiety. There have been so many bands who abandoned their most loyal defenders when success took them by surprise. In a way, I was afraid of becoming an orphan. And then I understood that I didn't owe anyone anything, that I needed to follow my natural path, without turning back. If certain fans feel dropped, if they can't share a band they love with others, they can fuck off. I have no sympathy for frustrated egoists. But as far as the larger public goes, all the people who bought *Nevermind* a few months after its release, I can't say anything about them. I don't know who they are, who they voted for, what they look like. Some of them might beat their wives, others might abandon their dogs when they move . . . Do I have anything in common with these people? So many totally missed the message of "Smells Like Team Spirit." The people who made the song a phenomenon buy the music that's on MTV: university and high school kids. They didn't understand that the message was aimed at them, that the song was an attack against the "youthful spirit" of universities and parties. I have to admit the obvious: the public at large hasn't understood much about the band.

COBAIN CLIP

Erica: How come you are so nice and you seem so comfortable with yourself—something must have really happened in the last couple of years. Is it just falling in love?

Kurt: [*Shaking head steadily as she spoke*] No.

Erica: What happened?

Kurt: I've always been a nice guy.

Erica: Maybe you were afraid to show it before—how's that?

Kurt: [*Laughs*] Well . . . I don't know, you've only just met me . . .

Erica: I've never met you before, but I know other people who had the opportunity to interview, and they said, "Aww, he hates doing interviews, he's not gonna want to talk about anything." I said, "Well, whatever, who knows?" And you're just like exactly the opposite of . . .

Kurt: It just depends on what mood I'm in. Really. I'm kind of a moody person, and a lot of time when someone's had the chance to talk to me, I've probably been on tour, or probably gone through an exhausted time where I've probably talked about myself for hours and hours, and this week I haven't had to talk about myself very much, so I'll be more cooperative.

—Interview with Erica Ehm broadcast on *Much Music* (Canada), August 1993

COBAIN CLIP

On Trying to Live in the Public Eye

One by one, these drunk, sarcastic twentysomething kids would come up to me and say, "Aren't you in the B-52s?" Just trying to start a fight. One guy came up, smacked me on the back and said, "Hey man, you got a good thing going, just get rid of your pissy attitude. Get off the drugs and just fucking go for it, man."

—from "Smashing Their Heads on the Punk Rock"

by Darcey Steinke, *Spin* (US), October 1993

NIRVANA SPARS WITH DEMON FAME

G. Brown | December 3, 1993 | *Denver Post* (US)

I met Kurt Cobain before a concert in late 1991, when Nirvana's *Nevermind* was a surprise success. With his shaggy hair and slight physique, he seemed shy, plagued with self-doubt. I worried about how he was dealing with the pressures of acclaim and money. Rumors flew about his heroin addiction. He was considering breaking up Nirvana.

But he jumped back into the circus. Why did the burden of popularity fall hard on twenty-seven-year-old alternative rockers? In the months before Cobain shot himself, I interviewed Eddie Vedder of Pearl Jam and Billy Corgan of Smashing Pumpkins. They said stardom was pure hell for them. The emotional Vedder was barely audible when he spoke, and a deep furrow formed between his eyebrows. He was mellow, but he wasn't happy. "So many things are fucked up, the way people manipulate us," he muttered, his mood darkening. "Betrayal is the worst. And I'm bad—I don't forget. I carry that stuff around down here." He clutched his stomach. "And I'm afraid it's going to come out in twisted ways."

Corgan was warm, articulate, and soft-spoken in our conversation, but he was notorious for manic mood swings. He said he had been nearly suicidal just prior to the release of the *Siamese Dream* album. "Now I'm pretty jaded. I can't even begin to list the things about the carnival that disturb me. Really, I can deal with all of the fucking bullshit better than I used to. But it's killing my desire to continue playing music. To me, what you stand for is pretty low on the totem pole of things that eventually get emphasized." I hoped Vedder and Corgan could take care of themselves. Cobain couldn't. May he rest in peace. —G. Brown

After a recent show in New Orleans, Nirvana's Chris Novoselic decided he hadn't had enough for the night. So at 2 a.m., the amiable bassist lounged in his hotel room and volunteered his take on returning to the music scene. "The rock 'n' roll industry has this whole machinery. You make records, you do video, this and that," Novoselic, 28, said.

"When it comes to the touring part, it's really easy now. We're traveling on buses and staying in hotels. But a few years ago, we toured in a Ford van—you couldn't sleep. We were pretty burned out on it, you can't imagine. But we did it for 24 months, easy. Before that."

"That" was the surprise success of *Nevermind*, Nirvana's 1991 major label debut—and the first punk album to make it to No. 1. It left the trio coping with the demons of fame. Novoselic admitted that, while stardom is sometimes tough for him, it's pure hell on singer-songwriter-guitarist Kurt Cobain.

Cobain and Novoselic come from the rural logging town of Aberdeen, 100 miles south of Seattle. They met soon after leaving high school, sharing an affection for early-'80s punk. They started up a cover band to make a few bucks.

"We were broke, but we couldn't bear to play country music," Novoselic laughed. "So we thought we'd play Creedence Clearwater Revival songs. I don't remember if we actually got a gig."

In 1987, they formed Nirvana and were signed by Sub Pop Records, an independent label that released *Bleach*. Recorded for a reported $600, the album eventually sold 35,000 copies and elevated the band's status among alternative rockers. After a procession of drummers, Cobain and Novoselic recruited Dave Grohl and hit the road.

When the punky, metallic threesome signed with Geffen Records and put out *Nevermind*, the members hoped it would put them on the level of indie kingpins Sonic Youth.

Instead, the album stormed to the top of the charts and sold 9 million copies worldwide.

MTV ran the sensational "Smells Like Teen Spirit" single day and night—Cobain screamed, "Here we are now, entertain us," and the sardonic hook line was construed as a youthful call to arms, the '90s equivalent of "I can't get no satisfaction."

Nirvana's career explosion resulted in a "feeding frenzy." Major labels scurried to sign any band that identified itself as "alternative" or "grunge," words that suddenly became valuable marketing tools. Every move that Nirvana made came under the media's scrutiny.

Friends worried about how the band was dealing with it all. Novoselic had a drinking problem but went on the wagon so he could stay on top of his good fortune.

But rumors flew about Cobain, who was plagued by self-doubt, the pressures of fame and money—and heroin addiction. He was acclaimed as rock's latest savior, but he was reluctant to be a spokesman for his generation, and he considered breaking up Nirvana. He refused to tour America and disappeared. Fans made do with *Incesticide*, a rarities collection.

"God, that whole period was nothing but ups and downs," Novoselic mused. "Kurt lived in Los Angeles for a year while everyone else was in Seattle."

Nirvana carried a lot of emotional baggage to the recording of the new *In Utero* album, but the followup to *Nevermind* isn't a compromise— it's loud, nasty, grinding noise. Cobain's abrasive growl is complemented with melody and texture. The first words out of his mouth on the opening "Serve the Servants" are "Teenage angst has paid off well/Now I'm bored and old."

"It's a raw record," Novoselic enthused. "We rehearsed a couple of weeks, then popped the tracks out. (Producer) Steve Albini has a lot of ethics. A band should sound on record like it sounds live. If you can't play the songs, you shouldn't record them. We had our chops down, then went in there and blasted off.

"I think we could have taken more time mixing. The guitar sound on the original 'Heart-Shaped Box' was like looking at a bloody abortion on the floor."

Novoselic expressed dissatisfaction with the media's portrayal of Nirvana as ill-mannered, annoying rockers simply reflecting the nihilism they rant against. The band makes sincere efforts to support feminist causes like Rock for Choice. In April, Novoselic organized a benefit concert for Balkan rape victims, and he's supported decriminalization of marijuana.

"We've always been interested, had a lot of discussions about sexism and other issues," Novoselic said. "Now they've bubbled to the surface in the songs."

The next challenge for the guys in Nirvana is to chase down a close connection with their audience. As Novoselic put it, many of the band's fans are the same "dumb heavy metal kids" who hassled Cobain in high school.

"For the most part, they look like they're pretty together on this tour. You see a few a—— grabbing girls by their breasts. But most kids look activist-type active. It might be a different climate coming around, where people seem to be a lot more open-minded."

Nirvana has also gained the opportunity to subvert from within and plug underground musicians.

"I don't have much use for the mainstream," Novoselic noted. "Before we came along, the people in power wanted to play it safe, didn't want to push—or maybe they had plain bad taste. Poison and Winger were making money, and it was like a chemical waste dump. They wanted to keep it going.

"Quality bands are out there, but they're suppressed somehow. You say the Fluid broke up in Denver? Aw, that's horrible news. But that's the music industry. It chews 'em up and spits 'em out."

He shrugged. "It almost happened to us."

THE NEGLECTED DESTRUCTION

David Dufresne | December 1993 | *Rage* (France)

A road trip through Nirvana's *In Utero* tour: David Dufresne sketches a cavalcade of towns, venues, audiences, and snatched moments with, or thoughts from, the band. What's striking is this picture of the band treading the roads once more, another tour as long as the spell that seemed to lead to so much fatigue and absent desire in 1991. Here also we have a subtle portrayal of the repetitiveness of performance as a profession rather than as a passion. —Ed.

Translated by Matthieu Page.

"When we said that *Nevermind* had experienced too great a success, it was out of sincere modesty." Krist Novoselic pauses. He brings a glass of wine to his lips. And continues, "But I'm not going to say it anymore. I'm glad of everything that happened; I wouldn't change anything. You know, I imagined a bunch of stuff before, about the independent punk rock bazaar. This humility, this embarrassment over success, affected me personally—being outside of the mainstream came with all that stuff. Then being absorbed and accepted by the mainstream, it was like being swallowed up—books, movies, music, politics, etc. Now I step back, I scrutinize the mechanism of the music industry. It's still a big pile of shit to me. MTV, the record labels, the press, they're all in cahoots. Everyone knows each other, praises each other, then backstabs each other. So this is where I am now, trying to make the best music and making as much money as possible out of it. I never want to work again in my life, you get that?" Krist has not abused this Californian wine he enjoys so much; he's simply lucid. Disillusioned. So long to his illusions from the early days. "Of course, I was very idealistic before, and I still am, as a matter of fact. I try to be generous and positive. The business has changed, but things still don't go the way you would like them to. How many times did we tell ourselves that we would have liked it if this had also happened to bands other than us? Today, *In Utero* is No. 20 (around two million sales in the United States) and Pearl Jam are No. 1. They make preformatted radio hits and we are supposed to take them for alternative rockers. That means there is room for . . . But, basically, what have we really changed?" Krist gets bored on tour. Only the stage excites him. "Being excited is all we have left. Jumping around, playing fast and loud, throwing our instruments in the air. The rest is routine and time to kill; hitting the road with the bus, getting clean, and taking a break at the hotel. (The band rarely stays over; there is no time for that. They sleep on the bus.) Before, we were just wandering in a van. Now, we have a tour manager, a sound team, a production company, a precise schedule. It used to be an adventure. It doesn't feel that way anymore." Are Nirvana dinosaurs in the making? What about the other grunge bands? That's the most dreadful outlook.

Dallas, Texas. Sunday, December 5, 1993. Nirvana has been touring throughout the United States for a month already and still has another thirty days to go. The Stoneleigh Hotel where we plan on staying seems fucking unfamiliar with our dirty hair and guitars. The place has bigger fish to fry; it welcomes the annual meeting of the county sheriffs— Stetsons, guns on the hip, cowboy boots and spurs, the whole arsenal. Fuck, here we are, surrounded by rednecks! Grunge against Guns. Amid this Alamo reenactment, the *Observer*, a free weekly (typical of Yankee towns) offers a meager break with all the good addresses from Dallas–Fort Worth. In a glimpse: The Sixth Floor, a museum dedicated to the Kennedy assassination in 1963, located on the same floor that Lee Harvey Oswald allegedly shot from (the Texas School Book Depository has since then been renamed the Dallas County Administration Building); the JFK Historical Tour (for twenty dollars you will experience a reenactment of the crime, from Oswald's apartment to the police station where he was shot by Jack Ruby); or the Million Dollar, a meeting club offering second-rate hostesses that boasts of their "inimitable" atmosphere (J. R. Ewing would have had memorable moments there . . .). Further inside, the newspaper advertises the gigs of the coming week. "Nirvana, Breeders, and Shonen Knife at Fair Park Arena, the lineup of the year for all alternative rockers."

Sitting downtown east on Martin Luther King Boulevard, the Fair Park is THE entertainment complex of the oil city. It comes with a giant aquarium, gardens, museums, a football stadium, and the arena, an ice rink turned into a concert hall for the event. In the huge parking area, some scalpers trade their extra tickets in a peaceful atmosphere. Their publisher, Ticket Masters, pretends to be "supporting children with AIDS." With a selling price of $22.75 (at face value), the venue is only a third full. The local security staff wears yellow T-shirts that can be easily seen from afar. Some cops in uniform also roam around the arena. 9:15 PM: spotlights light up the stage that has been decorated with two angel models (see the cover of *In Utero*), a bed of red plastic flowers, and three fake leafless trees, as seen in the clip for "Heart-Shaped Box." The decoration feels sober for a venue of this size and paradoxically out of touch for a garage band such as the Seattle trio; since the beginning of its stardom, the band has been struggling with a punk rock identity crisis. Sometimes anti-establishment, sometimes obedient. Their ambiguous relationship with MTV is a good illustration of this duality. Between sensational statements ("MTV is nothing more than an advertising network"), the chaotic MTV Awards from 1992 (the band began their live set with "Rape Me," previously unheard, despite pressures from Geffen and the channel before they eventually resigned themselves to playing "Lithium"), Nirvana has been featured on *Unplugged* and, even more troubling, has recently taken part in MTV's *Beavis & Butthead* compilation. So what, Krist? "We were very excited (excitation, again) at the idea of playing an acoustic set, and the *Beavis & Butthead* cartoon makes us laugh. That's all. That does not prevent me from criticizing MTV all the more. Our videos are notably among the wildest that the channel plays." Slightly pensive, Krist adds, "You know we're just a very small cog in the music industry's mechanism."

Teen Spirit and Traps for Kids

The group climbs on stage. There are four of them. Pat Smear, ex-L.A. punk from the Germs, joined the trio for the tour as an extra guitarist, giving Kurt the autonomy he needs to perform his solo front man act. And to manage the attention of the public he gets. Kurt is never in the dark, for that matter. The light follows each of his footsteps. He is also the only one with an air-con unit by his side. Awkwardness shines through this supergroup setup like the disco ball that sparkles on the megahit "Teen Spirit," triggering a public uprising. Second degree or not, lighters are taken out and lit up over their slow tracks. Nirvana would never have wanted it that way in their early days. There's a friendly atmosphere in the stands and a monstrous pogo in front of the stage—yet another proof of their duality. The band oscillates between pop and punk. And when he indulges in acoustic tracks, Kurt does not just grab a folk guitar, he sits down on a chair, soon imitated by Krist and Pat, who relax on the base of one of the models. Corny cliché, definitely unjustified. By chance the cellist that the band has hired for the quiet parts brings some relief to the show. The Blue Note, it's played with a fuzzbox and a bow. At least I think it is. 10:30 PM: the band greets the audience that literally screams for an "encore." By the way, the audience is young, very young (mainly made up of teenagers), mixed (girls, boys, 98 percent white), and aware of everything that rocks America (Soundgarden, Red Hot Chili Peppers, Mudhoney T-shirts . . .). Wait! Here they are, the kids! The glorious kids that all majors are chasing after. Nirvana is a trap for kids. Rock like teen spirit.

Suffice to say that there are fewer cowboys here than at the Stoneleigh Hotel (except for a few clean-cut couples who have gotten lost). Krist reappears on stage with . . . an accordion. Kurt, Pat, Dave, the cellist, and Krist then play a tune from the black bluesman Lead Belly, who coincidentally found refuge in Dallas a few decades ago. Krist introduces Kurt sarcastically as John Lennon, hinting at Cobain's ambitions to be fully recognized as a songwriter but also referring to Courtney Love, his wife whom the tabloid press has nicknamed "the Yoko Ono from Seattle." The song is called

"Where Did You Sleep Last Night," that same song that Kurt and Krist played on Mark Lanegan's (of Screaming Trees fame) solo album in 1990. "We've been playing pure rock 'n' roll for so long," recalls Krist, "things have become relatively simple. Playing acoustic excites us particularly. I think it sounds good. We play around, mixing hard rock with folk." At the end of their half-hour encore, which brought the whole gig up to two generous hours, Nirvana fades away through their usual smash of controlled feedbacks and abused sound equipment. The five merch booths discharge their junk at hardcore speed. T-shirts, caps, hats, pins, and even ink pads can be found at the prohibitive price of eight dollars. A sixth booth run by an average-looking student, Mike, displays pro-abortion and anti-racism petitions. But antimilitarist rear bumper stickers and "pro-choice" badges don't draw a lot of interest. What does abortion mean to a thirteen-year-old? We came to a gig to have fun, not to be made aware of such serious issues. Krist makes the observation, having tried to give a social-political reach to the band for a while: "I don't want to make a fuss anymore. I've gone too far in the past. Politics is boring. More and more rock bands talk about politics and forget about the music. They have their bit of influence, sure, but I think that rock newspapers and their readers don't care about that. Today I couldn't care less about politics. What could I do? Discourse on capitalism, communism, Clinton, Trotsky while I'm doing the dishes? I'm not an anarchist or a nihilist, though. I'm a nothing-ist. I have no ideology. As my parents said: 'An idea is simply a thought, while an ideology is a thought that owns you.'" This is a rather bitter observation in comparison to what the band said at the time of the release of *Nevermind*: "No one, especially from our generation, wants to look at the serious problems. Young people prefer to turn a blind eye to problems. Having said that, we're not really political. We may just be playing music, but we don't tell our listeners that they should just stop thinking. Rebellion's long gone from rock music. I hope that underground music can influence the market and shake up teenagers—it could change their lives and prevent them from turning into zombies. Maybe we need a new generation clash, who knows?" Unlike the Clash, the last rock band who knew world fame and tried to shake minds, Nirvana has known success almost instantly through a few video clips and an album. They haven't had the time to make up shortly before the concert carrying his already-famous daughter, Frances Bean, in his arms (she is a year and a half), followed by the nanny, a large man who looks astonishingly like the transvestite from the inlay booklet of *In Utero*. By the way, Krist, about the album . . . ? "Steve Albini, as a producer, is a man of principles. He knows absolutely how to work. His recording philosophy is strict. Key axiom: If you cannot record a song in three or four takes, you may as well leave it behind. It's a fast process. The recording felt like a rehearsal. Virtually everything was done live. First bass-drums-guitar, then the second layer of guitar for half of the album, then the solos and finally the voice. If you make a suggestion to Steve, you must arm yourself with patience; 'OK, Steve, lower the voices.' It takes him twenty minutes thinking about it . . ." Released in a rush, both to overshadow other books deemed "outrageous" by the group and in the event that the Nirvanamania would not last longer than a season, the official biography that the band ordered from a journalist for MTV and *Rolling Stone* (a disgrace!) tells us more about the recording of *In Utero*. Unlike *Nevermind*, on which we now know that Geffen had a say in the production, the third album is the offspring of the work behind closed doors of Nirvana and Albini only. No need for advice nor kindness this time around. Syndrome of former underground performers or merely a reaction to a perceived urgency, *In Utero* was canned faster and for even less money than their previous opus (twenty-four thousand dollars in studio operating costs plus one hundred thousand dollars for Albini, a miserly amount compared to the fifty million that *Nevermind* earned Geffen). Even better, the author of the biography reveals that Nirvana dropped the bass and substantially raised the voices during the mastering phase. You can also add the two remixes that Scott Litt produced. But the rawness and harshness remain. More disturbing are the similarities between "Heart-Shaped Box" and "Lithium," "Rape Me" and "Teen Spirit," or "Dumb" and "Polly." Coincidence? Formula? "Our songs come to us naturally. Kurt comes up with the guitar riffs and the lyrics. Dave and I add the rhythm. And we screw around. It doesn't get any deeper . . ." Kelley Deal appears, confused: the Breeders member is looking for an "all-access" pass for the whole tour. She lost hers. It will cost her a forty-dollar fine. The tour manager does not mess around with that; it is a matter of security. We speak of the past with Krist, of the days when these issues could be settled in ten seconds, when Nirvana performed in small venues: "I feel no nostalgia. There is no reason we should have stopped and started again under a new name. The small, stinking venues, the hassle, hmm . . . No. The only way forward is to continue to listen to our heart, to make the music we love. It's a good thing when people buy your records, not a bad one. I don't see why we should put out records that interest nobody . . . Why should I go back in the dark? I have the opportunity to express myself, and people buy my records through the promotion of mass media. I am very proud of our music. Why should I hide under the pretext that our music is better than 90 percent of the stuff that sells? I am more concerned with my ability to withstand the rock music business. It's a huge industry, a mass thing. And I do not have business acumen. I only want to invest myself in my music. I do it without compromises, without lies." It's not easy to assume such success, all the more so when you participated two years ago in a compilation entitled *Kill Rock Stars*. Impossible to make up for past choices, to overlook the master-crafted compromise they made with *Nevermind*, about which Krist admits openly that they "tried to find the right balance between sounding alternative and commercial." The stage is their only exit door. Facing the audience, without intermediaries, without media, labels, or anything else for that matter. And tonight, Monday, December 6, the Astro Arena earned its name. Kurt excelled in its picador role. "Oh—hey! How did you like the last Pearl Jam album?" he yelled before torturing his sky-blue Fender on "Territorial Pissings." It must have been around the same time when Thomas Lee Riley, seventeen, fell behind his cashier desk at the Whataburger where he worked on West Little Rock Avenue. Three bullets in the stomach. Whataburger immediately offered a five-thousand-dollar reward to anyone who could provide information on the shooter.

Snatched

Oklahoma City, Oklahoma. Far from Houston's flashiness, much more lost than Dallas, the city "Home of the Indians" is gray and bored to rot. At two o'clock in the morning, only the bus station and the office of Ken Boyer, "bail bonds" supplier (a pawnbroker for prison bails!), work through the night. Oklahoma is the lethargic part of America. The drive through the Christmas-decorated shop windows is the only entertainment the city has to offer according to the *Daily Oklahoman*. A little thin. No wonder that Shonen Knife–Breeders–Nirvana sold out at the Fairgrounds, this Wednesday, December 8, 1993. The public is framed by a rigid security service in front of the venue. "Everyone sit down!" Two sound-equipped trucks from two local radios play loud hard rock music ten meters from the line. "Now, get up! Hands up for the body search and have your ticket at hand." Along comes a fifty-year-old man carrying a placard for the legalization of marijuana. The security staff snatch it from his hands. His name is Clinton Real; he is a reverend and belongs to the Humanists of Central Oklahoma! This is America. For a time, Krist campaigned for the same cause: "The only reason why marijuana is illegal is money. Money talks, bullshit walks. The pro-cannabis folks do not emphasize the industrial benefits that hemp could have, notably as a textile fiber. If the capitalists knew the benefits they could make out of this plant, as they do for other natural substances, they would push for its development, force its legalization. Some will smoke, others won't. But it's not going to change tomorrow. I also do not want to waste my time in activism."

The concert is sold out (six thousand, five hundred people) and despite the length of the venue (about a hundred yards long), the atmosphere is contained. Much more so than in Houston or Dallas. For technical reasons, the light show has been simplified. No bleachers. The Fairgrounds almost feels like a club. Nirvana finds itself again. Nirvana frees itself. Nirvana rushes through its set, playing its tracks faster than in Houston or Dallas. The band gets back to its garage roots again, back to the days of *Bleach*. On "Stain" at the very end of the show, Kurt—who swapped his favorite guitar with another—wrecks an amp, throws his guitar, ravages another amp, then one of the two angel models (which loses its wings). Dave, Pat, and Krist leave the stage. Kurt looks around for something left to take down. He passes a few amps left intact, gets behind the drum kit, takes some chopsticks, plays along at the pace of the feedback, and eventually kicks the drums away. Strobe lights. Cheers.

Reverbs. Saturations. Feedback. Kurt, slightly bent, comes back to the front of the stage, approaches the microphone that his tornado miraculously spared, slips a hand in his pocket, smiles (yes, he smiles), and lets go a loving "Thank you, good night." Kurt Cobain, son of punk, is a call guy of destruction. That night, no murders were reported in Oklahoma.

COBAIN CLIP

On Christmas and Family

"It holds good memories. I've always had really good Christmases with my family—I have a very large family. Everyone has always gotten together and had a great blowout, at least until my grandfather died. He was usually the highlight of the ceremonies. He'd get really drunk, put on wacky hats, and sing for everyone . . . I only have one real sister and one half-sister, the rest of them are on my mom's side of the family. My mother had seven brothers and sisters and they all have children."

—from "Sleepless in Seattle"
by Everett True, *Melody Maker* (UK), December 1993

COBAIN CLIP

A "State of the Union" Address

"If there was a Rock Star 101 course, I would have liked to take it. It might have helped me. I still see stuff, descriptions of rock stars in some magazine—'Sting, the environmental guy' and Kurt Cobain, 'the whiny, complaining, neurotic, bitchy guy who hates everything, hates rock stardom, hates his life.' And I've never been happier in my life! Especially within the last week, because the shows have been going so well—except for tonight. I'm a much happier guy than a lot of people think I am."

—from "Kurt Cobain: The *Rolling Stone* Interview"
by David Fricke, *Rolling Stone* (US), January 1994

PART XI

February to April 1994—The Rest Is Silence

I MENTIONED THAT CATCHING SOMEONE UNAWARES is the fun of a surprise. Well, it's also the horror of a shock. As far as is known, Cobain spoke to the press only twice in 1994: a few inconsequential lines on Canadian radio, with Courtney Love and Krist Novoselic taking the strain, then a phone call with a journalist in the United States regarding his work on a guitar for Fender in February. Cobain's bandmates, in the interviews here, are cheerful, answering questions and making jokes—they display no foreknowledge.

Dave Grohl's shift to center stage is complete. In 1990 he had played junior to his two comrades; now, he's leading interviews single-handedly and discussing his own artistic endeavors, things he's been trying out, like the *Backbeat* soundtrack, given Nirvana's own inactivity in terms of creating new music. But Nirvana isn't over; the band members are clear that they are going to do the Lollapalooza tour, then perhaps the European festivals—and they claim they've got ideas for the next album.

But Dave and Krist are tentative. They're not sure what it's going to be or where it's heading, but they're real people; their mood isn't dependent on that of their lead singer. They've been through his lows before, and there's no indication that anything is different from what they've witnessed for two and a half years. You see them here acting normal because things *are* normal.

Twenty-six days after Nirvana's first appearance of the tour—a TV performance in Paris on February 4—Cobain canceled the remaining dates of the first leg. Fifteen days after the Rennes interview, on March 3, he was in a coma in Rome. Twenty-two days later, March 25, his loved ones were staging a drug intervention in Seattle. Eleven days later, on April 5, Kurt Cobain took his own life, leaving behind his final press statement.

"IT'S UP IN THE AIR RIGHT NOW. STILL A MYSTERY. TO US."

February 7, 1994 | 40 TV / Prisa Radio (Spain)

On February 7, 1994, Krist Novoselic and Dave Grohl visited the offices of 40 TV in Spain for an interview on Spanish radio, then a further interview with well-known music critic Joaquín Luqui. The band members were in fair form, Dave wearing a raincoat indoors, while Krist—in shades—played to the camera, removing a gold disc from the wall and giving a mock acceptance speech before introducing himself to people in his best "American tycoon" style: "Krist Novoselic here! Damn glad to meet you!" Ushered through the hallways, they met their interviewer, a popular music critic, who took over the tour until they could all settle together in a studio commanding views of the city.

The extended video clip indicates the draining experience of interviewing—the band starts in one studio for a bilingual radio broadcast, then transfers to another studio for a further discussion via a translator, then to yet another room for another interview—this time with the interviewer speaking relatively good English. Their cheerful enthusiasm always bounds back, as does their courtesy toward the staff, but at one point it's almost touching as Krist yawns and Dave turns and asks if he's OK, as they sit patiently for the third time watching people set up and prepare while awaiting yet more questions. The pair warm up across the interviews, and the level of joking rises, with a few moments standing out. Kurt Cobain is mentioned only twice in all. The bandmates point to a future on the Lollapalooza tour, then fudge and obfuscate their way through questions about recording plans and whether they have any new songs. The smiles fade for brief moments, but then they return to laughter. —Ed.

Krist Novoselic: We love Spain!
[*Female radio host continues to speak to the listeners in Spanish, explaining about the shows Nirvana would be playing the following night in Madrid and on the 9th in Barcelona.*]

KN: You can bring your parents too. [*Host speaks in Spanish.*] We play "Polly" and we play . . . (DG: "All Apologies") "All Apologies" . . . (DG: "Dumb") We have a song where I play an accordion . . .

Dave Grohl: Krist plays accordion too.

KN: I play accordion.

Host: [*Starts in Spanish*] At a Nirvana show, what do you recommend to have fun?

KN: Make sure you have a doctor's prescription. And ah . . . that's all I recommend.

Host: The last album, before *In Utero*, *Nevermind*—you worked with Andy Wallace. What do you think about this man who's about sixty years old?

DG: I dunno. He does Slayer records. He's pretty . . . he just looks like a friend of your dad's.

KN: Age is relative too.

DG: That's true.

KN: It doesn't really matter, it's how you feel. What sex you are . . . It's just all relative. You just have to be having a good time, have a feeling and passion for something.

Host: The way Andy Wallace works, he mixes the music at a very low volume, is that right?

DG: He's an old man, but he gets into it, he's pretty—

KN: You shouldn't necessarily say old as much as you should say mature, y'know?

DG: [*Pointing out of the window*] What is that? What is that green thing?

KN: Art Deco.
[*Interview cuts —Ed.*]

KN: . . . Americas. Well, he didn't discover anything. But who am I? Y'know? I'm no barometer of political correctness or anything. I'm just telling you how it is. What would he think of Chiapas or the Zapatistas, y'know? I dunno . . . He's a national hero . . . George Washington smoked pot!

DG: He grew it!

KN: He grew it!
[*Band members are walked through the station —Ed.*]

KN: What a beautiful city. See all the tile? Whoever seen a cedar roof here?

DG: Look at all the laundry drying . . .

KN: All the laundry hanging . . .
[*They enter the TV studio and spend time hanging out of the window while striking poses. KN: "El Duce!" He encourages Dave to take a turn impersonating Mussolini before they settle down to the interview —Ed.*]

Translator: Nirvana, the first time you came to Spain, did you have more sense of humor, less sense of humor, more music . . . What are the main differences?

KN: It just depends when you catch us and how you catch us, you know what I mean? I think last time we came to Spain we really didn't . . .

DG: I dunno. We're just . . . Last time we came to Spain was only like two weeks of touring. So we've been on tour now for about a little over two months.

KN: And a sense of humor can really be defining too . . . [*Interview cuts —Ed.*] In the United States he was going to be executed and his last name was French. And so they're walking him down the aisle—French Fries! And um . . .

Translator: The man was French?

KN: His last name was French. It was like Jim, Joe French or something. [*Entire joke repeated back to the host in Spanish.*] I'm just the bass player in a band, I don't make any policy decisions, but you know, I've come to the conclusion that the governments of the West are economically driven, they're not . . .
[*Cuts to a completely new interview in another studio —Ed.*]

KN: We just want to sell records. [*Yawns.*]

DG: How you feeling?

KN: Alright. [*Dave yawns while Krist continues to drum on the table.*]

Interviewer: Alright. I'll start with you?

DG: OK.

Interviewer: Can you talk a little about this tour and if it's true that this tour will be different from the one you're going to make in the United States back in the summer?

DG: Well, we already toured America for about two months. We began in October and we ended in . . . January, actually! So it was more than two months. We had a month off, we came over here, we'll be here for two months. We head through every country, pretty much, and we go back home and we're gonna do the . . . there's a tour in America called the Lollapalooza tour. And, uh, we're going to do the Lollapalooza tour this summer and then maybe come back for festivals so . . . [*shrugs*] not really sure. It's like your normal tour, just, like, about two months. It's the first time we've toured with a second guitar player—we have two guitar players now. Annnnnd . . . it's a lot more fun, it's a lot more exciting for me, so . . .

Interviewer: Are you referring to Pat? Pat Smear? Is he coming to this tour as well?

DG: Yeah, he's really great. He's really fun to watch—plus it makes it a lot easier for Kurt because Kurt doesn't have to concentrate as much on playing. So he can be really sloppy. And then, y'know, you just turn Pat up! [*All chuckle.*]

Interviewer: Why did you and the band decide to have Pat in the tour, in the band . . . Why?

KN: Because we were going to play bigger shows and we thought we'd have, like, a fatter, bigger sound . . . just fill it out.

Interviewer: Is he one of your influences?
[*Dave gives a Cheshire cat grin and nods emphatically.*]

KN: Oh, the Germs? Yeah, the Germs are amazing! Plus Pat's such a nice guy, I mean, it makes it so much more easier.

Interviewer: David, do you think people, the audience in Europe or in the United States, gave up on considering the Seattle sound a fashion and started now to consider every band as having its own identity and different?

DG: I hope so. I dunno. I think the people just listen to music—I don't know, it's hard to say, 'cause you know the whole grunge music came out, it's like, we don't sound like Alice in Chains . . . and Alice in Chains doesn't sound like Pearl Jam, really. Then Pearl Jam doesn't sound like us, so I think it was just more of, like, more of an image. It just wasn't heavy metal! Nobody knew what to call it, but you had to call it something.

KN: And it just looks like everybody has to root things on a regional basis. Like there's Manchester, or there's Minneapolis (DG: Liverpool!), Athens or . . . y'know?

DG: Or Kentucky. [*Sniggering between the pair.*]

KN: Or Smelterville, Idaho. Or Moosejaw, Saskatchewan.

DG: Yeah, 'cause now it's like when you want to get some chicken, you say you want some Kentucky Fried Chicken. So it's like, yeah, but it's not from Kentucky. It's fucked.

Interviewer: What have you learned of success? You have no more pressure than in the past—the past was more stressed than now?

DG: I think now is more stressed than the past.

KN: Think so?

DG: Sometimes. It goes back and forth. I mean, y'know . . .

KN: Stress is relative too.

DG: I had to learn to count 'cause I'm so rich.

KN: And what about that morning cup of coffee?

DG: Oooo. Yeah . . .

KN: Now our bags are on time.

DG: And I have so much luggage 'cause I'll, y'know, have so many nice clothes. [*Both openly chuckling now.*]

Interviewer: Does it mean that your life is no more complicated?

DG: In some ways, but there's some things that you can forget about and now there's some things that you have to worry about that you didn't have to before. So sometimes it's more comfortable, but sometimes it's not. It's back and forth.

Interviewer: The band has explained a lot of times about the psychology of your last album—and the ups and downs, optimism in some tracks, pessimism in other tracks. But is that Kurt's psychology, or is it the psychology of all the three members of the band? Did you agree with Kurt's lyrics, or did you find them sometimes a little deeper, a little . . .

KN: No, we pretty much, like, have discussions and see things—see eye-to-eye on a lot of things, y'know? And . . .

DG: We stand behind Kurt's lyrics 100 percent.

KN: And y'know, things like cynicism, I think cynicism is passé anymore. Because cynicism is hip and, ah, I've just been looking around and being really optimistic about a lot of things, y'know? People—seems like people tend to be cynical or dismiss a lot of things, but it's like a dead-end trap. It's fun to be cynical and to be comical or humorous about bad things in the world, but you can only go so far.

Interviewer: I've heard that you're going to release another album in several months. How will it be deeper or more poppy than this one?

DG: I don't know. We're still trying to figure it out. We're just experimenting. Might be really weird.

Interviewer: But have you already composed songs, or not yet?

DG: A few.

KN: Few, yeah.

DG: Just a couple. We're still—we don't know what we're going to do yet either. It's kind of—it's up in the air right now. Still a mystery. To us.

Interviewer: I've heard also you're going to work on the *Backbeat* film of the Beatles. Can you tell me a little more about your role in the film? What are you going to do in that film? *Backbeat.*

DG: I have a small part as a male prostitute from the streets of Hamburg. I'm only in about six or seven scenes and one of them I'm . . . I'm . . .

KN: It's so sexually explicit.

DG: I can't even explain it. I perform a sexual act on Pete Best [*mimes accordingly*], who was the drummer.

KN: That's why he got kicked out of the Beatles.

DG: That's why he got kicked out of the Beatles, 'cause they found out he liked to have his dick sucked by other guys! [*Both laughing uproariously.*] Actually, I'm not in the movie, I just play on the soundtrack! I just play drums on the soundtrack; they needed a band to play the music for the live sequences.

KN: Homophobic generalizations are a bad habit to get into.

DG: So I'm only on the soundtrack, not in the film. It's a good soundtrack, it's really good.

KN: If you like sucking dick.

DG: Yeah! It's like . . . [*Breaks down laughing again.*] S'OK, that's enough, sorry!

Interviewer: Krist, I think that you like to play covers of other groups—most of them not very well known in Europe or the United States and new bands. How many more bands will we get to know through Nirvana in the future?

KN: See, the only songs we call "covers" are the ones we're not—that we can't get away with ripping off and . . . I don't know. Covers are cool, but the first rule of songwriting is—the first rule of being in a band is never play a cover song that's better than your original. So . . . I don't know. We're doing a David Bowie song now, "The Man Who Sold the World"—that's an old song. So a lot of times, especially in the United States, there's a lot of people out there in the audience, a whole new generation who didn't even know that song—we didn't really get a good reaction from it.

DG: Oh! There was a band for the *MTV Unplugged* we did a few songs by: the Meat Puppets. And we had the guitar player and bass player of the Meat Puppets come play with us—that was good.

Interviewer: Was it your choice to have the Buzzcocks in this tour as support band?

KN: Yeah, oh yeah.

DG: They're great.

KN: Yeah, they're fantastic.

DG: Have you seen 'em before? Really great. They stir everything into a frenzy—it's great.

Interviewer: And why not the Breeders, as in the American tour?

DG: Everybody else is on tour.

KN: They weren't available.

DG: They weren't available.

KN: It's nice to go out with different bands, too, that you haven't played with before. Y'know, instead of playing with the same stable of bands. Might as well mix things up a little, keep things interesting—have new people to hang out with. Have them loan you money and buy you beers, and when they're tired of it, they're done with the tour, let's have a new band.

DG: We give 'em, like, a hundred bucks a night. They get to play in front of a couple thousand people and say that they know us. [*Whole room laughing behind the camera and in front of it.*]

Interviewer: OK, thank you very much. I see humor is important in Nirvana.

KN and DG: [*In unison*] Yeah.

KURT COBAIN: TRIBUTE
TO A RELUCTANT GUITAR HERO

Chuck Crisafulli | February 11, 1994 | *Fender Frontline* (US)

Fender is the world's leading guitar and musical instrument amplifier brand and a name that has been synonymous with popular music since its inception in Southern California in 1946. Fender instruments, such as the Telecaster, Precision Bass, Stratocaster, and Jazz Bass guitars, and Bassman, Twin Reverb, and Deluxe Reverb amplifiers, are known worldwide as the instruments that started the rock 'n' roll revolution, and they continue to be highly prized by today's musicians and collectors alike.

The last known interview with Kurt Cobain took place over the phone while he was in Paris on the final tour. The interview was published after Cobain's death, hence the introduction preceding the conversation. —Ed.

The music world suffered a tremendous and untimely loss this April when Nirvana's Kurt Cobain took his own life at the age of twenty-seven. The guitarist, singer, and songwriter was a troubled and fragile soul, but he was also an inspiring and talented artist, and his small, powerful legacy of work will no doubt continue to shape the sounds of rock for years to come.

A few weeks before his death, while the band was still on their last tour in Europe, Cobain agreed to answer some interview questions for *Fender Frontline*. Understandably, Kurt wasn't all that eager to submit to interviews at the time, but the idea was to get away from prodding him about any of the more sensational rumors swirling about the band and to just let him speak frankly about his music. He graciously consented. He was also beginning to work with special hybrid 'Jag-stang' guitars—half Jaguar, half Mustang—that he had helped design, so he was asked about his experiences with the new instrument.

Even the most jaded chart-watchers are going to have to concede that Nirvana made some thrilling sounds in its short history. *Bleach*, *Nevermind*, and *In Utero* hold up as potent, original works that, at their finest moments, deliver all the exhilarating thrills that rock and roll is supposed to. It is unfortunate and deeply saddening that Cobain chose to leave us so soon. He will be missed.

Having trouble figuring out the guitar that Kurt Cobain was sawing away at on stage? You're not suffering from double vision—or half vision, for that matter. Cobain worked with the Fender Custom Shop to develop the "Jag-stang," a very functional combination of Jaguar and Mustang design.

"Kurt always enjoyed playing both guitars," says Fender's Larry Brooks. "He took photographs of each, cut them in half, and put them together to see what they'd look like. It was his concept, and we detailed and contoured it to give him balance and feel."

"He was really easy to work with. I had a chance to sit and talk with him, then we built him a prototype. He played it a while and then wrote some suggestions on the guitar and sent it back to us. The second time around, we got it right."

The guitar features a Mustang-style short-scale neck on a body that borrows from both designs. There's a Dimarzio humbucking pickup at the bridge, and a Texas Special single coil at the neck, tilted at the same angle as on a Mustang. Cobain was quite satisfied with the guitar.

"Ever since I started playing, I've always liked certain things about certain guitars but could never find the perfect mix of everything I was looking for. The Jag-stang is the closest thing I know. And I like the idea of having a quality instrument on the market with no preconceived notions attached. In a way, it's perfect for me to attach my name to the Jag-stang, in that I'm the anti-guitar hero—I can barely play the things myself."

Chuck Crisafulli: Nirvana has become a Big Rock Story, but the music still seems to be the most important part of that story. How proud are you of the band's work?

Kurt Cobain: It's interesting, because while there's a certain selfish gratification in having any number of people buy your records and come to see you play—none of that holds a candle to simply hearing a song that I've written played by a band. I'm not talking about radio or MTV. I just really like playing these songs with a good drummer and bass player. Next to my wife and daughter, there's nothing that brings me more pleasure.

CC: Is it always a pleasure for you to crank up the guitar, or do you ever do battle with the instrument?

KC: The battle is the pleasure. I'm the first to admit that I'm no virtuoso. I can't play like Segovia. The flip side of that is that Segovia could probably never have played like me.

CC: With Pat Smear playing guitar in the touring lineup, has your approach to the instrument changed much?

KC: Pat has worked out great from day one. In addition to being one of my closest friends, Pat has found a niche in our music that complements what was already there without forcing any major changes. I don't see myself ever becoming Mick Jagger, but having Pat on stage has freed me to spend more time connecting with the audience. I've become more of a showman. Well, maybe that's going too far. Let's just say that having Pat to hold down the rhythm allows me to concentrate on the performance as a whole. I think it's improved our live show 100%.

CC: On *In Utero* and in concert, you play some of the most powerful "anti-solos" ever hacked out of a guitar. What comes to mind for you when it's time for the guitar to cut loose?

KC: Less than you could ever imagine.

CC: Krist [Novoselic] and Dave [Grohl] do a great job of helping to bring your songs to life. How would you describe the role of each player, including yourself, in the Nirvana sound?

KC: While I can do a lot by switching channels on my amp, it's Dave who really brings the physicality to the dynamics in our songs. Krist is great at keeping everything going along at some kind of an even keel. I'm just the folk-singer in the middle.

CC: You're a very passionate performer. Do you have to feel the tenderness and the rage in your songs in order to perform them?

KC: That's tough because the real core of any tenderness or rage is tapped the very second that a song is written. In a sense, I'm only recreating the purity of that particular emotion every time I play that particular song. While it gets easier to summon those emotions with experience, it's a sort of dishonesty that you can never recapture the emotion of a song completely each time you play it.

CC: It must be a very odd feeling for Nirvana to be performing in sports arenas these days. How do you get along with the crowds you're attracting now?

KC: Much better than I used to. When we first started to get successful, I was extremely judgmental of the people in the audience. I held each of them to a sort of punk rock ethos. It upset me that we were attracting and entertaining the very people that a lot of my music was a reaction against. I've since become much better at accepting people for who they are. Regardless of who they were before they came to the show, I get a few hours to try and subvert the way they view the world. It's not that I'm trying to dictate, it's just that I am afforded a certain platform on which I can express my views. At the very least, I always get the last word.

CC: Do you see a long, productive future for the band?

KC: I'm extremely proud of what we've accomplished together. Having said that however, I don't know how long we can continue as Nirvana without a radical shift in direction. I have lots of ideas and musical ambitions that have nothing to do with the mass conception of "grunge" that has been force-fed to the record buying public for the last few years. Whether I will be able to do everything I want to do as a part of Nirvana remains to be seen. To be fair, I also know that both Krist and Dave have musical ideas that may not work within the context of Nirvana. We're all tired of being labelled. You can't imagine how stifling it is.

CC: You've made it clear that you're not particularly comfortable being a "rock star," but one of the things that tracks like "Heart-Shaped Box" and "Pennyroyal Tea" on *In Utero* make clear is that you're certainly a heavyweight when it comes to rock songwriting. You may have a tough job sometimes, but is the writing process pleasurable and satisfying for you?

KC: I think it becomes less pleasurable and satisfying when I think of it in terms of being part of my "job." Writing is the one part that is not a job, it's expression. Photo shoots, interviews . . . that's the real job part.

NIRVANA

Sandrine Maugy | February 16, 1994 | *Uzine* (France)

By the time we performed this interview with Dave Grohl in 1994, there were only two of us—Aline Giordano and I—running the *Uzine* fanzine. It was also the end of *Uzine* as a written fanzine. Aline and I both moved to England later that year and, after a dormant period, *Uzine* became an online-only fanzine. Aline now runs the website and most of the interviews, while my participation is more sporadic and usually specializes in rare interviews with my favorite artists. I am now a visual artist while Aline works in academia.

Obtaining this Nirvana interview came about via a mixture of luck and sheer determination. Through the French tour manager I got the number of the American tour manager and somehow convinced him to give us two photo passes and eventually the interview, although Nirvana wasn't giving interviews or accepting photographers for this last tour. The photo passes were a last-minute thing, and as soon as we got them we rushed to the pit just in time to see the band arrive on stage. This means that we took what are among the very last pictures ever taken of Kurt Cobain and Nirvana on stage.

Dave Grohl arrived for the interview all smiles, sat on an amp, and we started. The guys in Nirvana were big, big stars, but he never showed anything other than kindness and sincerity, even pleasure, to be in our company. He is a really nice guy. After a few questions the interview turned more into a conversation as he asked me about how things were in France compared to the United States. We discussed politics, literature, and, of course, music.

Here is the conversation we had that evening in February 1994. —Sandrine Maugy

Translated by Carly Lapotre.

We interviewed Dave, the drummer of Nirvana, during the band's last stop in Rennes.

Sandrine Maugy: First, the new guitarist: Who is he?

Dave Grohl: He's from Los Angeles. He was playing in a band called Germs, which was part of the punk scene in L.A. They had an influence on us. They're really great. It was one of the first punk bands on the scene. He was their guitarist. We really liked them, and Kurt had been living in L.A. for about a year. He met him there. We always wanted to have a second guitarist in the band. We wanted Steve, the guitarist from Mudhoney, but he didn't want to. We asked Buzz from the Melvins, and he didn't want to either. And then we asked Pat, and he's perfect, he's really good. He's a really skilled musician, but he's sick of the punk sound, so it's a little weird. We like him, though; he's really good.

SM: Why did you want another guitarist?

DG: On the new album there were some things we'd recorded with two guitars—Kurt played one part and then he played another one—so we really needed two guitarists. There's a bigger sound on stage. And also I think Kurt wanted someone else to play so he'd have less responsibilities and could move around a little more.

SM: So is he just there for the show, or is he really part of the band now?

DG: Oh yeah, he's part of the band. Well, we don't talk about it, but I think he feels like an integral part of the band because we get along really well. He was writing songs for Germs that were great. He wrote most of their music. He can write really good songs. He also made some solo albums. I never heard them. I think we're probably going to write stuff with him in the future.

SM: Did you choose the Buzzcocks to open for you?

DG: Yes, they're a great band. They have some really good songs. It's fun. The lights go out, the kids are like "ooooohhhhh!!!" and the Buzzcocks come out. And a lot of these kids don't even know who they are. But they start to play and it works, it's cool, they put everyone in a good mood when they come out. They write happy-poppy-funny songs. They're cool.

SM: Were they one of the bands that influenced you?

DG: Yeah, I've been listening to the Buzzcocks for ten years. They've been around for a long time! When I started to listen to punk rock, it was mostly American stuff, hardcore from California. But then I started to listen to English groups like the Buzzcocks, the Sex Pistols, the Clash, 999 . . .

SM: And did you like Exploited's style?

DG: You know, Exploited's guitarist works for us! He's a technician on the tour. He played a show with us in New York. It was the first time we played with two guitarists in a while.

SM: Whose idea was it to have a cello on the last album?

DG: We'd already had it on *Nevermind*, on the song "Something in the Way." It's a really beautiful instrument. It's cool. It's very sad, kind of sober. It's weird; we like that. It was Kurt's idea. He wrote a song and thought we could have a cello during the mellow part, or maybe a violin.

SM: There was a cello on the album but not on stage . . .

DG: Yeah, but this time we really wanted to play the song with it, so we found a cellist. Melora [*Creager —Ed.*], the girl who plays, was classically trained. She's really good, so it's easy for her to do it.

SM: In *MTV Unplugged*, who were the two guitarists who played with you?

DG: They were from a band called the Meat Puppets, an old band from California, from Arizona, actually, an old punk band. But a weird punk band, a sort of country-western punk rock. They had some weird folk songs with a punk vibe. They had albums on the label SST Records, five or six albums. It's an old group, from the early 1980s, 1981, I think.

SM: And the two songs you played with them . . .

DG: Those were their songs. It's cool; they write really pretty songs. Kurt likes them a lot. I think it's because they write songs kind of the same way as him.

SM: Those two songs were kind of tribal—they sounded like Native American songs.

DG: Yes, it's weird. They take a lot of drugs! But they're very cool . . . You know they're from Arizona. There are a lot of Native Americans there. And they grew up there, in the desert. We did some concerts with them in Germany; they came on tour.

SM: Do you still live in Seattle?

DG: Yeah . . .

SM: Are bands still really prolific?

DG: Uh, it's weird, actually. There are a lot of bands. There are a lot of heavy metal bands. They want to be big, be on MTV, be rock stars like Tad or Mudhoney, a lot of old bands that still play.

SM: What do you think of the last Mudhoney?

DG: It's OK, but I've seen them so many times live . . . It's not easy for a band to stay together ten years. Actually, they haven't been together for ten years, but it's hard to play for a long time and continue to produce new, exciting things every year. Most of the good groups are ones that last three or four years; it's exciting for four years and then it gets boring. Hey, look, it's John from Exploited. This is Big John! There were some questions about Exploited tonight; they asked me if I liked them and I said no, they suck!

Big John Duncan: I was never cool enough to like Exploited. I was just pretending!

DG: Absolutely!

SM: Some band members in Seattle had common projects, like Temple of the Dog; did you have any?

DG: I did the soundtrack for a movie called *Backbeat*; it's a movie on the Beatles. I played drums, Thurston Moore from Sonic Youth played guitar, Dan Flemming plays guitar too, Mike from R.E.M. plays the bass, Greg Dulli from Afghan Whigs sings, Henry Rollins sings a song, and Dave Pirner sings a song.

SM: Who?

DG: The singer from Soul Asylum. Well, we only made the music for the movie. And it's only Beatles songs. We didn't really collaborate with any other group. Not really.

SM: Were you asked to participate in the Judgment Night compilation?

DG: No . . .

SM: What would you have said?

DG: We would have said yes to Disposable Heroes of Hiphoprisy. Cypress Hill, too. I love Cypress Hill. I love Public Enemy, too. Disposable Heroes are the best. Have you already seen them in concert?

SM: No . . .

DG: They're excellent! We played with them in San Francisco. They have machines, tools, huge circular saws, and they grind them on metal. It's great! There are groups that I like and groups that I really love: I love Melvins, the Breeders, and I love a lot of others like Rage Against the Machine, but I don't listen to them. I think they're good at what they do, but I don't listen to them. I don't listen to Pearl Jam either, but I think they're good. These are good rock groups. Rage has a powerful message and I think it's good. They propose an alternative to the public. They have a message, they're not only like, "Hey! . . ." We tried to do that too, to have a message, to abolish sexism, racism, all the *isms*, but it's hard and discouraging to get there and play for kids who are just like "Woooo, rock 'n' roooolll, punk rock!!!" It's hard, weird, uncomfortable, to be in a group that people consider famous; it's bizarre and stupid . . . I find it funny.

SM: You think that Nirvana is a politicized group?

DG: No . . . it was. But it isn't anymore. I know what I think: I'm against sexism, I'm against racism, I'm against the extreme right, against fascism, but I only play drums!

SM: Not necessarily in words but in action, benefit shows . . .

DG: Yeah, we do benefits, for AIDS, for pro-choice, and it's good to help raise money to help the homeless and those in need. But it's hard, if you want to do like Rage Against the Machine, to confront people with a political alternative, it's good. I agree with a large part of what they say. It's right. Everything they say is totally right. But us, I don't think it would work to do something like that. And it's hard for a group like Rage Against the Machine. If they come to Rennes, if they come to Paris, they do a concert in front of two, three, four thousand people. These people don't give a shit about American Indians, women's rights, things like race crime, they don't care; they came for, "Wooohoo, rock 'n' rooolll! Yeaaahh!!"

SM: But when they came last September, they stopped the concert to talk and people listened . . .

DG: They listened? Yeah, that's good, but it's hard to expect that. And it's another reason why I think it's important [to have] groups like RATM, it exposes people to something different. They see an MTV video, and RATM does videos, which is weird for a group who talks about destroying corporations—they contribute to these corporations, to the major labels, to MTV, which is one of the largest corporations in the world. They use it . . .

SM: Yes, but for their last video on the American Indian movement, they use it to get their message out . . .

DG: Yes, they use it for their message, that's right. But at the same time— and this is what's difficult, and what was difficult for us, too—when people ask us, "Do you think you've sold out to the majors?" we would say, "No, no, we didn't sell out, we use the machine to expose people to new ideas." And all the machine does is put your face on the cover of a magazine. It's strange, it's hard for me, because I really was unhappy because of the music industry with all this shit sometimes, simply because it's stupid . . . It's funny, and distracting, but trying to take it seriously can break your heart or make you feel like an idiot. For me, I would do better to be in school right now, instead of getting on stage every night. So it's hard. It's very hard because if you want to take it seriously, you can't . . . because sometimes it seems so stupid . . .

SM: On the album you thank Burroughs; are you a fan of the Beat Generation, Kerouac, etc.?

DG: Yeah. Kerouac, Ginsberg, Burroughs . . . In the United States they're . . . You go to high school and you learn everything about Charles Bukowski. I mean, you don't take classes on him, but growing up, most people discover Burroughs, Bukowski, Ginsberg, Kerouac . . . People who later are passionate about literature. Is he well known here?

SM: Bukowski, not so much, but Burroughs, yes. And what do you think about the idea that grunge stems from the Beat Generation?

DG: I don't know, grunge is confusing. I think grunge is made up of kids whose parents were part of the Beat Generation. Most people in Seattle are old hippies, you know! They're old, fuddy-duddy hippies from San Francisco. Really! They came to Seattle and now they're fucking parents, they're old, they're fifty . . .

SM: Your parents are hippies?

DG: No, not mine! I'm not from Seattle. I'm from Washington, DC. My mom is a teacher; my dad is a writer. My dad is really conservative Republican . . . he writes for the *Washington Post* and he's really . . . hmm . . . my mom is liberal and really cool.

SM: What was their reaction when you started to play?

DG: My mom thought it was really cool. Because I started to play, and the first time I came to Europe I was eighteen . . . I was in a punk rock group called Scream from Washington, DC. We toured, we played in squats, and some clubs in France. We didn't earn any money. All we did was smoke hash all day and play music. After that it was strange. My dad never approved.

SM: Even now?

DG: Now, obviously now that I'm earning more money than my dad, he thinks it's OK! But my mom was always OK with it. She came to concerts, and she came on stage.

SM: Have you ever tried a dreamachine?

DG: No! But, you know, once we tried to make one! It didn't work. It looked a little like one, but it didn't work at all. Most of the time when you start to read the writers of the Beat Generation, when you start to experiment with drugs, you take acid, you read Kerouac, Allen Ginsberg, their poetry, it makes you think . . . It's a different mentality. So you start thinking about the dreamachine. You try to do everything those writers talk about, and you can't. Sometimes you can do it, but . . . It's like William Burroughs, I don't want to go out and shoot a rifle, I don't want to do that! Might as well read Hunter S. Thompson. Do you know him?

SM: No . . .

DG: *Fear and Loathing in Las Vegas*—you haven't read that book?

SM: No . . .

DG: This guy is totally insane! He drinks tequila and he takes coke and he takes his gun and he writes. He's crazy! It's funny.

SM: Funny?

DG: Well, it's crazy! It's very strange. But in the same way Bukowski and Burroughs are very strange. Hunter S. Thompson was different than the Beat Generation. They thought a lot while he was just "bang! bang!" All he did was shoot at everything that moves. He was completely crazy. And he was a political correspondent in Washington, DC. He followed campaigns, like Richard Nixon's, and he went to press conferences, he was serious! But it's cool, you should read his stuff. I don't know if it's translated in French, but it's totally crazy.

SM: Did he kill a lot of people that way?

DG: I don't think he killed people; he wasn't really aiming at them.

SM: In *Unplugged*, you played a track titled "Jesus Don't Want Me for a Sunbeam." Where did that come from?

DG: It's a song by a group called the Vaselines, from Scotland. It's a song that we like a lot. It's acoustic. It's very cute. The group has two members, a girl, Frances, and a guy, they play acoustic guitar. It's really pretty.

SM: Do you know any French groups?

DG: I know a few. Treponem Pal and what's the group called—Désir . . .

SM: Noir Désir . . .

DG: That's it! Are they good or bad?

SM: Very good . . .

DG: Because I saw a video and it seemed cool, and I said to my fiancée, Jennifer, "Look at this, it's a French group . . ." Because usually French groups are weird.

[*Sandrine is silent —Ed.*]

DG: Well . . . sometimes . . . for me . . . There aren't that many French groups I really like. There was one that was called . . . oh, I forget.

SM: Les Thugs?

DG: Les Thugs, everyone knows Les Thugs in America. We played with them in Switzerland. They're not bad. And the other one, what was it again?

SM: Noir Désir.

DG: Yes, Noir Désir, I would have liked to play with them in France, but it's weird, too, because they seem to write good songs, they're a good group, but they could never get big in America because they sing in French.

SM: Do you like the Young Gods?

DG: Yes, I love them. They sing "Envoyé"; it was one of my favorite songs when I was young. They're great. Shit, who else? There was one I played with when I was with Scream. No, I can't remember anymore. But I really like Treponem Pal. And Noir Désir, they're really good, too. But I only heard one of their songs and I was surprised. It could have been American.

SM: Their producer is Ted Niceley . . .

DG: Ahhh, that's why.

SM: Have you heard the Tori Amos version of "Smells Like Teen Spirit"?

DG: [*Seemingly sorry*] I don't like Tori Amos . . . It's funny . . .

SM: It's ridiculous . . .

DG: It's totally ridiculous! But OK, it's smart, simply because it's a weird arrangement. But yes, it's ridiculous.

SM: What was the reaction in America to the cover of *In Utero*?

DG: It was OK. We had more of a reaction for the "Heart-Shaped Box" video because of the fetus. There were some fetuses that were hanging from tree branches. In Florida there's an anti-abortion group that kills people. Have you heard about that?

SM: No . . .

DG: There are abortion clinics in Florida, and people from these anti-abortion groups wait outside for people who try to get in and they spit on them, throw fetuses at them, and kill the doctors. And now the doctors in clinics where abortion is practiced are scared, they're stalked, threatened . . . We played in Florida and we got death threats. "We're going to kill you tonight!" We did outdoor concerts, so it was scary. We were expecting to get shot at! But no one ever said anything to us about that album, only that video. They're crazy. But America is really serious about censorship. There are always crazy people who can't accept change. They're stuck in the 1950s. It's starting to change now, but it's not easy. But the entire country has gone nuts. Everyone is killing each other and the violence is so bad; everyone has a gun, everyone. We aren't safe anywhere. But Seattle is a nice city!

COBAIN CLIP

"Press speculation can now cease. Kurt is restored to full health and is looking forward to touring the UK . . . Nirvana would like to apologize for any inconvenience and distress caused to their friends."

—from a press release rescheduling Nirvana's United Kingdom dates in 1994, March–April 1994

TO BODDAH

Kurt Cobain | April 1994

To BoddAH

Speaking from the tongue of an experienced simpleton who obviously would rather be an emasculated, infantile complainee. This note should be pretty easy to understand. All the warnings from the Punk Rock 101 courses over the years, since my first introduction to the, shall we say, ethics involved with independence and the embracement of your community has proven to be very true. I havent felt the excitement of listening to as well as creating music along with reading and writing for too many years now. I feel guilty beyond words about these things. For example when were back stage and the lights go out and the manic roar of the crowd begins. It doesnt affect me the way in which it did for Freddy Mercury, who seemed to love, relish in the love and adoration from the crowd, which is something I totally admire and envy. The fact is, I cant fool you. Any one of you. It simply isnt fair to you or me. The worst crime I can think of would be to Rip people off by faking it and pretending as if im having 100% fun. Sometimes I feel as if I should have a punch in time clock before I walk out on stage. Ive tried everything within my power to appreciate it (and I do. God, believe me I do, but its not enough). I appreciate the fact that I and we have affected and entertained a lot of people. I must be one of those ~~people who~~ narcissists who only appreciate things when theyre gone. Im too sensitive. I need to be slightly numb in order to regain the enthusiasm I once had as a child.

On our last 3 tours Ive had a much better appreciation for all the people Ive known personally and as fans of our music, but I still can't get over the frustration, the guilt and empathy I have for everyone. Theres good in all of us and I think I simply love people too much. So much that it makes me feel too fucking sad. The sad little, sensitive, unappreciative, pisces, Jesus man! Why dont you just enjoy it? I dont know! I have a goddess of a wife who sweats ambition and empathy and a daughter who reminds me too much of what I used to be. Full of love and joy, kissing every person she meets because everyone is good and will do her no harm. And that terrifies me to the point to where I can barely function. I cant stand the thought of Frances becoming the miserable, self destructive, death rocker that Ive become. I have it Good, very Good, and Im grateful, but since the age of seven Ive become hateful towards all humans in general. Only because it seems so easy for people to get along and have empathy. Empathy! Only because I love and feel sorry for people too much I guess. Thank you all from the pit of my burning nauseous stomach for your letters and concern during the past years. Im too much of an erratic, moody, baby! I dont have the passion anymore, and so remember, its better to burn out than to fade away. Peace love, Empathy. Kurt Cobain

Frances and Courtney, Ill be at your altar.

Please keep going Courtney.

for Frances

for her life, which will be so much happier

without me. I LOVE YOU I LOVE YOU!

COBAIN CLIP

"Kurt had an ethic toward his fans that was rooted in the punk rock way of thinking. No band is special, no player royalty."

—Krist Novoselic's eulogy for Kurt Cobain, April 10, 1994

COBAIN CLIP

"He left a note—it's more like a letter to the fucking editor . . . Some of it is to you. And I don't really think it takes away his dignity to read this considering that it's addressed to most of you."

—Courtney Love's recorded message played at the fans' memorial for Cobain,
April 10, 1994

COBAIN CLIP

The Cobain Media Dichotomy Summed Up

"Don't read my diary when I'm gone. OK, I'm going to work now, when you wake up this morning, please read my diary. Look through my things and figure me out."

—Undated entry from *Journals*, published by the Penguin Group/Viking in 2002

ABOUT THE CONTRIBUTORS

Jessica Adams worked as a freelance writer at *Select* and other music magazines before turning to novels, including the bestselling *Cool for Cats*, based on her time writing for rock newspapers. She is an astrologer for *Cosmopolitan* and *Harper's Bazaar* and also works as a medium. Jessica is also the editor of AMMP, the Australian Music Museum Project, where you can hear her original Kurt Cobain interview online. Her personal website is www.jessicaadams.com.

Jorge Aedo: Born in Valparaiso, Chile, Jorge holds a degree in cartography from the Metropolitan Technological University, though he has not worked in that field since graduating in 1982. At that time he started work as a radio announcer on a radio sports program. Then, in 1984, he started work with Canal 11 de Santiago, where he remained until 1990, when he commenced work at Televisión Nacional de Chile (TVN). He was hired to run the music show *Sábado Taquilla*, which he led until 1994, conducting weekly viewer video votes, adding animation, conducting outdoor interviews, and touring Chile and beyond to cover music events. He remains active in TV and radio today.

Lars Aldman has spent most of his working life with the Swedish national radio/TV public service company, doing everything from light daytime entertainment to social affairs, news, and youth programs. But in Sweden he is best remembered for his commitment to alternative music in the 1980s with radio shows *Bommen* and *Lilla Bommen*, which listeners credited as the place where new sounds and ideas could be heard. After being a bit too controversial, perhaps, Lars was sacked from the radio department of the company and was instead invited to do some TV shows in a style similar to what he had previously done on the radio. This TV gig brought him face-to-face with some of his favorite musicians on the planet—Nirvana.

Kevin Allman is the editor of *Gambit,* the New Orleans alt-weekly. His work has appeared in the *Los Angeles Times,* the *Washington Post,* Toronto's *Globe and Mail, Details,* and *Vogue,* among many other publications. He's also the author of two novels, *Tight Shot* and *Hot Shot,* the first of which was nominated for an Edgar Award by the Mystery Writers of America.

Cyrus Aman says of himself, "The greatest joy in writing is not the process, it's the before and after. Before I begin an article for my website (cyrusaman.com), I get to reach out to an artist I admire and see if he or she is up for an interview. If I didn't have the title 'writer,' potential interviewees wouldn't even open my e-mail, let alone read it. I get a nerdgasm at the response 'I'd be happy to talk!' from someone who's work I've drooled over since I was a kid. After I'm done writing (and, most important, editing) I get to read and reread my words, admiring my finished product and the byline 'by Cyrus Aman.' In the past two decades I've conducted interviews with Derek Riggs (creator of Iron Maiden's mascot, 'Eddie'), Jim Fitzpatrick (illustrator of the Che Guevara two-tone print and Thin Lizzy album covers), Gene Simmons, and more. But the crème de la crème interview was with Krist Novoselic of Nirvana."

Laura Begley Bloom is the editor in chief of Yahoo Travel and has written for a wide range of publications, including *Travel + Leisure, Wallpaper,* and the *New York Times.*

Frédéric Brébant was born in Mons, Belgium, in 1967 and graduated from the Institut des Hautes Études des Communications Sociales in 1988 with a degree in International Relations (UCL). In January 1991 he started working freelance for RTBF, a Belgian public TV network, and other magazines, eventually becoming coeditor-in-chief of *Le Vif Weekend* in 2005. Since then he has been working in business journalism and is currently at the economic magazine *Trends-Tendances* as well as being a radio commenter for La Première (RTBF Radio). He won a Citi Journalistic Excellence Award in 2011.

G. Brown has navigated the Rocky Mountain musical landscape for decades, both as a journalist and as a radio personality. He covered popular music at the *Denver Post* for twenty-six years, interviewing well over two thousand musicians, from Paul McCartney to Bruce Springsteen to Bono. Published in numerous national magazines, including *Rolling Stone* and *National Lampoon*, Brown also covered music news and hosted and programmed for myriad Denver-based radio stations. He is the author of three books; his work *Colorado Rocks!—A Half Century of Music in Colorado* was hailed as "the Centennial State's rock bible." He is currently the director of the Colorado Music Hall of Fame (www.cmhof.org).

Rafa Cervera started his own fanzine, *Estricnina*, in 1982, writing about artists like Siouxsie and the Banshees, Alan Vega, and John Cale. Mostly he covered the then-nascent phenomenon later called "Movida Madrileña," interviewing some of the artists that made history, such as Radio Futura, Alaska, and Pedro Almodóvar. Since then he's contributed to many Spanish newspapers and magazines, and collaborated on television and radio shows. Since 1993 he has written for the *El País* newspaper, as well as *GQ Spain*, *Vogue*, and *Rolling Stone Spain*, and also has been part of the Los Conciertos de Radio 3 radio/TV show team. Between 1985 and 1996 he worked with the cult Spanish magazine *Ruta 66*, writing about new acts like Nirvana, who played in his hometown of Valencia in 1992. Cervera has also written a book about the band— *Nirvana* (Editorial La Máscara, 1993)—and others about Lou Reed, Sonic Youth, and the Spanish Movida. A book compiling the now legendary fanzine *Estricnina* is available through www.efeeme.com.

Patrick Chng is probably best known as the front man of seminal Singapore indie rock band the Oddfellows, formed in 1988. He was also a member of Padres in the early 1990s and has been playing guitar for TypeWriter since 2001. Since the late 1980s Patrick has been a freelance music writer for various publications, and he worked at MTV Asia as an associate producer from 1995 to 1999 and as the editor of its website from 2002 to 2007. He currently works part-time for Gibson Guitar Singapore and produces bands at Thom's Loft.

Marc Coiteux: Having started his career as a lawyer, Marc chose to follow a passion for music and became a journalist for *MusiquePlus*, a French-speaking music TV channel in Montreal. Over the course of his six years there (1990–1996), he conducted some two thousand interviews with musicians from across the world and from every part of the spectrum of music. Since then he has worked for Radio-Canada, the public broadcasting network, where he continues today as a television producer and radio host. In his spare time he compulsively collects guitars.

Luca Collepiccolo has been writing for several monthly magazines since he was seventeen years old. He then went to work in the indie record business, where, since the mid-1990s, he has worked with the most famous US labels, including Touch & Go, Dischord, Alternative Tentacles, and Sub Pop.

Chuck Crisafulli is a journalist and the author of several books, including *Teen Spirit: The Stories Behind Every Nirvana Song* and *Go to Hell: A Heated History of the Underground*. As a freelance journalist, he has covered pop culture for the *Los Angeles Times*, the *Hollywood Reporter*, and *Rolling Stone*, and he was a contributing editor with *Option* magazine.

Giancarlo De Chirico is a music journalist, and at the time of the Nirvana interview he was working for *Tutti Frutti* magazine and collaborating with *Metal Shock*. He conducted interviews for a private channel named Video Music, which was broadcast all over Italy. At thirty-six he worked as a full-time teacher in an Italian public school, teaching English literature and language to the Rebibbia prisoners in Rome as part of the job. He regularly attended the women's session at the Rebibbia prison, then from there went to Terza Casa—a session for drug addicts—and to the G12 wing at the Nuovo Complesso building, where Mafia-related convicts were kept. After work, he started his second life as a rock 'n' roller! He still teaches English in the Italian public school, but no longer works with convicts. He teaches in the afternoons, works on interviews in the mornings, and goes to gigs at night.

Robyn Doreian: Born in Melbourne, Australia, Robyn's first concert was AC/DC fronted by Bon Scott. An art school introduction to the Ramones propelled a lifelong devotion to Da Bruddas. Her passion for gritty rock, punk, and riffs, coupled with a music magazine obsession, led to her first magazine editorship, *Hot Metal*, in Sydney. Four years later, in 1992, she moved to London and edited *Kerrang!* and then *Metal Hammer*. She has written for *RIP*, *Hard N' Heavy*, *Revolver*, *Alternative Press*, KNAC.com, *Kerrang!*, *Metal Hammer*, *Terrorizer*, and *Rolling Stone Australia*. Robyn continues to write about music and is working on her rock memoir, *I Was a Heavy Metal Mutha*.

David Dufresne was a longtime publisher of numerous French punk rock fanzines and worked for the Bondage alternative rock label in the 1980s. He has also published a dozen books of investigative journalism. The first one, *Yo Revolution Rap*, was published in 1991. He stopped writing about rock and music just after Kurt Cobain's suicide. David was one of the earliest innovators in online media in France, publishing the first webzine, *La Rafale*, in 1995. Now he is an award-winning independent writer and filmmaker. His latest film, *Fort McMoney*, an interactive game documentary, was named Best Web Documentary at the 2014 Festival du Film d'Environnement of Paris, was a finalist at the 2014 SXSW Festival, and won the 2014 Grimme Online Award in the Knowledge & Education category. The film was acclaimed by the *New York Times* as the "wedding of the film and the video game." In 2010, he authored and codirected *Prison Valley*, a Web documentary that won a host of international awards, including the 2011 World Press Photo award for Best Interactive Nonlinear Work of the Year. David lives in Montreal.

Anne Filson is an architect and professor. She still owns the first Shocking Blue album containing the original "Love Buzz," which she bought immediately after the interview with Kurt Cobain.

César Fuentes Rodríguez has a deep and well-respected background in the music business as a specialized writer. Fuentes Rodríguez started his writing career in the early 1980s in Buenos Aires City. He is the founder of *Madhouse* and *Epopeya* magazines, which were published in Argentina and had a great impact across South America. César is also recognized as the host and producer of *Power 30* and *MTL* on TV and *Ave Cesar* on radio. Nowadays, he hosts *Tiempos Violentos*, the biggest Argentine radio show dedicated to heavy metal. Fuentes Rodríguez contributes to a number of local and international magazines such as *Requiem* (Argentina), *Heavy Rock* (Spain), *Force Magazine* (Spain), *Hard Rock* (Australia), *Rock Brigade* (Brazil), *Maelstrom* (Argentina), *Hm Subterraneo* (Mexico), and *Iron Pages* (Germany). He has published three books in Spanish—*Iron Maiden: The Voyage of the Maiden*; *Hell and the Coelacanths*; and *Gothic World*.

Aline Giordano: Born in South Korea, adopted by a French family, educated in France, and now living in England, Aline has dedicated her life to music and creativity. On top of an MPhil in Irish studies, a degree in languages and commerce, plus a postgraduate diploma in health informatics, Aline also possesses a PhD in photography, which reflects her lifelong work photographing and writing about bands and music. She works at the University of Southampton. Visit her online at www.alinegiordano.net and www.uzinemusic.net.

Hanmi Hubbard's writing career resulted from a magical mix of being in the right place at the right time, an intense love of music, a bit of moxie, and very supportive parents. Her first assignment for her high school newspaper was to write about Mudhoney. She called Sub Pop Records expecting to get a press kit but instead was given lead singer Mark Arm's phone number, resulting in her first interview. She went on to write for *Backlash* magazine and *The Rocket*, but grew up to be a product designer and today is back to her first love, photography.

Eva Joory: When she left the University of Rio de Janeiro in the mid-1980s, Eva wanted to become a rock photographer. Before departing for London to pursue a master's in journalism, she was asked by a friend to contribute to a new music magazine called *Bizz* and ended up living in London for five years and acting as its official

UK correspondent. She attended a huge number of concerts: Siouxie, Everything But the Girl, Pretenders, New Order, Human League, Beastie Boys, Cramps, Cure. She soon began writing and got to interview the likes of Boy George, the Cult, and Paul Weller. Music, and rock in particular, became more than a passion for Eva, and when she returned to Brazil, she got a job in a daily newspaper and started writing about music full-time.

Lena Jordebo has worked as a journalist for most of her life, starting out as a music journalist in her early twenties. She worked on *Bommen*, a weekly radio show on Swedish public service radio dedicated to new independent music in the 1980s, interviewing many bands. In the 1990s she moved on, working as a culture journalist for radio, print, and eventually public service TV. One of the things she enjoys about television is finding the right music for a feature or interview.

Paul Kimball lived in Washington State from 1985 through early 1992. Paul played in bands, including AMQA, Lansdat Blister, and Helltrout, beginning in his senior year of high school in Puyallup and continuing through the years immediately after he graduated from Olympia's Evergreen State College. While at Evergreen, he cohosted two different shows on the college radio station, KAOS. From 1990 to 1991, Paul was also a contributing writer for the regional music and culture zine *Hype*.

Jens Kirschneck, born in 1966, was one of the founders of the music fanzine *What's That Noise* in the midsize German town of Bielefeld in 1988. In the early 1990s he was also manager of the post-punk band Hip Young Things. He later concentrated on journalism and today is editor of the football (soccer) monthly *11 Freunde*. He also writes stories about sports, music, and other stuff, and likes to read them in public.

David Kleijwegt, born in Rotterdam in 1965, has written about pop music since January 1985. He has interviewed David Bowie, Prince, Nick Cave, Paul McCartney, U2, and other big names in the industry. Kleijwegt also writes about authors. He has won several prizes for his journalistic work, but over the last few years he has been more focused on making documentaries, some also about music. His documentary on the band

Low, *You May Need a Murderer*, got a four-star review in *Uncut* magazine when it was released in 2008.

Edgar Klüsener worked as a journalist for local newspapers in Germany in the late 1970s and early 1980s. At that time he primarily focused on music and soccer. He became the editor of the German *Metal Hammer* in 1986 and held this position until 1990. Later, he wrote freelance for many renowned German publications, including *Spiegel*, *Frankfurter Rundschau*, and the *Financial Times*. He has also written or coauthored a number of books. In 1997, he moved from Germany to Manchester, England, where he still lives. Edgar is finishing a PhD in Middle Eastern studies. His academic interests include Iran's rock scene and the role of the international news agencies in a global media system.

Marcus Koehler was born and raised in Heidelberg, Germany, where, with a couple of friends, he founded the fanzine *No Trend Press* in 1987. Though only eighteen years old at the time, he had already accumulated tremendous experience in the underground music scene, where his dedication to early 1980s' NewWave of British Heavy Metal (NWOBHM) and speed/thrash metal soon led to his discovery of punk and grunge. Since then he has written for a number of other publications, including trade magazine *Musikmarkt* (the German equivalent of *Billboard*) and consumer publication *MusikExpress*.

Rodrigo Lariú was born in 1973 in Niterói, a seaside town close to Rio de Janeiro. In 1989 he started writing his fanzine called *Midsummer Madness*. Five years later it turned into mmrecords, a record label that is still running. Rodrigo is also a production manager at a cable TV channel in Brazil and works as a director, producer, and screenwriter.

Youri Lenquette: Initially a journalist before devoting himself full-time to photography, Youri has collaborated with some of the most famous artists of the last twenty-five years. His portraits of musicians have served to illustrate dozens of albums, concert posters, and magazine covers across five continents. Meanwhile, he has directed videos and documentaries for various artists (including Sergent Garcia, Youssou N'Dour, Yuri Buenaventura, and Havana Cultura), as well as numerous programs for French national TV. In 2013 a widely acclaimed exhibition entitled *The Last Shooting* was staged displaying his images from Kurt Cobain's last photo session. Parallel to his career as a portraitist, Youri has photographed and documented travels in numerous countries, leading to a large number of reports and reviews in the travel and leisure press. Youri currently splits his time between Paris and Dakar. His website is www.yourilenquette.com.

Sergio Marchi is a rock journalist who started his career in 1983 and has since worked at nearly every newspaper, magazine, and radio or television station that has at some point had anything to do with rock. He spent nine years with the newspaper *Clarín*—one of the biggest in Latin America—before becoming the editor at *Rolling Stone Argentina*. He has published seven books, teaches journalism and rock history, translates books into Spanish, and is a music consultant for several companies and agencies. He has two children, and in his spare time he works with abandoned dogs at the animal center in Buenos Aires.

Sandrine Maugy cofounded *Uzine* as a photocopied fanzine written by a group of students who were passionate about music and wanted to share that passion with others. The zine began by reviewing concerts and albums, and interviewing small bands and artists. Considering their lack of funds and experience, the group was surprised to land interviews with bands like Nirvana and New Model Army, and artists like Ice-T and Courtney Love. They prided themselves on bringing music fans interviews done by other fans rather than professional journalists. The photos accompanying the interviews were amateur work, but Sandrine, along with fellow *Uzine* photographer Aline Giordano, developed a signature style and became the fanzine's official photographers. Her website is www.sandrinemaugy.com.

Fraser McKay combined his love of alternative music and his desire to become a journalist by producing a number of fanzines, including *Eye Sore You*. During that fanzine's 1990–1993 run, he interviewed a host of bands who were legends in their own lunchtime or who are still around today—My Bloody Valentine, Spiritualized, the Wedding Present, and others. After twenty years as a journalist writing music columns for newspapers around East Anglia, Fraser turned to the dark side—the world of PR—but can still be seen at music venues waiting to be blown away by the next Nirvana.

Antonio Carlos Miguel, as with many teenagers of his generation, was converted by the Beatles and the Rolling Stones. Over four decades as a journalist, he has met many of his idols, including Kurt Cobain, Bossa Nova maestro Tom Jobim, Tropicalia founders Caetano Veloso and Gilberto Gil, Paul McCartney, Miles Davis, Hermeto Pascoal, George Clinton, and Samba masters Cartola and Dorival Caymmi. At twenty years old, in 1974, he began as copublisher of the magazine *Música do Planeta Terra*, the creation of a late friend, Julio Barroso. In the early 1980s, Antonio moved to the mainstream press. Since 2011, he has worked as a freelance writer and curator for music projects and released two books. He also writes a column about music at the G1 site and is a voting member of the Latin Grammys and Prêmio da Música Brasileira.

Monk—**Jim Crotty and Michael Lane:** Think big, don't give up—motto for the Monks. *Monk* magazine was a twelve-year odyssey, the world's first and only mobile magazine, following Jim and Mike's adventures as they drove across America providing interviews and monthly missives from waypoints across the country. Having welded passion to a sustainable business plan, the two gentlemen of the road journeyed far and wide meeting the great and the good (and the not-so-good) while each becoming published authors and respected cultural commentators. Today, Monk.com continues to spread wisdom far and wide about destinations wide and far. Around the travel reporting and think pieces of the site, Jim and Mike run Monk Host (a Web-hosting firm) and Monk Media (a design, marketing, and production agency) with the blend of professionalism, energy, personality, and endearing courtesy that always marked the Monk way. A way of life, not just words on paper.

Garth Mullins is a writer, broadcaster, and three-chord propagandist living in East Vancouver, Canada. He's still an albino. He's still punk. His website is www.garthmullins.com, and his Twitter handle is @garthmullins.

Carlos "Cake" Nunez wrote for *Flipside* fanzine from 1990 to 2000 and sang in the punk rock band DickTit from 1990 to 1996. DickTit's career highlights were playing with the Weirdos and Green Day at Raji's in Hollywood. Currently, Carlos performs with El Ron Hitler, now known as Nostradumass. The band's first album, *Eye: Being the Rebel*, will finally be released in 2015, having been recorded in 1999–2000. They are working on a second album.

Jen Oldershaw's career in radio commenced twenty-five years ago while she was studying for a bachelor of media studies degree. After two years at Melbourne community radio station 3RRR, she moved to Triple J, the national youth broadcaster. After eleven years with the station, she moved to become a founder of Sydney's Nova 969 station. Jen does regular voiceover work and can still be heard on continuity announcements for ABC TV to this day. She now lectures at the Australian Film, Television, and Radio School.

Sujesh Pavithran was an entertainment journalist from the mid-1980s to the mid-1990s. He covered the music, movie, art, and celebrity circuit in Malaysia for a variety of publications in the country, and joined the *Star*, Malaysia's widest read and highest circulation English-language daily, in 1989. He is currently news editor of the *Star Online*, the newspaper's website. He is also a musician, and fronts his own band with whom he has recorded a CD and gigs occasionally.

Push worked for *Melody Maker* from 1985 until 1995, when he left to become the launch editor of *Muzik*, an electronic music magazine. He edited *Muzik* for four years, after which he was the editor of *Mondo*, a male lifestyle magazine. From 2002 onward, he switched his attention from magazines to books, and has written four books, including *Rat Scabies and the Holy Grail*, the true story of two years spent grail hunting with punk legend Rat Scabies. Since 2012, he has been dragged into the digital world, and at the time of writing, he is the editor of *Electronic Sound*, a magazine app about electronic music.

Bill Reid was a Seattle disc jockey from 1983 to 2006. From 1988 to 1993 he hosted an independent label show called *The Independent Hour* that featured music and interviews from artists of the day. The program aired on KITS-FM (Live-105) in San Francisco and later on both KITS and KNDD-FM (The End) in Seattle.

John Robb is an award-winning journalist and the boss of *Louder Than War*. In a thirty-year music writing career, John was the first to write about bands such as Stone Roses and Nirvana and has several bestselling music books to his name. He constantly tours the world with Goldblade and the Membranes, playing gigs or doing spoken word, and speaking at music conferences. His website is www.louderthanwar.com.

Kenan Seeberg has worked in the Danish media since 1985, starting as a presenter at the contemporary youth program P4 in Denmarks Radio. During the following years he was educated as a radio and television journalist, covering a wide range of cultural and political issues. Since 1992 he has also worked on television as a host and as a reporter for the Danish Broadcast Corporation. Since 1999 he has been employed at Denmark's two biggest tabloid papers, *Ekstra Bladet* and *BT*, covering subjects such as international espionage, consumer journalism, and culture, but focusing primarily on music, movies, and TV. Over the years, he has interviewed a wide variety of Danish and international musicians and bands. Among them are Pete Townshend, Depeche Mode, Elton John, Frankie Goes to Hollywood, Sheryl Crow, Metallica, the Pet Shop Boys, and Chrissie Hynde.

Mark Shafer used to be the producer, programmer, and sound guy (loosely put as it relates to lack of equipment and knowledge) at WAIF Cincinnati 88.3 FM, on the program *An Electric Fence* and on the live show *Sunday Night Live*—a weekly program that included interviews and live performances from bands such as the Jesus Lizard, the Digits, Bikini Kill, Brainiac, Sun Ra, Sonic Youth, and Pere Ubu. He has been an adjunct instructor of art at many colleges and universities, and was the singer in the punk band the Twerps (702 Records). He has done a lot of experimental music, electronic arts, circuit bending, and hacking. He performs solo as 1/2 Mang and has been in a group collaborative called the Thriftsore Boratorium.

James Sherry has spent a lifetime loving music and has built a life with music at its core. At age sixteen, having already spent time writing and having released his fanzine *Phobia*, James was brought on board at *Metal Hammer*, where he spent half a decade running across the peak years of Nirvana and the Seattle craze. After a further long spell with *Kerrang!*, James and a friend chose to play an even deeper role in the industry based on a desire to bring great music into the light by starting Division Promotions. Since its founding, James has remained dedicated to nurturing bands worth hearing, helping to give artists a chance to be heard, get recognized, and make the most of their talent. What keeps him going is the simple fact that after all the trials and tribulations of the music industry, the result is an industry in which the people left standing are those who are truly passionate about making music—the same drive that led him to music so young is still what burns today. His website is www.divisionpromotions.com.

Lucio Spiccia studied at the Sapienza University of Rome and has a doctorate in Italian literature, with further specialization in medieval history and film studies. He worked for ten years as a freelance journalist with a variety of major Italian music magazines, including *Il Mucchio Selvaggio*, *Ciao 2001*, and *Music & Arts*. During his career he often worked as a correspondent in London dealing mainly with the British and American indie scenes. Currently, his focus is on historical studies, which has led him to publish three books on the subject.

Phil Sutcliffe has worked as a freelance journo for thirty-five years. He wrote about music for *Sounds*, *Smash Hits*, *The Face*, *Q*, *Mojo*, the *Los Angeles Times*, and others. Now he is in a state of grace self-designated as "semi-retirement" and is pursuing enthusiasms in book form. Available now is *Nobody of Any Importance: A Foot Soldier's Memoir of World War I* by Sam Sutcliffe—Phil's father—edited by Phil. See the blog footsoldiersam.blogspot.co.uk for details. Promoting the work will be a five-year commitment through to the centenary of the July 1919 peace parade. But, in parallel, Phil writes and intermittently self-publishes chunks of a socio-historico-politico-artistico biographo on Bruce Springsteen, the man who pulls it all together. Even Nirvana . . .

Emmanuel Tellier was part of the small team of music lovers who started the music magazine *Les Inrockuptibles* in 1986—joining the staff in 1988 and working there for the next eleven years while the magazine advanced from one success to another. He also found time to be a founding member of the indie band 49 Swimming Pools and now lives in Paris, where he works for France's biggest weekly magazine, *Telerama*, covering cultural topics and disruptive technologies.

Annemiek van Grondel lives and works in Amsterdam. She started out as a music journalist. The interview with Dave Grohl in 1991 was her first ever. As a music journalist for the Netherlands' biggest music magazine, *OOR*, and newspaper, *NRC Handelsblad*, she interviewed the likes of Lemmy, Black Sabbath, and Chris Cornell, plus many more. After ten years she explored other fields of journalism and became an editor, later sub-editor, and editor-in-chief. She also was a copywriter for a design and photography agency and still writes in the fields of photography, design, art, architecture, theater, fashion, and culture. She is a part-time senior sub-editor of the fashion magazines *L'Officiel NL* and *L'Officiel Hommes NL*. In the 1990s she sang and played guitar in the all-female band Bitchcock (which performed at Hole's infamous 1995 Paradiso gig). She continues to sing, anonymously playing the shy singer-songwriter in the attic and performing with her (this time, male) band. Her website is www.avgrond.nl.

Bram van Splunteren worked as a rock journalist and DJ before he started making rock documentaries for Dutch national television. In the past twenty-five years he has made documentaries about Nick Cave, Iggy Pop, Beck, Public Enemy, Loudon Wainwright, and the Red Hot Chili Peppers, among others. The footage he shot with the Red Hot Chili Peppers between 1987 and 1994—as a friend of the band—is legendary among RHCP fans all over the world. Van Splunteren was the only filmmaker to film the band's guitar player John Frusciante during the mid-1990s in California—when Frusciante had left the band and was down and out on drugs. Van Splunteren's hip-hop documentary *Big Fun in the Big Town* (1986) recently gained international recognition as one of the best hip-hop documentaries of all time.

Phil West started his professional writing career with the *Daily* of the University of Washington in 1986 and the *Seattle Times* in 1989, covering music and theater. He's since written for a number of other publications, including the *Los Angeles Times*, the *San Antonio Express-News*, and the *Austin Chronicle*, and he currently writes about soccer for *Howler*, *PasteSoccer*, and *SB Nation*, with a book in the works on his twelve-thousand-mile journey across the United States to watch the 2014 World Cup with fans in a different city each day.

Sebastian Zabel worked for the (then) Cologne-based pop magazine *Spex* throughout the era from *Bleach* to *In Utero*. Today he lives in Berlin and is the editor-in-chief of the German edition of *Rolling Stone* magazine.

Angela Zocco is a journalist from Bologna, Italy, a city known above all for incredibly tasty food. (Remember—"Spaghetti Bolognese" is a fake!) But there is one thing that defines Bologna today: it is, and has always been, Italy's Rock City. She was born and raised there. She began as a presenter on local rock radio stations when she was sixteen, around 1980. She had her own programs and wrote for the radio fanzine; occasionally, she was also involved in putting some concerts together. Everything was done with a total DIY attitude, for fun, for passion (and usually for free!). Slowly, things started to become more professional; she served time as one of the first female rock DJs and worked as a press agent for a couple of rock clubs. In the early 1990s she got a three-year contract with BMG Record Company for realizing the first music "house organ" in Italy called *Ain't—Amazing Internoise* magazine (named after BMG sub-label Internoise). That's where I did my first "important" interviews: Aerosmith, John Peel, Rick Rubin, Joey Ramone, the Black Crowes . . . Kurt Cobain was not in the Rock 'n' Roll Olympus, not yet, when she got the chance to talk with him. Recently, she worked as head press agent for a network of museums, and she writes for *La Repubblica*, one of the main Italian newspapers.

CREDITS

A very sincere thank-you to each of the individuals who allowed this work to exist. I genuinely hope the result vindicates the trust you placed in me and that you're proud to see your piece as part of a greater whole. In addition, I'd like to thank the team at Swedish Radio P3, Sybil Augustine at WORT Radio, and Robin Alam at CiTR Radio for their support.

INDEX